New York City Opera Sings

New York City

by NEW YORK CITY OPERA GUILD
ARCHIVES COMMITTEE

Harold J. McKenna, Editor
Robert Nash
Emma D. Nordsiek
Pauline Ortega
Martha Moore Sykes

Opera Sings

Stories and Productions of the
New York City Opera 1944–79

RICHARDS ROSEN PRESS, INC., NEW YORK, N.Y. 10010

Published in 1981 by Richards Rosen Press, Inc.
29 East 21st Street, New York, N.Y. 10010

Copyright 1981 by New York City Opera Guild

First Edition

Library of Congress Cataloging in Publication Data
Main entry under title:

New York City Opera sings.

  Includes index.
  1. New York City Opera. 2. Operas—Stories,
plots, etc. I. New York City Opera Guild. Archives
Committee.
ML1711.8.N3N56   782.1'07'3   81–10533
ISBN 0–8239–0544–6   AACR2

Manufactured in the United States of America

Contents

-»»*«<-

Contents

Contents

Listing of Photographs

→))*(((←

COLOR PHOTOGRAPH SUPPLEMENT

Acknowledgments

-»»*«««-

The Committee would like to thank those who have assisted in the production of this book, particularly the many volunteers who helped in developing, organizing, and writing the text. Since it is impossible to include every person involved in the production of the text, we wish to recognize all of the volunteers whose contributions will long be remembered, especially the following: Barbara Adelman, Miriam Adelman, Jay Ferrara, Stephen A. Maguire, June Peters, Meredith Reid, Janet Russo, and Robert Sheldon.

The Committee would also like to acknowledge their indebtedness to George Louis Mayer, principal librarian of the General Library of the Performing Arts, Lincoln Center, for his assistance in detailed researching. In addition, we wish to give special thanks to Fred Fehl for permitting us to use his magnificent photographs of the New York City Opera. His contribution is greatly appreciated. Furthermore, we wish to thank past Guild director Robert Porter and present Guild director Dick Webster and the administrator, Shirley Barton, for their assistance and constant support of our work. The book could not have been produced without them.

Lastly, the Committee wishes to thank the members of the management who also assisted in the development of the book. Very special thanks to J. Edgar Joseph, Ruth Hider, Thomas Martin, and Felix Popper for their patience and understanding.

Harold J. McKenna,
editor

All black and white photographs except where indicated were graciously supplied Courtesy of Fred Fehl.

Overture

-»»*«««-

By JULIUS RUDEL

Hanging in my library, on a wall dotted with mementos, is the first program of the New York City Opera, announcing one week of eight performances. At the very bottom of the program, last and least, I am listed as "repetiteur," a euphemism for general factotum and jack of all the things no one else wanted to do. I played, for free, six months of auditions prior to that one week and then received the nice round sum of $50. Like so many American dreams, this one too was made up of often contradictory elements: harsh pragmatism and lofty ideals, penny-pinching in the production of the most expensive performing art that exists, and exploitation of talent hand in hand with its development.

I was, in a sense, a Viennese Horatio Alger, a refugee armed with only my American conducting diploma and the intuition that a new cultural enterprise, in a city whose Mayor had an Italian name, would include opera. Without influential friends or favor I got a job, and it remained one of my ideals to listen attentively to anyone who thought he had something to offer. I find that I can smile now at the many torments of my years of apprenticeship, for I grew as the company grew. As even the most loving child learns from his parents what he is determined never to do to his own children, I learned much from my predecessors, particularly from the company's founder, Laszlo Halasz, that intrepid pragmatist and organizer. The Halasz regime was followed by those of Joseph Rosenstock and Erich Leinsdorf. I assumed the directorship in 1957.

It was because Halasz could not raise the $50-a-week salary of my friend Larry Deutsch that Larry went off to Los Angeles and became a millionaire. He brought our company to perform there at the Music Center, beginning in 1967, a bit of the mountain coming to Mohammed. He became our most ardent supporter and most astute critic. I cherished our friendship up to his untimely death in 1977 and still cling to many memories. There have indeed been many wonders in my 22-year tenure as director.

Among them I recall first those giants who headed our board, Newbold Morris and Morton Baum, civic-minded idealists who wanted only to help build our company, to bring the art they loved to as many people as possible. Baum was quite proficient on the piano and could play through any opera we discussed (I drew the line when he tried to sing). So many of the people who supported us were models of what great patrons should be: Martha Baird Rockefeller, Ralph and Pat Corbett, Jean Tennyson, and more recently, Les and Fan Samuels. There was the Ford Foundation, under MacNeil Lowry, who gave us sustenance through some of our most daring experiments, entire seasons of nothing but contemporary opera. Wonder of wonders was Martha Sykes, a soft-spoken Southerner who turned 12 friends into a Guild of 4,000.

A world mesmerized by the "best this" and the "record-breaking that" is always curious about what I consider my greatest accomplishments. In those first lean seasons, when I took over a company bankrupt of everything except determination, it was a source of pride merely to survive. But very quickly I knew that survival was nothing. Like the human organism, a company must continue to grow, change, win a few, lose a few, and develop new perspectives. With only survival as a goal, someone sooner or later pulls the plug.

What I did best, I think, was to allow artists to develop from an ensemble, to balance individual growth with a community spirit, and as I look back, I marvel at the number of stars we launched into the operatic firmament. For those given to counting, it is noteworthy that we provided a podium for fifty (50!) American conductors, a fact that, in retrospect, bears its own grim mortality statistic.

Certainly, we blazed a trail of innovation in opera production, and if, occasionally, we lighted fires under the traditionalists, what light we shed, what a glow! Our bold use of film, the restoration of reality to "verismo," the insistence on interpersonal interaction on stage, the use of a chorus as individuals, and most of all, the emphasis on style had their impact around the opera globe. We experienced the heady excitement of innovators and occasional dismay at the flattery of poor imitation. For me personally, the fact that I led so many of these productions from the pit, as well as with the critical eye (and often harsh hand) of director, added immeasurably to the creative excitement of those years. By happy coincidence this book concludes with the end of my reign.

Among my cherished souvenirs I count plaques, commendations, doctorates (I was, courtesy of Adolf Hitler, a high-school dropout), awards, and life-time tenure as director of the New York City Opera, voted me in 1968 by the board. These 35 years, 22 of them as director, were more lifetime than I ever expected to give. I emerge from them grateful and free to be the only thing I ever intended to be, a musician and conductor.

General Directors of the New York City Opera

-»»*«««-

Laszlo Halasz, 1944–Spring 1952
Joseph Rosenstock, Fall 1952–Spring 1956
Erich Leinsdorf, Fall 1956
Julius Rudel, 1957–Spring 1979
Beverly Sills, Fall 1979–

Introduction

-»»*«««-

New York City Opera Sings is an adventure into the 161 works produced by the New York City Opera since its inception in 1944 to the Spring Season 1979. The project was begun in 1975 by a group of volunteers on the Archives Committee of the New York City Opera Guild, who met to conceptualize and develop this anthology. These dedicated volunteers have given countless hours of time to researching, writing, organizing, typing, and editing the book that you now hold in your hands. Words cannot express the many thanks the editor has for the endurance and understanding of the Committee.

The purpose of the book is to introduce you to the New York City Opera through productions it has staged over the first 35 years of its operation. Of the 161 operas included in this book, many are favorites from the standard repertory, but many are unique to the City Opera. These "unique" works—contemporary, unknown, or obscure—have been commissioned, discovered, and even rediscovered by the company. This is in part what City Opera is all about. It is an adventuresome company willing to undertake the challenge of such works in order to introduce them to opera-going audiences.

In addition to the stories of the operas included in this book, you will find premiere performances, casts and dates, composers, librettists, scenic designers, costumers, conductors, and the languages in which the works were sung.

Other unique features of the book are:

• an alphabetical listing of all works done by the City Opera from 1944 to 1979.
• a chronological listing of all the works.
• a listing of premiere casts, the voice type of each character, and the order of their appearance.
• a collection of photographs of the productions and the performers.

The book is a guide to the world of opera: for the newcomer who wants to be adventuresome and know the stories and characters of each opera; for the student who needs data on world premieres, American premieres, composers, librettists, voice types, and characters; and for the opera buff who wants to gain further insight into the City Opera. It is also a guide to the "uncommon" operas, many of which were performed for the first time by the New York City Opera.

As you browse through the book, it is hoped that you will find it informative, enjoyable, and educational. It was written so that opera lovers everywhere can share the great adventures that the City Opera chartered at its inception 35 years ago. The editor hopes all who read the book will use it as a reference guide to the accomplishments of the past, as well as a prelude to the new adventures that lie ahead for our company.

Harold J. McKenna,
editor

New York City Opera Sings

The Abduction from the Seraglio

→))) ✳ (((←

MUSIC BY: Wolfgang Amadeus Mozart

WORLD PREMIERE: Vienna, Austria,
   July 16, 1782

LIBRETTO BY: Christoph Friedrich Bretzner
ENGLISH TRANSLATION BY: John Bloch
NEW YORK CITY OPERA PREMIERE:
   (Sung in English) October 30, 1957

CONDUCTOR: Peter Herman Adler (debut)
STAGE DIRECTOR: Michael Pollock
SETS and COSTUMES: Robert Fletcher*

CHARACTERS (In order of appearance)	VOICE (type)	PREMIERE CAST (New York City Opera)
Belmonte	Tenor	Robert Rounseville
Osmin	Bass	Richard Humphrey
Pedrillo	Tenor	David Lloyd
Pasha Selim	Speaking	Carlton Gauld
Constanza	Soprano	Phyllis Curtin
Blonda	Soprano	Virginia Haskins

Servants and Guards

SYNOPSIS OF STORY
TIME AND PLACE: Turkey, 16th century

✳

ACT I

SCENE 1—Outside the palace

Somewhere on the high seas, Belmonte and his beloved Constanza, together with their servants Pedrillo and Blonda, were happily voyaging when pirates attacked their ship and took them prisoner. Belmonte escaped. The others were sold in the Turkish slave markets to the powerful Pasha Selim, who made Pedrillo an assistant gardener and put the women into his seraglio.

Belmonte, losing no time, equipped a ship and set sail for Turkey to find Constanza.

SCENE 2—The garden of the palace

As our story begins, Belmonte is discovered before the walls of the seraglio. The gate opens and a fat figure appears. It is Osmin, commander of the palace guard and, in his spare time, chief gardener. An attempt by Belmonte to elicit information from this surly individual proves fruitless,

---

* The sets and costumes were borrowed from the Stratford, Connecticut, Shakespeare Festival, where the opera had been given the previous year.

and when threatened with Osmin's whip he is forced to retreat. The gardener resumes his work, only to be interrupted by Pedrillo. This young man, having insinuated himself into the graces of the Pasha, feels safe enough to tease Osmin on occasion. Osmin, in turn, gives vent to his own feelings about upstarts like Pedrillo. At last Osmin disappears into the palace. Belmonte rushes from his hiding place and embraces his faithful servant. With relief he hears that Constanza is well, but he also learns that the Pasha has fallen in love with her and, quite contrary to the habits of an oriental potentate, is courting her with the propriety natural to a refined and gentle ruler. Pedrillo conceives a plan to introduce his master into the palace. He presents him to the Pasha as a famous architect eager to enter his service. The Pasha is pleased by Belmonte and orders Pedrillo to show him inside the palace; as they prepare to enter, however, they find the doorway blocked by Osmin, who bellows that as long as he has not given the order, no one shall pass. In spite of his determination, the two friends succeed in entering. Osmin is furious, and when he is furious he takes it out on his personal servants. However, Blonda has an answer for him, "He who wants to capture a woman's heart must treat her quite differently." Her theories are considered highly dangerous and subversive by Osmin. "We are here in Turkey," he bellows, "and in Turkey women have to obey orders." Blonda is not to be won by commands. One more step and she offers to scratch his eyes out. Osmin retreats in a hurry. Pedrillo enters and outlines his plan for the escape. The absence of the Pasha affords the lovers an opportunity for a brief but joyous reunion.

ACT II

SCENE 1—Outside the seraglio

As the Pasha's love for Constanza is rapidly outweighing his patience, he decides to give her until sunrise either to accept his love or be subjected to torture. Pedrillo must now complete his plans for the abduction. First he must dispose of Osmin. He decides to get Osmin to drink some wine in which he has put a sleeping potion, but his ingenuity is sorely tested by the realization that wine is forbidden to Turks. However, Osmin is soon snoring happily, and Pedrillo, placing a ladder against the tower, sings a serenade, the prearranged signal for the abduction to begin. The escape is thwarted by the premature awakening of Osmin, and guards capture the lovers. Osmin boasts that this time nothing will keep him from getting his revenge.

SCENE 2—The throne room of the Pasha

The accused are brought before the Pasha knowing that they can no longer hope for his magnanimity. The Pasha reveals that Belmonte's father had in former times committed a grievous wrong against him. Therefore, to die together is all the lovers can hope for. The Pasha, however, has his own ideas about revenge and sets the lovers free, thereby repaying evil with good. As for himself he says, "I shall woo that mistress who will not deny me her healing favors—time." All sing his praises, and the story ends happily with the words of Constanza, "The noble man forgives all wrong. This is the moral of our song."

4

Aida

→))∗(((←

Music by: Giuseppe Verdi
World Premiere: Cairo, Egypt,
December 24, 1871

Libretto by: Antonio Ghislanzoni
New York City Opera Premiere:
(Sung in Italian) October 28, 1948

Conductor: Laszlo Halasz
Stage Director: Theodore Komisarjevsky
Scenery and Costumes: H. A. Condell
Ballet Choreographer: George Balanchine

CHARACTERS (In order of appearance)	VOICE (type)	PREMIERE CAST (New York City Opera)
Ramphis, High Priest of Egypt	Bass	Oscar Natzka
Radames, an Egyptian Chieftain	Tenor	Ramon Vinay
Amneris, daughter of the King of Egypt	Mezzo	Suzy Morris
Aida, daughter of Amonasro and slave of Amneris	Soprano	Camilla Williams
The King of Egypt	Bass	James Pease
An Egyptian Messenger	Baritone	Edwin Dunning
Amonasro, King of Ethiopia	Baritone	Lawrence Winters (debut)
Priestess (offstage only)	Mezzo	Frances Bible
Dancers		Maria Tallchief
		Nicholas Magallanes (debut)

and Misses Dushock, Gilbert, Karlin, LeClerq, McBride, Sundsten; Messrs. Beard (debut), Bigelow (debut), Jackson (debut), Tobias (debut)

Priests, Priestesses, Egyptian chieftains, the King's bodyguards, Amneris' girl servants, Slaves, Ethiopian chieftains taken prisoner

SYNOPSIS OF STORY

Time and Place: Period of the Pharaohs; Memphis and Thebes

∗

ACT I

SCENE 1—The interior of the Temple of Phtah

Radames learns from Ramphis that the Ethiopians have attacked Egypt and that Isis has chosen the general who is to lead the Egyptian attack. Ramphis leaves to inform the King of the name of this man, and Radames hopes that

5

he is the chosen one so that he may return in glory and marry his beloved Aida. Amneris enters; she is in love with Radames and seeing his joy tries to learn its cause, hoping it is love for her. He tells her it is his hope of being named the Egyptian general, but then Aida enters and the troubled glances between the two cause Amneris to suspect that it is Aida whom Radames loves. Aida protests that her tears are for fear of war with the Ethiopians.

The King, Ramphis, and the court enter. A messenger announces that the Ethiopians have invaded, led by their King, Amonasro. The King then announces that Radames has been chosen to lead the Egyptian armies, and he is hailed by all with wishes for his victorious return. After all have left, Aida remains, berating herself for joining in the wish for victory, since this would mean defeat for her own country and for her father; then she recalls that Ethiopian victory could also mean death for her beloved Radames. Her only wish is that she might die and be set free, and she begs the gods to have pity on her.

The priests enter the temple, an offstage priestess intones a prayer to Phtah, and sacred dances are performed. Radames is led in, and Ramphis prays for his victory and presents him with the sacred sword as symbol of victory.

SCENE 2—Chamber of Amneris

Amneris is prepared by her slaves for the triumphal return of the Egyptians. She is entertained by the dancing of Moorish slaves, whom she dismisses at Aida's entry. Although she pretends sorrow at the defeat of the Ethiopians, she is determined to learn if Aida is her rival for Radames. Aida's anguished cry upon being told of Radames' death confirms her suspicions. Amneris accuses Aida of being in love with Radames and then tells her that he is alive. At Aida's joyous outburst, Amneris threatens Aida and orders that she follow her to the triumphal ceremonies. As Amneris leaves, Aida again asks the gods to pity her.

SCENE 3—Inner courtyard of the King's Palace

To the rejoicing of the crowd, the victorious Egyptian army passes in review before the King and Amneris. The spoils of war are brought in, and victory dances are performed. Radames is

borne in triumphant and receives the victory wreath from Amneris. The Ethiopian prisoners are then brought in, and Aida recognizes her father among them. Warning her to be silent, he announces that Amonasro, the Ethiopian King, was killed in battle, and that he is but a defeated warrior. He begs that the King have mercy on the prisoners and pleads for their freedom. Ramphis and the priests are opposed to the plea, but Radames and the crowd plead for their freedom. The King releases all prisoners, keeping only Amonasro as hostage. The King then announces that Radames will marry Amneris, to her joy but to the dismay of Radames and of Aida, who is consoled by her father.

ACT II

SCENE—On the banks of the Nile by the temple

On the eve of her wedding, Amneris, accompanied by Ramphis, comes to pray at the temple. After they have entered the temple, a heavily veiled Aida enters for a final meeting with Radames. She recalls her happy days in her homeland, which she has lost hope of ever seeing again. Amonasro enters with the news that the Ethiopians have rearmed, and he promises Aida that she will return to her home. But he must know the route of the Egyptian army, and he demands that Aida learn this from Radames. Aida first refuses, but she succumbs to the threats of Amonasro and reluctantly agrees. Amonasro hides as Radames enters. Radames proclaims his love for Aida and promises to marry her after the new battle with the Ethiopians. Aida urges that they flee immediately; Radames at first refuses, but he soon agrees to flee with her, telling her how they may avoid the Egyptian armies. Amonasro reveals himself, and Radames realizes that he has betrayed a military secret. Amneris and Ramphis emerge from the temple, and as Aida and Amonasro escape, Radames surrenders to Ramphis.

ACT III

SCENE—A subterranean hall and the prison in the temple

Although condemning Radames as a traitor, Amneris still loves him and is resolved to make one last effort to save him. She has him brought in by the guards; she begs him to defend himself and offers to plead with the King for his life if he will only renounce Aida and marry her. Radames rejects her offer even when he learns that Aida has escaped, preferring death to life without Aida. Radames is led out by the guards. Amneris, at first furious with him, is overcome with remorse for having condemned him. The priests enter the hall of justice and charge Radames with treason, rebellion, and desertion. He refuses to defend himself and is condemned to die by being buried alive near the altar of the gods. As the priests file out, Amneris curses them for their evil verdict.

The scene changes to the vault in which Radames has been entombed. Above is the temple. Radames is dreaming of Aida when he is distracted by a noise. Aida, who had earlier hidden herself in the tomb, appears to share death with him. Failing to dislodge the stone that has sealed the crypt, Radames joins Aida in their farewell to earth. While the priests and priestesses chant a prayer, Amneris, prostrating herself above the tomb, prays for forgiveness.

Albert Herring

→))) * (((←

MUSIC BY: Benjamin Britten

WORLD PREMIERE: Glyndebourne,
England, June 20, 1947

LIBRETTO BY: Eric Crozier
From a short story by Guy de Maupassant
NEW YORK CITY OPERA PREMIERE:
(Sung in English) September 15, 1971

CONDUCTOR: Mario Bernardi
STAGE DIRECTOR: Anthony Besch
SETS and COSTUMES: Lloyd Evans

CHARACTERS (In order of appearance)	VOICE (type)	PREMIERE CAST (New York City Opera)
Lady Billows, an elderly autocrat	Soprano	Ellen Faull
Florence, Lady Billow's housekeeper	Mezzo	Beverly Evans
Miss Wordsworth, teacher at the Church School	Soprano	Sandra Darling
Mr. Gedge, the Vicar	Baritone	Thomas Jamerson
Mr. Upfold, the Mayor	Tenor	John Lankston
Superintendent Budd, of the local Constabulary	Bass	Richard T. Gill
Emmie	Girl Soprano	Beth Glick (debut)
Cis	Girl Soprano	Mary Ann Clatworthy
Harry	Boy Soprano	Colin Duffy (debut)
Sid, the butcher's assistant	Baritone	Dominic Cossa
Albert Herring, the greengrocer's son	Tenor	John Stewart
Nancy, the baker's daughter	Mezzo	Kay Creed
Mrs. Herring, Albert's mother	Mezzo	Muriel Greenspon

SYNOPSIS OF STORY
TIME AND PLACE: A small market town in England, in the Spring of 1910

*

ACT I

SCENE 1—Lady Billow's drawing room, an April morning

It is time for the little town of Loxford to select a Queen of the May. The members of the committee to decide between the rival candidates are Miss Wordsworth, the Vicar, the Mayor, and Superintendent Budd. They have discussed the qualifications of the candidates and are reporting to Lady Billows.

All are distressed by what each considers unde-

Albert Herring, 1971

sirable characteristics of the young ladies in the town. Suddenly Superintendent Budd suggests that they select a King of the May. He nominates Albert Herring, considered by all a rather backward boy who works in his mother's greengrocery. This nomination meets with the complete agreement of the committee.

SCENE 2—Mrs. Herring's greengrocery, later the same day

Some children are playing outside the shop. Sid, a friend of Albert's, calls for Albert to come along with him, but Albert keeps on with his work.

Nancy, Sid's girl friend, comes to shop. She and Sid make a date to meet that night for a walk in the moonlight. If she is late, he will whistle under her window. Albert observes all this and is left alone to think about what he has seen and heard.

The Committee comes to advise Mrs. Herring of the decision to award the prize money to Albert and to crown him King of the May. At first Albert refuses to take part in the festivities,

but his mother forcefully makes him change his mind.

ACT II

SCENE 1—The vicarage garden, May Day

A table is being set with food for the celebration. The children are rehearsing the anthem they are to sing. Sid confides in Nancy that he has a scheme to help poor Albert. He pours rum into the glass of lemonade at Albert's place at the table. All is now ready for the reception.

The guests arrive. Lady Billows presents Albert with the prize money, and there are numerous speeches. Albert is called on to reply, but all he can say is thank you very much.

Albert drinks his lemonade, likes what he tastes, and asks Nancy to refill his glass. He gets hiccups.

SCENE 2—Mrs. Herring's shop, that evening

Albert returns to the shop from the feast and the celebration. He has become aware of Nancy's

9

charms and of how much more exciting life could be.

For the first time, Albert sees himself as others see him and decides to change that image. With the prize money in his pocket, he goes off to find out what he has been missing.

ACT III

SCENE—Mrs. Herring's shop, the next afternoon

Albert has disappeared, and everyone is searching for him. Superintendent Budd leads the search but is making little progress. Albert's orange blossom wreath is found on the road to Campey Ash, crushed by a cart.

In the midst of this confusion, Albert walks in. He is bombarded with questions and demands for an explanation. He tries to explain what has changed him, and everyone realizes he is no longer the backward boy they thought he was. He joins Sid and Nancy, the children and the townspeople, with whom he now feels more at ease.

Amahl and the Night Visitors

-»»*«‹-

MUSIC BY: Gian Carlo Menotti

WORLD PREMIERE: NBC-TV Opera Theatre,
   December 24, 1951

First stage performance,
   New York, April 27, 1952

LIBRETTO BY: Gian Carlo Menotti

NEW YORK CITY OPERA PREMIERE:
   (Sung in English) April 9, 1952

CONDUCTOR: Thomas Schippers (debut)
STAGE DIRECTOR: Gian Carlo Menotti
SCENERY and COSTUMES: Eugene Berman (debut)
CHOREOGRAPHER: John Butler (debut)

CHARACTERS (In order of appearance)	VOICE (type)	PREMIERE CAST (New York City Opera)
The Mother	Soprano	Rosemary Kuhlmann (debut)
Amahl	Boy soprano	Chet Allen (debut)
King Kaspar	Tenor	Michael Pollock
King Melchior	Baritone	Lawrence Winters
King Balthazar	Bass	Richard Wentworth
A Shepherdess	Dancer	Mary Hinkson (debut)
Two Shepherds	Dancers	Marc Breaux (debut)
		Glen Tetley (debut)
A Page	Baritone	William Starling (debut)
	Shepherds and Villagers	

SYNOPSIS OF STORY
TIME AND PLACE: Interior of a cottage near Bethlehem

*

ACT I

SCENE—Interior of a cottage

Somewhere in the world lives a crippled little shepherd called Amahl, with his mother, an impoverished widow. Nothing is left to them of the little they ever had, and they are now faced with hunger and cold in their empty home.

Three Wise Men, on their way to Bethlehem, stop at the hut and ask to be taken in for the night. Amahl and his mother welcome them as well as they can and are much astonished at the splendor of their robes and the wealth of gifts they are carrying with them.

When Amahl's mother realizes that the Three Kings are looking for a newborn babe and that the expensive gifts are all destined for him, she becomes bitter and envious. She cannot under-

11

stand why at least some of these gifts are not to be bestowed upon her own child who is so poor and sickly.

Under cover of darkness, while the Three Kings are asleep, she steals some of the gold from them—and is caught red-handed. When she explains to the Three Kings that she needs the gold to feed her starving child, she is readily forgiven. With great tenderness they try to explain to her who this newborn child is and how much he needs the love of every human being to build his coming kingdom. Touched by their words, the poor widow not only gives back the stolen gold but wishes she could add a gift of her own. Little Amahl comes to her rescue. He impulsively gives to the Three Kings his wooden crutch, his most precious possession, and in doing so he is miraculously cured of his lameness.

As dawn appears in the sky, the Three Kings make ready to resume their journey. Amahl begs his mother to let him join them, and he is finally allowed to follow the Kings to Bethlehem to adore and give thanks to the Christ-Child.

Note: This work was staged without any attempt at historical validity, but rather with poetical anachronism, as if it were seen by a Dutch or Italian primitive.

Amelia Goes to the Ball

-»»*«««-

MUSIC BY: Gian Carlo Menotti

WORLD PREMIERE: Philadelphia, Pennsylvania,
April 1, 1937

LIBRETTO BY: Gian Carlo Menotti
English translation by: George Mead
NEW YORK CITY OPERA PREMIERE:
(Sung in English) April 8, 1948

CONDUCTOR: Laszlo Halasz
STAGE DIRECTOR: Gian Carlo Menotti
SCENIC DESIGNER: H. A. Condell
COSTUMES*

CHARACTERS (In order of appearance)	VOICE (type)	PREMIERE CAST (New York City Opera)
Amelia	Soprano	Frances Yeend
1st Maid	Soprano	Leonore Portnoy
2nd Maid	Soprano	Ruth Shor (debut)
The Friend	Mezzo	Betty Dubro
The Husband	Baritone	Walter Cassel
The Lover	Tenor	William Horne
The Police Commissioner	Bass	Gean Greenwell
	Neighbors	

Note: This opera performed with "The Old Maid and the Thief."

SYNOPSIS OF STORY
TIME AND PLACE: Amelia's boudoir, Milan, 1905

*

Amelia is discovered dressing for the ball. Her husband enters flourishing an intercepted letter from her lover and demands to know his name. Amelia, afraid that her husband will refuse to take her to the ball, tells him that her lover lives on the floor above. The husband rushes out. . . Amelia then calls to her lover from the balcony and urges him to escape.

The lover instead slides down a rope to the balcony and asks Amelia to elope. She refuses . . . Meanwhile the husband returns and discovers the lover. They are about to fight but think it better to discuss matters. Amelia reminds her husband that it is time to start for the ball. He is so engrossed in his discussion on marriage with the lover that he pushes her aside.

Furious, she breaks a vase over his head, knocking him unconscious. The police and neigh-

---

* By Kate Friedheim

Amelia Goes to the Ball, 1948. Left to right: Frances Yeend, Walter Cassel, William Horne

bors arrive, whereupon Amelia accuses her lover of being a burglar and of having attacked her husband.

The police hustle him out, and the husband is taken away in an ambulance. Amelia bursts into tears. The chief of police consoles her, saying that her husband is not seriously hurt. Amelia tells him she is not crying because of her husband, that all she wants is to be taken to the ball. The chief of police gallantly offers to escort her. Amelia exits, smiling, on the arm of the chief of police.

14

El Amor Brujo

-»»*«««-

MUSIC BY: Manuel de Falla
WORLD PREMIERE: Madrid, Spain,
    April 15, 1915

BOOK BY: G. Martinez Sierra
NEW YORK CITY OPERA PREMIERE:
    (Sung in Spanish) October 16, 1957

CONDUCTOR: José Iturbi
STAGE DIRECTOR: Jean Dalrymple
SCENIC DESIGNER: Manuel Muntanola*
COSTUMES: Peggy Clark
CHOREOGRAPHER: Antonio Triana (debut)

CHARACTERS (In order of appearance)	VOICE (type)	PREMIERE CAST (New York City Opera)
Candelas	Dancer	Rita Vega (debut)
Carmelo	Dancer	Antonio Triana (debut)
The Singer	Mezzo	Mignon Dunn
Lucia	Dancer	Teresita Osta (debut)
The Spectre	Dancer	Don de Natale (debut)
The Witch	Dancer	Georgia Simmons (debut)

Corps de Ballet: Maria Alba, Silvia Camargo, Don de Natale, Victoria Flores, Paco Gallo, Carmen Gomez, Maria-Christina, Andrea Mora, Rolando Pernas, Clarissa Talve, Juanita Traves

Note: This performance was preceded by *La Vida Breve* by Manuel de Falla.

SYNOPSIS OF STORY
A Ballet-Pantomime of Andalucia

*

Candelas, a beautiful gypsy, once loved a wicked but fascinating man who, though now dead, still haunts her and forbids her to love another. But she does love another, Carmelo, who is devoted to her and who tries to rid her of her hallucinations. Her friend Lucia also feels the presence of the Spectre, although she cannot see him, and she, too, tries to free Candelas from the evil spirit that seems to possess her. Even the midnight "ritual of fire," joined in by Candelas' friends and neighboring gypsies, fails, and the Spectre returns to taunt them, luring Candelas away from Carmelo's embrace. But then the Spectre's attention is taken by Lucia, who delib-

* Scenery loaned through the courtesy of the Barcelona Opera Company, Teatro Liceo, Barcelona, Spain.

erately tries to intrigue him, although she cannot see him. Faithless to Candelas even in death, he becomes absorbed in Lucia, and his power over Candelas weakens. When at last Candelas is able to exchange a kiss of perfect love with Carmelo, the Spectre is banished forever by El Amor Brujo, "Love, the Sorcerer." A new day is born, and Candelas and Carmelo are able to start a new life to the joyful pealing of the bells of morning.

Andrea Chénier

-»»*«««-

MUSIC BY: Umberto Giordano
WORLD PREMIERE: Milan, Italy,
   March 28, 1896

LIBRETTO BY: Luigi Illica
NEW YORK CITY OPERA PREMIERE:
   (Sung in Italian) April 9, 1947

CONDUCTOR: Laszlo Halasz
STAGE DIRECTOR: Theodore Komisarjevsky
SCENIC DESIGNER: H. A. Condell
COSTUMES*
BALLET CHOREOGRAPHER: William Dollar

CHARACTERS (In order of appearance)	VOICE (type)	PREMIERE CAST (New York City Opera)
Carlo Gérard	Baritone	Enzo Mascherini
Contessa de Coigny	Mezzo	Lydia Edwards
Maddalena de Coigny	Soprano	Vivian Della Chiesa (debut)
Bersi	Mezzo	Rosalind Nadell
Fléville	Bass	Arthur Newman
Andrea Chénier	Tenor	Vasso Argyris
L'Abate	Tenor	Allen Stewart
Mathieu	Baritone	Desire Ligeti (debut)
Vecchia (Madelon)	Mezzo	Mary Kreste
Incredibile	Tenor	Nathaniel Sprinzena
Roucher	Bass	Grant Garnell
Fouquier	Baritone	Edwin Dunning (Debut)
Dumas	Bass	Arthur Newman
Schmidt	Bass	Paul Dennis

Aristocracy, Peasants, Revolutionaries, Common People, and
Prisoners Dancers

Note: Major Domo added to program on April 18.

SYNOPSIS OF STORY
TIME AND PLACE: Paris, France, before and during the French Revolution

*

---

* By Kate Friedheim; additional costumes by Stivanello.

ACT I

SCENE—Hall of the Contessa de Coigny's castle

As the curtain rises, preparations are being made for a ball at the country estate of Contessa de Coigny in prerevolutionary France. Gérard, servant of the Contessa and secretly in love with her daughter Maddalena, has been imbued with the revolutionary spirit. On seeing his aged father still slaving, he curses the old order. The guests arrive, and among them is a young poet, Andrea Chénier. Maddalena jokingly asks him to recite a poem on the subject of love, and Chénier agrees. But overcome by the revolutionary spirit, he recites instead a poem depicting the misery of France. After his departure the ball continues, only to be interrupted by Gérard leading a group of beggars.

ACT II

SCENE—Square in Paris outside the Cafe Hottot

Act II takes place in the midst of the Revolution, of which Gérard is now a leader. Roucher comes to his friend Chénier with a passport and endeavors to induce him to flee since he does not agree with the extremists who are in control. Chénier, however, has been receiving letters from an unknown woman, and, believing in destiny, he refuses to flee. Maddalena enters and identifies herself as the writer of the letters. Incredibile calls Gérard, who fights a duel with Chénier. Gérard is wounded.

ACT III

SCENE—Seat of the Revolutionary Tribunal

Gérard asks the people to sacrifice their families and meager possessions for the fight against all Europe. Incredibile informs him that Chénier has been captured, sarcastically remarking that now Maddalena will come to them. He leaves, asking Gérard to write the denunciation of Chénier. Gérard, left alone, throws aside the pen in disgust and expresses his great unhappiness. Maddalena approaches him and offers herself in return for Chénier's freedom. Gérard, inspired by her self-sacrifice, pleads in vain with the tribunal for Chénier's life, but Chénier is sentenced to death.

ACT IV

SCENE—The prison yard of Saint Lazare

On the morning of the execution, Chénier reads his last verses to his friend Roucher. Maddalena bribes the jailer to permit her to die with Chénier by taking the place of another woman. Together once more, the lovers express an acceptance of their fate as they are led to the guillotine.

Anna Bolena

→))) * (((←

MUSIC BY: Gaetano Donizetti
WORLD PREMIERE: Milan, Italy,
December 26, 1830

LIBRETTO BY: Felice Romani
NEW YORK CITY OPERA PREMIERE:
(Sung in Italian) October 3, 1973

CONDUCTOR: Julius Rudel
STAGE DIRECTOR: Tito Capobianco
SCENIC DESIGNER: Ming Cho Lee
COSTUMES: José Varona

CHARACTERS (In order of appearance)	VOICE (type)	PREMIERE CAST (New York City Opera)
Giovanna (Jane Seymour), lady-in-waiting to the Queen	Mezzo	Susanne Marsee
Anna Bolena (Anne Boleyn), wife of Henry VIII	Soprano	Beverly Sills
Smeton, Queen's page	Mezzo	Hilda Harris
Enrico (Henry VIII), King of England	Bass	Robert Hale
Lord Riccardo Percy	Tenor	Enrico di Giuseppe
Lord Rochefort, Queen's brother	Bass	Samuel Ramey
Sir Hervey, an officer of the King	Tenor	Jerold Siena

Courtiers, Officers, Pages, Hunters and Soldiers

SYNOPSIS OF STORY
TIME AND PLACE: England, 1536

*

ACT I

SCENE 1—Hall of Windsor Castle

The gossip among waiting courtiers is that their fickle King has turned to another woman. Jane Seymour, Anne Boleyn's favorite lady-in-waiting and the secret object of Henry's affection, is torn between her love for him and the unhappiness she is causing her mistress. When the Queen enters, she asks Smeton to sing for them. His song distresses Anne, and as she dismisses the court she cautions Jane to remember her heartbreak if ever Jane should be tempted by the splendor of a royal throne.

Jane's guilty thoughts are interrupted by the King's arrival. Jane begs him to let this be their last meeting, but Henry accuses her of offering him her love solely to gain the throne, as he feels Anne had once done. As Jane tearfully denies this, the King tells her that she will soon have marriage and the throne, since Anne's day of punishment is near. Although Henry tries to reassure her, Jane is further troubled that her happiness will come from Anne's sorrow.

SCENE 2—Park of Windsor Castle

Lord Percy has returned from exile upon order of the King. Rochefort, Anne's brother, warns him to be careful about talking so openly of his love for the Queen. The royal hunting party gathers, and Percy comes forward to thank Henry for his pardon. The King replies that it is only through Anne's belief in his innocence that Percy has been allowed to return. Percy's emotional greeting to the Queen betrays his true feelings for her, which alarms Anne and her brother. Henry, who has brought Percy back to trap Anne into an indiscretion, tells Sir Hervey to keep constant watch over Anne and Percy. Requesting that Percy be in faithful attendance at the court, the King orders the hunt to continue.

SCENE 3—Antechamber of Anne's apartment at Windsor

Smeton professes his secret love for the Queen to the portrait of her that he has stolen. As Rochefort and Anne enter, Smeton hides. Rochefort finally persuades Anne to see Percy for a moment while he stands guard at the door. Anne implores Percy to be brief, but when he proclaims his undying love for her, she urges him to leave, to flee England for his sake and for hers. She admits that she was ambitious; she obtained the throne she wanted, and although she now lives in fear of a King who does not love her, she is still his wife. The devoted Percy pleads with her to see him again; when she refuses, he draws his sword to kill himself. Rochefort's entrance is followed quickly by the King's. The King summons the guards and the court and asks them to bear witness to the shameful scene. When Smeton boldly offers to die as protest of their innocence, Henry sees the portrait of Anne and calls it proof of her infidelity. Anne begs her husband to listen to the truth; he answers that she would be better off dead. Rochefort and Smeton rue the part they have played in Anne's downfall; Percy believes Smeton to be a rival and the reason Anne rejects him; Jane Seymour is horrified by what has happened. The King commands that Anne and the others be taken to separate prisons

and tells the Queen that the judges will hear what she has to say.

ACT II

SCENE 1—Antechamber in the Tower of London

Anne's attendants feel that everyone has abandoned the unfortunate Queen, and when she appears they attempt to console her. The Council sends Sir Hervey to summon Anne's ladies-in-waiting to testify. Jane Seymour finds the Queen alone in prayer and urges her to admit her guilt and thereby save her life. Anne refuses to buy her life with infamy and presents the distraught Jane with visions of the horrors she hopes will befall the King's new wife. Suddenly the Queen realizes that Jane is that woman. Jane pleads for the Queen's understanding and receives Anne's pardon, which only adds to Jane's remorse.

SCENE 2—Outside the Council Chamber

The assembled courtiers are informed by Sir Hervey that Smeton has admitted his guilt to the Council. The King enters and talks to Hervey. He tries to avoid Anne and Percy, who are being brought to the Council Chamber, but Anne stops him and again begs him to spare her the disgrace of a trial. Percy accuses the King of having stolen Anne's love from him. Anne is outraged to learn that Smeton has been tricked into confessing. She declares that her only crime was to believe that she would find happiness with Henry rather than with Percy, which leads Percy to proclaim that he and Anne were once married. Anne is too upset to confirm or deny this, and Henry, whose vanity has been hurt, is now more determined that they both should die. He summons the guards to lead them before the Council and asserts that Anne will be forever disgraced and will be replaced by a worthier woman on the throne.

Henry is pondering what he has just learned when Jane Seymour appears. She asks Henry to allow her to go away; she loves him but cannot bear the guilt of Anne's death. Her distress causes Henry to despise Anne more, but his protests are interrupted by Hervey's announcement that the Council has annulled Anne's marriage to

Henry and condemned her and the others to death. The courtiers and Jane appeal to Henry for clemency, but the King leaves, followed by his court.

SCENE 3—The Tower of London

Rochefort and Percy refuse to accept the King's pardon, preferring to die with their Queen.

SCENE 4—Anne's apartments in the Tower of London

The Queen's attendants are disturbed by her pitiful condition and are further moved when she enters, distracted and confused. Anne's mind wanders; she thinks it is her wedding day, then she believes that Percy is there, and finally her thoughts turn to her childhood. The entrance of Percy, Smeton, and Rochefort brings her to her senses for a moment, but when Smeton confesses he lied to the Council in hopes of saving her, she returns to her delirium. She hears the cannon and bells and is told that they acclaim the new Queen. Declaring that only the shedding of her blood is needed to complete the crime, she refuses to invoke vengeance upon the guilty couple; she pardons them in hopes of mercy for herself.

Ariadne auf Naxos

→))）＊（（←

MUSIC BY: Richard Strauss

WORLD PREMIERE: Stuttgart, Germany,
October 25, 1912

LIBRETTO BY: Hugo von Hofmannstahl
English translation of the Prologue:
Lewis Sydenham
NEW YORK CITY OPERA PREMIERE:
(Sung in English and German) October 10,
1946

CONDUCTOR: Laszlo Halasz
STAGE DIRECTOR: Leopold Sachse
SCENIC DESIGNER: H. A. Condell
COSTUMES*

CHARACTERS (In order of appearance)	VOICE (type)	PREMIERE CAST (New York City Opera)
PROLOGUE		
Major-domo	Speaking	Gene Greenwell
Music Master	Baritone	James Pease
Lackey	Bass	Arthur Newman
Officer	Tenor	Lawrence Harwood
Composer	Soprano	Polyna Stoska
Tenor	Tenor	Vasso Argyris
Wigmaker	Bass	Grant Garnell
Zerbinetta	Soprano	Virginia MacWatters
Prima Donna	Soprano	Ella Flesch
Dancing Master	Tenor	Allen Stewart
Harlequin	Baritone	Ralph Herbert
Scaramuccio	Tenor	Hubert Norville
Truffaldino	Bass	Paul Dennis
Brighella	Tenor	Nathaniel Sprinzena
THE OPERA		
Naiad	Soprano	Lillian Fawcett
Dryad	Contralto	Rosalind Nadell
Echo	Soprano	Lenore Portnoy
Ariadne	Soprano	Ella Flesch
Zerbinetta	Soprano	Virginia MacWatters
Harlequin	Baritone	Ralph Herbert

* By Kate Friedheim; additional costumes by Stivanello.

CHARACTERS (In order of appearance)	VOICE (type)	PREMIERE CAST (New York City Opera)
Scaramuccio	Tenor	Hubert Norville
Truffaldino	Bass	Paul Dennis
Brighella	Tenor	Nathaniel Sprinzena
Bacchus	Tenor	Vasso Argyris

SYNOPSIS OF STORY

PROLOGUE

TIME AND PLACE: An improvised theater in the garden house of Jourdain's estate; 18th century

*

Monsieur Jourdain, a "nouveau riche," is giving a gala dinner party and to impress his guests has commissioned an opera seria for the occasion. He has also planned various other entertainments.

The great night has arrived. Nerves are on edge; last-minute touches are being made to scenery and costumes. The young Composer is beside himself with excitement. He does not notice that the dressing room of the Prima Donna who is to sing Ariadne has been shifted to make room for Zerbinetta, the leading lady of a commedia dell'arte troupe that has been engaged to perform after the opera.

The Composer, the Music Master, and all the members of the Opera Seria company are outraged and indignant when they learn that the opera is to be followed by such a vulgar frolic. The Prima Donna tries unsuccessfully to reach her friend Count Dorante to register a protest. Zerbinetta complains facetiously to a young officer (her current lover) that it might be better if the comedy were to take place first, as the audience will surely fall asleep during the long and boring opera and will be difficult to arouse.

The major-domo appears with astounding orders. As the hour is getting late, M. Jourdain wishes the opera and the comedy to be presented simultaneously! How this is to be arranged he leaves to the skill of the directors of each troupe, with the admonition that M. Jourdain expects his money's worth. Also, the curtain must fall precisely at nine o'clock, as the entertainment is to be followed by a display of fireworks in the garden. The Composer is desperate and wants to leave; the Music Master points out that the Composer needs the money promised by Jourdain in order to live. The Dancing Master proposes that cuts be made in the opera and explains that his actors are skilled at improvisation and will find moments to take part in the action. Zerbinetta flirts with the Composer, who, in his youthful naiveté, imagines that she has fallen in love with him and truly understands his innermost thoughts. He is momentarily cheerful but is rudely awakened when the whistling band of comedians rushes onstage to participate in his opera.

THE OPERA

TIME AND PLACE: Exterior of a cave on the desert island of Naxos; Antiquity

Ariadne has been abandoned by her lover, Theseus, on the island of Naxos. Because she has given her heart to him completely and cannot think of loving anyone else, she lies in a grotto sobbing and weeping, waiting only for Death. Nature, personified by three nymphs—Naiad of the waves, Dryad of the woods, and Echo of the winds and clouds—grieves for her. She gropes to find her sanity again, to reach the girl she once was, but can find comfort only in her conviction that the god of death will come and take her away. Zerbinetta and the members of her troupe, Harlequin, Scaramuccio, Brighella, and Truffaldino, try in various ways to reason with Ariadne. Harlequin sings a gentle song, but she fails to react. The comedians dance and clown

23

Ariadne auf Naxos, 1973

in an effort to make her smile, but she will not. Zerbinetta speaks to Ariadne woman to woman. Zerbinetta has had many lovers and on occasion has been in love with two at once, she confesses. Each lover seemed to her like a god. Surely a new lover will appear for Ariadne. Ariadne does not respond. Giving up, Zerbinetta and her colleagues perform a sequence from a play they had originally planned for the evening. "The Faithless Zerbinetta and Her Four Lovers." Each comedian tries to outdo his comrades in efforts to woo Zerbinetta. Harlequin triumphs.

A ship is sighted on the horizon by the nymphs. It is the ship of the young god Bacchus, who has just escaped the charms of the enchantress Circe. Ariadne believes Bacchus to be the god of death. Donning the robes in which she has planned to be buried, she receives him.

Because of his encounter with Circe, Bacchus is at first wary of the beautiful young Ariadne. She is fearful, but tells him she is ready for Death and mistakes his words of love for those words that will transport her to the nether world. Bacchus tries to reassure her that no harm will come to her and leads a nearly swooning Ariadne into her grotto to make love.

Zerbinetta enters to point out that Ariadne, like all women, has found another lover. But if we are to believe the young Composer, Ariadne dies. She and Bacchus are transported into the heavens to form a constellation of stars.

Ashmedai

→))) ✶ (((←

MUSIC BY: Josef Tal

WORLD PREMIERE: Hamburg, West
Germany, November 9, 1971

LIBRETTO BY: Israel Eliraz
English version by: Alan Marbe
NEW YORK CITY OPERA PREMIERE and
    AMERICAN PREMIERE: (Sung in English)
    April 1, 1976

CONDUCTOR: Gary Bertini (debut)
STAGE DIRECTOR: Harold Prince (debut)
SCENIC DESIGNER: Eugene Lee (debut)
COSTUMES: Franne Lee (debut)
CHOREOGRAPHY: Ron Field (debut)
DIRECTOR FOR ELECTRONIC SOUND: Eckhard Maronn (debut)

CHARACTERS (In order of appearance)	VOICE (type)	PREMIERE CAST (New York City Opera)
The Sergeant	Actor	Ed Nolfi
The Army	Actors	Steve Anthony (debut)
		John Calvert (debut)
		Fred Mann (debut)
		Wayne Mattson (debut)
The Fire Eater	Mute	"Presto"
The Knife Thrower	Mute	Michael Rubino
The Juggler	Mute	Jay Green
Ashmedai	Tenor	John Lankston
The Counsellors	Tenor	David Griffith
	Baritone	Thomas Jamerson
	Baritone	David Ronson
The Firechief	Baritone	Alan Baker
The Prince	Tenor	Richard Taylor
The Queen	Soprano	Eileen Schauler
The Executioner	Baritone	Philip Steele
The King	Baritone	Paul Ukena
The Tailor	Tenor	Jerold Siena
The Daughter	Soprano	Gianna Rolandi
The Mistress of the Inn	Soprano	Patricia Craig
The Citizen	Bass-baritone	Don Yule
The Soldier	Tenor	Howard Hensel
The Townspeople	Sopranos	Pegge Daly
		Joyce Lynn
		Rita Metzger

Ashmedai, 1976. Left to right: Richard Taylor, Eileen Schauler, Paul Ukena.

CHARACTERS (In order of appearance)	VOICE (type)	PREMIERE CAST (New York City Opera)
The Trumpeter	Mute	Dan Kingman
The Drummer	Mute	Ralph Williams
The Officer	Baritone	Robert Fisher
The Runner	Tenor	Gary Pool (debut)
The Rooster	Actor	Don Swanson (debut)

SYNOPSIS OF STORY
TIME AND PLACE: A mythical kingdom, Once Upon a Time

*

ACT I
At peace—Ashmedai arrives

Ashmedai is a folkloric villain who first appeared (as "Ashmodeva") in Persian and Babylonian mythologies. He played an important part in Hebrew legends concerning the relationship between him (Ashmedai, King of the Devils) and King Solomon.

The opera is rooted in these talmudic anecdotes but transcends them into an abstract and fabulous time and place.

Ashmedai intrudes upon the life of a land that has enjoyed peace and harmony for 500 years, ruled by a benevolent and beloved king. He perceives that these 500 years without war have left the king's wife, son, counselors, and army restless.

26

ACT II
At war

Capitalizing on their boredom, Ashmedai offers the king a year of freedom from the responsibilities of his crown; a year away from the nagging of his wife and the bickering of his court; a year in the arms of his mistress and the company of their illegitimate daughter.

The king accepts the offer, and Ashmedai in the guise of the king ascends the throne and makes the people his disciples.

The Ballad of Baby Doe

→))) * (((←

MUSIC BY: Douglas Moore
WORLD PREMIERE: Central City, Colorado,
  July 7, 1956

LIBRETTO BY: John Latouche
NEW YORK CITY OPERA PREMIERE:
  (Sung in English) April 3, 1958

CONDUCTOR: Emerson Buckley
STAGE DIRECTOR: Vladimir Rosing
SETS and COSTUMES: Donald Oenslager (debut)

CHARACTERS (In order of appearance)	VOICE (type)	PREMIERE CAST (New York City Opera)
An Old Silver Miner	Tenor	Howard Fried
A Saloon Bartender	Baritone	Chester Ludgin
Horace Tabor, Mayor of Leadville	Bass-baritone	Walter Cassel
Sam Bush, Barney, Jacob: cronies and associates of Tabor	Tenor	Keith Kaldenberg
	Tenor	Jack De Lon (debut)
	Baritone	George Del Monte
	Baritone	Arthur Newman
Augusta, wife of Horace Tabor	Mezzo	Martha Lipton
Mrs. Elizabeth (Baby) Doe, a miner's wife	Soprano	Beverly Sills
Kate and Meg, dance hall entertainers	Soprano	Naomi Collier
	Mezzo	Helen Baisley
Samantha, a maid	Mezzo	Lou Rodgers (debut)
A Clerk in the Clarendon Hotel	Tenor	Keith Kaldenberg
Albert, a bellboy	Baritone	Arthur Newman
Sarah, Mary, Emily, Effie: old friends of Augusta	Sopranos and Contraltos	Mary Lesawyer
		Jennie Andrea
		Anita Alpert (debut)
		Barbara Lockard (debut)
McCourt Family	Sopranos, Tenor, and Baritone	Helen Baisley
		Naomi Collier
		Nicola Barbusei (debut)
		William Zakariasen
Mama McCourt, Baby Doe's mother	Contralto	Beatrice Krebs
Four Washington Dandies	Tenors and Baritones	Edson Hoel
		William Elliot (debut)
		Peter Sliker (debut)
		John Dennison (debut)

CHARACTERS (In order of appearance)	VOICE (type)	PREMIERE CAST (New York City Opera)
Father Chappelle, priest at the wedding	Tenor	Howard Fried
A Footman at the Willard Hotel	Baritone	Arthur Newman
Chester A. Arthur, President of the United States	Tenor	Jack De Lon
Elizabeth and Silver Dollar, children of Horace and Baby Doe Tabor	Soprano Mime	Lynn Taussig (debut) Barbara Becker (debut)
Mayor of Leadville	Tenor	Robert Ruddy
William Jennings Bryan, Democratic Presidential Candidate	Bass	Joshua Hecht
Stage Doorman of the Tabor Grand Theatre	Tenor	Howard Fried
A Denver Politician	Baritone	Chester Ludgin
Silver Dollar (grown up)	Mezzo	Helen Baisley

Dance Hall Girls, Guests at the Clarendon, Baby Doe's Family and Foreign Diplomats at the Wedding Reception, Miners and Miners' Wives

SYNOPSIS OF STORY
TIME AND PLACE: Leadville and Denver, Colorado, 1880–99

*

ACT I

SCENE 1—Outside the Tabor Opera House, Leadville, 1880

During a concert at the new opera house, Tabor and his cronies escape and mix with the girls from the saloon. Augusta and the other women, in search of their husbands, are horrified by the scene. After everyone except Tabor has returned to the concert, Baby Doe arrives from Central City.

SCENE 2—Outside the Clarendon Hotel, later that evening

After the concert, Augusta and Horace Tabor return to the Clarendon. After Augusta has retired, Tabor has a romantic meeting with Baby Doe, and his passion is aroused.

SCENE 3—The Tabor apartment, several months later

When Augusta discovers evidence of the affair between Tabor and Baby Doe, she is determined to destroy Baby Doe.

SCENE 4—The lobby of the Clarendon Hotel, shortly thereafter

Baby Doe is about to leave Tabor and writes a letter to her mother explaining the reasons. When Augusta enters, Baby Doe tells her that the affair is over and that she is leaving; but when Augusta belittles her husband's accomplishments, Baby Doe is horrified and determines to remain with Tabor.

SCENE 5—Augusta's parlor in Denver, a year later

Augusta learns from her friends that Tabor has divorced her, and she is determined to have her revenge.

ACT II

SCENE 1—The Windsor Hotel, Denver, 1893

At the Governor's Ball, Baby Doe is snubbed by Augusta's friends, treatment she has been given for the ten years since her marriage to Tabor. Augusta arrives to warn Baby Doe that the

The Ballad of Baby Doe, 1966. Left to right: Walter Cassel, Beverly Sills, Muriel Costa-Greenspon.

silver standard is about to collapse and that Tabor will be ruined if he does not sell his silver mine. When Tabor enters, he orders Augusta out and obtains a promise from Baby Doe that she will never, under any circumstances, sell the Matchless Mine.

SCENE 2—A club room in Denver, 1895

Tabor has been ruined by the collapse of silver, and he seeks financial assistance from his old cronies. He tells of William Jennings Bryan, who is seeking the Presidency on the free silver platform, but his friends laugh at him for his support. Tabor angrily reminds them that it is silver that made them rich.

SCENE 3—The Matchless Mine, 1896

Bryan addresses the miners at the Matchless Mine.

SCENE 4—Augusta's parlor, November, 1896

As the newsboys announce Bryan's defeat, Mama McCourt comes to Augusta to seek aid for Tabor and his family. But an embittered Augusta refuses to help.

SCENE 5—The stage of the Tabor Grand Theatre, April, 1899

Tabor, completely ruined, old and ill, returns to the theatre that he built. In his dying moments he relives his past: the opening of the theatre, his courtship of Augusta, his rise to wealth and power. But Augusta also describes his ruin and foretells the ruin of his daughter, Silver Dollar. Baby Doe appears to comfort her dying husband and sings of their love; as Tabor dies, she is shown as a white-haired old woman entering the Matchless Mine to await her death.

Un Ballo in Maschera

->>>*<<<-

MUSIC BY: Giuseppe Verdi
WORLD PREMIERE: Rome, Italy,
  February 17, 1859

LIBRETTO BY: Antonio Somma
NEW YORK CITY OPERA PREMIERE:
  (Sung in Italian) March 21, 1971

CONDUCTOR: Julius Rudel
STAGE DIRECTOR: John Hirsch (debut)
SCENIC DESIGNER: Eoin Sprott (debut)
COSTUMES: José Varona
CHOREOGRAPHY: Thomas Andrew

CHARACTERS (In order of appearance)	VOICE (type)	PREMIERE CAST (New York City Opera)
Count Horn	Bass	Michael Devlin
Count Ribbing	Bass	Will Roy
Oscar, page to the King	Soprano	Patricia Wise
Gustavo (Gustavus III, King of Sweden)	Tenor	Enrico di Giuseppe
Renato (Count Anckarstrom), counselor to the King	Baritone	Louis Quilico
The Chief Justice	Tenor	Bernard Fitch
Ulrica, a fortune teller	Contralto	Muriel Greenspon
Silvano, a sailor	Baritone	William Ledbetter
Servant to Amelia	Baritone	Jack Bittner
Amelia, wife of Renato	Soprano	Gilda Cruz-Romo
Solo Dancer		Juliu Horvath

Noblemen, Court Ladies, Sailors, Fishermen

SYNOPSIS OF STORY
TIME AND PLACE: 1792, Stockholm and its environs

*

ACT I

SCENE 1—Reception hall in the Royal Palace

King Gustavus III of Sweden, who has fallen in love with Amelia, the beautiful wife of his loyal counselor Renato, is very pleased to see Amelia's name among the list of guests invited to a masked ball at the Royal Theater. Renato warns his master that there is a conspiracy afoot, but he has not as yet learned the names of the traitors. They are interrupted by the arrival of the Chief Justice, who asks for a decree of banishment against the sorceress Ulrica. The King is loath to banish one of his subjects, and Oscar, the page, who believes implicitly in the fortune teller's powers, adds his entreaties. The result is a reprieve for Ulrica, and Gustavo decides that he and his friends, in disguise, shall pay her a surprise visit and test her predictions. The anti-King faction, led by Counts Horn and Ribbing, sees in this proposed excursion a possibility of furthering their plans.

SCENE 2—Ulrica's den

Ulrica's den is filled with fishermen and sailors, fascinated with the sorceress' summoning of the spirit of evil. They all crowd in, and the first client who comes forward is Silvano, a sailor in the King's service. He is told, "Be cheerful! Soon riches and rank will come to you." Gustavo overhears this and, turning aside, scribbles a note on a piece of paper and slips it and a purse of money into Silvano's pocket. The simple sailor finds them immediately and reads the note aloud: "From Gustavo, to his dear friend and officer, Silvano." A knock is heard at the outer door, and a servant appears to tell Ulrica that his mistress must consult with her privately. Ulrica then bids the onlookers to depart. Gustavo stays behind unnoticed and overhears Amelia beg Ulrica for a potion to erase from her memory her love for Gustavo. Ulrica commands the conscience-stricken Amelia to go outside the city gates. There beneath the gallows she will find a herb; if she plucks it at midnight and drinks the juice, all will be well. Gustavo, learning that Amelia also has a secret love for him, joyfully swears to himself to protect her.

After Amelia has left, the disguised courtiers arrive and call for a prophecy. Ulrica warns them that her powers are real and not for amusement. They persist and she reluctantly predicts that Gustavo will be slain by a friend—the next to grasp his hand. The King, to show how little he believes her, calls on his assembled friends to take his hand. They all refuse. His consternation is cut short by the arrival of Renato, who rushes in and clasps his hand. Gustavo generously rewards Ulrica, even though he believes her prophecy has been proven false, and accepts

the praise of his subjects as his true identity is revealed.

ACT II

SCENE 1—Midnight, near the gallows

Amelia is startled by the appearance of Gustavo, who has followed her on her mission in order to protect her. Although he has resolved not to reveal his feelings, he weakens and declares his love for her. Suddenly Amelia's husband, Renato, appears to warn the King that his enemies are on their way to kill him. He does not recognize Amelia, who is heavily veiled. Gustavo makes Renato swear a solemn oath to conduct the veiled lady to the city gates without trying to discover her identity. The King then makes his escape just as Horn and Ribbing and their band of conspirators appear. They demand to know who Renato and his companion are. There is a struggle in which Amelia's veil falls to the ground, and Renato sees his wife. His horror quickly changes to anger and then to hatred of both Gustavo and Amelia, as the laughter of the conspirators mocks him. He makes a decision and asks Horn and Ribbing to call upon him the next day.

SCENE 2—Renato's library, the next day

Amelia pleads with her husband, who will not listen to her but insists that she must die for the disgrace she has brought upon him. He is willing to grant one last favor, that she see their little son, and as she departs, Horn and Ribbing arrive to keep their appointment. At first they do not trust the sudden change that has come over Renato, but he convinces them of his sincerity and they agree to work together for the King's death. Since each wants to be the chosen instrument, they decide to draw lots and place three names in a vase. Amelia returns to announce the King's page bringing invitations to a masked ball. Renato decides that he will not kill his wife, but that she shall share in her lover's death by unknowingly drawing the name of his assassin. She does so, and draws the name of Renato. Oscar is then admitted with the invitations, and the conspirators rejoice at the perfect opportunity to carry out their plan.

32

ACT III

SCENE 1—The King's box at the Royal Theater

The King writes a letter authorizing Renato to leave for a foreign country as his ambassador, taking Amelia with him. He signs the order and hides it in his shirt when he is interrupted by Oscar, who hands him a letter given to him by an unknown woman with instructions to place it, secretly, in the King's own hand. Gustavo reads it, and finds a warning of danger if he goes to the ball. Fearing an accusation of cowardice if he stays away, he orders his page to prepare to attend him.

SCENE 2—The Royal Theater

The masked ball has begun, and the guests and the conspirators have arrived in costume. Oscar recognizes Renato, who retaliates by unmasking him and accusing him of idling at the ball while his master is at home sleeping. Oscar retorts that the King is indeed at the ball and, finally yielding to Renato's taunts, describes in detail the King's disguise. Gustavo appears, followed by Amelia, who whispers a warning. The King recognizes her and realizes that it was she who sent the warning letter. He tells her that he is sending her and her husband away, and as they say goodbye, Renato mortally wounds Gustavo. The guests rush to attack the assassin, but they are restrained by Gustavo, who gives Renato the orders for his safe departure, telling him that Amelia is not to blame. Gustavo pardons both Renato and his associates as his last act as their King. He bids them and his beloved country farewell and dies.

Il Barbiere di Siviglia

-»»*«««-

MUSIC BY: Gioacchino Rossini

WORLD PREMIERE: Rome, Italy,
February 5, 1816

LIBRETTO BY: Cesare Sterbini
Based on Beaumarchais' comedy
NEW YORK CITY OPERA PREMIERE:
(Sung in Italian) October 5, 1947

CONDUCTOR: Laszlo Halasz
STAGE DIRECTOR: Elemer Nagy
SCENIC DESIGNER: H. A. Condell
COSTUMES*

CHARACTERS (In order of appearance)	VOICE (type)	PREMIERE CAST (New York City Opera)
Fiorello	Baritone	Arthur Newman
Count Almaviva	Tenor	Luigi Infantino
Figaro	Baritone	Enzo Mascherini
Rosina	Soprano	Virginia Haskins
Doctor Bartolo	Bass	Richard Wentworth
Berta	Mezzo	Terese Gerson
Don Basilio	Bass	Gean Greenwell
An Officer	Tenor	Nathaniel Sprinzena
Serenaders and Soldiers		

Note: Miss Haskins sang "L'inutile precauzione" by Pietro Cimara in The Lesson Scene.

SYNOPSIS OF STORY
TIME AND PLACE: Seville in the 18th century

*

ACT I

SCENE—A square in Seville

While visiting in Seville, Count Almaviva has a glimpse of a beautiful girl, Rosina, and vows to win her. She, however, is kept a virtual prisoner in the house of her guardian, Dr. Bartolo, who wants to marry her himself. One night Almaviva comes with a band of musicians to serenade her. When she fails to answer his song, he pays the musicians, who thank him profusely, and sends them away. He hides as Figaro, the

* By Kate Friedheim; additional costumes by Stivanello.

34

Il Barbiere di Siviglia, 1976

barber, approaches and boasts of his busy life as the neighborhood "Jack-of-all-trades." When Almaviva steps forward, Figaro, who is currently employed by Bartolo, recognizes him and promises (for a fee) to help him win Rosina. Almaviva then sings a second serenade to Rosina, describing himself as Lindoro, a poor creature who can offer her only his love. Rosina appears and replies that she will take him as he is, but she is suddenly interrupted and pulled inside. Figaro suggests that Almaviva might gain access to the house by disguising himself as a drunken soldier. The Count sings of his love; Figaro anticipates his coming reward.

ACT II

SCENE—A room in Dr. Bartolo's house

Rosina, alone in the house, dreams of Lindoro and decides to oppose Bartolo by whatever tricks are necessary to have her way. Figaro joins her, but they rush away at the sounds of footsteps. Bartolo, having learned of Almaviva's interest in his ward, enters with the music master, Basilio,

Il Barbiere di Siviglia, 1965. Sherrill Milnes

35

who suggests slandering the Count's reputation. Bartolo agrees, but Figaro, overhearing the plot, warns Rosina that Bartolo plans to marry her the next day and promises to take a letter she has written to Lindoro. Rosina listens to Bartolo's pompous boasting that he is far too clever to be outwitted by her. A violent knocking is heard at the door, and Berta, the maid, returns with Almaviva, disguised as a drunken soldier in search of a night's lodging. During a long argument with Bartolo, whose name he pretends not to understand, the Count slips a love letter to Rosina. The hubbub has attracted a large crowd in the street, and Figaro rushes in to warn that the police are coming to quiet the disturbance. They arrive and are about to arrest Almaviva when he reveals his true identity to the officer in charge and is released. Bartolo is stupefied by such trickery, and everyone comments merrily on this sudden turn of events.

ACT III

SCENE—Same as Act II

Bartolo receives the new music teacher, Don Alonso (the Count, again disguised), who says he is replacing the ailing Basilio. Rosina quickly recognizes her suitor, and the singing lesson begins while Bartolo dozes in his chair. Figaro arrives and then Basilio, who looks the picture of health. Almaviva, however, bribes Basilio to feign illness and leave. While Figaro shaves Bartolo, the Count and Rosina plan to elope that night. Bartolo overhears them and drives Almaviva from the house and Rosina to her room. Berta, overcome by the confusion, complains that she is going mad. During a violent thunderstorm, Bartolo has sent Basilio for a notary and has convinced Rosina that her suitor is really a servant of Almaviva. When Lindoro (the Count) and Figaro climb through the window, Rosina at first rejects her lover but then joyously falls into his arms when she learns that he and the Count are one and the same. As Figaro urges them to hurry, the ladder falls away and Basilio enters with the notary. Though summoned to join Rosina and Bartolo, the notary is instructed to marry the two young lovers instead. Arriving too late to stop the ceremony, Bartolo generously bestows his blessing on the happy couple.

The Bartered Bride

→))) * (((←

MUSIC BY: Bedrich Smetana

WORLD PREMIERE: Prague, Czechoslovakia,
May 30, 1866

LIBRETTO BY: Karel Sabina
English version by Joan Cross and
    Eric Crozier, after the translation by Rosa
    Newmarch
NEW YORK CITY OPERA PREMIERE:
    (Sung in English) October 3, 1945
    (Note: Performed with spoken recitatives)

CONDUCTOR: Laszlo Halasz
STAGE DIRECTOR: Eugene S. Bryden
SCENIC DESIGNER: Richard Rychtarik
BALLET CHOREOGRAPHER: Carl Randall
COSTUMES: Van Horn & Son

CHARACTERS* (In order of appearance)	VOICE (type)	PREMIERE CAST (New York City Opera)
Jenik	Tenor	Morton Bowe (debut)
Marenka	Soprano	Polyna Stoska
Kecal	Bass	Carlton Gauld
Kruschina	Baritone	Grant Garnell
Ludmilla	Soprano	Enid Szantho
Vashek	Tenor	Hubert Norville
Principal Circus Director	Tenor	Gil Gallagher
Esmeralda	Soprano	Lillian Fawcett
An Indian	Tenor	Allan Winston
Hata	Mezzo	Mary Kreste
Tobias Micha	Bass	Arthur Newman

Villagers, Children, Circus Performers

SYNOPSIS OF STORY
TIME AND PLACE: A Bohemian village about 1850

*

---

* Characters are listed according to the original Slavic-language spelling.

ACT I

SCENE—A square in the village

The story is that of a village romance in the Bohemia of a former day, involving the ancient custom of the marriage contract arranged by the village matchmaker through the parents, and the various ruses employed by Jenik and Marenka, the hero and heroine, to outwit the parents, the matchmaker—and the cruel stepmother.

It is the Spring Carnival, and everyone is very gay except Marenka, daughter of the rich peasant Kruschina. She is sad because this is the day when the unknown bridegroom, chosen by her parents, will claim her. She loves Jenik, a new arrival in the village, whom she knows as a poor servant. In reality he is the half-brother of the bridegroom. Jenik consoles her and explains, without giving his real name, that he is the son of wealthy parents, that his mother died and his father married again, and that the stepmother estranged him from his father.

Meanwhile, Marenka's parents approach with the matchmaker, Kecal, who has already obtained Kruschina's consent to his daughter's marriage to Vasek, son of the rich farmer Micha by a second marriage. Marenka's mother has insisted that her daughter's wishes be consulted, much to the annoyance of Kecal who, while excusing the bridegroom's absence, loudly sings his praises and proposes to Marenka according to custom. She repulses him and confesses to him her love for Jenik. Kecal determines to talk Jenik over to renouncing her in favor of a wealthier bride.

ACT II

SCENE—A room in the inn

Vasek meets Marenka, whom he does not know, and tells her of his purpose. She, without revealing her identity, tells him that he should be ashamed to woo a girl who does not love him but loves another man. Vasek, easily intimidated, finally swears never to claim Kruschina's daughter. Meanwhile, Kecal offers bribes to Jenik to give up Marenka. When Jenik learns from Kecal that the marriage contract is worded as being "Micha's son" he agrees, provided that "Micha's son" and none other shall claim the bride.

ACT III

SCENE—A square in the village

Vasek is entranced by some tightrope dancers, and especially by the Spanish dancer Esmeralda. The director of the troupe, needing a dancing bear, hires Vasek by promising him Esmeralda in marriage. Just as Vasek is putting on the bearskin, his parents come to him with the marriage contract, which he now refuses to sign.

Marenka, in the meantime, has heard of Jenik's fickle renunciation and is much grieved. During the course of events Jenik confronts his parents, is recognized as Micha's elder son, and claims his rights as son—and heir—much to Marenka's surprise and joy and to the stepmother's rage, and everything ends happily.

Beatrix Cenci

→))) * (((←

MUSIC BY: Alberto Ginastera

WORLD PREMIERE: Washington, D.C.,
September 10, 1971

LIBRETTO BY: William Shand and
Alberto Girri

NEW YORK CITY OPERA PREMIERE:
(Sung in Spanish) March 14, 1973

CONDUCTOR: Julius Rudel
PRODUCTION DEVISED and DIRECTED BY: Gerald Freedman
SCENIC DESIGNER: John Conklin
COSTUMES: Theoni V. Aldredge
CHOREOGRAPHY and ENSEMBLES STAGED BY: Joyce Trisler (debut)

CHARACTERS (In order of appearance)	VOICE (type)	PREMIERE CAST (New York City Opera)
Count Francesco Cenci	Bass	Justino Diaz (debut)
Andrea, a servant	Baritone	Irwin Densen
Beatrix Cenci	Soprano	Arlene Saunders
Lucrecia, her stepmother	Contralto	Gwendolyn Killebrew
Orsino, a prelate	Tenor	Gary Glaze
1st Guest	Tenor	Robert Manno
2nd Guest	Bass	Ron Bentley
3rd Guest	Baritone	Raymond Papay
Bernardo, brother of Beatrix	Tenor	Colin Duffy
Giacomo, brother of Beatrix	Bass-baritone	J. B. Davis
Olimpio ⎫ two assassins	Speaking	Ernesto Gonzalez (debut)
Marzio ⎭	Speaking	Juan Canas (debut)
Guard	Bass	Ron Bentley

Nobles, Guards, Judges, Servants

SYNOPSIS OF STORY

TIME AND PLACE: Rome and Petrella at the end of the 16th century

ACT I

SCENE 1—Outside the Cenci Palace in Rome

A throng of people are waiting for Count Francesco Cenci. They comment in hushed voices on his acts of violence and his contempt for his fellow man.

SCENE 2—A room in the Cenci Palace

The Count appears. He receives a message containing news of his two older sons in Spain and orders his servant Andrea to arrange a banquet. He orders his wife, Lucrecia, and his daughter, Beatrix, to be present, for at the banquet he intends to make an announcement.

39

Beatrix Cenci, 1973. Left to right: Arlene Saunders, Justino Diaz.

SCENE 3—Lucrecia's chambers in the Cenci Palace

Lucrecia, Beatrix, and their ladies-in-waiting embroider and sing while the child Bernardo listens. Andrea arrives and tells them of the Count's order. After he leaves, Beatrix expresses her foreboding of Cenci's evil intentions.

SCENE 4—Garden in the Cenci Palace

Beatrix secretly meets Orsino, her former suitor, who has taken holy orders. She begs him, as her only friend, to deliver a message to the Pope, seeking his aid in escaping the tyranny of her father. After Beatrix hands him the letter and leaves, Orsino reveals his intention not to deliver the message and tears up the letter.

SCENE 5—A masked ball in the banquet hall of the Cenci Palace

Unknown to each other, the Count and Beatrix are partners in a sensuous dance. The dance ends, the masks are removed, and Beatrix flees, aghast.

At the height of the festivities, Cenci announces with a toast that the reason for the celebration is the death of his two sons. The guests are horrified. A bacchanal follows, and the guests begin to leave. Beatrix pleads with them not to abandon her, Lucrecia, and Bernardo to the hands of a madman. The nobles sympathize but fear Cenci, and leave. Beatrix runs away terrified when Cenci tries to approach her. Alone, the Count muses that his desire for her will be fulfilled.

SCENE 6—Beatrix' bedroom

Beatrix is praying before the statue of the Virgin. Orsino enters, frightened, having escaped Cenci's watchdogs. Lying, he tells her that the Pope has rejected her plea without reading it. He declares his passion for her, but she no longer believes him. The Count calls her from outside the door. Beatrix begs Orsino to stay and defend her, but he leaves. Cenci enters, drunk, and moves toward Beatrix; she faces him, trembling with fear. He forces her into an embrace and drags her to the bed.

40

SCENE 7—Bernardo's room

Lucrecia is trying to calm Bernardo. They are both awake and troubled by the howling of Cenci's dogs. Beatrix' heartrending scream is heard. Bernardo hides. Lucrecia stands paralyzed with horror.

ACT II

SCENE 1—A terrace in the isolated castle of Petrella

Beatrix, in anguish as a prisoner of the decaying castle and of her defiled body, is being consoled by Lucrecia. Giacomo, Cenci's eldest son, says that Beatrix can only be freed by avenging this most heinous of crimes.

SCENE 2—An underground passage in the castle of Petrella

Olimpio and Marzio, who have been hired by Giacomo to assassinate the Count, arrive. Beatrix hands them the dagger and a purse containing the agreed sum. They leave and Beatrix, alone, dwells on her hatred for her father.

SCENE 3—Dining room of Petrella castle

The Count is dining, attended by Lucrecia. He calls for more wine. Lucrecia hands him a glass into which she has secretly put a sleeping potion. He orders her to drink first. She hesitates, then drinks. Cenci drinks. As the wine takes effect he sees visions and hears the voices of his enemies in the howling of the mastiffs.

SCENE 4—Bedroom of Count Cenci in Petrella

The Count staggers into the room. In his delirium the ghosts of his victims appear. He falls to the bed in a drugged sleep. Giacomo, Beatrix, Olimpio, and Marzio enter. At the sight of the sleeping Cenci, the two assassins lose their courage. Beatrix threatens to kill Cenci herself and accuse them. At this, Olimpio and Marzio stab the Count and leave in terror. Beatrix moves toward the bed. The dying Count sits up, tears at her dress, then falls back, dead.

SCENE 5—Room in the Cenci Palace in Rome

Months later, Bernardo tells of the peace he has felt since the Count's death. Orsino rushes in to announce that Cenci's body has been found and the guards are coming to arrest all of them. One of the assassins has been killed, and the other has confessed under torture. Orsino flees. Lucrecia finds new strength in her anguish as the guards come for them.

SCENE 6—Prison in the Castel Sant' Angelo

A bloodthirsty crowd is assembled expecting to witness Beatrix' confession. She is brought in bound to a huge wheel and tortured. The judges accuse her, but she cries out that she is not guilty and pleads for her life.

SCENE 7—Beatrix' cell

Bernardo is with Beatrix. She tells him that she is consoled by the deed for which she must forfeit her life. She feels pure again and is prepared to die. The guards enter to take her to the scaffold, and she gives Bernardo a farewell embrace. As she walks toward the door of the cell, she has a vision and recoils in horror: "I am afraid of Hell! There I shall meet my father . . ." She recovers her composure and walks out calmly to her death.

La Belle Hélène

→))) * (((←

MUSIC BY: Jacques Offenbach

WORLD PREMIERE: Paris, France,
December 17, 1864

LIBRETTO BY: Henri Meilhac and
  Ludovic Halévy
English version by Geoffrey Dunn,
  revised by Julius Rudel
NEW YORK CITY OPERA PREMIERE:
  (Sung in English) September 21, 1976

CONDUCTOR: Julius Rudel
DEVISED and DIRECTED BY: Jack Eddleman
SCENIC DESIGNER: Lloyd Evans
COSTUMES: Patton Campbell
CHOREOGRAPHY: Thomas Andrew

CHARACTERS (in order of appearance)	VOICE (type)	PREMIERE CAST (New York City Opera)
Calchas, Grand Augur of Jupiter	Baritone	Richard McKee
Philocomos, his servant	Tenor	Joaquin Romaguera
Euthycles, a blacksmith	Baritone	Don Yule
Helen, Queen of Sparta	Soprano	Karan Armstrong
Daphne, Helen's attendant	Mezzo	Puli Toro
Orestes, son of Agamemmon	Tenor	David Griffith
Daughters of Joy:		
Jocanthis	Soprano	Vicki Groff
Anthea	Soprano	Valeria Orlando
Phantis	Soprano	Madeleine Mines
Chloe	Soprano	Joyce Tomanec
Paris, son of King Priam	Tenor	Henry Price
Ajax I, King of Salamis	Tenor	Jerold Siena
Ajax II, King of the Locrians	Tenor	Melvin Lowery
Achilles, King of Phthiotis	Tenor	John Lankston
Menelaus, King of Sparta	Baritone	James Billings
Agamemnon, King of the Kings	Baritone	David Holloway
Living Statues	Dancers	Sandra Balestracci
		Mikhail Korogodsky (debut)

Princes and Princesses, Courtiers, Mourners of Adonis, Helen's Attendants, Guards,
People, Slaves

SYNOPSIS OF STORY
TIME AND PLACE: Ancient Greece, time of Homer

"THE ARGUMENT"

The plot and the music of this opera, pertaining to the mythological history of Paris and Helen as described by Homer, Apollodorus, and others, have made it the most popular burlesque of modern times. It has been represented more than five hundred times in Paris.

*

ACT I

SCENE—THE ORACLE—Sparta, the Temple of Jupiter

In a gay and brilliant scene, worshippers place their offerings at the shrine of Jupiter and depart. Then the augur, Calchas, with his attendants, enters upon a discussion of the situation and prepares the way for the fair Helen. When her suite retires, she is left alone with Calchas, and they confer on the means to be employed to save her from the decree of the oracle, which has declared that, although she is the wife of King Menelaus, she must abandon her husband and fly to Troy with the son of Priam. No decision is made, and Helen enters the temple while Calchas greets Orestes, the son of Agamemnon. Soon Paris appears, disguised as a shepherd, and, disclosing himself, states the decree of Venus. In a comical episode, Paris tells the celebrated "apple story," in which he was an actor. Calchas, of course, perceives the kind of nobility that he has to deal with and takes no special pains to guard Helen from an interview with the Prince of Troy. Helen and Paris are now alone. The former declares her love in a burlesque style. The lovers part, agreeing to meet at a grand tournament, to which soon come Achilles, Menelaus, Agamemnon, the two Ajaxes, and the court. Prizes for the best conundrums mark this "court of love," that institution of the Middle Ages being ridiculed by this laughable contest. Paris is victorious. He proclaims his name and lineage. Helen is delighted. To accommodate matters, Calchas oracularly bids Menelaus depart for Crete. Helen and Agamemnon urge him to yield, and he makes his exit to very striking music.

ACT II

SCENE—THE CARAVEL OF VENUS—The beach at Nauplia

Helen struggles against the decree of Venus, but her efforts avail little. Paris has another interview. He tells his plans and asks if Helen will love him. She says she will not. Paris leaves her, and she is more alarmed at her position than ever. The interlude, in the form of the Game of Goose, places Calchas in an awkward plight, he being charged with fraud at the game. Calchas now aids his ally, Paris, and the latter appears by the side of the slumbering queen. The beautiful music at this point is abridged by the unexpected arrival of Menelaus. The incident is highlighted by the rage of the king and the bacchanalian chorus. An absurd song by Helen would persuade Menelaus that he should have announced his return, while Paris defies all the Grecian heroes. The mixed feelings here produce a peculiarly jolly scene, closing with the retreat of Paris and with Helen's despair.

ACT III

SCENE—THE CARAVEL OF VENUS—The beach at Nauplia

Orestes and others are in the full tide of fashionable excitement. Menelaus and his wife have a domestic altercation. He charges her with being false; she declares her innocence, and that he is deluded by a dream, in return for which she threatens him with a reality. Agamemnon and Calchas appear. They deplore the pass to which things have been brought and announce that an epidemic of love has broken out because the will of Venus has not been obeyed. A new grand augur is announced. A golden galley approaches the shore, and it is discovered that the soothsayer is no other than Paris himself. He names the conditions on which Venus will relent. Helen is to return with him to Cythera and must sacrifice white heifers at the shrine of the goddess. She does not wish to do so, but on discovering that the grand augur is the Prince of Troy, consents to depart in obedience to destiny. She enters the galley with Paris, and they depart amid a storm of indignation and threats.

Bluebeard's Castle

->>>*<<<-

MUSIC BY: Béla Bartók

WORLD PREMIERE: Budapest, Hungary,
May 24, 1918

LIBRETTO BY: Béla Belasz
U.S. STAGE PREMIERE and
NEW YORK CITY OPERA PREMIERE:
(Sung in English) October 2, 1952

CONDUCTOR: Joseph Rosenstock
STAGE DIRECTOR: John Butler
SETS and COSTUMES: Rouben Ter-Arutunian (debut)
CHOREOGRAPHY: John Butler

CHARACTERS (In order of appearance)	VOICE (type)	PREMIERE CAST (New York City Opera)
Prologue	Spoken	Arnold Moss (debut)
Bluebeard	Bass	James Pease
Judith	Mezzo	Ann Ayars
Judith's Inner Self	Dancer	Mary Hinkson
First Door	Dancer	Murray Gitlin (debut)
Second Door	Dancer	Jim Smith
Third Door	Dancer	Mary Anthony (debut)
Fourth Door	Dancers	Anneliese Widman and Alvin Schulman (debut)
Fifth Door*		
Sixth Door	Dancer	Glen Tetley
Seventh Door	Dancers	Una Kai (debut) Yvonne Mounsey (debut) Patricia Savoia (debut)

Note: This performance was followed by *L'Heure Espagnole*.

SYNOPSIS OF STORY
TIME AND PLACE: Bluebeard's castle hall, with seven doors

*

After a spoken Prologue, the scene opens onto the gloomy hall of Bluebeard's castle. Bluebeard and his bride, Judith, enter. She has forsaken her family and her promised husband to marry Bluebeard. The hall is dark, and all that can be seen are the figures of Bluebeard and Judith

---

* In the New York City Opera production, there was no character representing the Fifth Door.

and seven doors. Judith proclaims her love for Bluebeard, even upon discovery of the gloom, and insists she will bring air and light to the castle, but Bluebeard asserts that no light may enter the castle. In the gloom, she discovers the seven locked doors and insists that they be opened at once. He reluctantly gives her the keys. As she opens the doors the first reveals a torture chamber; the second, the weapons of war; the third, a treasure chamber; the fourth, a garden; and in each she finds blood everywhere. The fifth door opens to reveal, in bright light, Bluebeard's vast domain. With the light now pouring into the castle, Judith insists that the last two doors must be opened for her. Bluebeard reluctantly consents to open the sixth door, which reveals a lake of teardrops. He at first refuses to open the last door but succumbs to Judith's pleas and gives her the last key. As this door opens to reveal Bluebeard's three former wives, the fifth and sixth doors gently close and the hall is once again steeped in darkness. Judith marvels at the beauty of each of the former wives and realizes that she must follow them. She pleads for mercy but Bluebeard answers her pleas only by taking a crown, a cloak, and jewels from the third door, which then closes. He places these upon Judith and she, nearly collapsing under their weight, joins the other wives behind the seventh door. This door now also closes and Bluebeard is engulfed in darkness.

La Bohème

-»»*«««-

MUSIC BY: Giacomo Puccini

WORLD PREMIERE: Turin, Italy,
February 1, 1896

LIBRETTO BY: Giuseppe Giacosa and
Luigi Illica

NEW YORK CITY OPERA PREMIERE:
(Sung in Italian) May 4, 1944

CONDUCTOR: Laszlo Halasz
STAGE DIRECTOR: José Ruben
SCENIC DESIGNER: H. A. Condell
COSTUMES*

CHARACTERS (In order of appearance)	VOICE (type)	PREMIERE CAST (New York City Opera)
Marcello	Baritone	John DeSurra (debut)
Rodolfo	Tenor	Mario Berini
Colline	Bass	Ralph Leonard
Schaunard	Baritone	Emile Renan
Benoit	Bass	Hamilton Benz (debut)
Mimi	Soprano	Irma Gonzalez (debut)
A Hawker	Bass	(not listed)
Parpignol	Tenor	(not listed)
Alcindoro	Bass	Hamilton Benz (debut)
Musetta	Soprano	Natalie Bodanya (debut)

Citizens, Students, Street Vendors, Soldiers

SYNOPSIS OF STORY
TIME AND PLACE: Paris, 1838

*

ACT I

SCENE—An attic studio in Montmartre

Rodolfo, the poet, and Marcello, the painter, are freezing in their Paris garret. Colline, the philosopher, enters, having unsuccessfully tried to pawn some books. In order to warm themselves, they burn a manuscript of Rodolfo's. Suddenly Schaunard, the musician, enters with ample provisions. Benoit, the landlord, knocks

---

* Costumes supplied by Van Horn & Son.

at the door, trying to collect the rent. Cleverly the four friends manage to get him drunk and chase him out without having paid. Everyone leaves to celebrate Christmas in the Latin Quarter except Rodolfo, who stays behind to finish an article. Mimi, a young seamstress and neighbor, calls from the outside, asking for her candle to be relit. Rodolfo hurries to comply. To his delight a charming girl enters. A sudden attack of faintness forces her to sink into a chair. Rodolfo revives her with a bit of wine. Delighting in her company, he detains her, and Mimi, finding her new friend charming, agrees to spend the evening with him in the Latin Quarter.

ACT II

SCENE—The Cafe Momus

The four friends and Mimi meet at the Cafe Momus. Musetta, a former love of Marcello, arrives, richly dressed, followed by an elderly admirer, Alcindoro. As soon as she becomes aware of Marcello's presence, she decides to win him back, and after several unsuccessful attempts, pretends to have a pain in her foot. Screaming loudly, she sends Alcindoro to fetch another pair of shoes. While he is gone, Marcello and Musetta embrace. It is quickly decided to let Alcindoro pay the bill for all. While the drum major and his tattoo march on, the Bohemians disappear in the crowd.

ACT III

SCENE—The gates of Paris

A tavern at the gates of Paris. Deep winter.

Mimi, now gravely ill, appears. Marcello, who has been working for the innkeeper as a painter while Musetta entertains the guests, meets her. She confesses to him that a separation from Rodolfo is unavoidable. Marcello promises to give him the message. Rodolfo joins him and confesses that his poverty prevents him from providing for Mimi. He realizes her fatal illness and feels guilty of accelerating her end. Mimi, who had been listening from behind a tree, is discovered. A reconciliation takes place, and the lovers decide to stay together until springtime. Meanwhile Marcello has been angered by the sound of frivolous laughter from Musetta and rushes back into the inn. After a brief fight, Musetta leaves in anger.

ACT IV

SCENE—Same as Act I

Rodolfo and Marcello are reminiscing. Mimi has left Rodolfo, improving her lot in the company of a Viscount. Colline and Schaunard enter, bringing a scanty meal which they share in mock humor. Suddenly Musetta enters and announces excitedly that she has found Mimi in a desolate condition, trying to reach Rodolfo, wishing to die near him. Mimi is brought in and quickly made comfortable on the bed. It is soon obvious that her life is almost at an end. The friends depart on various errands, leaving Rodolfo alone with Mimi. She reassures him that she has loved only him and then sinks into sleep. The friends return, soon recognizing the graveness of the situation. While Rodolfo darkens the room, Mimi dies.

Bomarzo

->))*((←-

MUSIC BY: Alberto Ginastera
WORLD PREMIERE: Washington, D.C.,
May 19, 1967

LIBRETTO BY: Manuel Mujica Lainez
NEW YORK CITY OPERA PREMIERE:
(Sung in Spanish) March 14, 1968

CONDUCTOR: Julius Rudel
PRODUCTION DEVISED and DIRECTED BY: Tito Capobianco
SCENIC DESIGNER: Ming Cho Lee
COSTUMES: José Varona
CHOREOGRAPHY: Jack Cole (debut)

CHARACTERS (In order of appearance)	VOICE (type)	PREMIERE CAST (New York City Opera)
Shepherd Boy	Boy Soprano	Robert Harwood (debut)
Pier Francesco Orsini, Duke of Bomarzo	Tenor	Salvador Novoa
Silvio de Narni, Astrologer	Baritone	Richard Torigi
Nicolas Orsini, nephew of Pier Francesco	Tenor	Joaquin Romaguera
Diana Orsini, grandmother of Pier Francesco	Contralto	Claramae Turner
Pier Francesco as a child	Mute	Patricio Porras (debut)
Maerbale, brother of Pier Francesco, as a child	Mute	Manuel Folgar (debut)
Girolamo, brother of Pier Francesco, as a child	Mute	Emilio Crespo (debut)
Gian Corrado Orsini, father of Pier Francesco	Bass	Michael Devlin
Skeleton	Dancer	Buzz Miller (debut)
Messenger	Tenor	Nico Castel
Pantasilea, courtesan of Florence	Mezzo	Joanna Simon
Abul, manservant of Pier Francesco	Dancer	Charles Moore (debut)
Girolamo, brother of Pier Francesco	Baritone	Robert Gregori (debut)
Julia Farnese, wife of Pier Francesco	Soprano	Isabel Penagos (debut)
Maerbale, brother of Pier Francesco	Baritone	Raymond Gibbs (debut)
Alter Ego of Pier Francesco	Dancer	Buzz Miller
Solo Dancers		Carmen de Lavallade, Robert Powell

Courtiers, Prelate, Pages, Servants, Peasants, Astrologers

SYNOPSIS OF STORY
TIME AND PLACE: Bomarzo, Florence, and Rome; 16th century

*

ACT I

SCENE 1—Park of the Castle of Bomarzo

"The Potion"—I, Pier Francesco Orsini, Duke of Bomarzo, on the last day of my life, left my castle with my nephew and my astrologer, Silvio de Narni, carrying a chalice with a potion that would make me immortal. They left me. After drinking the potion, I heard the voice of my dead grandmother saying I was going to die. And I saw, passing before my eyes, all the events of my strange life, which, like the hump on my back, encumbered my soul.

SCENE 2—Room in the Castle of Bomarzo

"Pier Francesco's Childhood"—Thus, I saw my brothers Girolamo and Maerbale when we were playing. Girolamo, the eldest, decided that since he was to be the Duke, I would be the Duchess of Bomarzo. I tried to resist and he angrily pierced my ear. My father came in, but instead of helping me he insulted me and dragged me into a haunted room in the castle, where I saw a skeleton. I know not whether I dreamt it, but the skeleton stood up and started dancing, till it fell on me.

SCENE 3—Pier Francesco's study, Castle of Bomarzo

"The Horoscope"—I next saw myself with the astrologer, who told me that my horoscope revealed that I would be immortal. I argued that my father wouldn't let me outlive him, but Silvio answered that he could avoid that. He wove a terrible incantation, and as he was about to finish, my grandmother appeared on the terrace filled with premonition as the peacocks' cries were heard. Then a messenger announced my father's return from battle badly wounded.

SCENE 4—Chamber of the courtesan Pantasilea, in Florence

"Pantasilea"—As a young man, my father sent me to Florence to a famous courtesan, Pantasilea,

attended by Abul, my slave, whom I dearly loved. I remember the terror I felt when I was left alone with her in a room of mirrors peopled by my shameful image. I gave her my jeweled necklace and asked her to let me go. She led me to a cupboard and I was revolted by its contents: skulls, bones, and dreadful aphrodisiacs. I ran away as the peacocks echoed the ominous cries I had heard in the castle.

SCENE 5—Countryside in Bomarzo, by the Tiber

"By the Tiber"—Memory then took me to a place near the Tiber, where my grandmother told me the story of the Orsinis and assured me that I had nothing to fear. Suddenly I saw Girolamo; he was about to bathe in the river and laughed at the promise of my horoscope. As he stepped back, he fell into the river and hit his head on a rock. My grandmother would not let me help him. She held out her arms, saying to me: "Come, Duke of Bomarzo forever."

SCENE 6—Great Hall, Castle of Bomarzo

"Pier Francesco Orsini, Duke of Bomarzo"—After my father died and I succeeded to the Dukedom, we held the ceremony in the castle, where my grandmother introduced me to the beautiful Julia Farnese. To my annoyance, Julia left with my brother, Maerbale. I remained alone with Abul and saw the ghost of my father approaching. My grandmother then told me that I should marry Julia.

SCENE 7—Terrace and garden, Castle of Bomarzo

"Fiesta at Bomarzo"—The courtiers were dancing, and I hardly managed to mumble the love I felt for my Bomarzo. I passed from one dream to another and had the impression that Abul, Julia Farnese, and Pantasilea were trying to take possession of me, till the dream became a nightmare.

49

Bomarzo, 1968. Left to right: Salvador Novoa, Claramae Turner.

SCENE 8—Pier Francesco's study, Castle of Bomarzo

"The Portrait by Lorenzo Lotto"—I next remember returning from battle and admiring my beautiful, idealized portrait by Lorenzo Lotto. Then I noticed a large mirror. There appeared the reflection of my painful body, which was suddenly transformed into the terrifying image of the Devil.

ACT II

SCENE 1—Palace of Galeazzo Farnese, Rome

"Julia Farnese"—The beautiful Julia Farnese was an obsession with me. I saw her singing with Maerbale while I, hidden, interpolated phrases of bitterness. When they were about to drink a glass of wine, I spilt it on Julia's dress and divined in that a premonition of death.

SCENE 2—The Bridal Chamber, Castle of Bomarzo

"The Bridal Chamber"—Julia and I were mar-

ried in Bomarzo. We retired to the bridal chamber and I pointed out to Julia the mosaics with our heraldic designs; I saw one that represented the face of the Devil, invisible to Julia.

SCENE 3—The same, at a distance

"The Dream"—I couldn't possess Julia that night and sank into despair. I dreamt that my courtiers captured Julia and myself in their dances, offering me through imagination what reality had denied me.

SCENE 4—Gallery, Castle of Bomarzo

"The Minotaur"—Like a madman I left the chamber and made my way along the corridor to the statue of the Minotaur. On recognizing a fated brother, I kissed its marble lips. The castle trembled with passion yet I found solace only in that sweet Minotaur.

SCENE 5—Garden, Castle of Bomarzo

"Maerbale"—The years went by, and I

50

couldn't erase from my mind a suspicion that Julia and Maerbale were deceiving me. To ascertain the truth, I induced Silvio to bring the suspected lovers together. I hid, and when Maerbale passed by, Silvio convinced him that Julia was awaiting him. I didn't realize that Nicolas was also watching the scene. The lovers kissed; I ordered Abul to pursue him, and Maerbale met his end.

SCENE 6—Silvio's studio, Castle of Bomarzo

"The Alchemy"—At last Silvio found a formula that would win eternity for me. In his studio we were surrounded by the statues of famous alchemists, and while he prepared the supreme potion it seemed to me that those shapes danced, helping him. Nicolas, who had sworn to avenge his father, was watching.

SCENE 7—Park of the Castle of Bomarzo, Continuation of ACT I, Scene 1

"The Park of the Monsters"—And now I know I am going to die. Nicolas has poisoned the potion. The shepherd boy has returned and kissed my forehead. That kiss means Bomarzo forgives me. I have accomplished the tremendous task of transforming the rocks in the park into gigantic monsters. It is my "Sacred Wood"— my immortality.

Boris Godunov

→))) ∗ (((←

MUSIC BY: Modeste P. Moussorgsky
Arranged and Instrumented by:
  N. Rimsky-Korsakoff
WORLD PREMIERE: St. Petersburg, Russia,
  February 8, 1874

LIBRETTO BY: Modeste P. Moussorgsky
English translation by: Joseph Machlis

NEW YORK CITY OPERA PREMIERE:
  (Sung in English) October 1, 1964

CONDUCTOR: Walter Susskind
STAGE DIRECTOR: Allen Fletcher
SCENERY and LIGHTING: Will Steven Armstrong
COSTUMES: Freddy Wittop (debut)
CHOREOGRAPHER: Thomas Andrew

CHARACTERS (In order of appearance)	VOICE (type)	PREMIERE CAST (New York City Opera)
Constable	Baritone	William Ledbetter
Peasants	Soprano	Barbara Beaman (debut)
	Mezzo	Charlotte Povia
	Tenor	Anthony Safina (debut)
	Baritone	John Smith
Andrei Schtschelkalow, Secretary of the Duma	Baritone	Ron Bottcher
Prince Schuiskij, Court Adviser to Boris Godunov	Tenor	Norman Kelley
Boris Godunov	Bass	Norman Treigle
Pimen, a monk and historian	Bass	Thomas Paul
Brother Gregori (false Dimitri)	Tenor	Jon Crain
Innkeeper	Mezzo	Muriel Greenspon
Missail, mendicant friar (heard offstage first)	Tenor	Kellis Miller
Varlaam, mendicant friar (heard offstage first)	Bass	Spiro Malas
First Guard	Baritone	Dominic Cossa
Xenia, daughter of Boris	Soprano	Carol Bergey
Nurse to Xenia	Mezzo	Beverly Evans
Feodor, son of Boris	Mezzo	Marlena Kleinman
Boyar Guard	Tenor	Harris Davis
Marina, Mnishek, daughter of a Polish landowner	Mezzo	Tatiana Troyanos
Rangoni, Jesuit priest	Baritone	William Chapman
An Idiot	Tenor	Richard Krause

CHARACTERS (In order of appearance	VOICE (type)	PREMIERE CAST (New York City Opera)
Lowitsky	Bass	Don Yule
Tschernjakowsky	Bass	David Smith
Solo Dancers		Rochelle Zide
		Michael Maule (debut)

Crowds, Boyars, Soldiers

Note: Boys' Choir from Epiphany Church trained by Mildred Hohner

SYNOPSIS OF STORY
TIME AND PLACE: Russia and Poland, 1598–1605

*

PROLOGUE

SCENE 1—Outside a convent in Moscow

Boris accepts the crown of Russia after the people—ignorant, superstition-ridden, and apathetic—have been forced into staging demonstrations of support.

SCENE 2—A Square in the Kremlin

At his coronation, Boris enters upon his reign with foreboding.

ACT I

SCENE 1—A cell in the Convent of Miracles

In a monastery cell the aged monk Pimen is writing his chronicles. The young monk Gregori speaks of his desire to emulate the old chronicler's brilliant and warlike past, but he is gently reminded that the pursuit of power and glory does not often bring content, as many monarchs have found. However, he does elicit from Pimen the information that had the murdered Tsarevich Dimitri lived, he would now be about Gregori's age.

SCENE 2—An inn near the Lithuanian border

Gregori determines to pose as the missing Tsarevich Dimitri. Journeying to Poland, he enters an inn on the Lithuanian border in the company of two vagabond monks, Varlaam and Missail, who settle down to carousing. Presently guards burst in, searching for the escaped monk Gregori, who is pursued by order of the Tsar.

Gregori, who is recognized from the description in a warrant, escapes, and makes his way over the border into Poland, where he raises forces to march against Boris.

SCENE—A room in the Tsar's Palace

Six years have passed since Boris' accession. He is shown in the company of his children, but the workings of conscience soon put an end to the peaceful domestic scene. As it seems to him, all the evils and misfortunes of his reign can be laid at the door of his crime. In the midst of his troubled meditations, the ambitious Prince Schuiskij arrives to report the uprising in Lithuania of the Pretender, Dimitri, to whose standard the nobles and peasants are flocking. Boris dismisses Schuiskij, whom he has reason to suspect of complicity in the plot. The chiming of a clock seems like the accusing voice of conscience, and his disordered imagination conjures up before him a vision of the murdered child in all its dreadful detail. Near collapse, Boris prays heaven for mercy on his guilty soul.

ACT III

SCENE 1—A castle in Poland, Marina's boudoir

The heart of the Princess Marina of Poland has been won by Gregori, now the false Dimitri. Marina longs to reign as Queen in Moscow and is persuading her countrymen to support her lover.

SCENE 2—The Palace gardens

The scene is set near a fountain. While Dimitri

awaits Marina, Rangoni appears to assure him of her love. Dimitri hides as Marina and her guests appear in the garden. The guests leave after dancing a polonaise honoring Marina. Dimitri and Marina are then alone; after first repulsing him, she capitulates to his promises of love and power.

ACT IV

SCENE 1—The forest near Kromy

At an emergency meeting of the Council of Boyars, the chronicler Pimen is brought before Boris to tell of a blind shepherd's vision of the murdered Tsarevich's grave. Boris is seized with pains that warn him that his end is near, and he sends for his son. He bids farewell to his son, to whose youthful hands he must resign his scepter. Feeling the nearness of death, he points to his son crying, "There is your Tsar—" and dies.

SCENE 2—The Duma

Gregori, the Pretender, appears in Russia and is acclaimed by the oppressed and rebellious people as the rightful Tsar Dimitri.

Le Bourgeois Gentilhomme

(A Ballet)

-»»*«««-

MUSIC BY: Richard Strauss
WORLD PREMIERE and NEW YORK CITY
OPERA PREMIERE: April 8, 1979

BASED ON Molière's comedy of the same name

CONDUCTOR: Cal Stewart Kellogg
CHOREOGRAPHY: George Balanchine and Jerome Robbins
SETS and COSTUMES: Rouben Ter-Arutunian

CHARACTERS	PREMIERE CAST (New York City Opera)
Lucile	Patricia McBride
M. Jourdain	Jean-Pierre Bonnefous (debut)
Cléonte	Rudolf Nureyev (debut)
Divertissement	Darla Hoover
	Michael Puleo
	Miriam Mahdaviani
	Allison Woodward
	Sarah Bard
	Cynthia Lochard
	Michelle Lanzet
	Antonia Franceschi
Maid	Leslie Saunders
Lackeys	David Keary
	Johan Bager
	Paul Frame
	Afshin Mofid
	Daniel Quinn
	Espen Giljane
Cooks	Robert Tracy
	Carl Hause
	Donald Dawson
	Ethan Brown
Attendants to Cléonte	Robert Weigel
	Sean Musselman

Note: This ballet followed the opera *Dido and Aeneas* (Purcell).

Le Bourgeois Gentilhomme, 1979. Left to right: Patricia McBride, Rudolf Nureyev, Jean-Pierre Bonnefous.

SYNOPSIS OF STORY

*

SCENE—Paris, Monsieur Jourdain's home

Based on the central episode in Molière's comedy of the same name, *Le Bourgeois Gentilhomme* introduces Cléonte, a young man in love with Lucile, the daughter of Monsieur Jourdain.

A would-be gentleman, Jourdain has rejected Cléonte as Lucile's suitor because he is not of noble birth. Cléonte disguises himself as the dancing master, fencing master, and tailor whom Jourdain has summoned to teach him the ways of the aristocracy in his attempts to shed his bourgeois manners. Finally, Cléonte impersonates the fictitious "son of the Great Turk," who seeks Lucile's hand and promises to confer a Turkish title upon Jourdain. Delighted, his host offers him a divertissement, a classical pas de sept.

In a ludicrous initiation ceremony in which he is mocked by all, Jourdain is dubbed a "mamamouchi." Dinner is served. Lucile expresses her sadness when ordered by her father to marry the Turkish stranger—until she recognizes Cléonte. During their pas de deux, Cléonte takes off his disguise. Jourdain accepts the situation and gives his blessing to the young lovers.

56

Capriccio

-»»*«««-

MUSIC BY: Richard Strauss

WORLD PREMIERE: Munich, Germany,
October 28, 1942

LIBRETTO BY: Clemens Kraus
English translation by: Maria Pelikan
NEW YORK CITY OPERA PREMIERE:
(Sung in English) October 27, 1965

CONDUCTOR: Ernst Maerzendorfer (debut)
STAGE DIRECTOR: Christopher West
SCENIC DESIGNER: Howard Bay
COSTUMES: Patton Campbell
CHOREOGRAPHER: Thomas Andrew

CHARACTERS (In order of appearance)	VOICE (type)	PREMIERE CAST (New York City Opera)
Flamand	Tenor	David Lloyd
Olivier	Baritone	John Reardon
LaRoche	Bass	Guus Hoekman (debut)
The Countess	Soprano	Donna Jeffrey
The Count	Baritone	Robert Trehy
Clairon	Contralto	Marijia Kova
Young Dancer	Dancer	Sandra Ballestracci (debut)
Italian Tenor	Tenor	Enzo Citarelli
Italian Singer	Soprano	Ellen Faull
Eight Servants	Tenors	Paul Corder, Harris Davis
	Baritones	Don Henderson, Robert Kelly
	Basses	Alan Olsen (debut),
		Richard Park, Anthony Safina,
		Don Yule
Major-domo	Bass	Ara Berberian
Monsieur Taupe	Tenor	Nico Castel

Musicians on stage: Harpsichord, Violin, Cello

SYNOPSIS OF STORY

TIME AND PLACE: A château outside Paris at the time of Gluck's operatic reform, about 1775

*

Guests in the house of the charming Countess, a composer, Flamand, a poet, Olivier, and a theatrical producer, LaRoche, discuss the relative merits of their contributions to the arts. The composer and the poet are both in love with the Countess, and each hopes to impress her in his

Capriccio, 1965

own metier—Olivier with a sonnet from his play (which is being rehearsed at the château by the Countess' brother and the famous actress Clairon); Flamand with a musical setting to the poem. The rivals embellish the theme "Prima le parole, dopo la musica." The Count professes interest in the stage only so far as it concerns Clairon, whereas LaRoche defends his practical approach to the arts and his services in putting the works of the artists on the stage. Of course, no one gives in or alters his own viewpoint. To solve the impasse, the Count suggests that Olivier and Flamand write an opera, using the events of the day as the basis for the libretto. LaRoche then presents some of his artists for the amusement of the guests. When they have all departed for Paris, the Countess is left to decide the end of the opera. However, she realizes that a decision between music and poetry also represents a personal choice. She muses, "Is there an ending which is not trivial?" For the moment she cannot decide and leaves the answer unresolved as the curtain falls.

Carmen

→»»∗«««

MUSIC BY: Georges Bizet

WORLD PREMIERE: Paris, France,
  March 3, 1875

LIBRETTO BY: Ludovic Halévy and
  Henri Meilhac

NEW YORK CITY OPERA PREMIERE:
  (Sung in French) February 24, 1944

CONDUCTOR: Laszlo Halasz
STAGE DIRECTOR: Hans Wolmut
SCENIC DESIGNER and ADVISOR: Richard Rychtarik*
COSTUMES†

CHARACTERS (In order of appearance)	VOICE (type)	PREMIERE CAST (New York City Opera)
Morales, an Officer	Baritone	Hugh Thompson (debut)
Andres, a Captain[1]	Bass	--
Micaela	Soprano	Mary Martha Briney (debut)
Zuniga, a Captain	Bass	Sidor Belarsky
Don José, a Corporal	Tenor	Mario Berini
Carmen	Mezzo	Jennie Tourel (debut)
Frasquita	Soprano	Regina Resnik (debut)
Mercedes	Mezzo	Rosalind Nadell (debut)
Lillas Pastia, an Innkeeper[1]	Tenor	--
Escamillo	Baritone	George Czaplicki
El Dancairo, a Smuggler	Baritone	Emile Renan
El Remendado, a Smuggler	Tenor	Henry Cordy (debut)
Guide[1]	Tenor	--
Solo dancers		Pilar Gomez
		Giovanni Rozzino

Children, Officers, Dragoons, Gypsies, Cigarette
Girls, Smugglers, Street Urchins

SYNOPSIS OF STORY
TIME AND PLACE: Seville, Spain; early 19th century

∗

* Sets loaned by the St. Louis Grand Opera Association.
† Supplied by Van Horn & Son.
[1] These characters were not included in the premiere cast of the New York City Opera production.

ACT I

SCENE—A square in Seville

Micaela, looking for her beloved, Corporal Don José, questions the townspeople and soldiers in the square near the cigarette factory but is told to come back later. Don José arrives, with the changing of the guard, and is told of the girl who has been seeking him. The people in the square are joined by the girls from the cigarette factory. All the men try to get the attention of one of the girls, Carmen, but she ignores them and directs most of her words to the young corporal. She throws a flower to him and goes back into the factory as the bell signals the return to work. Micaela comes back, bringing Don José news of his mother. Suddenly, a disturbance in the cigarette factory sends all the girls back into the square. When they accuse Carmen of attacking one of the girls with a knife, Captain Zuniga orders Don José to arrest her. After Zuniga has left, Carmen persuades her captor to loosen her bonds so that she can escape and promises to meet him later at Lillas Pastia's tavern if he does. When Captain Zuniga returns with the soldiers and townspeople, he orders Carmen taken to jail. Her wrists now untied, Carmen flees, and the Captain arrests Don José for aiding her escape.

ACT II

SCENE—Lillas Pastia's tavern

A month later, Carmen and her friends Frasquita and Mercedes entertain the gypsies and smugglers. The famous bullfighter Escamillo and his entourage enter, and he becomes very much interested in Carmen. Although she is impressed by his attentions, she is more concerned about Don José, who, she has heard, was just released from jail. When the tavern closes, she informs the smugglers that she will not be able to join them on their latest venture since she is in love with Don José, but she promises to ask him to join them. Don José arrives and Carmen dances for him, but when he starts to leave as the bugle call sounds from the barracks, she becomes enraged. Don José tells her that he wants to stay but cannot, and he shows her the withered flower that she had tossed him that first day. When

he confesses his love for her, Carmen tries to persuade him to join her and the smugglers. Captain Zuniga appears and makes advances to Carmen, deliberately provoking Don José. Don José attacks him; the smugglers come to his aid; and Don José has no choice but to desert the army and join the smugglers.

ACT III

SCENE—Smugglers' camp in the mountains

The smugglers, Carmen and Don José among them, are gathering in the hills. Don José is unhappy with life as a deserter, but he refuses to leave Carmen. Even though she has grown indifferent to him by now, he swears that he will never let her go. Frasquita and Mercedes amuse themselves by telling their fortunes from the cards, finding predictions of handsome men and riches. When Carmen joins them, she finds only death in her cards. Micaela, still looking for Don José, appears just as Don José fires at an approaching stranger. Micaela hides, and the stranger turns out to be Escamillo, who has come to see Carmen. He and Don José start to fight but are separated by the gypsies. Led in from her hiding place, Micaela begs Don José to return to their village to see his dying mother. He goes with her, but warns Carmen that they will meet again.

ACT IV

SCENE—Outside the bullring

Carmen waits with the crowd at the entrance to the bullring for the procession of bullfighters into the arena. After the other participants in the corrida pass by, Escamillo enters. He and Carmen profess their love for each other, and Escamillo goes into the arena. Carmen is warned by Frasquita and Mercedes that Don José has been seen looking for her, but she ignores them. Don José appears and Carmen faces him fearlessly, throwing away the ring he had given her. She is defiant as he pleads with her, her attention distracted by the shouts of the crowd inside the arena where Escamillo is fighting. As she goes toward the entrance, Don José stabs her.

Carmina Burana

Cantiones profanae

-»»*«««-

MUSIC BY: Carl Orff

WORLD PREMIERE: Frankfurt am Main,
Germany, June 8, 1937

LIBRETTO: Based on the Songs
of the Goliards

NEW YORK CITY OPERA PREMIERE:
(Sung in Latin) September 24, 1959

CONDUCTOR: Leopold Stokowski (debut)
PRODUCTION DIRECTED and CHOREOGRAPHED BY: John Butler
SCENIC DESIGNER: Paul Sylbert
COSTUMES: Ruth Morley

CHARACTERS (In order of appearance)	VOICE (type)	PREMIERE CAST (New York City Opera)
Singers	Soprano	Reri Grist (debut)
	Tenor	John Alexander
	Baritone	John Reardon
Solo Dancers		Carmen de Lavallade (debut
		Veronika Mlakar (debut)
		Scott Douglas (debut)
		Glen Tetley (debut)

Note: This opera was performed with *Oedipus Rex.*

SYNOPSIS OF STORY

Carmina Burana, literally, "Songs of Benediktbeuern," is a musical setting of the secular poems from the Middle Ages found in the monastery of Benediktbeuern in Bavaria. These poems, "carmina," are the songs of the goliards—vagabond students, seminarians, and disenchanted monks—who devoted their lives to singing, drinking, making love, and graphically describing these pleasures in their poetry.

*

FORTUNA IMPERATRIX MUNDI
(Fortune, Empress of the World)
1. *O Fortuna* (Chorus) Fortune, like the ever-

changing moon, brings happiness and, just as quickly, brings sadness.
2. *Fortune plango vulnera* (Chorus) As the

wheel of fortune turns, the happy ones at the top are thrust to the bottom in disgrace and another is raised to the top.

I
PRIMO VERE
(Springtime)

3. *Veris leta facies* (Chorus) A paean to the return of spring.
4. *Omnia sol temperat* (Baritone) With the return of spring come thoughts of the pleasures of love.
5. *Ecce gratum* (Chorus) A welcome to spring, which heralds the return of summer and the delights of love.

UF DEM ANGER
(On the Green)

6. *Tanz* (Dance)
7. *Floret silva* (Chorus) A maiden's lament for a lover who has ridden off on horseback.
8. *Chramer, gip die varwe mir* (Soprano and Chorus) The maidens request paint to color their cheeks red to make the young men love them.
9. *Reie* (Round Dance)
   Swaz hie gat umbe (Chorus)
   Chume, chum, geselle min (Chorus)
   The longings of youth for each other's love.
10. *Were diu werlt alle min* (Chorus) The lover would trade all the joys of the world to have the Queen of England lie in his arms.

II
IN TABERNA
(In the Tavern)

11. *Estuans interius* (Baritone) A driftless youth seething with rage and bitterness turns to a life of vice and lust.
12. *Olim lacus colueram* (Tenor and Chorus) The lament of a swan, roasted black, ready to be eaten.
13. *Ego sum abbas* (Baritone and Chorus) The Abbot of Cucany describes the pleasure of drinking and gambling, when all those he meets lose everything to him.
14. *In taberna quando sumus* (Chorus) In the tavern everybody drinks and toasts all from the prisoners to the Pope and King.

III
COUR D'AMOURS
(The Court of Love)

15. *Amor volat undique* (Soprano and Chorus) Reflections on the plight of a girl without a lover.
16. *Dies, nox et omnia* (Baritone) The lament of a young man whose love has a heart made of ice.
17. *Stetit puella* (Soprano) Description of a young girl wearing a red dress and its provocative sound as she moves.
18. *Circa mea pectora* (Baritone and Chorus) The yearning of a young man for his sweetheart.
19. *Si puer cum puellula* (Baritone and Chorus) Description of the passions of young lovers.
20. *Veni, veni, venias* (Chorus) Young man's description of the beauties of his sweetheart.
21. *In trutina* (Soprano) Reflections of a young woman on the sweetness of love.
22. *Tempus est iocundum* (Soprano, Baritone, and Chorus) A paean to spring and the passionate delights of love.
23. *Dulcissime* (Soprano) Surrender of a young woman to her lover.

BLANZIFLOR ET HELENA
(Blanziflor and Helena)

24. *Ave formosissima* (Chorus) A hymn to Venus comparing her to Blanziflor and Helena, two mythological sorceresses.

FORTUNA IMPERATRIX MUNDI

25. *O Fortuna* (Full company) A repeat of the opening chorus.

Carry Nation

-»»*«««-

MUSIC BY: Douglas Moore
WORLD PREMIERE: Lawrence, Kansas,
    April 28, 1966

LIBRETTO BY: William North Jayme
NEW YORK CITY OPERA PREMIERE:
    (Sung in English) March 28, 1968

CONDUCTOR: Samuel Krachmalnick
STAGE DIRECTOR: Frank Corsaro
SCENIC DESIGNER: Will Steven Armstrong
COSTUMES: Patton Campbell
CHOREOGRAPHY: Maria Grandy (debut)

CHARACTERS (In order of appearance)	VOICE (type)	PREMIERE CAST (New York City Opera)
1st Man in Saloon	(unavailable)	Dan Kingman
2nd Man in Saloon	(unavailable)	Don Carlo
Piano Player	Musician	Byron Dean Ryan
Carry Nation	Mezzo	Beverly Wolff
City Marshal	Baritone	Don Yule
Carry's Father	Bass-baritone	Arnold Voketaitis
Carry's Mother	Soprano	Ellen Faull
Ben	Tenor	Kellis Miller
Charles	Baritone	Julian Patrick (debut)
Preacher	Baritone	Edward Pierson
Young Man at Hoedown*	Tenor	John Stewart
Young Girl at Hoedown	Soprano	Arlene Adler
A Boy	Child	Michael Ahearn
A Girl	Child	Colette Martin (debut)
Toaster at Hoedown	Baritone	Jack Bittner
1st Lady of Auxiliary	Mezzo	Joan August
2nd Lady of Auxiliary	Mezzo	Maria West
3rd Lady of Auxiliary	Soprano	Lila Herbert
4th Lady of Auxiliary	Soprano	Hanna Owen
1st Man at Reunion	Tenor	Harris Davis
2nd Man at Reunion*	Baritone	Douglas Hunniken
Waiter	Mime	Luis Espinosa
Caretaker	Baritone	Jack Bittner

SYNOPSIS OF STORY
TIME AND PLACE: Kansas and Missouri, mid-19th and turn of the 20th century

*

Deep within any fanatic there is usually a wound, often self-inflicted, that has never properly healed. At the turn of the century such a wounded soul swept out of Kansas—behind her a trail of shattered saloon glass, before her a niche in history. More than anyone else, it was Carry

* A 2nd Young Man at Hoedown and 3rd Man at Reunion were added to the program on April 2, 1968.

63

Nation who roused the passions that led to Prohibition. Carry was fifty-three when she launched her crusade—to the applause of many. A dozen years later she died—ridiculed by all. What caused fervor to turn into fanaticism? Her autobiography, with its touching title *The Use and Need of the Life of Carry A. Nation,* provides what may be an answer: Many years before, this garrulous, self-righteous meddler had loved, had married, had given birth to a child. Her husband was a dashing young doctor just returned from the Civil War. He was also an alcoholic.

PROLOGUE

SCENE—A plush joint in Topeka

The Prologue takes place in 1901 in a barroom in Topeka, but it might be Kansas City, Washington, New York, London. "Joints" in countless cities had the misfortune to meet up with Carry's hatchet.

ACT I

SCENE 1—The parents' home, Belton, Missouri, 1865

The Civil War is over, Missourians are impoverished, the family is taking in a boarder. As Carry readies the parlor, the father recalls her conversion. Disappointed in marriage, Carry's mother lives increasingly in the past. Her sensibilities are offended at the idea of a boarder, but learning that he is a physician, she agrees to receive him—as a guest. The boarder, too, finds reality a burden. Charles leans on alcohol to forget the war. When he is ushered in by the stationmaster, his hangover shows. The bell sounds for evening prayer. The father shames Charles into kneeling.

SCENE 2—A churchyard, the following spring

Disdaining fire and brimstone, Charles has escaped from Sunday service. When Carry sneaks out, too, he conveys his love by acting a scene from Shakespeare. The father discovers them and takes from the gravestones the text for a sermon on sin. He accuses Charles of alcoholism. Charles responds by raising a flask.

SCENE 3—A hoedown, that autumn

After a summer of meeting secretly, Carry and Charles can now marry. Charles is establishing a practice. Carry's parents arrive. As Charles organizes a line to welcome the mother, the father begs Carry to end the romance. Charles asks for her hand, and Carry accepts. The mother begins a toast, but the father cuts her short. The crowd takes up the toast.

ACT II

SCENE 1—Carry's new home, Holden, Missouri, 1867

The Auxiliary Ladies read *Wuthering Heights* as they sew. The gossip is that Carry's husband is often too drunk to care for patients. He arrives home sober, but Carry is incensed. The gossip is true. Now he must really stop drinking, for she is having a baby. When she tries to use the baby to pledge Charles to abstinence, it is more than he can bear.

SCENE 2—Early autumn, the mother's bedroom

Alone in her bedroom, the mother is packing toys for Carry's baby. With the birth not far off, Carry has written for money. The father learns of the letter and sees a chance to get his daughter back. In a last burst of sanity, the mother pleads with him not to interfere.

SCENE 3—A men's club in Holden

Charles' chums revel in Civil War memories, but he remembers when his courage was tested, and found wanting, by a dying soldier. Carry pushes past the boy at the door, but finds Charles too far gone to take home. Her father arrives and goads her into leaving Charles.

SCENE 4—The churchyard, Easter Monday, the following spring

Carry cannot wait for the caretaker to finish putting Easter flowers on the graves so she can reread Charles' letter. Her mother no longer comprehends, but the baby can share the good news. Charles says he is getting well and they can soon be together again. The father arrives with a telegram: Charles has died the night before. First blaming herself for Charles' death, then angrily calling on God to give her a reason to go on living, Carry prefigures the crusader of the Prologue who styled herself "Your Loving Home Defender."

Catulli Carmina

→))) * (((←

MUSIC BY: Carl Orff
WORLD PREMIERE: Leipzig, Germany,
 November 6, 1943

LIBRETTO BY: Carl Orff
NEW YORK CITY OPERA PREMIERE:
 (Sung in Latin) October 30, 1969

CONDUCTOR: Julius Rudel
PRODUCTION CONCEIVED, DIRECTED, and
CHOREOGRAPHED BY: John Butler
SETS and COSTUMES: Jac Venza

CHARACTERS (In order of appearance)	VOICE (type)	PREMIERE CAST (New York City Opera)
Singers	Soprano	Patricia Wise
	Tenor	William Du Pree
Lesbia		Carmen De Lavallade
Caelius		Buzz Miller
Catullus	Dancers	Robert Powell
Ipsitilla		Lynn Kothera (debut)

Note: This followed the opera *L'Heure Espagnole.*

SYNOPSIS OF STORY
TIME AND PLACE: Rome, before Christ

*

The Roman poet Gaius Valerius Catullus (87–54 B.C.) specialized in the subject of love—its appetites, its tragedies. In many of his poems he expressed his infatuation and final disillusionment with a patrician lady whom he called Lesbia. Catullus died in Rome at the age of 33, a victim of his own obsessions. The life and poems of Catullus are the basis of Orff's work.

A chorus of old men comments throughout the work on the futility of earthly passion; young couples express their exuberance with the first experiences of love. The soloists carry out Catullus' own story of love and tragedy: his passion for Lesbia; his discovery that his best friend, Caelius, has betrayed him with Lesbia; the confrontation of the two men when Catullus tries to find solace with the courtesan Ipsitilla; his failure to break the spell of Lesbia.

The young couples, ignoring the old men's warnings and the example of Catullus' tragic love, return to their own ritual of love.

Cavalleria Rusticana

→))) * (((←

MUSIC BY: Pietro Mascagni

WORLD PREMIERE: Rome, Italy,
May 17, 1890

LIBRETTO BY: Giovanni Targioni-Tozzetti,
Guido Menasci

NEW YORK CITY OPERA PREMIERE:
(Sung in Italian) May 5, 1944

CONDUCTOR: Hans Schwieger (debut)
STAGE DIRECTOR: Hans Wolmut
SCENIC DESIGNER: Richard Rychtarik
COSTUMES*

CHARACTERS	VOICE	PREMIERE CAST
(In order of appearance)	(type)	(New York City Opera)
Turiddu (heard offstage first)	Tenor	Edward Kane
Mamma Lucia	Mezzo	Sura Aronovich
Santuzza	Soprano	Dusolina Giannini
Alfio	Baritone	Francis Row (debut)
Lola	Mezzo	Alice Howland

Villagers, Children, Priest

Note: This opera was performed with *Pagliacci.*

SYNOPSIS OF STORY

TIME AND PLACE: The square in a Sicilian mountain village, late 19th century

*

Before the curtain rises, Turiddu, a young Sicilian peasant, is singing a serenade extolling the beauty of Lola, the girl he loved before going into military service. When he returned, he found that she had married Alfio, a coachman, whose business keeps him away most of the year. Turiddu consoled himself by starting a love affair with Santuzza, another village girl, but soon tired of her and returned to Lola. Santuzza confronts Turiddu in one more attempt to win him back, but her pleading only infuriates him. Enraged, Santuzza swears to pay him back. The village is celebrating Easter. Alfio has returned, is greeted by the peasants, and joyfully anticipates the reunion with his wife. Santuzza tells him of Lola's unfaithfulness and, in true Sicilian fashion, he swears vendetta. When Turiddu joins the crowd, unaware of what has happened, he is challenged by Alfio to a duel with knives. Turiddu, conscious of his guilt, accepts. Sensing his impending death, he bids goodbye to his mother, Mamma Lucia, and rushes to the orchard to meet Alfio. Santuzza reappears, only to hear the outcry of the peasant women; Turiddu has been murdered.

---

* Supplied by Van Horn & Son.

66

La Cenerentola

–>))∗(((–

MUSIC BY: Gioachino Rossini
WORLD PREMIERE: Rome, Italy,
    January 25, 1817

LIBRETTO BY: Jacopo Ferretti
NEW YORK CITY OPERA PREMIERE:
    (Sung in Italian) March 26, 1953

CONDUCTOR: Joseph Rosenstock
STAGE DIRECTOR: Otto Erhardt
SCENIC DESIGNER and COSTUMES: Rouben Ter-Arutunian

CHARACTERS (In order of appearance)	VOICE (type)	PREMIERE CAST (New York City Opera)
Clorinda,	Soprano	Laurel Hurley
Tisbe,	Mezzo	Edith Evans
and		
Angelina (Cinderella), daughters of Don Magnifico	Contralto	Frances Bible
Alidoro, a philosopher	Bass	Arthur Newman
Don Magnifico, a nobleman	Bass	Richard Wentworth
Prince Ramiro	Tenor	Riccardo Manning (debut)
Dandini, his servant	Bass	George Gaynes
Courtiers and Ladies		

SYNOPSIS OF STORY
TIME AND PLACE: Salerno, 18th-century manners and customs

∗

ACT I

SCENE 1—A hall in the house of Don Magnifico

Angelina (called Cinderella) has two stepsisters, Clorinda and Tisbe, and a stepfather, Don Magnifico, who keep her in constant servitude. Don Magnifico has squandered the dowry left her by her mother and allowed her estate to fall into disrepair. The cruelty of the stepsisters is shown by their disregard of a beggar while Cinderella, in contrast, gives him bread and coffee. The beggar is Alidoro, a court philosopher and tutor to Prince Ramiro, come in disguise to examine all the marriageable girls in the vicinity, for Ramiro must marry immediately or be disinherited. Having been told by Alidoro that he

67

Le Cenerentola, 1970. Left to right: Spiro Malas, Lois Crane, Beverly Evans, Frances Bible, Enrico d'Giuseppe.

will find an ideal wife there, Ramiro also comes in disguise and falls in love with Cinderella at first sight. He thinks that Alidoro meant him to admire one of the sisters, for Cinderella, by her appearance, seems to him to be a servant. She, for her part, falls in love with the supposed groom. Dandini, the Prince's valet, comes as well, and he is dressed as the Prince. Clorinda and Tisbe fawn on him, and he pretends to be completely taken by them. Don Magnifico is certain that one of his daughters will succeed in marrying the Prince, thus repairing the family fortunes. When the sisters go off to the Prince's palace, where the most beautiful girl of the province is to be selected to marry him, Cinderella begs her stepfather to let her go, too. He waves her aside and threatens her with a beating. Ramiro, still present in his disguise, has observed this with great anger. When all have left, Alidoro returns again, with a gown and jewels, to take Cinderella to the ball.

SCENE 2—A park and the palace of Don Ramiro*

Dandini, still dressed as the Prince, appoints Don Magnifico chief butler. Tisbe and Clorinda pursue the "prince," who suggests that as he can marry only one of them, the other should marry his valet. They are both indignant at such a suggestion. Alidoro announces the arrival of an unknown lady, wearing a mask. When she is persuaded to show her face, the sisters are struck by her resemblance to Cinderella.

ACT II

SCENE 1—The palace

Ramiro, who has fallen in love with the mysterious lady, suspects that Dandini entertains similar feelings for the beautiful stranger. When Dandini does in fact make advances to her, she

---

* Scene 3 of Act I was combined with Scene 2 in this production.

68

tells him she loves another, his valet. Ramiro (still disguised as his valet) reveals himself to her, but she tells him that before she agrees to marry him, he must discover her identity. She gives him one of the pair of bracelets she is wearing, so that he may eventually recognize her when he finds her. Dandini now tells the Baron that he is not really the Prince, but his valet. The Baron and the sisters leave in indignation.

SCENE 2—Don Magnifico's house

Don Magnifico and his daughters, furious at the deception, vent their anger on Cinderella because she reminds them of the unknown beauty who spoiled things for them at the ball. Later, Ramiro, who has left the palace to find the unknown beauty, is obliged to take shelter in the house of Don Magnifico because his coach is upset in a storm. This time he enters in his true character of the Prince. His discovery of the bracelet on Cinderella's arm sets things right for the lovers, and Ramiro declares that he will marry her. Her cruel relatives then beg mercy of the new Princess.

SCENE 3—The palace

Cinderella, now the bride of Don Ramiro, forgives her stepsisters and father, and all ends happily amid general rejoicing.

The Consul

→)))∗(((←

MUSIC BY: Gian Carlo Menotti
WORLD PREMIERE: New York, New York,
March 15, 1950

LIBRETTO BY: Gian Carlo Menotti
NEW YORK CITY OPERA PREMIERE:
(Sung in English) October 8, 1952

CONDUCTOR: Thomas Schippers
STAGE DIRECTOR: Gian Carlo Menotti
SETS and COSTUMES: Horace Armistead (debut)
CHOREOGRAPHER: John Butler

CHARACTERS (In order of appearance)	VOICE (type)	PREMIERE CAST (New York City Opera)
The Voice on the Record		Mabel Mercer
John Sorel	Baritone	Richard Torigi
Magda Sorel	Soprano	Patricia Neway
The Mother	Contralto	Mary Kreste
Secret Police Agent	Bass	Emile Renan
First Plainclothesman	Mute	Charles Kuestner
Second Plainclothesman	Mute	Thomas Powell
The Secretary	Mezzo	Gloria Lane (debut)
A Young Professor	Mute	Glen Tetley
A Nightclub Performer	Mute	Mary Hinkson
Mr. Kofner	Bass-baritone	Jon Geyans
The Foreign Woman	Soprano	Maria Marlo (debut)
Anna Gomez	Soprano	Vilma Georgiou (debut)
Nika Magadoff, Magician	Tenor	Norman Kelley (debut)
Vera Boronel	Contralto	Edith Evans
Assan	Baritone	Arthur Newman
Plainclothesmen	Mute	Jerry Decker
		Alvin Schulman
		Jim Smith

SYNOPSIS OF STORY
TIME AND PLACE: A European country; the present

∗

70

The Consul, 1960

ACT I

SCENE 1—The Home

As the curtain rises, John Sorel stumbles through the door calling for his wife. A member of the underground, John has been wounded in a raid and is still being pursued. He barely has time to hide when the Secret Police Agent enters with two henchmen. After a violent search and questioning, they leave, threatening that they will return. John comes out of hiding, advises Magda to seek help at the Consulate, and reluctantly leaves his family.

SCENE 2—The Consulate

Magda goes to the Consulate. There she is confronted by a meticulously efficient Secretary who rules in a kingdom of applications, request forms, and endless documents. With the other applicants, Mr. Kofner, a Foreign Woman, Magadoff the Magician, and two other women, Magda submits her case to the unyielding Secretary and meets with failure and delay.

ACT II

SCENE 1—The Home

The days of waiting have lengthened into months. Magda watches helplessly as the Mother tries to comfort the sick child. In a moment of nightmare, Magda sees both her husband and child threatened by death. A few moments later a visit from the Secret Police Agent coincides with the first message from John, brought by Assan the Glasscutter. Knowing the police are becoming impatient and learning that John threatens to return to help her, Magda decides to return to the Consulate.

SCENE 2—The Consulate

At the Consulate, the stage is held by Nika Magadoff, the Magician, who attempts to win a visa with feats of prestidigitation and hypnotism. When Magda can at last appeal to the Secretary, her request is denied. Finally defiant, Magda cries out against the senseless chains of paper that bind all the hopeless who come to the Consulate. Relenting, the Secretary offers to see the Consul. But this last hope is destroyed a moment later.

ACT III

SCENE 1—The Consulate

Magda sits alone in the Consulate. Ignoring the Secretary's insistence that she is wasting her time, Magda watches one fortunate woman receive her papers and visa. Then Assan hurries in to tell her that John will return unless she can find a way to stop him. Knowing what she must do, Magda writes a note to John and sends Assan to deliver it. In a moment she, too, leaves the Consulate.

Left alone, the Secretary has a frightening vision of the myriad names and faces that pass in endless procession before her. Suddenly John

Sorel enters and begs her for news of his wife and for help. Almost immediately, the Secret Police enter and force John to go with them, but not before the Secretary, moved for the first time, promises to call his wife.

SCENE 2—The Home

Magda enters her home an instant too late for the call. In hopeless resignation, she shrouds the windows and the door and turns on the gas. As she dies, she sees again John, his mother, and the people she has watched in the Consulate. She hears them urging her to join them but struggles futilely, unable to move. At last the Magician appears and with great compassion leads her once more to her place at the stove.

The ringing of the phone shatters the dream. Magda makes one more effort to answer, but death has freed her. The curtain falls.

Les Contes d'Hoffmann

->>>*<<<-

MUSIC BY: Jacques Offenbach

WORLD PREMIERE: Paris, France,
February 10, 1881

LIBRETTO BY: Jules Barbier and
Michel Carré

NEW YORK CITY OPERA PREMIERE:
(Sung in French) April 6, 1949

CONDUCTOR: Jean Morel
STAGE DIRECTOR: Leopold Sachse
SCENIC DESIGNER: Herbert Brodkin (debut)
BALLET CHOREOGRAPHER: George Balanchine
COSTUMES*

CHARACTERS[1] (In order of appearance)	VOICE (type)	PREMIERE CAST (New York City Opera)
Lindorf	Bass-baritone	Carlton Gauld
Andres	Tenor	Luigi Vellucci
Luther	Bass-baritone	Richard Wentworth
Hermann	Bass-baritone	Arthur Newman
Nathaniel	Tenor	William Stanz
Hoffmann	Tenor	Robert Rounseville
Nicklausse	Mezzo	Rosalind Nadell
Spalanzani	Baritone	Edwin Dunning
Cochenille	Tenor	Luigi Vellucci
Coppelius	Bass-baritone	Carlton Gauld
Olympia	Soprano	Virginia MacWatters
Giulietta	Soprano	Wilma Spence
Schlemil	Baritone	Edwin Dunning
Pittichinaccio	Tenor	Luigi Vellucci
Dappertutto	Bass-baritone	Walter Cassel
Antonia	Soprano	Ann Ayars
Crespel	Bass-baritone	Norman Scott
Franz	Tenor	Luigi Vellucci
Dr. Miracle	Bass-baritone	Carlton Gauld
The Mother	Mezzo	Frances Bible

Students, Guests

SYNOPSIS OF STORY
TIME AND PLACE: Germany and Italy; 19th century

*

---
* By Kate Friedheim.
[1] The role of Stella in Act IV was not identified in the premiere performance.

PROLOGUE

SCENE—Luther's tavern in Nuremberg

The poet Hoffmann (waiting for the arrival of his latest love, Stella) falls into an argument with the evil genius Lindorf. Carried away by his passion, he tells the story of his three loves.

ACT I

SCENE—Spalanzani's studio

Hoffmann has become enamoured of Olympia, the beautiful "daughter" of the scientist Spalanzani. He gains entrance to his mansion posing as a student. At a party, Olympia sings a strangely mechanical song for the guests and dances with Hoffmann until he drops from exhaustion. The evil Coppelius enters, accusing Spalanzani of having paid for his "daughter" with a worthless draft, and in a fit of anger smashes Olympia to bits. The guests laugh as Hoffmann discovers that his passion has been for an automaton.

ACT II

SCENE—Giulietta's villa on a canal in Venice

In Venice, Hoffmann has become fascinated with the courtesan Giulietta. Under the spell of Dappertutto, she has already procured the shadow of Schlemil, and she soon wins for him the reflection of Hoffmann. The jealous Schlemil enters into a duel with Hoffmann and is killed by the sword that Dappertutto proffers to the poet. Hoffmann's disillusionment is complete when he sees Giulietta leaving, protected by Pittichinaccio and Dappertutto.

ACT III

SCENE—Crespel's home in Munich

Hoffmann is betrothed to Antonia, daughter of Crespel. The girl, like her mother who died at an early age, has a beautiful voice but is afflicted with consumption. Crespel forbids her to sing, knowing this would be fatal for her. Soon, however, the evil Doctor Miracle, aided by the counsel of her mother, persuades the girl to sing. She does so and, quickly exhausted, dies in front of her desperate father. Once more Hoffmann's love has been thwarted.

EPILOGUE

SCENE—Luther's tavern in Nuremberg

Back at the tavern, with Hoffmann completely drunk, Lindorf walks off arm in arm with Stella, Hoffmann's latest love.

Le Coq d'Or

-»»*«««-

MUSIC BY: Nikolai Rimsky-Korsakov

LIBRETTO BY: Vladimir Bielsky
English version by: Antal Dorati and
James Gibson after a fairy tale by
Alexander Pushkin

WORLD PREMIERE: Moscow, Russia,
October 7, 1909

NEW YORK CITY OPERA PREMIERE:
(Sung in English) September 21, 1967

CONDUCTOR: Julius Rudel
PRODUCTION DEVISED and DIRECTED BY: Tito Capobianco
SCENIC DESIGNER: Ming Cho Lee
COSTUMES: José Varona

CHARACTERS* (In order of appearance)	VOICE (type)	PREMIERE CAST (New York City Opera)
Astrologer	Tenor	Enrico di Giuseppe
King Dodon	Bass	Norman Treigle
Prince Guidon	Tenor	Nico Castel
Prince Afron	Baritone	David Smith
General Polkan	Bass	Noel Jan Tyl
The Golden Cockerel	Soprano	Joan Summers
Amelfa	Contralto	Muriel Greenspon
Queen of Shemakha	Soprano	Beverly Sills

Ministers, Peasants, Pages, Guards, Eunuchs, Slaves, Animals

SYNOPSIS OF STORY
TIME AND PLACE: King Dodon's kingdom, legendary times

*

PROLOGUE

The Astrologer warns the audience to heed the moral of the story.

ACT I

SCENE 1—The King's court

Once upon a time in a legendary kingdom,
King Dodon held court, spending his time in luxurious pursuits, giving little care to affairs of state. His two sons, the princes Guidon and Afron, are much more concerned with the enemies that are attacking the nation from all quarters. A war council is called by the ministers of state; many suggestions are made, but a disagreement arises between the King, his General, Polkan, and his sons. As they wrangle, an Astrologer appears; he presents the king with a Golden

* Two Ministers were added to program of October 1, 1967 (matinee).

Cockerel, which has the power to foretell events and gives warning when danger threatens. The King is delighted and asks the Astrologer to name his price. The Astrologer declares that he will name his reward at a later time.

SCENE 2—The siesta and dream

The King and his household settle down for a nap. The King dreams of a lovely maiden. Twice the Cockerel gives warning of danger, and twice Polkan has to wake the King.

SCENE 3—The declaration of war

The princes Guidon and Afron go off to battle, followed by King Dodon and General Polkan.

ACT II

SCENE 1—The battlefield, death of the sons

When the King reaches the scene of battle, he finds his two sons dead, having slain each other by mistake due to the magic of the witch Fata Morgana. King Dodon is overcome with grief but is soon distracted by an astonishing event.

SCENE 2—The apparition of the Queen

A tent draped in lovely silks has risen magically; Fata Morgana, disguised as the beautiful Queen of Shemakha, appears. The King is so overpowered by her beauty and singing that he forgets his grief and his enemies and proposes to the lovely Queen. She consents to be his bride.

SCENE 3—The wedding procession

A magnificent welcome awaits the royal couple at the palace. As soon as they arrive in pomp and splendor, the Astrologer appears to claim his reward for the Golden Cockerel—he demands the Queen herself. The King flies into a rage and strikes the Astrologer with his scepter.

SCENE 4—The death of the King

The Cockerel flies toward Dodon and kills him with its beak. Thunder sounds, and darkness descends upon the city. When light returns, the Cockerel, the Astrologer, and the Queen have disappeared. The grieving people are left with their dead King.

EPILOGUE

The Astrologer reappears and reminds us that what we have seen is only an illusion, a fairy tale for our enjoyment.

Così fan Tutte

-»»*«-

MUSIC BY: Wolfgang Amadeus Mozart

WORLD PREMIERE: Vienna, Austria,
January 26, 1790

LIBRETTO BY: Lorenzo Da Ponte
English version by Ruth and Thomas Martin
NEW YORK CITY OPERA PREMIERE:
(Sung in English) October 8, 1959

CONDUCTOR: Julius Rudel
STAGE DIRECTOR: William Ball
SCENERY and COSTUMES: Robert Fletcher

CHARACTERS (In order of appearance)	VOICE (type)	PREMIERE CAST (New York City Opera)
Ferrando, Officer, betrothed to Dorabella	Tenor	John Alexander
Guglielmo, Officer, betrothed to Fiordiligi	Baritone	John Reardon
Don Alfonso, an old Philosopher	Bass	James Pease
Fiordiligi } Ladies from Ferrara and sisters, living	Soprano	Phyllis Curtin
Dorabella } in Naples	Mezzo	Frances Bible
Despina, chambermaid to the Ladies	Soprano	Judith Raskin (debut)

Soldiers, Wedding Guests, Servants, Boatmen

SYNOPSIS OF STORY
TIME AND PLACE: Naples, 1790

*

ACT I

SCENE 1—Terrace of a cafe

Don Alfonso, a cynical old man, is having an argument with two young officers, Ferrando and Guglielmo, over the faithlessness of women. He says that Fiordiligi and Dorabella, sisters to whom they are engaged, will never be faithful. "Così fan tutte!", he says—all women are the same.

Don Alfonso offers to prove his point if the two young officers will agree to a bet. They accept. For twenty-four hours, they must act out whatever Don Alfonso tells them to do.

SCENE 2—Garden of Dorabella's and Fiordiligi's house

The sisters are in the garden expecting their young men, but it is Don Alfonso who appears.

77

Così fan Tutti, 1959. Left to right: James Pease, Judith Raskin, John Reardon, John Alexander, Frances Bible, Phyllis Curtin.

He says the officers have been ordered to report for active duty. The young people sing of their sorrow at being parted.

SCENE 3—The ladies' boudoir

Despina, the maid, helps Don Alfonso with his scheme. She finds her mistresses very sad but is not at all sympathetic. She urges them to have a good time while their sweethearts are away.

SCENE 4—In the garden

Almost at once, Ferrando and Guglielmo appear, disguised in beards and dressed as rather fearsome Albanians. The girls are reluctant to receive their new admirers. After some persuasion, they decide to accept the attentions of the strange young men, especially after a scene in which the men pretend to take poison and must be revived by Despina, disguised as someone from Dr. Mesmer's school. To make it even funnier, the young men woo each other's sweetheart.

ACT II

SCENE 1—The ladies' boudoir

Fiordiligi and Dorabella decide that there is no harm in a little flirtation. Dorabella is more receptive to the attentions of her new lover, Guglielmo. Fiordiligi does not welcome the attentions of Ferrando at first, but finally agrees when he proposes marriage. Naturally the young officers are upset when their sweethearts agree so quickly to marry someone else. However, Don Alfonso repeats to them, "Così fan tutte!"—all women act like that.

SCENE 2—Garden of the ladies' house

Arrangements are made for a double wedding. Despina, disguised this time as a notary, appears with the marriage contracts. The ceremony is just beginning when Don Alfonso rushes in to say that the officers are returning. The young men hide, remove their disguises, and reappear in their military uniforms. The two sisters are confused and embarrassed, but finally admit their guilt.

SCENE 3—Terrace

Fiordiligi, unconvinced of love and disapproving of the way her sister has behaved, decides to go off to fight by her lover's side. Her intentions evaporate as her lover Ferrando appears dressed as an Albanian. Ferrando is determined to avenge himself on Guglielmo and Dorabella and threatens to kill himself. Fiordiligi succumbs to his advances. This in turn arouses the fury of both soldiers, since it is apparent that neither of their lovers has remained faithful. Don Alfonso persuades the soldiers to marry their lovers, since the hearts of all women are unpredictable.

SCENE 4—Banquet hall

Finally, Don Alfonso explains everything, and the lovers are reunited with their own sweethearts. He pockets the bet. All ends happily.

The Cradle Will Rock

→))) * (((←

MUSIC BY: Marc Blitzstein
WORLD PREMIERE: New York, New York,
   June 16, 1937

LIBRETTO BY: Marc Blitzstein
NEW YORK CITY OPERA PREMIERE:
   (Sung in English) February 11, 1960

CONDUCTOR: Lehman Engel (debut)
STAGE DIRECTOR: Howard Da Silva (debut)
SCENIC DESIGNER: David Hays
COSTUMES: Ruth Morley
DANCE DIRECTION: Billy Parsons (debut)

CHARACTERS (In order of appearance)	VOICE (type)	PREMIERE CAST (New York City Opera)
Moll	Soprano	Tammy Grimes (debut)
Gent	Baritone	Seth Riggs
Dick	Bass	Arnold Voketaitis
Cop	Baritone	Dan Merriman
Reverend Salvation	Bass	Kenneth Smith
Editor Daily	Tenor	Jack Harrold
Yasha	Actor	Michael Wager (debut)
Dauber	Actor	Chandler Cowles (debut)
President Prexy	Bass	John Macurdy
Professor Trixie	Actor	Philip Bruns
Professor Mamie	Tenor	Maurice Stern
Professor Scoot	Tenor	Howard Fried
Dr. Specialist	Bass	Joshua Hecht
Harry Druggist	Actor	William Griffis (debut)
Clerk	Musician Actor	Lehman Engel
Mr. Mister	Tenor	Craig Timberlake
Mrs. Mister	Mezzo	Ruth Kobart
Junior Mister	Tenor	Keith Kaldenberg
Sister Mister	Soprano	Nancy Dussault
Steve	Tenor	Frank Porretta
Bugs	Baritone	George Del Monte
Sadie Polock	Soprano	Sophie Ginn (debut)
Gus Polock	Baritone	Robert Kerns
Larry Foreman	Baritone	David Atkinson
Ella Hammer	Mezzo	Jane A. Johnston (debut)
Reporters	Baritone	Seth Riggs
	Tenor	William Saxon

Townspeople

The Cradle Will Rock, 1960

SYNOPSIS OF STORY
TIME AND PLACE: Steeltown, U.S.A., 1931, during a union drive

*

ACT I

SCENE 1—Street corner
SCENE 2—Night court
SCENE 3—Mission
SCENE 4—Lawn of Mr. Mister's home
SCENE 5—Drugstore
SCENE 6—Hotel lobby

The scene is Steeltown, USA; a night in 1931, during a union drive. The Moll is arrested by the Dick for plying her trade. At the same time, the overzealous and clumsy Cop arrests, by mistake, the Liberty Committee, which consists of the elite of the town: Reverend Salvation, Editor Daily, Yasha (violinist), Dauber (artist), President Prexy and Professors Mamie and Trixie of College University, and Dr. Specialist. They are all hauled off to night court, where the Moll makes friends with Druggist, a derelict to whom night court is a second home. The Clerk reads off the names of the defendants. As they step forward, each appears in a scene showing his subservience to the Mister family, who own the town and its steel factory. The act ends with the scene of Yasha and Dauber, rivals for the attentions of Mrs. Mister, their mutual patroness.

ACT II

SCENE 7—Night court
SCENE 8—Faculty room
SCENE 9—Dr. Specialist's office
SCENE 10—Night court

Now Larry Foreman is brought into court. It was because of his speech that the Cop made the mistake of arresting the Liberty Committee; they had been listening with considerable antagonism to Larry, speaking in behalf of the union drive. More defendants come forward; each again has his scene with Mr. Mister, in flashback style.

Now Mr. Mister actually appears in night court, worried that the union drive seems to be succeeding. He makes a direct bid to buy off Larry Foreman, but is refused in no uncertain terms. We hear the sounds of bugles, fifes, and drums; the union drive is a success.

The Crucible

-»»*«««-

MUSIC BY: Robert Ward
WORLD PREMIERE and NEW YORK CITY OPERA PREMIERE: October 26, 1961 (Sung in English)

LIBRETTO BY: Bernard Stambler
Based on the play by Arthur Miller

CONDUCTOR: Emerson Buckley
STAGE DIRECTOR: Allen Fletcher
SCENIC DESIGNER: Paul Sylbert
COSTUMES: Ruth Morley

CHARACTERS (In order of appearance)	VOICE (type)	PREMIERE CAST (New York City Opera)
Betty Parris	Mezzo	Joyce Ebert (debut)
Reverend Samuel Parris	Tenor	Norman Kelley
Tituba	Contralto	Debria Brown
Abigail Williams	Soprano	Patricia Brooks
Ann Putnam	Soprano	Mary LeSawyer
Thomas Putnam	Baritone	Paul Ukena
Rebecca Nurse	Contralto	Eunice Alberts
Francis Nurse	Bass	Spiro Malas
Giles Corey	Tenor	Maurice Stern
John Proctor	Baritone	Chester Ludgin
Reverend John Hale	Bass	Norman Treigle
Elizabeth Proctor	Mezzo	Frances Bible
Mary Warren	Soprano	Joy Clements
Ezekiel Cheever	Tenor	Harry Theyard
Judge Danforth	Tenor	Ken Neate
Sarah Good	Soprano	Joan Kelm
Ruth Putnam	Soprano	Lorna Ceniceros (debut)
Susanna Walcott	Contralto	Helen Guile (debut)
Mercy Lewis	Contralto	Nancy Roy
Martha Sheldon	Soprano	Elizabeth Schwering
Bridget Booth	Soprano	Beverly Evans

Neighbors, Townspeople, Jailer

SYNOPSIS OF STORY
TIME AND PLACE: Salem, Massachusetts; 1692

*

The Crucible, 1961

ACT I

SCENE 1—Parlor of the home of the Reverend
  Samuel Parris; a spring morning

The town of Salem is in turmoil over what
is considered evidence of witchcraft. Several of
the young girls have been stricken with a mysterious illness. The Reverend Parris, minister
in Salem, is praying at the bedside of his ill
daughter, Betty. His niece, Abby Williams,
denies that the illegal dancing in the woods
the previous evening was the cause of the illness.

Thomas and Ann Putman report that their
daughter Ruth is also ill. They send for the
Reverend Hale, an acknowledged expert on
witchcraft. Other neighbors enter to inquire
about Betty. A quarrel ensues, each accusing the
others of some misconduct.

On his arrival, the Reverend Hale starts an
inquiry into the case. Tituba, Parris' Negro slave,
is accused of witchery and confesses that she
has had dealings with the Devil.

SCENE 2—Kitchen-dining room of John Proctor's house, eight days later

John and Elizabeth Proctor are greatly distressed over the witch trials. Elizabeth believes
that her husband could stop the whole witch
business if he would reveal that Abby is a fraud,
but he is unwilling to do so because Abby had
been his mistress during a time when Elizabeth
was ill.

Mary Warren, the Proctors' current servant,
is one of the accusing girls. Judge Danforth is
presiding at the trials, where confession brings
freedom and denial brings further imprisonment,
torture, and finally hanging.

The Reverend Hale and Ezekiel Cheever enter
with a warrant for Elizabeth, and she is taken
away.

ACT II

SCENE 1—The woods near the Reverend Parris'
  house

John pleads with Abby to end her wicked fraud, but she only adds further nonsensical ideas to what she plans to do. When John refuses her amorous advances, she threatens that Elizabeth's death will be his fault.

SCENE 2—The town meeting house, the same afternoon

Judge Danforth maintains that he, a judge-minister-governor, is the voice of God delivering harshly cleansing judgments upon a troubled and sinful land. Giles Corey is the first witness to be jailed. Proctor brings Mary Warren to testify that the girls are frauds, but Abby turns the testimony around, and in the end John Proctor is accused.

ACT III

SCENE—The town blockhouse and jail, fall of the same year

Sarah Good and Tituba are half crazed by their long imprisonment. Abby bribes the jailer to let John Proctor escape, but John makes no response to her pleas.

Executions are scheduled for dawn. Elizabeth Proctor is brought in to persuade John to confess, but she refuses to ask him to lie. There is a complete reconciliation and resolution of their differences.

Danforth tries unsuccessfully to get Rebecca Nurse and John to confess. He sends them out to be hanged.

Danton's Death

-»»*«« -

MUSIC BY: Gottfried von Einem

LIBRETTO BY: Boris Blacher and
Gottfried von Einem
English version by: Ruth and Thomas Martin

WORLD PREMIERE: Salzburg, Austria,
August 6, 1947

NEW YORK CITY OPERA PREMIERE:
(Sung in English) March 9, 1966

CONDUCTOR: Ernst Maerzendorfer
STAGE DIRECTOR: Adolf Rott
SCENIC and PROJECTION DESIGNER: Wolfgang Roth
COSTUMES: Ruth Morley

CHARACTERS (In order of appearance)	VOICE (type)	PREMIERE CAST (New York City Opera)
George Danton	Baritone	John Reardon
A Woman	Soprano	Helen Guile
Hérault de Séchelles	Tenor	Richard Krause
Julie	Mezzo	Kay Creed
Camille Desmoulins	Tenor	William Dupree
Simon	Bass	Herbert Beattie
Simon's Wife	Mezzo	Muriel Greenspon
A Young Man	Tenor	Nico Castel
Robespierre	Tenor	Mauro Lampi
St. Just	Bass	Malcolm Smith
Lucille	Soprano	Sylvia Grant
Herman	Baritone	William Ledbetter
An Executioner	Tenor	Kellis Miller
An Executioner	Bass	Edward Pierson

Guests, Dandies, Crowds, Terrorists, Guards

SYNOPSIS OF STORY
TIME AND PLACE: Paris, 1794, during the Reign of Terror

*

ACT I

SCENE 1—A room

As Danton and his wife, Julie, look on, his fellow revolutionist Hérault de Séchelles plays cards with several ladies, exchanging pleasant conversation in luxurious surroundings. Camille Desmoulins enters. The execution of the Hébertists (former heroes of the Revolution) causes alarm among these men who favor an

86

end to the Terror and would like to see the Republic function and the Revolution reorganized.

SCENE 2—A street

Simon and his wife quarrel violently. People gather. Their fury is soon diverted toward the aristocrats, and a passing nobleman is about to be hanged on a lamppost. Robespierre appears. His flattery calms the people. He invites them to the Jacobin Club, headquarters of the radical party in favor of the Terror. Danton criticizes Robespierre for his views. After he leaves, Robespierre decides to sacrifice his former friend. St. Just, a member of the Committee of Public Safety, joins Robespierre. Together they plot the execution of Danton and his sympathizers, Camille and Hérault.

SCENE 3—A room

Danton had learned of his forthcoming arrest. He takes the news calmly. Camille, urged by his wife, Lucille, decides to intervene with Robespierre, not knowing that he himself is also to meet the same fate. Lucille, alone, has a crazed premonition of death for Camille.

ACT II
SCENE 1—The Conciergerie—Inside the Prison

The people acclaim Danton, but Simon soon turns their minds against him in favor of Robespierre. Danton and Camille, both imprisoned, reflect on their impending death. Danton is strong and heroic, but Camille in despair is on the verge of breaking down. Lucille appears outside the prison, calling Camille. Her mind is deranged.

SCENE 2—The Revolutionary Tribunal

The accusation against Danton is read. Danton defends himself with all the force of his personality against the falsified document. While the court is in recess, St. Just produces further forged charges against the accused. The session is resumed. The people hail Danton and momentarily denounce Robespierre and the Decemvirs. Nevertheless, the death sentence is pronounced for all the accused.

SCENE 3—Place de la Revolution

The crowd, in great excitement, watches the tumbril with the condemned arrive, jeering and ridiculing them. The victims mount the scaffold courageously and are guillotined. The crowd disperses, and the executioners leave. Lucille appears, forlorn and distracted. Suddenly she cries out, "Long live the King," and is arrested.

The Daughter of the Regiment

->>> * <<<-

MUSIC BY: Gaetano Donizetti

WORLD PREMIERE: Paris, France,
February 11, 1840

LIBRETTO BY: Vernoy de Saint-Georges and
Jean François Bayard
English Version by Ruth and Thomas Martin
NEW YORK CITY OPERA PREMIERE:
(Sung in English) September 7, 1975

CONDUCTOR: Charles Wendelken-Wilson
PRODUCTION CONCEIVED and DIRECTED BY: Lotfi Mansouri (debut)
STAGE DIRECTOR: Bruce Donnell (debut)
SCENERY and COSTUMES: Beni Montresor

CHARACTERS (In order of appearance)	VOICE (type)	PREMIERE CAST (New York City Opera)
Hortensius, servant of the Marquise	Baritone	David Ronson
The Marquise of Berkenfield	Mezzo	Muriel Costa-Greenspon
A Peasant	Tenor	James Sergi
Sergeant Sulpice	Baritone	Spiro Malas
Marie	Soprano	Beverly Sills
Tonio, a young peasant	Tenor	Enrico Di Giuseppe
The Corporal	Baritone	William Ledbetter
The Dancing Master	Mute	Michael Rubino
The Duchess of Krackenthorp	Soprano	Ethel Barrymore Colt
The Notary	Tenor	Melvin Lowery

French Soldiers, Tyrolean Peasants, Ladies and Gentlemen, Servants of the Marquise

SYNOPSIS OF STORY
TIME AND PLACE: The Tyrol, 1850, at the time of Napoleon I

*

ACT I

SCENE—A village in the Tyrol

Marie, the adopted "daughter" of Napoleon's 21st Regiment, has been raised since infancy by Sergeant Sulpice and the other men of the regiment. As mascot of the group she finds herself in the Tyrol with the advancing French army. As a result, she encounters her real family, in the person of the Marquise of Berkenfield, who soon insists that she give up the life and the people she loves. In addition, Marie has fallen in

The Daughter of the Regiment, 1979. Left to right: Bruce Reed, Ashley Putnam, Richard McKee.

love with a young Tyrolean peasant, Tonio, whom she persuades to join the French regiment to be with her.

ACT II

SCENE—Drawing room of the Château Berkenfield

The Marquise attempts to reeducate Marie as befits a member of the nobility; Tonio struggles to adapt to being a soldier in the enemy army and to obtain permission to marry Marie; and Sergeant Sulpice reluctantly agrees that Marie must forget her beloved regiment. All of this causes unhappiness to everyone involved. Finally, however, the Marquise relents, and Marie is reunited with Tonio, Sergeant Sulpice, and her regiment.

The Devil and Daniel Webster

→⟫*⟪←

MUSIC BY: Douglas Moore
WORLD PREMIERE: New York, New York,
May 18, 1939

LIBRETTO BY: Stephen Vincent Benét
NEW YORK CITY OPERA PREMIERE:
(Sung in English) April 5, 1959

CONDUCTOR: Max Goberman (debut)
STAGE DIRECTOR: John Houseman (debut)
SCENERY and COSTUMES: Rouben Ter-Arutunian
CHOREOGRAPHY: Robert Joffrey

CHARACTERS (In order of appearance)	VOICE (type)	PREMIERE CAST (New York City Opera)
A Fiddler	Speaking	Keith Kaldenberg
Jabez Stone	Bass	Joshua Hecht
Mary Stone	Mezzo	Adelaide Bishop
Daniel Webster	Baritone	Walter Cassel
Mr. Scratch	Tenor	Norman Kelley
Justice Hawthorne	Speaking	Emile Renan
Clerk	Baritone	Arthur Newman
The Voice of Miser Stevens	Tenor	Grant Williams
Jury of the Dead:		
Walter Butler	Speaking	Chester Ludgin
Blackbeard Teach	Baritone	George Del Monte
King Phillip	Baritone	Arnold Voketaitis
Simon Girty	Tenor	Grant Williams
Others of the Jury	Tenor	Jack De Lon
	Tenor	Howard Fried
	Baritone	Andrew Frierson
	Tenor	Paul Huddleston
	Bass	John Macurdy
	Baritone	Dan Merriman
	Tenor	William Nahr
	Tenor	Harry Theyard (debut)

Note: An old man and an old woman added to the program on April 17.
Note: This opera was performed with *The Scarf.*

SYNOPSIS OF STORY
TIME AND PLACE: The home of Jabez Stone, Cross Corners, New Hampshire, in the 1840's

*

The neighbors of Cross Corners are celebrating the marriage of Jabez and Mary Stone. The Stones were always poor, but Jabez has prospered amazingly and they are talking of running him for governor. Everything goes well at first; Daniel Webster, the great New England hero, appears as a guest and is given a real New Hampshire welcome. There is another guest, an unexpected one who carries a black collecting box under his arm. His appearance terrifies Jabez, the song he sings horrifies the neighbors, and when a lost soul—in the form of a moth—flies out of the collecting box, panic ensues. The neighbors realize that Jabez has sold his soul to the Devil; they denounce him and flee. Left alone with Mary, he tells how he came to make his hideous bargain. They appeal to Daniel Webster, who promises to help them. But the Devil—Mr. Scratch—is an excellent lawyer, too. When Webster demands a trial for his client, Scratch summons a Jury of the Dead of famous traitors and renegades and a hanging judge who presided at the Salem witch trials. Webster seems about to lose not only the case but his own soul's salvation. But his powerful oratory finally turns the tables on Scratch and rescues Jabez. The neighbors rush in to drive the Devil out of New Hampshire, and the case ends with a New England pie breakfast.

The Dialogues of the Carmelites

->>>*<<<-

MUSIC BY: Francis Poulenc

WORLD PREMIERE: Milan, Italy,
January 26, 1957

LIBRETTO BY: George Bernanos
English Text By: Joseph Machlis
NEW YORK CITY OPERA PREMIERE:
(Sung in English) March 3, 1966

CONDUCTOR: Alain Lombard (debut)
STAGE DIRECTOR: Nikos Psacharopoulos
SCENIC DESIGNER: John Conklin (debut)
COSTUMES: Ruth Morley

CHARACTERS (In order of appearance)	VOICE (type)	PREMIERE CAST (New York City Opera)
The Chevalier, son of the Marquis de la Force	Tenor	David Thaw (debut)
Marquis de la Force	Baritone	William Ledbetter
Blanche, his daughter	Soprano	Donna Jeffrey
Thierry	Baritone	Kellis Miller
Madame de Croissy, Prioress of the Carmelite Convent	Contralto	Claramae Turner
Sister Constance of Saint-Denis	Soprano	Anne Elgar
Mother Marie of the Incarnation	Mezzo	Marguerite Willauer
M. Javelinot, a doctor	Baritone	Don Henderson
Madame Lidoine, the new Prioress	Soprano	Ellen Faull
Chaplain of the Convent	Tenor	William Dembaugh
Sister Mathilde	Mezzo	Helen Guile
Mother Jeanne of the Child Jesus	Contralto	Beverly Evans
1st Commissioner	Tenor	Nico Castel
2nd Commissioner	Baritone	Jack Bittner
Officer	Tenor	L. D. Clements
Jailer	Baritone	Jack Bittner

Officials of the Municipality, Officers, Policemen, Prisoners, Guards, Townfolk

SYNOPSIS OF STORY
TIME AND PLACE: Paris, April 1789, the start of the French Revolution

*

The Dialogues of the Carmelites, 1966. Left to right: Anne Elgar, Harry Thaw, Donna Jefferies.

ACT I

SCENE 1—A room in the house of the Marquis de la Force

The Marquis and his son, the Chevalier, are discussing the Marquis' daughter, Blanche, a sensitive, high-strung girl who cannot conquer her fear of life. Blanche enters, pale and overwrought. Her carriage had been stopped by a mob of angry peasants. Thoroughly shaken by the experience, she retires to her apartment to rest. The unexpected entrance of a servant suffices to throw her into a state of panic. The incident, trifling though it is, impels her to a step she has long wished to take. She confesses to the Marquis her decision to become a nun. She no longer wishes to struggle with a world in which she feels herself to be a stranger.

SCENE 2—The parlor of the Carmelite Convent at Compiègne

Blanche is interviewed by the Mother Superior, who explains to her that the Order is not a refuge from life and cannot give her the courage she lacks. What she seeks can be attained only through discipline and self-mastery.

SCENE 3—The workroom of the Convent

Blanche and a very young nun, Sister Constance of Saint-Denis, go about their chores. Blanche chides Sister Constance for chattering unconcernedly even though the Mother Superior lies critically ill. Constance artlessly confides to Blanche a strange premonition she has had, that Blanche and she are going to die together, on the very same day.

SCENE 4—The infirmary

The Mother Superior is attended by the sub-Prioress, Mother Marie of the Incarnation. The Mother Superior is appalled at her own weakness. She has meditated on death every day of her life, yet now that she must face it she is afraid. In an affecting scene the dying woman takes leave of Blanche and entrusts her to the care of Mother Marie.

ACT II

SCENE 1—The chapel

Blanche and Constance stand watch beside the bier of the Mother Superior. When Blanche, left alone with the body, is overcome by fear and retreats to the door, she is confronted by Mother Marie. The latter realizes that Blanche has failed in her duty but, seeing how distraught the girl is, accompanies her to her cell.

SCENE 2—The entrance of the chapel

Blanche and Constance discuss the Mother Superior's death. Blanche is baffled by the fact that the woman she had worshipped should have met so mean an end. Constance advances an artless explanation of her own. God gives each of us the death that fits him, but sometimes, as in a cloakroom, there is a mistake. The Prioress had received a death much too small for her, which could only mean that some little person somewhere, when his time came, would be astonished at what a large death he was having and how easily and bravely he entered into it.

SCENE 3—The chapter room

The community assembles for the ceremony of obedience to the new Prioress, Mme. Lidoine, a plainspoken woman of humble birth.

SCENE 4—The entrance to the parlor

The Chevalier is forced to leave France. He comes to the Convent in order to take leave of Blanche.

SCENE 5—The parlor

Both Blanche and her brother are constrained. He urges her to return to their father, who is now alone. Blanche, despite her love for her brother, makes it clear that life in the Convent has wrought a great change in her. Although aware of her duty to her father, she now acknowledges a higher loyalty.

SCENE 6—The sacristy

The Chaplain of the Convent informs the assembled nuns that he has been relieved of his duties by the revolutionary regime and must leave them. The Revolution reaches the Convent when a mob gathers at the gate demanding admittance. An official reads the decree of the Legislative Assembly: all religious orders are to be dissolved. An older nun tries to comfort Blanche by entrusting to her the statue of the Little King. Blanche, overcome with fright at the sound of the *Ca ira,* lets fall the sacred image, which breaks against the flagstones.

ACT III

SCENE 1—The chapel

The Convent has been pillaged by the mob. The nuns welcome the Chaplain, who has surreptitiously returned to them. In the absence of the Mother Superior, Mother Marie takes charge. She proposes that the nuns take the vow of martyrdom, but makes it clear that the decision can be binding only if it is unanimous. Each nun passes behind the altar and makes known her decision to the Chaplain. Blanche emerges with haggard face. The Chaplain informs Mother Marie that there was one vote against. The nuns

have good reason to suspect whose that was. At this point, to their amazement, Sister Constance announces that it was she who cast the dissenting vote, but that she now wishes to reverse herself. The Chaplain grants her permission to do so. Thus Mother Marie's proposal is accepted. The nuns advance two by two—Blanche and Constance, as the youngest, come first—to take the vow of martyrdom administered by the Chaplain.

SCENE 2—A street outside the Convent

The Carmelites, led by the Mother Superior, leave the Convent.

SCENE 3—A room in the house of the Marquis de la Force

The room bears the marks of pillage and disorder. Blanche, dressed as a woman of the people, works as a servant in the mansion of her ancestors. Mother Marie, also in civilian costume, comes looking for her and tries to persuade her to return to the nuns. Blanche refuses, feeling that she is safer where she is. We learn that the Marquis has been guillotined a week earlier.

SCENE 4—A cell in the Conciergerie

The nuns come to the end of their first night in prison. Sister Constance still believes that Blanche will return to join them. The jailer arrives and reads to them the decree sentencing them to death for crimes against the Republic. The Mother Superior gives them her blessing and places them "under obedience for the last time, once and for all . . ."

SCENE 5—A street

Mother Marie learns of the sentence from the Chaplain. She feels she ought to rejoin the sisters in death. But the Chaplain reminds her that it is God who decides which of us shall live and which shall die.

SCENE 6—Place de la Revolution

The Carmelites, led by the Mother Superior, go to the guillotine chanting the *Salve Regina.* As each ascends the scaffold, the voices are diminished by one. Presently only one voice is left,

94

that of Sister Constance. At this point, from the other end of the square, Blanche makes her way through the crowd toward the scaffold. When Constance's voice is cut off, Blanche's takes up the hymn. She mounts the scaffold without a vestige of fear, achieving in death that victory toward which her whole life had aspired.

Dido and Aeneas

->>>*<<<-

MUSIC BY: Henry Purcell
Realized and edited by Benjamin Britten
  and Imogen Holst
WORLD PREMIERE: London, England, 1689*

LIBRETTO BY: Nahum Tate

NEW YORK CITY OPERA PREMIERE:
  (Sung in English) April 8, 1979

CONDUCTOR: Cal Stewart Kellogg
STAGE DIRECTOR: Frank Corsaro
PANTOMIME SCENES DIRECTED IN COLLABORATION WITH: George Balanchine
SETS and COSTUMES: Rouben Ter-Arutunian
CHOREOGRAPHER: Peter Martins (debut)

CHARACTERS (In order of appearance)	VOICE (type)	PREMIERE CAST (New York City Opera)
Belinda, Lady-in-Waiting	Soprano	Janice Hall (debut)
Dido, Queen of Carthage, sometime Elissa	Mezzo	Sandra Browne (debut)
Lady-in-Waiting	Soprano	Gwenlynn Little
Aeneas, a Trojan Prince	Baritone	David Holloway
Sorceress	Mezzo	Rosemarie Freni
Witches	Soprano	Martha Thigpen
	Mezzo	Eunice Hill
Spirit	Child Soprano	Robert Sapolsky
Sailor	Tenor	John Lankston

Witches, Sailors, Attendants, Torch Bearers, and animals

Note: This opera was performed with *Le Bourgeois Gentilhomme.*

SYNOPSIS OF STORY
TIME AND PLACE: Ancient Greece

*

---

* Because of the early date the exact date of first performance is unknown.

ACT I

SCENE 1—The palace

Dido, Queen of Carthage, enters with her attendants. Her lady-in-waiting Belinda urges the Queen to drive away her present mood of dejection by revealing its cause: "Grief increases by concealing." Belinda has in fact guessed Dido's torment; she is in love with Aeneas, the Trojan prince who has landed in Carthage en route from his vanquished homeland to a new home divinely ordained in Italy. Belinda and the attendants assure Dido that her love is returned. Aeneas enters to plead his cause: "Let Dido smile and I'll defy the feeble stroke of destiny!" As the scene ends, the attendants sing and dance in celebration of love's triumph.

SCENE 2—The cave

While the royal party is hunting, a sorceress summons her "wayward sisters," a band of witches, to plot the ruin of Dido. A spirit in the shape of Mercury will be sent to Aeneas, charging him to sail at once for Italy. As an additional exercise of power, the witches will first arrange a storm "to mar their hunting sport."

ACT II

SCENE —The grove

During the hunt, the royal party pauses at the spot where Actaeon was punished for gazing upon the bathing Diana. The fatal storm comes on. As the others flee back to town, the spirit calls Aeneas to remain. By "great Jove's command," the Trojan prince is instructed to sail that evening for Italy. A regretful Aeneas agrees to comply, and goes off. The witches enter and celebrate.

ACT III

SCENE—The ships

A Trojan sailor summons his companions from their dalliance on shore. The sorceress and her companions enter and gloat: "Our plot has took, the Queen's forsook!" Further to torment Aeneas, they will send him a storm at sea. They leave; Dido and the court enter. Aeneas begs forgiveness: "How, royal fair, shall I impart the god's decree, and tell you we must part?" Dido calls him a hypocrite and rejects his offer to defy the gods and remain: "'Tis enough . . . that you had once a thought of leaving me." When he has gone, Dido realizes that she is doomed: "Death is now a welcome guest." She charges Belinda to "remember me, but ah! forget my fate." The attendants call upon Cupids to watch over her tomb.

Don Giovanni

-»»*«««-

MUSIC BY: Wolfgang Amadeus Mozart
WORLD PREMIERE: Prague, Czechoslovakia,
   October 29, 1787

LIBRETTO BY: Lorenzo Da Ponte
NEW YORK CITY OPERA PREMIERE:
   (Sung in Italian) October 23, 1947

CONDUCTOR: Laszlo Halasz
STAGE DIRECTOR: Theodore Komisarjevsky
SCENIC DESIGNER: H. A. Condell
COSTUMES*
BALLET DIRECTOR: William Dollar

CHARACTERS (In order of appearance)	VOICE (type)	PREMIERE CAST (New York City Opera)
Leporello	Bass	Norman Cordon (debut)
Donna Anna	Soprano	Ellen Faull (debut)
Don Giovanni	Baritone	James Pease
Commendatore	Bass	Gean Greenwell
Don Ottavio	Tenor	Eugene Conley
Donna Elvira	Soprano	Brenda Lewis
Zerlina	Soprano	Virginia Haskins
Masetto	Baritone	Edwin Dunning

An Innkeeper, a Night Watchman, Elvira's Maid, Lackeys, the Commendatore's Servants, Peasants

Note: A new production in 1963, designed by Allen Fletcher, was presented in the English translation of Ruth and Thomas Martin.

SYNOPSIS OF STORY
TIME AND PLACE: In and near Seville, mid-17th century

*

ACT I

SCENE 1—Courtyard of the Commendatore's palace

Don Giovanni flees the bedchamber of Donna Anna, who follows, shocked and confused by her encounter with the masked intruder. The Commendatore, Donna Anna's father, appears, challenging Don Giovanni to a duel. Donna Anna rushes off to bring help. Upon her return

---

* By Kate Friedheim; additional costumes by Stivanello.

with her betrothed, Don Ottavio, she finds her father dead and the killer gone. Grief-stricken, Donna Anna and Ottavio vow vengeance.

SCENE 2—A public square in Seville

It is carnival time. Leporello, worried about his master's scandalous life, enters and calls up to the Don. To placate his angry servant, the Don asks Leporello to join him in observing the arrival of a lady of fashion. She is Donna Elvira, one of Don Giovanni's former conquests. Urged by the Don, Leporello offers excuses to Donna Elvira for the Don's desertion on the eve of their nuptials. Leporello elaborates at length on Don Giovanni's past seductions. Elvira swears she will destroy the fickle Don.

SCENE 3—A barn near Don Giovanni's country villa

The marriage of Masetto and Zerlina is about to be celebrated. Don Giovanni, finding Zerlina attractive, orders Leporello to invite the peasants to his villa. As Zerlina resists the Don's advances, Donna Elvira appears to denounce him and leads the bewildered girl away. Donna Anna and Ottavio come upon the Don and ask his help in tracking down the murderer of Donna Anna's father. Donna Elvira appears, pleading that Anna and Ottavio not misplace their trust in the treacherous Don. Anna suddenly realizes that it was the Don who killed her father and calls upon Ottavio to renew his vow of vengeance. Meanwhile, Don Giovanni instructs Leporello to prepare a wild party for all the villagers and to invite as many girls as he can.

SCENE 4—Garden of Don Giovanni's villa

During the celebration, Masetto quarrels with Zerlina over her flirtation with the Don, but he finally forgives her. Anna, Elvira, and Ottavio join the other masked guests and enter the ballroom.

SCENE 5—Inside the villa

As the guests dance the minuet, Don Giovanni draws Zerlina into another room. Moments later her outcries are heard by the guests. The Don returns dragging Leporello, whom he accuses of having made advances to Zerlina. The ruse fools no one, and the masqueraders approach threaten-

ingly. Don Giovanni overcomes the incensed Ottavio and is forced to flee.

ACT II

SCENE 1—The square in Seville

Don Giovanni and the ladies of the town are trying to persuade Leporello not to leave the Don's service. As they succeed, Don Giovanni informs Leporello that his next adventure will be to seduce Elvira's young maid. Don Giovanni persuades Leporello to exchange cloaks with him. Leporello, disguised as the Don, lures Elvira from the inn, leaving the Don free to attempt another seduction. Masetto, searching for the Don, is fooled into thinking he has enlisted Leporello's aid. Caught off guard, Masetto is beaten severely by the Don. Zerlina arrives to console the injured bridegroom.

SCENE 2—Garden of the Commendatore's Palace

Still disguised as the Don, Leporello is confronted by Ottavio, Anna, Elvira, Zerlina, and Masetto. To avoid punishment, Leporello reveals his identity and slips away from the avengers.

SCENE 3—A graveyard

Don Giovanni and Leporello meet near the statue of the slain Commendatore, exchanging news of their latest adventures. Amused by the inscription on the statue, "Here I await vengeance on the wicked man who brought me to my death," Don Giovanni mockingly orders Leporello to invite the statue to dine with him. To Leporello's horror, the statue nods in acceptance.

SCENE 4—Donna Anna's chambers

Don Ottavio begs Donna Anna to marry him, but she replies that she cannot be his wife until she is freed from her terrible grief over her father's unavenged death.

SCENE 5—Banquet hall in Don Giovanni's villa

As the Don defiantly enjoys a lavish meal with an empty suit of armor representing the Commendatore, Donna Elvira enters, begging him to reform his evil ways. As she runs to a door, she shrieks and rushes out. Leporello investigates the source of Elvira's terror and discovers to his horror that the statue of the Commendatore has come to keep his appointment. Leporello refuses to answer the knock, and Don Giovanni welcomes the man of stone. The statue refuses the food of mortals and invites Don Giovanni in turn to dine with him, demanding the Don's hand as a pledge. The statue, clasping Don Giovanni, orders him to repent his sins. The Don refuses. The statue announces that the time has come for vengeance. He departs as flames envelop the Don. Don Giovanni, with a final scream, vanishes amid smoke and hellfire. As the opera ends, the principals learn of Don Giovanni's fate and proclaim together that his death befits the wicked life he has led.

Note: This 1947 production was done in 6 scenes instead of the usual 10 scenes as above.

Don Pasquale

-»»*«««-

MUSIC BY: Gaetano Donizetti
WORLD PREMIERE: Paris, France,
   January 3, 1843

LIBRETTO BY: Giacomo Ruffini
NEW YORK CITY OPERA PREMIERE:
   (Sung in Italian) March 24, 1955

CONDUCTOR: Joseph Rosenstock
STAGE DIRECTOR: Leopold Sachse
SCENIC DESIGNER: John Boyt
ARTISTIC ADVISER: Salvatore Baccaloni (debut)
COSTUMES*

CHARACTERS (In order of appearance)	VOICE (type)	PREMIERE CAST (New York City Opera)
Don Pasquale	Bass	Richard Wentworth
Doctor Malatesta	Baritone	Richard Torigi
Ernesto	Tenor	Davis Cunningham
Norina	Soprano	Adelaide Bishop
Notary	Tenor	Michael Pollock[1]
House Servants		

SYNOPSIS OF STORY
TIME AND PLACE: Rome, early 19th century

*

ACT I

SCENE 1—A room in Don Pasquale's house

Don Pasquale's nephew, Ernesto, is in love with the young widow Norina but has not won the approval of his uncle. The young people look to a friend, Dr. Malatesta, for assistance in winning approval of their marriage. Together they work out a plot to fool the uncle and get his consent. Dr. Malatesta tells Don Pasquale of an imaginary, very beautiful sister who is in love with him. Without having seen her, Don Pasquale falls in love with the girl who is described to him. He wishes to marry her, which would eliminate Ernesto as his heir. When Ernesto hears this, he feels betrayed.

SCENE 2—In Norina's house

Dr. Malatesta and Norina discuss the plans for fooling Don Pasquale. Norina is to masquerade as the sister, pretending to be a shy country

---

* Executed by Manhattan Costume Co., Inc.
(1) Substituted for an indisposed Arthur Newman.

girl, and to go through a mock wedding ceremony with the old Don Pasquale. Meanwhile, Ernesto, who is heartbroken, has sent a letter to Norina telling her he is leaving the country. Dr. Malatesta promises to give Ernesto the details of the plot and to keep him from leaving.

ACT II

SCENE—Don Pasquale's house

Ernesto realizes that without his inheritance he will not be able to marry Norina, and he leaves the house. Dr. Malatesta arrives with Norina dressed as the bride. A mock marriage ceremony is performed, which Ernesto returns to witness. As soon as the ceremony is over, Norina changes character, becoming a hot-tempered shrew. She refuses to let Don Pasquale embrace her and prepares to do everything possible to upset him. She completely disrupts the setup of the household and the staff of servants. Don Pasquale bemoans his fate.

ACT III

SCENE 1—Don Pasquale's house

Don Pasquale is distraught. His supposed new wife is making life unbearable. Deliveries of her purchases keep arriving, and he is appalled at the bills. Norina leaves for the opera, purposely dropping a love letter addressed to her. Don Pasquale reads the letter and believes that his "wife" is meeting someone in the garden. He calls for Dr. Malatesta to put things right and is advised to surprise the young people in the garden.

SCENE 2—The garden of Don Pasquale's house

Norina and Ernesto meet in the garden and declare their love for each other. Don Pasquale and Dr. Malatesta enter the garden and Ernesto, as prearranged, escapes. Norina, Don Pasquale, and Dr. Malatesta discuss the situation, finally admitting the truth of the arranged plot. Ernesto returns. Don Pasquale is so relieved when he learns the truth that he consents for Ernesto to marry Norina. He gives them his blessing and agrees that an old man should not marry a young girl.

Don Rodrigo

-»»*«««-

MUSIC BY: Alberto Ginastera
WORLD PREMIERE: Buenos Aires, Argentina, July 24, 1964

LIBRETTO BY: Alejandro Casona
UNITED STATES and NEW YORK CITY OPERA PREMIERE: (Sung in Spanish) February 22, 1966

CONDUCTOR: Julius Rudel
PRODUCTION DEVISED and DIRECTED BY: Tito Capobianco
SCENIC DESIGNER: Ming Cho Lee (debut)
COSTUMES: Theoni V. Aldredge (debut)

CHARACTERS (In order of appearance)	VOICE (type)	PREMIERE CAST (New York City Opera)
Fortuna, servant to Florinda	Mezzo	Kay Creed
Florinda, daughter of Count Don Julian	Soprano	Jeannine Crader
Doncella, 1st lady-in-waiting	Soprano	Helen Guile
Doncella, 2nd lady-in-waiting	Mezzo	La Vergne Monette (debut)
Teudiselo, tutor to Don Rodrigo	Bass	Spiro Malas
Don Julian, Governor of Ceuta	Baritone	David Clatworthy
Don Rodrigo, King of Spain	Tenor	Placido Domingo
Obispo, bishop	Baritone	Malcolm Smith
Paje, page	Tenor	Nico Castel
Paje, page	Baritone	Edward Pierson
Herrero, 1st locksmith	Tenor	Kellis Miller
Herrero, 2nd locksmith	Baritone	Richard Park
Voz Del Sueno, voice of sleep	Bass	Noel Jan Tyl
Mensajero, 1st messenger	Tenor	Kellis Miller
Mensajero, 2nd messenger	Baritone	Edward Pierson
El Joven Mensajero, young messenger	Mezzo	Beverly Evans
Rapaz, young boy	Child	Robert Puleo (debut)
Zagala, young girl	Child	Providenzia Casado (debut)
Ermitano, hermit	Baritone	Michael Devlin (debut)

Heralds, Pages, Maids, Ladies, Noblemen, Captains, Soldiers and Watchmen, Arab Soldiers, Monks, Peasants, Shepherds, Woodcutters, Craftsmen

SYNOPSIS OF STORY
TIME AND PLACE: Toledo, Spain; 8th century

*

103

ACT I

SCENE 1—The Victory

The scene is Toledo, capital city of Gothic Spain. Having defeated the rebels who had taken his father prisoner and pulled out his eyes, young Rodrigo returns in triumph. On entering his palace he meets Florinda, daughter of his comrade-at-arms Count Don Julian, Governor of Ceuta, who has crossed the sea in order to assist him in battle. Rodrigo asks the Count to allow Florinda to stay in the Spanish court and promises to treat her as his daughter. The people acclaim the avenger, asking the crown for him.

SCENE 2—The Coronation

Rodrigo is crowned king in the Basilica. He swears to take Spain as his wife and consecrates his ring to her. He is anointed on head, breast, and arms. A Maid of the Court gives him the Scepter; a second one, the Cross. Florinda offers him the Crown, but it falls and rolls across the floor as a sinister omen. However, Rodrigo picks it up and proudly raises it over his head. The atmosphere of evil omen breaks as the people glorify their King.

SCENE 3—The Curse

In the Vault of Hercules, in Toledo, there is a chest to which each king must add a new lock, swearing never to try to find out the secret hidden in it. There have been thirty-two kings, and there are thirty-two locks. Rodrigo, burning with curiosity, does not add his lock but orders the locksmith to break the chest open. Inside the chest is an Arab flag and a message predicting that the King who profanes the mystery shall be the last of his dynasty and his country shall be laid waste by the Moors. Everybody draws back, filled with superstitious fear. Captains and locksmiths run away. Rodrigo falls, as if struck by the prophecy.

ACT II

SCENE 4—Love

Rodrigo comes back from hunting, attended by Teudiselo, his tutor. He enters a summerhouse in his gardens by the River Tajo, in order to take a rest. Florinda and her Ladies-in-Waiting come to the gardens, laughing and singing love songs. It is early afternoon. Florinda disrobes in order to bathe in the cool fountain as her Maids keep watch. Rodrigo catches a glimpse of her and is fascinated by her beauty. He calls to her and Florinda, as the hunting horns sound, flees like a wounded gazelle.

SCENE 5—The Outrage

Florinda, ready for bed, is singing by the light of the stars. Rodrigo, who has had her personal guard withdrawn, enters her chamber and confesses his love for her. In vain, Florinda tries to cool his ardor, telling him that his behavior is outrageous and reminding him that her father left her in his custody. She tries to defend herself with the dagger that Rodrigo himself has given her, asking for Love or Death. Her strength fails her, and she falls in Rodrigo's arms.

SCENE 6—The Message

Florinda has been forsaken. In a fit of anger, she writes to her father, urging him to cross the sea and avenge her dishonor. But she is uncertain herself as to which is the cause of her fury—her dishonor, or her jealousy. She decides it does not matter. Let the avenging ships come from Africa! Let Rodrigo burn with Spain!

ACT III

SCENE 7—The Dream

Rodrigo has a premonitory dream, in which he is warned that a woman's hand will set his country on fire. The dream comes true in Africa, where a messenger delivers Florinda's letter. Count Don Julian, in blind fury, rouses his troops against the King. The Arab ships set sail with cries of rebellion. Don Rodrigo wakes up in a hallucinatory state, calling his captains to battle.

SCENE 8—The Battle

On the battlefield of Guadalete, the African troops have charged seven times against Don Rodrigo, who has been seriously wounded in the right arm. Trumpets are blown for the eighth assault, which will be decisive. Don Julian's battalion is charging. In a frenzy, Rodrigo grasps his sword with his left arm and orders his wounded soldiers to follow him. They all rise to their feet. On the battlefield, in the red sunset, only Teudiselo remains waiting for the end of the battle. A trumpet announcing the defeat is heard in the distance.

SCENE 9—The Miracle

Having lost the battle and the crown, a weary Rodrigo comes to a small hermitage; his arrival is announced by two children. He asks to be accepted as a penitent, making a public confession of his sins. He accuses himself of having caused the death of his people. He bows his head and beats his breast three times. Florinda, who has been looking for Rodrigo, arrives. She has come to tell him that in "the verdant Asturias" his soldiers have raised his cross and his banner and that Spain will be born again. Reassured by her words, Rodrigo dies in Florinda's arms. Then, miraculously, the bells of Spain ring out in the quiet dawn. As the bells fill the air, Florinda cries, "It is all Spain that is answering— it is the hand of the Lord."

Die Dreigroschenoper

-»»*«««-

MUSIC BY: Kurt Weill
WORLD PREMIERE: Berlin, Germany,
   August 31, 1928

LIBRETTO BY: Bertold Brecht
NEW YORK CITY OPERA PREMIERE:
   (Sung in German) March 11, 1965

CONDUCTOR: Julius Rudel
STAGE DIRECTOR: Adolph Rott (debut)
PRODUCTION DESIGNER: Wolfgang Roth
COSTUMES: Ruth Morley

CHARACTERS (In order of appearance)	VOICE (type)	PREMIERE CAST (New York City Opera)
Ansager (Narrator)	Baritone	George S. Irving
Jonathan Jeremiah Peachum	Bass	Stefan Schnabel (debut)
Mrs. Peachum	Mezzo	Lilia Skala (debut)
Polly Peachum	Soprano	Anita Hoefer (debut)
Macheath	Bass-baritone	Kurt Kasznar (debut)
Brown	Baritone	Ralph Herbert
Lucy	Actress	Marion Brash (debut)
Filch	Actor	Matthew Anden (debut)
Die Platte (The Gang)		
Hakenflingerjakob		Sol Frieder (debut)
Munzmatthias		John Garson (debut)
Traverweidenwalter	Actors	Paul Andor (debut)
Ede		Michael Haeusserman (debut)
Sagerobert		Claus Jurgens (debut)
Jimmy		Curt Lowens (debut)
Die Spelunken—Jenny	Mezzo	Marta Schlamme (debut)
Huren (Ladies of Ill Repute)	Actresses	Constance Conrad (debut
		Carla Huston (debut)
		Erna Rossman (debut)
		Ruth Sobotka
		ᴣmilla Tchor (debut)
Smith	Bass-baritone	David Smith
Pastor Kimball	Actor	Henry Cordy

SYNOPSIS OF STORY
TIME AND PLACE: Soho, just before the coronation of Queen Victoria.

*

Die Dreigroschenoper, 1965. Left to right: Anita Hoefer, Ralph Herbert, Kurt Kasznar.

ACT I

SCENE 1—A fair in Soho.

At a fair in Soho, the beggars are begging, the thieves are thieving, and the prostitutes are prostituting themselves. A singer of penny-dreadful ballads tells of the exploits of the notorious Macheath, known as Mack the Knife.

SCENE 2—The shop of Jonathan Jeremiah Peachum.

At his shop, the Beggar's Friend, Inc., Peachum, uncrowned king of London's beggars, prepares to meet the day. Mrs. Peachum announces that Polly, their daughter, again has not returned home. They fear she has fallen prey to the wiles of Mack the Knife and are worried that she might even be foolish enough to marry him.

SCENE 3—The stable.

In an abandoned stable, Mack and his gang are preparing a wedding feast. Polly does not find the site appropriate, but she is soon calmed by the lavish wedding gifts, stolen by the gang from the finest homes in London. The gang is alarmed by the entry of Tiger Brown, Chief of Police. However, it turns out that Brown is an old friend of Mack's. They reminisce about their past adventures. His wedding gift to the newlyweds is the news that all incriminating records of Mack's deeds have been removed from the police files.

SCENE 4—Peachum's shop.

When Polly returns to her parents with the news of her marriage, they urge immediate divorce. She refuses, mocking her parents' plot to denounce Mack to the police.

ACT II

SCENE 1—The stable.

Mrs. Peachum, taking matters into her own hands, seeks out Jenny, one of Mack's favorites in a certain house of ill repute. Mrs. Peachum bribes Jenny to inform on Mack, knowing that his dependency on women will bring him to the bordello even though he is hiding from the police.

SCENE 2—A bordello in Turnbridge.

When Smith, the policeman, comes to arrest Mack, who has appeared to visit Jenny on schedule, he escapes momentarily but is captured by the other policemen waiting outside with Mrs. Peachum.

SCENE 3—A cell in the Old Bailey prison.

At the Old Bailey, Tiger Brown bemoans the arrest of his old friend and urges Mack to make himself as comfortable as possible, explaining that anything can happen as long as Mack has enough money to pay for it.

Mack's life is further complicated by the appearance of Lucy, Brown's daughter, to whom he has also promised marriage. Polly arrives, and the two young ladies engage in a fierce battle for Mack's attention. As she is more useful to him at the moment, Mack sides with Lucy, who then helps him to escape.

ACT III

SCENE 1—Street outside Peachum's shop.

Peachum tells Brown that if Mack is not rearrested immediately, all the beggars in London will march to disrupt the coronation ceremonies of the new queen. Peachum and the beggars work through the night.

SCENE 2—Death cell in Old Bailey prison.

Brown admits defeat, and Mack is again in prison, this time to be executed immediately so as not to interfere with the coronation.

SCENE 3—The gallows.

On the scaffold, Mack makes several biting comments about the present social order and lack of it and says his farewell. Suddenly a messenger is heard, and Peachum prepares the audience for the happiest of all endings: Mack is to be reprieved and to be granted honors besides. Mack, reunited with Polly, and Mr. and Mrs. Peachum each express their own reactions to the extraordinary news. The crowd mills about, and the street singer reappears with the final verses of the story of Mack the Knife.

The Dybbuk

→)))＊(((←

MUSIC BY: David Tamkin
WORLD PREMIERE and **NEW YORK CITY OPERA PREMIERE:** October 4, 1951
(Sung in English)

LIBRETTO BY: Alex Tamkin
Based on a play by S. Ansky

CONDUCTOR: Joseph Rosenstock
STAGE DIRECTOR: Irving Pichel (debut)
SCENIC DESIGNER: Mstislav Doboujinsky
COSTUMES: Ruth Morley
CHOREOGRAPHER: Sophie Maslow (debut)

CHARACTERS (In order of appearance)	VOICE (type)	PREMIERE CAST (New York City Opera)
The Messenger	Baritone	Lawrence Winters
Meyer	Bass-baritone	Emile Renan
First Batlon	Tenor	Nathaniel Sprinzena
Second Batlon	Baritone	Richard Wentworth
Third Batlon	Tenor	Michael Pollock
Rabbi Schmelke	Dancer	Joseph Gifford (debut)
A Poor Man	Dancer	John Fealy (debut)
A Rich Man	Dancer	Donald McKayle (debut)
Channon	Tenor	Robert Rounseville
Elderly Woman	Contralto	Eunice Alberts (debut)
Chennoch	Baritone	Arthur Newman
Gittel	Soprano	Shirley Russell
Leah	Soprano	Patricia Neway (debut)
Frade	Contralto	Frances Bible
Asher	Tenor	Keith Kaldenberg
Sender	Bass	Carlton Gauld
A Wedding Guest	Tenor	Michael Pollock
Bassia	Mezzo	Edith Evans
The Old Woman	Dancer	Carroll Taussig
Rabbi Mendel	Tenor	Luigi Vellucci
Menashe	Tenor	Armand Harkless (debut)
First Chassid	Tenor	Nathaniel Sprinzena
Second Chassid	Tenor	Luigi Vellucci
Third Chassid	Bass-baritone	Emile Renan
Michoel	Baritone	Arthur Newman
Rabbi Azrael	Baritone	Mack Harrell
Nachmon	Dancer	Earl James (debut)

CHARACTERS (In order of appearance)	VOICE (type)	PREMIERE CAST (New York City Opera)
	Dancers	Beria, Clark, Genkel, Harrison, Kirpich, Manings, Widman, Zeiger, Decker, Lemmon, Smith, Wood
	Beggars	

SYNOPSIS OF STORY
TIME AND PLACE: Eastern Europe, 1850's

*

ACT I

SCENE—A synogogue at Brainitz

Channon, an impoverished Talmudic student, loves Leah, who returns his love. But her father, the rich Sender, plans a match for her with the son of a wealthy man. To win the riches that would make him eligible in Sender's eyes, Channon studies the Kabala and masters the power to call upon the Evil One, but the knowledge costs him his life.

ACT II

SCENE—The street between Sender's house and the synagogue

The day of Leah's wedding to the bridegroom chosen by her father. According to custom, the beggars of the town are given a feast and insist upon dancing with the bride. Leah visits the grave of her mother to ask her to stand with her under the wedding canopy, and, seeing the grave of Channon, her dead love, mourns for him and shrinks from the thought of the loveless marriage that lies ahead of her. As the bridegroom places the veil over her face, the spirit of Channon takes possession of her body, to find fulfillment through her. This is the Dybbuk.

ACT III

SCENE—Miripol. A study in the house of Rabbi Azrael

Leah's distracted father takes her to Azrael, a "wonder-working" rabbi, who summons the spirit of Channon's father and learns from him that Sender had pledged him, when they both were young, that their children should be married when they reached maturity. Sender has broken the pledge. He is judged and accepts the penalty imposed upon him. Thereupon Azrael, on threat of excommunication, exorcises the Dybbuk from the body of Leah and orders her father to prepare the marriage. But Leah, calling upon Channon, dies and is united with her lover.

Eugene Onegin

→))) * (((←

MUSIC BY: Peter I. Tchaikovsky

WORLD PREMIERE: Moscow, Russia,
March 29, 1879

LIBRETTO BY: Konstantin Shilovsky
and the composer
Based on a poem by Pushkin
NEW YORK CITY OPERA PREMIERE:
(Sung in Russian) November 14, 1946

CONDUCTOR: Laszlo Halasz
STAGE DIRECTOR: Theodore Komisarjevsky (debut)
SCENIC DESIGNER: H. A. Condell
COSTUMES*

CHARACTERS (In order of appearance)	VOICE (type)	PREMIERE CAST (New York City Opera)
Larina, a widow, owner of a large farm	Mezzo	Lydia Edwards
Filipievna, the nurse	Mezzo	Mary Kreste
Tatiana ⎤ Larina's	Soprano	Brenda Miller (debut)
Olga ⎦ daughters	Mezzo	Margery Mayer
Eugene Onegin ⎤ Larina's	Baritone	Ivan Petroff
Vladimir Lenski ⎦ neighbors	Tenor	William Horne
A Captain	Bass	Grant Garnell
Triquet, a French tutor	Tenor	Nathaniel Sprinzena
Saretski	Bass	Arthur Newman
Prince Gremin	Bass	Gean Greenwell

Peasants, Ball Guests, Landowners, Officers. Solo dancer added to program November 24.

SYNOPSIS OF STORY
TIME AND PLACE: St. Petersburg, Russia; about 1830

*

ACT I

SCENE 1—In front of Larina's country house

Larina, a landowner, is preserving fruit in the garden before her house. From within she hears the voices of her two daughters, Tatiana and Olga, singing, as she and the old nurse Filipievna reminisce of the old days. Lenski arrives with his friend Onegin. Tatiana is immediately greatly attracted to Onegin, but he remains distant and

---

* By Kate Friedheim; additional costumes by Stivanello.

111

aloof. He is a man of cold personality, proud and arrogant. The conflict within himself is so great and his unhappiness so intense that he can find no peace.

SCENE 2—Tatiana's bedroom

The same night, thinking of Onegin, Tatiana cannot sleep; to divert herself she asks Filipievna to tell her about her past. Suddenly she confesses that she is in love and sends the old woman away. Instead of sleeping, however, she writes a feverish love letter to Onegin. When Filipievna enters next morning, Tatiana sends her to Onegin with the letter.

SCENE 3—Same as Scene 1

Later Onegin meets her; torn between love and the knowledge that he could never make her happy, Onegin rejects her and leaves.

ACT II

SCENE 1—Chamber in the home of Larina

A ball is being given by Larina. Onegin arrives with Lenski. Bored with the company, Onegin flirts with Olga, who responds with mischievous simplicity. Lenski is annoyed with Olga's flirtatiousness and starts an argument with Onegin, which develops into a real fight. In that moment of fury Lenski challenges Onegin to a duel.

SCENE 2—A wintry morning on the banks of a stream

The two men meet for the duel. The erstwhile friends regret that they are now enemies, but the duel commences. Lenski is killed instantly, and Onegin is overwhelmed with grief.

ACT III

SCENE—Ballroom in Prince Gremin's mansion

Years pass, during which Onegin has wandered restlessly over the world. He attends a ball being given by an old friend, Prince Gremin, in St. Petersburg, and there he discovers that Tatiana is now the Princess. The Prince tells Onegin that he loves his wife passionately and then brings her forward to meet him. Her indifference rekindles his love anew, and he declares that she belongs to him. She upbraids him and reminds him of their conversation years ago in the garden. His ardor at last wrings from her the admission that she loves him, but she insists that her duty is to her husband. She asks Onegin to depart and not to return. Despite his outburst of passion and her own disturbed feelings, she remains firm in her decision and leaves him alone. Completely dejected, Onegin rushes off in despair.

Falstaff

-»»*«««-

MUSIC BY: Giuseppe Verdi

WORLD PREMIERE: Milan, Italy,
February 9, 1893

LIBRETTO BY: Arrigo Boito
English translation by Chester Kallman
NEW YORK CITY OPERA PREMIERE:
(Sung in English) April 15, 1954

CONDUCTOR: Joseph Rosenstock
STAGE DIRECTOR: Otto Erhardt
SCENERY and COSTUMES: John Boyt

CHARACTERS (In order of appearance)	VOICE (type)	PREMIERE CAST (New York City Opera)
Sir John Falstaff	Baritone	Richard Wentworth
Dr. Caius, a Physician	Tenor	Michael Pollock
Bardolph } Followers of Falstaff	Tenor	Luigi Vellucci
Pistol }	Bass	Norman Treigle
Mistress Alice Ford	Soprano	Phyllis Curtin
Mistress Meg Page	Mezzo	Rosemary Kuhlmann
Nannetta, Daughter of Mistress Ford	Soprano	Madeline Chambers
Dame Quickly	Mezzo	Margery Mayer
Fenton, a young Gentleman	Tenor	Jon Crain
Ford, a wealthy Burgher	Baritone	Walter Cassel

Burghers and Street Folk, Ford's Servants, Maskers as elves, fairies, witches

SYNOPSIS OF STORY
TIME AND PLACE: Windsor, early 15th century

*

ACT I

SCENE—Inside the Garter Inn

At the Garter Inn, where Sir John Falstaff holds court attended by Bardolph and Pistol, old Dr. Caius accuses them of theft and outrages upon his property. Falstaff airily dismisses him, and then reveals his plans to woo Alice Ford and Meg Page, two married women of Windsor who he imagines are in love with him. Bardolph and Pistol refuse to carry his letters because it offends their honor. After expatiating on honor, Falstaff angrily drives them out.

ACT II

SCENE—Inside the Garter Inn

Bardolph and Pistol, feigning repentance, introduce Quickly to Falstaff. The rendezvous, between two and three that afternoon, is arranged. Falstaff exults, and his exultation increases when

113

Ford, under the name of Brook, gives him money and asks him to seduce Alice Ford so that he too may have a chance with her. When he hears that Falstaff already has an appointment, he gives full vent to his jealousy.

The women set the stage for their comedy, and when Falstaff arrives to woo Alice, the others are hiding nearby. Ford, however, enters unexpectedly in a fury, and Falstaff is hidden first behind the screen and then in a laundry hamper. During the general riot Nannetta and Fenton hide behind the screen, and Ford, hearing them kiss and thinking to find Falstaff and Alice, knocks the screen down. Then he orders Fenton to abandon all hopes of marrying his daughter. A moment later, servants enter to a prearranged signal and empty the laundry and Falstaff into the river.

ACT III

SCENE 1—In front of the Garter Inn

Falstaff laments the degradation of the world, as exemplified by his watery fate. But reanimated by wine, he again agrees to meet Alice when Quickly brings him another message. The meeting is to take place by Herne's Oak in Windsor Forest at midnight, a time and place legend designates as haunted, and Falstaff is to come disguised as Herne. Alice and the others plan to come costumed as supernatural beings in order to frighten Falstaff, and Ford thinks to take advantage of the masquerade and betroth his daughter to Dr. Caius, but Quickly overhears them.

SCENE 2—Windsor Forest

Falstaff arrives at the meeting place and tries to make love to Alice, but a shriek from Meg interrupts them. The goblins are coming. Led by Nannetta, dressed as Queen of the Fairies, the rest enter; Falstaff, "a mortal," is discovered, and they set upon him unmercifully. During the melee, Bardolph's mask falls off and the joke is revealed. Later, when Ford's plot is foiled by the women and he unwittingly joins Nannetta and Fenton with his blessing, Alice laughingly points out that they—Ford, Falstaff and Dr. Caius—have all been equally duped. The opera ends with the wise laughter of pardon and repentance: "Life is the joke we make it."

La Fanciulla del West

→))∗((←

MUSIC BY: Giacomo Puccini

LIBRETTO BY: Carlo Zangarini and Guelpho Civinini
Based on the play of the same name by David Belasco

WORLD PREMIERE: New York, New York, December 10, 1910

NEW YORK CITY OPERA PREMIERE: (Sung in Italian) October 16, 1977

CONDUCTOR: Sergiu Comissiona (debut)
STAGE DIRECTOR: Frank Corsaro
SCENIC DESIGNER: Robert O'Hearn (debut)
COSTUMES: Suzanne Mess (debut)

CHARACTERS (In order of appearance)	VOICE (type)	PREMIERE CAST (New York City Opera)
Nick, bartender of the Polka saloon	Tenor	John Lankston
Jack Rance, the sheriff	Bass-baritone	Charles Long
Jim Larkens	Baritone	William Ledbetter
Billy Jackrabbit, an Indian	Baritone	Don Yule
Joe	Tenor	Howard Hensel
Bello	Baritone	James Sergi
Harry	Tenor	David Griffith
Happy	Bass-baritone	Irwin Densen
Sid	Baritone	Harlan Foss
Sonora	Baritone	Thomas Jamerson
Trin	Tenor	Melvin Lowery
Jake Wallace, a ballad singer	Baritone	Andrew Smith (debut)
Ashby, a Wells Fargo agent	Baritone	Richard McKee
Minnie, owner of the Polka saloon	Soprano	Maralin Niska
A Post Rider	Tenor	Joaquin Romaguera
Dick Johnson, the disguised bandit Ramerrez	Tenor	Ermanno Mauro
José Castro, a member of Ramerrez' gang	Baritone	James Billings
Wowkle, Billy's Squaw	Mezzo	Kathleen Hegierski

Men of the Camp

SYNOPSIS OF STORY
TIME AND PLACE: California, during the Gold Rush, 1849

∗

La Fanciulla del West, 1977. Left to right: Maralin Niska, Ermanno Mauro.

ACT I

SCENE—The Polka saloon

At dusk in a small California mining camp, the Polka saloon fills with boisterous miners. The distant voice of Jake Wallace, an itinerant minstrel, is heard approaching; when he enters the men join him in his nostalgic ballad. After money has been collected for young Jim Larkens, who longs to return home, Ashby, a Wells Fargo agent, arrives to tell the sheriff, Jack Rance, that he is about to close in on the bandit Ramerrez and his gang. As the bartender, Nick, serves drinks courtesy of Minnie, the Polka's owner and camp schoolteacher, Rance solemnly announces that she will soon be his wife. The miner Sonora jealously protests, and the ensuing brawl brings forth Minnie herself. After threatening to close the school if the men do not behave, she reads to them from the Bible. The mail arrives, and the miners go off to the dance hall to celebrate. Rance tells Minnie of his bitter life, empty of love and ruined by cards; in contrast, Minnie recalls the happy childhood she knew in her par-

ents' saloon. Suddenly a handsome stranger enters, claiming to be Dick Johnson of Sacramento but in reality Ramerrez. Remembering him from a brief romantic encounter on the road to Monterey, Minnie welcomes him. Suspicious, Rance and the miners challenge his presence, but Minnie vouches for Johnson and further infuriates the sheriff by dancing with him. Just then Ashby drags in Ramerrez' accomplice, José Castro, who, recognizing Johnson, sends the posse on a false chase. When the men entrust their gold to Minnie, the love-struck Johnson, impressed with the girl's devotion to the miners, discards his plan to rob the Polka. Instead, he accepts Minnie's invitation to her cabin and leaves, kissing her hand. Alone, the girl muses ecstatically on his words of love.

ACT II

SCENE—Minnie's cabin

Minnie's maid Wowkle sings her papoose a lullaby as the father, Billy Jackrabbit, comes to

116

propose marriage. Soon Minnie enters; dismissing Billy, she excitedly dresses for Johnson's visit. When he arrives, full of compliments and advances, she begs him to slow down but, soon forgiving him, tells him of the joy of life. After Wowkle leaves, Johnson takes Minnie in his arms and kisses her. A mounting snowstorm leads her to suggest that he stay the night; he retires to a bunk, and Minnie curls up on a bearskin beside the fireplace. As shots announce the posse's approach, Johnson hides. Rance, checking to see that Minnie is safe, tells her the stranger is Ramerrez, lover of the notorious Nina Micheltorena. Shocked, she sends the men away and turns on Johnson. Admitting his identity, he tells how his father made him a bandit; since meeting her, however, he has changed. Touched, she nevertheless sends him away. Almost at once a shot rings out, and Johnson staggers back, wounded. Scarcely has Minnie hidden him in the loft than Rance bursts in, hot on the trail. Not finding his prey, he makes advances toward Minnie, who orders him to leave. But drops of blood fall on his hand from the loft, revealing the bandit's hiding place. When Johnson climbs down, Minnie plays on Rance's gambling instinct by offering herself and her lover as stakes at poker. First hiding a full house in her stocking, she begins the game. Both win a round, but when Rance draws three kings in the third hand, Minnie pretends to faint; pulling forth the concealed cards, she defeats the sheriff, who leaves in fury.

ACT III

SCENE—A deserted mining camp

By a dawn campfire, Rance regrets his pact with Minnie. Harry and Bello report the near capture of Johnson as savage outcries signal his continued pursuit; others shortly lead in the outlaw. From the vengeful miners, determined to hang him, Johnson begs one last favor: Minnie must not know his fate. Just as the noose is slipped around his neck, Minnie rides to the rescue. Holding the mob at bay, she reminds them of her years of devotion, in return claiming Johnson as her own. As a gesture of faith, she throws down her gun. All the men except Rance are won to her side. Johnson, freed from his bonds, thanks the miners, and he and Minnie leave to begin a new life.

Faust

→))) ∗ (((←

MUSIC BY: Charles François Gounod

WORLD PREMIERE: Paris, France,
    March 9, 1859

LIBRETTO BY: Michel Carré and
    Jules Barbier

NEW YORK CITY OPERA PREMIERE:
    (Sung in French) April 16, 1945

CONDUCTOR: Jean Morel
STAGE DIRECTOR: José Ruben
SCENIC DESIGNER: H. A. Condell
COSTUMES*

CHARACTERS (In order of appearance)	VOICE (type)	PREMIERE CAST (New York City Opera)
Faust	Tenor	Joseph Laderoute (debut)
Mephistopheles	Bass-baritone	Roberto Silva (debut)
Marguerite	Soprano	Dorothy Kirsten
Wagner	Baritone	Richard Rivers (debut)
Valentin	Baritone	Daniel Duno
Siebel	Baritone	Henry Cordy†
Marthe	Mezzo	Enid Szantho

Soldiers, Villagers, Entertainers

SYNOPSIS OF STORY
TIME AND PLACE: Germany, 16th century

∗

PROLOGUE

SCENE—Faust's laboratory and study

No longer able to bear his empty life, the old scholar Faust contemplates taking poison. Instead, in a fit of despair, he invokes the help of Satan. Mephistopheles appears and offers Faust his services in return for his soul. Faust yearns to regain his youth but hesitates. In order to persuade him, Mephistopheles conjures up the image of a lovely girl, Marguerite. Faust signs a pact and, transformed into a young man, departs with Mephistopheles.

ACT I

SCENE—A street fair (Kermesse)

The townspeople gather in the market square as soldiers, including Valentin, Marguerite's

---

* Supplied by Van Horn & Son, with certain costumes donated by Mrs. Cornelius Dresselhuys.
† Usually sung by mezzo-soprano.

brother, prepare to go off to war. Mephistopheles entertains the crowd and amuses, then frightens, them with his magic. The town band begins to play a waltz. Faust, searching for the Marguerite he has seen in the vision, tries to speak to her as she passes by but is firmly though gently reproved. Mephistopheles laughingly promises him better luck in the future.

ACT II

SCENE—Marguerite's house and garden

Siebel, a young admirer of Marguerite, places a bouquet of flowers on her doorstep and leaves. Faust enters the garden and is enchanted by the charm of the surroundings. Mephistopheles goes off, to return with a box of jewels, which he places next to Siebel's modest flowers. Marguerite, deep in thought about the man she had met in the market square, enters and discovers the gifts. Unable to resist opening the jewel box, she is delighted with its precious contents and hastens to adorn herself with the jewels. Her old housekeeper, Marthe, advises her to keep them. Mephistopheles appears with Faust and, in the following scene, distracts Marthe by pretending to court her, as Faust persuasively woos Marguerite. Marguerite finally surrenders to Faust's ardent advances.

ACT III

SCENE 1—A street near Marguerite's house

Valentin returns from war with the victorious soldiers, only to learn from Siebel of his sister's misfortune. Faust, now remorseful, also returns to Marguerite but is met by Valentin, who challenges him to a duel. Faust then slays him with the aid of Mephistopheles. The townspeople, drawn by the clamor, arrive to hear Valentin's dying curse upon Marguerite.

ACT IV

SCENE 1—A church

Deserted by Faust and carrying his child, Marguerite prays in church. Instead of consolation,

Faust, 1978. Samuel Ramey (courtesy Sally Cooney).

she hears the voices of demons and of a mocking Mephistopheles cursing her, and flees in terror.

SCENE 2—A prison

Faust enters the prison in which Marguerite, having killed her child, now lies completely insane. He pleads desperately with her to follow him, but to no avail. When she spies Mephistopheles in the shadows, she recoils in horror and prays for deliverance. The dawn breaks, and with it, Marguerite's fate is sealed.

119

La Favola d'Orfeo

→))) * (((←

MUSIC BY: Claude Monteverdi
WORLD PREMIERE: Mantua, Italy,
    February 24, 1607

LIBRETTO BY: Alessandro Striggio
NEW YORK CITY OPERA PREMIERE:
    (Sung in Italian) September 29, 1960

CONDUCTOR: Leopold Stokowski
STAGE DIRECTOR: Christopher West (debut)
SETS, COSTUMES, and LIGHTING: Donald Oenslager
CHOREOGRAPHER: Robert Joffrey

CHARACTERS (In order of appearance)	VOICE (type)	PREMIERE CAST (New York City Opera)
La Musica	Soprano	Doris Yarick (debut)
Shepherds	Tenors	Maurice Stern
		John Dennison
Ninfa (Nymph)	Soprano	Mary LeSawyer
Orfeo	Baritone	Gerard Souzay (debut)
Euridice	Soprano	Judith Raskin
Messaggera (Messenger)	Mezzo	Regina Sarfaty
Speranza (Hope)	Mezzo	Joy Clements
Caronte	Bass-baritone	Andrew Frierson
Proserpina	Contralto	Evelyn Sachs
Plutone (Pluto)	Bass	Joshua Hecht
Plutone's Chamberlain	Tenor	Maurice Stern
Apollo	Tenor	Frank Porretta
Solo Dancers:		
Musica's Attendants		Françoise Martinet
		Carolyn Borys (debut)
		Brunilda Ruiz
Shepherd Boy		Jonathan Watts
Caronte Spirit		Françoise Martinet
Shepherds and Nymphs		

Note: This performance preceded *The Prisoner* by Dallapiccola.

SYNOPSIS OF STORY
TIME AND PLACE: Legendary Greece; classical times

*

La Favola d'Orfeo, 1960. Left to right: Gerard Souzay, Frank Porretta, and dancers.

PROLOGUE

The prologue consists of a recitation by La Musica of her powers.

ACT I

SCENE—A pastoral scene

Shepherds and nymphs are rejoicing over the wedding of Orfeo and Euridice. The act ends with a beautiful chorus praying that their happy state may bring no misfortune to the lovers.

ACT II

SCENE—Another pastoral scene

The mood is one of contentment and happiness, which is suddenly broken by the advent of the Messenger with the news of Euridice's death. The unclouded happiness and serenity that seemed to be Orfeo's have aroused the envy of the gods. The first reaction of horror comes from the Shepherds. They mourn the tragedies of Euridice and of Orfeo transfixed by grief.

ACT III

SCENE—The banks of the River Styx

Orfeo is comforted by Hope. He resolves to seek Euridice in Hades.

ACT IV

SCENE—Hades

Proserpina and Pluto discuss Orfeo's plight and, prompted by his wife and urged by captive spirits, the King of the Underworld agrees to release Euridice to her husband. Orfeo is triumphant but looks back to see if Euridice is following. Her short-lived freedom is snatched from her by her husband's transgression of Pluto's stipulation.

ACT V

SCENE—The plains of Thrace

Orfeo, wandering on the plains of Thrace, laments his broken heart. Apollo, Orfeo's father, descends from Heaven and tells his son that he will be translated to divine immortality and among the stars will be able to see his Euridice. Father and son ascend to Heaven.

The Flaming Angel

(L'Ange de Feu)

➤➤➤✳◀◀◀

MUSIC BY: Serge Prokofiev

WORLD STAGED PREMIERE: Venice, Italy,
    September 14, 1955
(Performed in concert form in
Paris on November 25, 1954)

LIBRETTO BY: Serge Prokofiev
Based on a tale by Valery Bryusov
English translation by Joseph Machlis
NEW YORK CITY OPERA PREMIERE:
    (Sung in English) September 22, 1965

CONDUCTOR: Julius Rudel
STAGE DIRECTOR: Frank Corsaro
SCENERY and LIGHTING: Will Steven Armstrong
COSTUMES: Patricia Zipprodt

CHARACTERS (In order of appearance)	VOICE (type)	PREMIERE CAST (New York City Opera)
The Innkeeper	Mezzo	Beverly Evans
Ruprecht, a Knight	Baritone	Sherrill Milnes
Renata	Soprano	Eileen Schauler
Pot boy	Mute	Gary Finkelstein (debut)
A Waiter at the Inn	Baritone	William Beck (debut)
The Fortune Teller	Mezzo	Muriel Greenspon
Jacob Glock	Tenor	Luigi Vellucci
Agrippa of Nettesheim	Tenor	Jon Crain
Three Men of Cologne	Tenor	Don Henderson
	Baritone	Richard Park
	Bass	Don Yule
Count Heinrich	Mute	Lester James (debut)
Matthew, a friend of Ruprecht	Baritone	William Beck (debut)
Nuns	Soprano	Iris Bala (debut)
	Soprano	Carol Bergey
	Mezzo	Kay Creed (debut)
	Mezzo	Beverly Evans
	Mezzo	Rosalind Hupp (debut)
	Mezzo	Marlena Kleinman
	Soprano	Donna Precht
	Mezzo	Joan Summers

The Flaming Angel, 1965. Eileen Schauler (center) and members of the ensemble.

CHARACTERS (In order of appearance)	VOICE (type)	PREMIERE CAST (New York City Opera)
A Physician	Tenor	Richard Krause
Mephistopheles	Tenor	Norman Kelley
Dr. Faustus	Baritone	Robert Trehy
A Tavernkeeper	Baritone	Jack Bittner
The Abbess	Mezzo	Muriel Greenspon
The Inquisitor	Bass	Malcolm Smith (debut)

Guards, Skeletons, Servants

SYNOPSIS OF STORY

TIME AND PLACE: Germany in the 16th century

*

ACT I

SCENE 1—An attic room in a highway inn

Ruprecht is trying to get to sleep but is disturbed by Renata, who, in an adjoining room, is having one of her hallucinations. When Ruprecht breaks into Renata's room to calm her, she tells him her story.

She had her first vision of a Flaming Angel when she was eight. Renata called him Madrid and had dreams of him until she was eighteen, when he no longer appeared to her. Then she met Count Heinrich, to whom she transferred her love because she believed him to be the mortal incarnation of Madrid. After a year together, the Count left her.

The Innkeeper quiets the disturbance and cautions Ruprecht about the strange things that have been happening since Renata came to the village. Renata persuades Ruprecht to go with her to Cologne to look for Count Heinrich. A Fortune Teller says she sees blood in Renata's future.

SCENE 2—A room in a lodging house in Cologne, one week later

Ruprecht is in love with Renata. She insists that she is still seeking Count Heinrich. Jacob Glock involves Renata in further magic but does not tell her how to find the Count.

SCENE 3—The study of Agrippa of Nettesheim, a famous alchemist

Agrippa tries to dissuade Ruprecht from becoming involved in the occult. However, Ruprecht is greatly enlightened by what he is told and shown.

ACT II

SCENE 4—A street outside Count Heinrich's house in Cologne

Renata finally finds Count Heinrich, but he rejects her. At first she is angry and asks Ruprecht to challenge the Count to a duel, which Ruprecht does. Later, when she again sees the Count as the Flaming Angel, Renata remembers only her love. She tells Ruprecht she will never forgive him if he harms the Count.

SCENE 5—A steep bank of the Rhine

Ruprecht is seriously wounded in the duel with the Count. Ruprecht's devotion makes Renata realize that she really loves him.

ACT III

SCENE 6—A quiet square in Cologne

Renata has nursed Ruprecht back to health. Her feelings change, and she decides to renounce the world and enter a convent. Ruprecht's love for her is undiminished.

Faust and Mephistopheles meet Ruprecht, who is heartbroken over the loss of Renata's love. They persuade him to join them in a stroll around Cologne.

SCENE 7—A vaulted crypt in a convent

Renata, a novice, is questioned by the Mother Superior about former contacts with the Devil. The nuns have been disturbed by visions since Renata has joined them.

The Inquisitor arrives and questions Renata, who proclaims her innocence of any contact with the Devil. The nuns believe themselves possessed by the Devil because of Renata's presence. The Inquisitor pronounces Renata guilty and sentences her to be tortured as a witch and burned at the stake.

Die Fledermaus

→))) * (((←

MUSIC BY: Johann Strauss

LIBRETTO BY: Carl Haffner and
Richard Genee
English book and lyrics by: Ruth and Thomas
Martin

WORLD PREMIERE: Vienna, Austria,
April 5, 1874

NEW YORK CITY OPERA PREMIERE:
(Sung in English) April 8, 1953

CONDUCTOR: Thomas P. Martin
STAGE DIRECTOR: James Westerfield (debut)
SCENIC DESIGNER: (unavailable)*
COSTUME SUPERVISOR: Robert Fletcher (debut)
BALLET CHOREOGRAPHER: John Butler

CHARACTERS (In order of appearance)	VOICE (type)	PREMIERE CAST (New York City Opera)
Alfred, an operatic tenor (heard offstage)	Tenor	Jon Crain
Adele, chambermaid to Gabriel von Eisenstein and his wife, Rosalinda	Soprano	Elaine Malbin
Rosalinda	Soprano	Laurel Hurley
Gabriel von Eisenstein, a banker	Tenor	Jack Russell (debut)
Dr. Blind, Eisenstein's lawyer	Tenor	Luigi Vellucci
Dr. Falke, a friend of the Eisensteins	Baritone	William Shriner (debut)
Frank, the prison warden	Baritone	Richard Wentworth
Sally, Adele's sister, a ballet dancer	Mezzo	Jeanne Beauvais (debut)
Prince Orlofsky, a wealthy Russian prince	Baritone	Donald Gramm†
Ivan, servant to Orlofsky	Speaking role	Michael Arshansky
Frosch, the jailer	Speaking role	Ernest Sarracino (debut)

Guests, Servants, Dancers

SYNOPSIS OF STORY
TIME AND PLACE: Vienna, 1870

*

---

* The sets and costumes were borrowed from various sources and productions, including a Sol Hurok touring production
of *Die Fledermaus* and the 1952 Broadway show *My Darlin' Aida.*
† Usually sung by mezzo-soprano.

ACT I

SCENE—Sitting room of the Eisensteins

Gabriel von Eisenstein has been sentenced to jail, and Alfred, an itinerant operatic tenor, uses the opportunity to renew his former relationship with Eisenstein's wife, Rosalinda. Adele, the maid, receives an invitation from her sister to go to a fancy ball and, pleading a dying relative, tries to get the evening off. Highly flattered by Alfred's attentions, Rosalinda agrees to see him later when her husband suddenly returns from court. He and his lawyer, Dr. Blind, argue furiously over which of them is to blame for the judge's extending of Eisenstein's sentence. Eisenstein prepares to report to jail after a farewell dinner with his wife, but Dr. Falke persuades him to attend Prince Orlofsky's ball (without Rosalinda's knowledge) and to surrender himself to the prison warden the following morning. The two old friends reminisce about a previous masquerade when Eisenstein left Dr. Falke (drunk and costumed as a bat) passed out on a park bench—to awaken in broad daylight surrounded by Sunday strollers. Eisenstein laughs as he remembers the trick he played on Falke, and Falke laughs also, but he is thinking of the revenge he will have later that night at the ball. As the wealthy and eccentric Prince Orlofsky's social adviser, Falke has prepared the guest list, inviting Rosalinda, Adele, and the prison warden, all in disguise.

Alfred reappears to continue his pursuit of Rosalinda, who has changed her mind and given the puzzled Adele permission to leave. When a note arrives from Falke informing her that her husband has not gone to jail but to Orlofsky's party, Rosalinda tries to get rid of Alfred so she too can go to the ball. Frank, the prison warden, comes to escort Eisenstein to jail, and Rosalinda persuades Alfred (whom Frank has mistaken for her husband) to save her reputation and go off to jail as Eisenstein.

ACT II

SCENE—Ballroom of Prince Orlofsky's palace

Prince Orlofsky's party is in full progress as Adele enters dressed in one of Rosalinda's gowns. She soon recognizes the "Marquis Renard" as Eisenstein. Eisenstein and Frank (as Marquis Renard and Chevalier Chagrin) have been amusing themselves with Adele and Sally when the masked Rosalinda is announced as a Hungarian countess. Eisenstein pursues the lovely countess, unaware that she is his own wife. Throughout all of the intrigue moves Falke, playing one person against another for his own enjoyment. Even the perpetually bored Orlofsky begins to take an interest in Falke's machinations. The dancing, gambling, and entertainment continue throughout the night, with the party breaking up as the sun rises.

ACT III

SCENE—The jail

Alfred, after a night in jail as Eisenstein, insists upon seeing a lawyer. Frosch, the drunken jailer (whom Alfred has driven further to drink by his constant singing), sends for Dr. Blind. Frank, also drunk, arrives at the jail directly from Orlofsky's. Adele and her sister (thinking they have followed "Chevalier Chagrin" to his mansion) soon appear to ask help in furthering Adele's career as an actress. Eisenstein also arrives to surrender himself to the warden and begin his jail term, only to discover that "Eisenstein" is already in jail. In rapid succession, Rosalinda, Dr. Blind, and Prince Orlofsky and the party guests show up at the jail. After a great deal of confusion, everyone's true identity is revealed, and Falke confesses his scheme of revenge. All is forgiven, and everyone joins in a toast to the night and champagne.

Der Fliegende Holländer

-»»*«««-

MUSIC BY: Richard Wagner
WORLD PREMIERE: Dresden, Germany
    January 2, 1843

LIBRETTO BY: Richard Wagner
NEW YORK CITY OPERA PREMIERE:
    (Sung in German) April 12, 1945

CONDUCTOR: Laszlo Halasz
STAGE DIRECTOR: José Ruben
SCENIC DESIGNER: Richard Rychtarik
COSTUMES*

CHARACTERS (In order of appearance)	VOICE (type)	PREMIERE CAST (New York City Opera)
Daland	Bass	Sidor Belarsky
Steersman	Tenor	Giulio Gari (debut)
Dutchman	Baritone	Frederick Destal (debut)
Mary	Mezzo	Enid Szantho (debut)
Senta	Soprano	Doris Doree (debut)
Erik	Tenor	William Horne
Sailors, Village Girls		

SYNOPSIS OF STORY
TIME AND PLACE: Coast of Norway, 18th century

*

ACT I

SCENE—Seashore with steep cliffs

If the translators had been a little less literal, *The Flying Dutchman* might have been called "The Roaming Dutchman," which would have been more in the vein of its tragic theme. At any rate, the story concerns a Dutchman marked by the gods for doom. He has vowed to round the Cape of Good Hope if it takes him all eternity.

They condemn him to roam the seas forever unless he meets a girl who not only would be faithful to him but would be willing to die in order to save him. To fulfill his quest he is allowed to touch land for twenty-four hours every seven years. The first act of the opera opens with one of these landings. At first we see a Norwegian ship owned by a captain named Daland, who has sought refuge in a cove a few miles from his home port to escape a violent storm. Presently

---

* By Van Horn & Son.

the Dutchman's ship, often referred to as the Ghost Ship, anchors alongside it. Daland and his steersman vainly hail the mysterious craft for a signal of identification. Eventually they spot a solitary figure on the shore who seems to be her captain. Daland and the Dutchman strike up an acquaintance. The odd-looking mariner begs the Norwegian's hospitality for one night, offering to repay him with fabulous treasures. At sight of the riches, Daland's eyes gleam. He tries to be very friendly with the owner of such treasures, whose aloofness intrigues him. However, upon hearing that Daland has an unmarried daughter, the Dutchman thaws and asks for her hand. Daland is elated at the prospect of the lucrative match, and as a favorable wind rises, the two men decide to set sail at once for the Norwegian's home.

ACT II

SCENE—A large room in Daland's home

Senta, Daland's daughter, and her companions are spinning, but she hardly touches her wheel. Her eyes are fixed on a portrait of the Dutchman hanging over the door. Evidently the legend of the Flying Dutchman has spread far afield, for a popular ballad has been written about his plight. The romantic and mystic quality of Senta's nature has turned the legend into an obsession. A feeling of deep compassion arouses in her the desire to save him from his fate even though she has allowed Erik, a young hunter, to court her. Goaded by her companions, she confesses her yearning. She is overheard by Erik, entering the room unnoticed; he and the girls look upon her obsession as a form of madness. Erik has come to announce the arrival of her father's ship. On hearing the news, the girls rush out to welcome their sweethearts. Left alone with Senta, Erik begs her to give up her wild dream and settle down with him in a sensible and peaceful marriage. His entreaties ignored, he runs off with a cry of despair.

Senta reverts to her morbid ecstasy when the door suddenly opens and the legendary figure appears on the threshold. The spell of the meeting is broken by the entrance of Daland. The greedy father, having already acquired some of the jewels, shows them to his daughter and exhorts her

to give her hand to the wealthy stranger. His efforts being ignored, he turns to the Dutchman, coaxing him to propose. Finally realizing that the best thing he can do is to leave the two alone, he picks up his hat and leaves. For a long while Senta and the Dutchman remain motionless, transfixed. Out of fairness, the Dutchman reveals to Senta that her desire to save him would bring her death. But the magnitude of the sacrifice does not frighten her, and she renews her vow. Daland returns to tell them that the sailors and the girls have heard the good news and are anxious to see the engagement celebrated at once. Senta takes the Dutchman by the hand and with supreme happiness leads him out to join the expectant throng.

ACT III

SCENE—A bay, with rocky shores; Daland's house in the foreground

The two ships are anchored side by side. The night is clear. Lights shine on the Norwegian ship, but the Dutch craft is enveloped in an unnatural darkness with the stillness of death reigning over it. The crew on Daland's ship is singing and dancing—a constant flow of wine adds to their gaiety. After a while the girls enter carrying baskets of food and liquor for the Dutch sailors, but their efforts to attract attention are of no avail. There is no sign of life on the phantom ship. The Daland crew laugh at the girls' failure and persuade them to give them the baskets instead. Then they in turn hail the mysterious craft. For an answer they hear a shrill and ghostly laughter that fills them with awe. They draw back, making the sign of the cross, and disappear below.

Senta enters from the house, greatly agitated. She is followed by Erik, who once more pleads his cause. He reminds her that her own father, before the Dutchman's arrival, had urged her to give him her heart. The Dutchman enters unobserved and hears Erik's protestation of love. Convinced that Erik has a claim on Senta, he cries out his defeat and prepares to board his ship. But Senta stops him and begs him to stay, assuring him that she will carry out her promise. The Dutchman refuses her sacrifice and swiftly runs onto his ship. Senta tries to follow him but is held back by her people. As the Dutch ship moves out to sea, she climbs on a cliff and wildly calls after him. Then with a poignant cry she casts herself into the sea. At that very moment the Dutchman's ship is seen to sink with all her crew. The Dutchman and Senta have landed on the only shore where they could be together, the shore of the beyond.

The Four Ruffians*

-»»*«««-

MUSIC BY: Ermanno Wolf-Ferrari

WORLD PREMIERE: Munich, Germany,
March 19, 1906

LIBRETTO BY: Giuseppe Pizzolato
English version by: Edward Dent*
UNITED STATES and NEW YORK CITY OPERA
PREMIERE: (Sung in English) October 18, 1951

CONDUCTOR: Laszlo Halasz
STAGE DIRECTOR: Otto Erhardt
SCENIC DESIGNER: Mstislav Doboujinsky
COSTUMES and MASKS BY: Ruth Morley
CHOREOGRAPHER: Charles Weidman

CHARACTERS (In order of appearance)	VOICE (type)	PREMIERE CAST (New York City Opera)
Lucieta, daughter of Lunardo by his first wife	Soprano	Dorothy MacNeil
Margarita, second wife of Lunardo	Mezzo	Margery Mayer
Lunardo, dealer in antiques	Bass	Gean Greenwell
Maurizio, a merchant	Bass	Richard Wentworth
Marina, wife of Simon	Soprano	Ellen Faull
Maid to Marina	Mezzo	Edith Evans
Filipeto, son of Maurizio and nephew of Marina	Tenor	David Lloyd
Simon, a broker	Bass	George Jongeyans
Felice, wife of Canciano	Mezzo	Frances Bible
Canciano, an apothecary	Bass	Emile Renan
Count Riccardo Arcolai, a gentleman from Florence	Tenor	Armand Harkless

SYNOPSIS OF STORY
TIME AND PLACE: Venice, 1800

*

ACT I

SCENE 1—A room in Lunardo's house

It is carnival time in Venice. Lucieta, daughter of Lunardo, is at home with her stepmother, Margarita. Both bewail the fact that they are kept confined to their household tasks and never given opportunity for pleasure or amusement. Lucieta learns that a marriage is being planned for her. Lunardo is making arrangements for her

---

* *I Quattro Rusteghi.* The translation was a modification of Edward Dent's adaptation for the Sadler's Wells Theatre in London, where the work was staged under the title *School for Fathers.*

131

to marry Filipeto, the son of his friend Maurizio. The young people have not met, and both fathers tyrannically disregard the romantic aspects of the union, basing their contract on the old-fashioned *mariage de convenance.*

SCENE 2—The roof terrace of Simon's house

Filipeto, whose father has told him of the forthcoming marriage, is horrified at not being allowed to see his bride and visits his Aunt Marina to tell her his troubles. Marina, whose own experience with another tyrannical husband, Simon, gives her a ready understanding of the boy's problem, promises to help. She enlists the aid of Felice, a wealthy and attractive lady of fashion, who arrives with her "attendant," Count Riccardo, followed by her husband, Canciano. The two ladies plan to bring the young people together.

ACT II

SCENE—A large room in Lunardo's house

Felice and Marina bring Filipeto into Lunardo's house masked, as is customary for carnival time, and dressed as a girl, escorted by Count Riccardo. Filipeto sees Lucieta and falls in love immediately; he unmasks and a love scene begins between the two, which is interrupted by the arrival of Lunardo with Simon and Canciano. Riccardo and Filipeto are hurried into another room while the ladies distract the men with stories of seeing a mouse. Maurizio arrives, discovers his son, and there is general turmoil.

ACT III

SCENE—Lunardo's antique shop

The men discuss ways to punish their respective wives. When they have concluded that it will do no good as they cannot live without them, Felice appears and gives them a lecture on how to treat women. The others return, and the young people are united with the blessing of both fathers.

Gentlemen, Be Seated!

→》》*《《-

MUSIC BY: Jerome Moross
WORLD PREMIERE and NEW YORK CITY
  OPERA PREMIERE: October 10, 1963
  (Sung in English)

LIBRETTO BY: Edward Eager

CONDUCTOR: Emerson Buckley
STAGE DIRECTOR: Robert Turoff (debut)
SCENIC DESIGNER: William Pitkin (debut)
COSTUMES: Henry Heymann (debut)
CHOREOGRAPHY: Paul Draper (debut)

CHARACTERS*	VOICE (type)	PREMIERE CAST (New York City Opera)
Mister Interlocutor	Baritone	Dick Shawn (debut)
Mister Tambo	Tenor	Avon Long (debut)
Mister Bones	Baritone	Charles Atkins (debut)
The Comedienne	Speaking	Alice Ghostley (debut)
The Contralto	Contralto	Carol Brice
Johnny Reb	Tenor	William McDonald
Bill Yank	Baritone	Richard Fredricks
Southern Girl	Soprano	June Card (debut)
Northern Girl	Mezzo	Mary Burgess
Mister Banjo	Speaking	Bernard Addison (debut)
The Character Actor	Speaking	Richard Krause
Mister Taps	Dancer	Paul Draper (debut)
Ermyntrude	Chorus	Charlotte Povia
Farmer McLean	Baritone	David Smith
Florida Cotton	Dancer	Michele Hardy (debut)
Two Soldiers	Chorus	Kellis Miller
		Don Henderson
Drill Team	Dancers	Bob Bernard (debut)
		John Tormey (debut)
		Rec Russel (debut)
		Bob Ellis (debut)
Horse		Bob Bernard
		Rec Russel
Two Other Soldiers	Chorus	Kellis Miller
		Don Yule

* Not in order of appearance.

133

Gentlemen, Be Seated!

CHARACTERS*	VOICE (type)	PREMIERE CAST (New York City Opera)
Two Girls	Chorus	Joyce Miko Beverly Evans
Four Nurses	Chorus	Joyce Miko Beverly Evans Charlotte Povia Candida Pilla

Minstrels, Waltzers, Soldiers, Nurses, Spectators, Slaves

SYNOPSIS OF STORY
TIME AND PLACE: A History of the Civil War (a minstrel show)

*

This is a one-act opera with popular songs, dialogues, and soft-shoe dances, following the sequence of the Civil War. Included are the following scenes:

Picnic at Manassas—A series of gay luncheons did take place on the Bull Run Battlefield, given by Washington's social set, who thought the war was going to be a one-battle affair.

The Ballad of Belle Boyd—Miss Boyd, after the war, went on a theatrical tour of the United States recounting her exploits for an enrapt audience. This is an attempt to recreate the kind of act she might have presented, basing it factually upon incidents in her career.

Mr. Brady Takes a Photograph—This is the one piece of fiction in *Gentlemen, Be Seated!* It

is an explanation of a peculiar gap in the otherwise remarkably complete photographic documentation of the war by Mathew B. Brady and his assistant.

Atlanta to the Sea—The incident that forms the basis of this number caused a wave of protest in the North when news of it arrived shortly after General William T. Sherman and his Army entered Savannah. Secretary of War Edwin M. Stanton went down to Georgia with a Commission of Inquiry to investigate the facts. In the end, they verified the happening but exonerated Sherman's troops of malicious intent.

The Dialogues—All the jokes used in the dialogues were culled from joke books printed during the Civil War.

---

* Not in order of appearance

Gianni Schicchi

⇥⟫∗⟪⇤

MUSIC BY: Giacomo Puccini
WORLD PREMIERE: New York, New York,
   December 14, 1918

LIBRETTO BY: Giovacchino Forzano
NEW YORK CITY OPERA PREMIERE:
   (Sung in Italian) October 5, 1961

CONDUCTOR: Julius Rudel
STAGE DIRECTOR: Christopher West
SCENERY and COSTUMES: Rouben Ter-Arutunian

CHARACTERS (In order of appearance)	VOICE (type)	PREMIERE CAST (New York City Opera)
Zita, Buoso's cousin	Mezzo	Claramae Turner
Simone, Buoso's cousin	Bass	John Macurdy
Rinuccio, Zita's nephew	Tenor	Frank Porretta
Marco, his son	Baritone	Richard Fredricks
La Ciesca, Marco's wife	Mezzo	Joan Kelm (debut)
Gherardo, Buoso's nephew	Tenor	Maurice Stern
Nella, his wife	Soprano	Mary LeSawyer
Betto, Buoso's brother-in-law	Bass	Fredric Milstein (debut)
Gherardino, Gherardo and Nella's son	Child's voice	Richard Buckley (debut)
Gianni Schicchi	Bass	Norman Treigle
Lauretta, his daughter	Soprano	Doris Yarick
Maestro Spinellochio, a Doctor	Bass	Spiro Malas (debut)
Amantio Di Nicolao, a Notary	Baritone	Herbert Beattie
Pinellino, a Shoemaker	Bass	Norman Grogan
Guccio, a Dyer	Bass	Glen Dowlen

Note: This performance was presented with *Suor Angelica* and *Il Tabarro* as part of *Il Trittico*.

SYNOPSIS OF STORY
TIME AND PLACE: The bedchamber of Buoso Donati in Florence, 1299

∗

In medieval Florence, the relatives of Buoso are assembled, bemoaning his death. When the will is read, it becomes apparent that he had willed all his possessions to a convent. In their distress, the "mourners" ask Gianni Schicchi, a citizen of the lower classes, to help them. Gianni, whose daughter Lauretta is in love with Rinuccio, Buoso's nephew, finally consents to come to their aid. The body of Buoso is removed, and Gianni Schicchi takes his place. After warning

135

Il Tritico, 1961. Il Tabarro (left to right), Placido Domingo, Arlene Saunders, Malcolm Smith, Claramae Turner. *Suor Angelica* (left to right), Claramae Turner, Maria Di Gerlando. *Gianni Schicchi.*

the relatives of the dire consequences if the plot is discovered, the lawyer is called and a new will is dictated by the "dying Buoso." After having disposed of trifles for the relatives, Gianni Schicchi wills all the prize possessions to himself. When the lawyer has gone, he chases the outraged relatives out of his newly acquired house and unites his daughter with Rinuccio. At the end of the comedy, Gianni begs the audience to forgive him for this prank.

Giulio Cesare

-»»*«««-

MUSIC BY: George Frederick Handel
WORLD PREMIERE: London, England,
  February 20, 1724

LIBRETTO BY: Nicolá Francesco Haym
NEW YORK CITY OPERA PREMIERE:
  (Sung in Italian) September 27, 1966

CONDUCTOR: Julius Rudel
PRODUCTION DEVISED and DIRECTED BY: Tito Capobianco
SCENIC DESIGNER: Ming Cho Lee
COSTUMES: José Varona (debut)

CHARACTERS (In order of appearance)	VOICE (type)	PREMIERE CAST (New York City Opera)
Giulio Cesare	Bass-baritone	Norman Treigle
Curio	Bass	William Beck
Cornelia	Contralto	Maureen Forrester (debut)
Sextus	Mezzo	Beverly Wolff
Achilla	Baritone	Dominic Cossa
Cleopatra	Soprano	Beverly Sills
Nireno	Bass	Michael Devlin
Tolomeo	Bass	Spiro Malas

Romans, Egyptians, Slaves, Attendants of Cleopatra

SYNOPSIS OF STORY
TIME AND PLACE: Egypt, 48 B.C.

*

ACT I

SCENE 1—Near Alexandria

Caesar has ousted Pompey. He enters Egypt in a victorious procession. Pompey's wife, Cornelia, and their son, Sextus, approach Caesar and ask for peace. Caesar is willing to grant this and summons Pompey. Achilla, the leader of Tolomeo's troops, arrives and proffers the head of Pompey to the horrified Caesar. Tolomeo had ordered Pompey's death in hope of gaining Caesar's favor, but instead incurs his wrath. Achilla, on seeing the distraught Cornelia, becomes passionately attracted to her. Sextus vows to avenge his father's murder.

SCENE 2—Cleopatra's room in Tolomeo's palace

Cleopatra is vying with her brother, Tolomeo, for the throne of Egypt. She decides to woo Caesar in order to secure his help, not only to win the throne but also to gratify her sense of power

138

Giulio Cesare, 1966. Left to right: Norman Treigle, Beverly Sills, Maureen Forrester.

over men. Tolomeo, aware of his sister's ambitions, derides her. Cleopatra retorts flippantly.

SCENE 3—Caesar's camp

Caesar is standing by the grave of Pompey when Cleopatra, disguised as her own maid, Lydia, enters and asks his help in rectifying the injustices done her by Tolomeo. Caesar, enthralled by her beauty, agrees. As she is about to leave, Cornelia and Sextus arrive to mourn for Pompey. Cleopatra overhears Cornelia's despair and, still in the guise of Lydia, offers to help them avenge the murder.

SCENE 4—Tolomeo's palace

Caesar and his aides are greeted by Tolomeo. Caesar, knowing of Tolomeo's treachery, confronts him. Achilla suggests that Tolomeo have Caesar killed and, as a reward for this, demands Cornelia as his wife. Cornelia and Sextus are also at the palace. Sextus challenges Tolomeo to a duel, but Tolomeo orders him imprisoned

and Cornelia taken to his seraglio. Achilla promises their freedom if Cornelia will submit to his ardor. She rejects him. The act ends with a duet by Cornelia and Sextus taking leave of each other and lamenting their fate.

ACT II

SCENE 1—The "Monte Parnasso"

Cleopatra, still in the guise of Lydia, arranges to have Caesar brought to her palace, where she has devised a *scène d'amour.* She completely enchants him.

SCENE 2—The seraglio garden in Tolomeo's palace

Cornelia sings of her despair. Achilla confronts her with his declaration of love and gives her an ultimatum. She rejects him. Tolomeo enters. He, too, is enamored of Cornelia and forces his attentions on her, expecting her to submit. At the height of her despair, she is saved from suicide by Sextus, who has escaped with Nireno's aid. Sextus now actively plans vengeance against Tolomeo.

SCENE 3—The "Monte Parnasso"

Curio enters and warns Caesar that a plot for his murder is afoot and that, in fact, the assassins are now on their way to kill him. Cleopatra reveals her true identity to Caesar and begs him to flee. He refuses and rushes to confront the assassins. Cleopatra is left with misgivings, fearing the death of her lover.

ACT III

SCENE 1—At the shore of the Mediterranean

Cleopatra has sent her troops against Tolomeo's. His forces are victorious, and Cleopatra is taken prisoner. Caesar, though thrown into the sea and presumed dead, has saved himself. Achilla, betrayed by Tolomeo, has been mortally wounded in battle. Sextus, still looking for Tolomeo, comes upon the dying Achilla, who confesses that he had advised the murders of Pompey and Caesar in order to win Cornelia for himself. To avenge himself before he dies, Achilla gives Sextus a ring bearing the seal that will make him the commander of Egyptian soldiers still loyal to Achilla. He hopes that Sextus will free Cornelia and kill Tolomeo. Caesar steps from his hiding place, seizes the ring, and promises to free both Cornelia and Cleopatra.

SCENE 2—Tolomeo's camp

Cleopatra, still a prisoner, bids farewell to her faithful servants when Caesar and his forces arrive and free her. Caesar promises to win Egypt for her.

SCENE 3—Tolomeo's seraglio

Tolomeo is about to force Cornelia to submit to him when Sextus enters with sword in hand. He kills Tolomeo and frees Cornelia.

SCENE 4—Alexandria

Caesar and Cleopatra are triumphant. Cornelia and Sextus have been avenged; they approach Caesar bearing the scepter. He receives them warmly and accepts the scepter, which he then gives to Cleopatra. She is now the reigning queen of Egypt.

The Golden Slippers*

-»»*«««

MUSIC BY: Peter I. Tchaikovsky

LIBRETTO BY: J. Polensky
Based on Gogol's story "Christmas Eve"
English version by Ruth and Thomas Martin
NEW YORK CITY OPERA PREMIERE:
  (Sung in English) October 13, 1955

WORLD PREMIERE: St. Petersburg, Russia,
  December 6, 1876
Revived in a new version called *Chere Vichki*,
  performed in Moscow on January 31, 1887.
  This is essentially the version used at the
  New York City Opera.

CONDUCTOR: Joseph Rosenstock
STAGE DIRECTOR: Vladimir Rosing
SCENIC DESIGNER: Nicolai Remisoff (debut)
COSTUMES†
CHOREOGRAPHY: Ray Harrison

CHARACTERS (In order of appearance)	VOICE (type)	PREMIERE CAST (New York City Opera)
Solocha, mother of Vakula	Mezzo	Margery Mayer
Devil	Bass	Donald Gramm
Tschub, an elderly Kossak	Bass	Richard Wentworth
Schoolmaster	Tenor	Michael Pollock
Oxana, his daughter	Soprano	Jean Fenn
Vakula, a blacksmith	Tenor	Richard Cassilly (debut)
Village Mayor, friend of Tschub	Baritone	Lloyd Harris[1]
Wood-Demon	Bass	Joshua Hecht
Old Kossak	Tenor	Thomas Powell
Czarina	Mezzo	Rosemary Kuhlmann
Majordomo	Bass	John Reardon

Villagers, Watersprites, Demons, Courtiers

SYNOPSIS OF STORY
TIME AND PLACE: A village in the Ukraine, 1850's

*

---

* In Western Europe, also known as *Oxana's Caprices*.
† Supplied by Helene Pons Studios, Braznick; Czarina's Golden Slippers by I. Miller.
[1] Lloyd Harris substituted for Arthur Newman, who was indisposed.

ACT I

SCENE 1—Village square

A Ukrainian village on a clear winter night. The moon shines brightly. The Devil discovers Solocha in front of her hut and makes love to her. Solocha, being half witch, flies off on her broomstick, the Devil pursuing her. The Devil has a bone to pick with Vakula, Solocha's son, and plans revenge. He conjures up a tremendous snowstorm and steals the moon from the sky, thus plunging the village into darkness. He hopes to break up Vakula's courtship of the beautiful Oxana by preventing Tschub, Oxana's father, from finding his way to the tavern.

SCENE 2—Tschub's house

Vakula visits Oxana, but his pleas for her love are rejected. Tschub, covered with snow and tipsy, enters. Vakula, who does not recognize him, chases him out. Oxana, infuriated, throws Vakula out. The villagers arrive and sing Christmas carols, but Oxana, now repenting her action, is too dejected to join them. She loves Vakula and suffers through her own capriciousness.

ACT II

SCENE 1—Solocha's hut

Solocha has returned from her flight with the Devil, and their flirtation is continued. Solocha is attractive not only to the Devil but also to quite a number of villagers. First the arrival of the Village Mayor causes the Devil to hide in an empty coal sack. The Schoolmaster enters, and now the Mayor hides in another sack. The Schoolmaster is forced to hide in a third sack

by the entrance of Tschub. Hearing Vakula knock at the door, Tschub joins the Schoolmaster in the third sack. The lovelorn Vakula, in a distressed mood, removes all the sacks, not knowing their contents.

SCENE 2—Village square

The carolers assemble and sing, receiving presents. Oxana mockingly declares that she will marry Vakula if he brings her the golden slippers of the Czarina. Vakula, driven by despair, takes one of the sacks and leaves. The rest of the villagers open the other sacks and find their strange contents.

ACT III

SCENE 1—Riverbank

Watersprites are tempting Vakula to drown himself. The Devil leaps out of the sack and grabs Vakula, but Vakula outwits him and gets the Devil in his power. Vakula now orders the Devil to take him to the palace of the Czarina.

SCENES 2 and 3—Anteroom in the Palace

In the palace of the Czarina, Vakula manages to get the golden slippers from the Czarina and returns with the Devil to the village.

SCENE 4—Village square

It is Christmas morning. Solocha and Oxana, believing that Vakula is dead, bemoan his fate. There is general rejoicing when Vakula unexpectedly returns. Tschub forgives him, and Oxana, happy at his return, gladly accepts him as her husband.

142

The Golem

→)))*(((←

MUSIC BY: Abraham Ellstein
WORLD PREMIERE and NEW YORK
  CITY OPERA PREMIERE: March 22, 1962
  (Sung in English)

LIBRETTO BY: Abraham Ellstein
  and Sylvia Regan
Based on the work of H. Leivick;
  a Jewish myth

CONDUCTOR: Julius Rudel
STAGE DIRECTOR: Allen Fletcher
SCENIC DESIGNER: Lester Polakov
COSTUMES: Ruth Morley
CHOREOGRAPHY: Sophie Maslow

CHARACTERS (In order of appearance)	VOICE (type)	PREMIERE CAST (New York City Opera)
Rabbi Levi Bar Bezallel, the Maharal	Tenor	Jon Crain
Avrom, the Shames	Bass-baritone	John Fiorito
The Golem	Baritone	Chester Ludgin
Yacov, disciple of Rabbi	Tenor	William Dupree
Isaac, disciple of Rabbi	Baritone	Dominic Cossa
The Rabbi's wife	Mezzo	Gladys Kriese
Deborah, Rabbi's granddaughter	Soprano	Lee Venora
Rabbi Bashevi	Bass	John Macurdy
Tanchum, the madman	Tenor	Maurice Stern
Beggars		
Hunchback	Baritone	Frederic Milstein
Blind One	Tenor	Arthur Graham
Peg-Leg	Baritone	George Del Monte
Tall	Tenor	Harris Davis (debut)
Short	Tenor	George McWhorter (debut)
Red	Tenor	Kellis Miller
Sick Old Woman	Soprano	Pearle Goldsmith (debut)
Tadeus	Bass	Paul Ukena
The Old Man, Elijah	Tenor	Richard Krause

Citizens, Beggar Women, Guards, Tadeus' Men

SYNOPSIS OF STORY
TIME AND PLACE: Prague, 1580

*

143

ACT I

SCENE 1—A riverbank

The Maharal, Rabbi Levi Bar Bezallel, through mystical formulas deciphered in the Caballah, derives the Preeminent Name of God, the SHEM HAMA FORASCH, said to be the secret of all creation. Believing himself counseled by Heaven to save his persecuted people, he molds from the clay of the riverbank the figure of a man. He will employ the Holy SHEM to create a being with the superhuman strength to overcome their enemies.

In a vision, the Spirit of the Golem warns the Maharal against creating an instrument of force. Determination overcomes the Maharal's doubts. In a spiritual rite, aided by his disciples, Yacov and Isaac, he injects the SHEM into the skull of the clay figure, endowing his Golem with life.

SCENE 2—The Maharal's house

The Maharal brings the giant, cretinlike Golem into his home, names him Yossef, and gives him his first lessons in human behavior. The Rabbi's wife views the Golem with fear, but his granddaughter, Deborah, feels compassion for the ungainly stranger. He is accepted in their midst as a servant, a wood-chopper and water-carrier. As the Golem sleeps, the Maharal muses on how little he resembles the Messenger of his dreams.

SCENE 3—Outside the Maharal's house

Yacov reads from the Book of Psalms. Deborah, his betrothed, relates a dream in which the Prophet Elijah appeared to her. Yacov interprets this as a good omen, but Deborah feels a foreboding.

In deep distress, the old Rabbi Bashevi and several pious citizens inform the Maharal that their enemy, the fanatic monk Tadeus, is preparing a new ritual murder accusation against them. Tanchum, the ghetto madman, adds to their fears as he describes the death of his son in an earlier pre-Passover terror. Bashevi begs the Maharal to proclaim a period of fasting and prayer to help them. The Maharal taxes them with their dependence on prayer; in extremity they must use stronger means to defend themselves. As the Golem appears, ax over shoulder, on his way

to chop wood, the Maharal knows the means he will use to save his afflicted people.

ACT II

SCENE—The Fifth Tower, a desolate ruined castle

The beggars huddle against the fierce cold and plead to the God of Abraham, Isaac, and Jacob to help them in their wretchedness. Tadeus appears with his guards, a pair of soldiers of fortune who assist him in his iniquitous work. Unseen by the beggars, he derides their disabilities and affirms his intention to destroy them.

The Maharal finds the beggars chasing and mocking the Golem. Admonishingly, he sends them to the ghetto to warn the people of their impending danger. Told to find safer shelter in the caves under the synagogue, the beggars leave the Fifth Tower.

Once again, the Maharal is assailed by doubt. In a vision, Elijah appears and offers to usher in the Messiah to help them. The Maharal renounces the age-old pious dream of the Messiah's promise to raise the dead. He will rely on his man of clay to watch over the living.

Deborah enters seeking her grandfather. Out of compassion for the friendless Golem, she invites him to her impending wedding. As she describes its joys, the dancing, the wine, the Golem, overcome by her warmth, embraces her. Her cries attract the Maharal and his disciples. Yacov fiercely demands that the Golem be driven out.

Alone with the Golem, the Maharal reveals to him the meaning of his existence, his wondrous powers. In a hypnotic trance, the Golem traces Tadeus and his false evidence, two sacks containing the remains of a murdered Christian child and a flask of blood. Commanded to apprehend the enemy and bring back the sacks, the Golem magically disappears to carry out his mission. Exalted by the miracle, the Maharal gives thanks to the Almighty One.

ACT III

SCENE 1—The caves beneath the synagogue

Tadeus and his men emerge from a secret tunnel to plant their false evidence. The Golem appears. Radiating with the light of his newfound

144

powers, he attacks the terrified men. Routed, they leave behind them the two sacks. The Golem enjoys a moment of victory, but suddenly, as if drained, the power goes out of him and he is once again the cretinlike Golem, afraid of his own shadow. Seeking a clue to where he is and why, he opens the small sack and draws out the flask of blood. Lighting up with recognition, he recalls Deborah's description of a wedding. Certain the flask contains the wine she described, he puts it to his lips.

SCENE 2—The caves, some time later

The Shames leads the beggars down into the caves. They find the Golem asleep, the empty flask by his side, and mistakenly believe he is in a drunken stupor from wine. The Golem awakes. He has tasted blood and is no longer the Maharal's docile servant. A wild power rages in him. Inflamed beyond control, he strangles Tanchum before the horrified beggars. In the ensuing commotion, he disappears.

Confronted by the murder committed by his Golem, the Maharal, in his growing madness, attempts to justify the foul deed, revealing the Golem to be their savior. As Rabbi Bashevi and the beggars go up into the synagogue reciting the prayer for the dead, Yacov confides to Isaac his fears for the Maharal's sanity.

Alone with Tanchum's body, the Maharal once again voices his inner doubts. In a vision of his now-disordered mind, the dead Tanchum suddenly comes to life. Thrice he blows his ram's horn, signifying the coming of the Messiah. Affirming that he gave life to a stone, why not to Tanchum, the Maharal is surrounded by many dead who arise to proclaim him their Redeemer. In an apotheosis of his Messianic madness, Maharal is carried off by the dead in a triumphal procession.

ACT IV

SCENE—The attic of the synagogue

As the last wraithlike figure disappears, the Maharal is seen standing over Tanchum's body, lost in his dream.

The Good Soldier Schweik

→)))✳(((←

MUSIC BY: Robert Kurka
WORLD PREMIERE and NEW YORK CITY
OPERA PREMIERE: April 23, 1958
(Sung in English)

LIBRETTO BY: Lewis Allan
Based on the novel by Jaroslav Hasek

CONDUCTOR: Julius Rudel
STAGE DIRECTOR: Carmen Capalbo (debut)
SCENIC DESIGNER: Andreas Nomikos
COSTUMES: Ruth Morley
CHOREOGRAPHY: Robert Joffrey

CHARACTERS (In order of appearance)	VOICE (type)	PREMIERE CAST (New York City Opera)
A Gentleman of Bohemia	Speaking	George S. Irving
Joseph Schweik	Tenor	Norman Kelley
Mrs. Muller, his landlady	Soprano	Mary LeSawyer
Palivec, owner of a tavern	Baritone	Chester Watson
Bretschneider, a plainsclothes policeman	Tenor	Jack DeLon
Police Officer	Bass	Arthur Newman
A Guard	Tenor	Keith Kaldenberg
First Prisoner		Robert Atherton
Second Prisoner	Tenors,	George Del Monte
Third Prisoner	Baritones,	William Zakariasen
Fourth Prisoner	Basses	Robert Ruddy
Fifth Prisoner		Edward Ghazal (debut)
First Psychiatrist	Tenor	Howard Fried
Second Psychiatrist	Baritone	Chester Ludgin
Third Psychiatrist	Bass	Joshua Hecht
First Doctor	Baritone	Chester Ludgin
Second Doctor	Tenor	Robert Ruddy
A Consumptive	Bass	Peter Sliker
First Malingerer	Tenor	William Elliott
Second Malingerer	Tenor	Edson Hoel
Third Malingerer	Bass	John Dennison
Fourth Malingerer	Bass	Edward Ghazal
A Sergeant	Bass	Arthur Newman
An Army Doctor	Baritone	Emile Renan
The Baroness von Botzenheim	Contralto	Ruth Kobart
An Army Chaplain	Tenor	Jack DeLon
Lieutenant Henry Lukash	Baritone	David Atkinson

146

CHARACTERS (In order of appearance)	VOICE (type)	PREMIERE CAST (New York City Opera)
Fox, a dog	Speaking	Emile Renan
Katy Wendler	Soprano	Helen Baisley
Colonel von Zillergut	Bass	George S. Irving
Mr. Wendler, Katy's husband	Tenor	Keith Kaldenberg
General von Schwarzburg	Baritone	Chester Watson
Voditchka	Speaking	Chester Ludgin
Mr. Kakonyi	Baritone	Emile Renan
Madama Kakonyi, his wife	Soprano	Naomi Collier
Sergeant Vanek	Speaking	Howard Fried

Prisoners, Malingerers, Wounded Soldiers, the Baroness' Retinue, Tavern Patrons, Guards and Suspects at Police Headquarters, Attendants and Inmates of the Insane Asylum

SYNOPSIS OF STORY
TIME AND PLACE: Prague, 1914

*

ACT I

SCENE 1—Schweik's flat, June 28, 1914

Joseph Schweik hears about the assassination of Archduke Ferdinand at Sarajevo from his cleaning woman, Mrs. Muller, and receives the news with characteristic good-natured calm.

SCENE 2—The Flagon, a tavern

He goes, as usual, to The Flagon, a tavern occupied at the moment by Palivec, the landlord, and Bretschneider, a plainclothes policeman on secret service who is hoping to pick up some anti-Austrian expressions of opinion in the wake of the assassination. He leads the conversation into political channels and arrests Schweik and Palivec for some harmless remarks.

SCENE 3—Police headquarters

Schweik is taken to police headquarters, where he is interrogated and thrown into a cell among other innocent victims of the war hysteria, including Palivec.

SCENE 4—A cell

Schweik, always the optimist, points out how much better off they are than in the days of medieval torture.

SCENE 5—Another room in police headquarters

As he is expounding his ideas, Schweik is dragged out to be examined by a commission of medical authorities consisting of three psychiatrists of divergent schools of thought. Schweik's bland good nature convinces them that he is an idiot, and they commit him to a mental institution.

SCENE 6—An insane asylum

In contrast to the world outside, Schweik enjoys the advantages of a public institution. He is examined again by two other doctors, who become convinced that he is feigning the role of a happy simpleton and is in reality a malingerer seeking to escape military service. They have him thrown out of the asylum, despite his resentful and vigorous protests.

SCENE 7A—Schweik's flat

Back home again, in bed with an attack of chronic rheumatism, Schweik informs Mrs. Muller that he has received his draft call and patriotism impels him to report for induction immediately. His excited behavior and feverish enthusiasm alarm Mrs. Muller.

The Good Soldier Schweik, 1958.

SCENE 7B—The street

She obeys his wishes and tearfully pushes Schweik along the street in a wheelchair while he brandishes his crutches and shouts enthusiastically, "On to Belgrade!" followed by an appreciatively gleeful crowd.

ACT II

SCENE 1—An army infirmary

Schweik and a group of other suspected malingerers, including Palivec, are confined to a hut used as an infirmary, where an Army Doctor tries to convince them by various unorthodox methods that serving the Emperor is preferable to malingering.

SCENE 2A—A prison compound

As the Doctor is engaged in this practical group therapy, the Sergeant ushers in Baroness von Botzenheim, followed by her retinue bearing hampers of food and gifts. She has come to see Joseph Schweik, whose patriotic gesture in reporting for the draft in a wheelchair and with crutches has captured the attention of the newspapers. Schweik and his companions devour the food with ravenous appetites. When the Baroness and her retinue have gone, the furious Doctor has them all thrown into the guardhouse.

SCENE 2B—The army chapel

Schweik and his companions attend a sermon by the Army Chaplain, who storms at them for their enslavement to carnal appetites at the expense of the spirit. Schweik breaks into tears and sobs audibly.

SCENE 2C—The chaplain's quarters

The Chaplain appoints Schweik his orderly. Shortly after, the Chaplain loses Schweik to Lieutenant Henry Lukash during a spirited game of poker.

SCENE 3—Lieutenant Lukash's flat

In his first day of service, the good-natured Schweik amiably complicates Lieutenant Lukash's life. He lets the canary out of its cage to become friends with the cat, whereupon the cat gobbles up the bird. Annoyed at the cat's unfriendly disposition, he chases it out of the house. In order to replace the cat, he steals a monstrous dog. At the same time, Mrs. Katy Wendler, one of the Lieutenant's paramours, arrives bag and baggage. Schweik puts her up in the Lieutenant's bedroom, but to facilitate her early departure, he notifies her husband. When Lieutenant Lukash arrives home, he is caught in the center of a vortex involving the dog, Mr. Wendler, and, of course, Schweik. As a result, the furious Colonel orders Lieutenant Lukash and Schweik sent off immediately to the front.

SCENE 4—A second-class compartment and corridor of the Prague–Budejovice Express

En route to their destination, Schweik gets the Lieutenant into further difficulties with a bald General von Schwarzburg, whom he mistakes for a bald Mr. Purkabek. The Lieutenant gives Schweik a wrathful dressing down for the mistaken identity, at the conclusion of which Schweik accidentally pulls the emergency brake, bringing the train to a sudden stop. Schweik is arrested and taken off the train, to the great relief of Lieutenant Lukash, who now sees a tranquil future ahead of him, even though at the front.

SCENE 5—A private room in a small cafe in Budejovice

During the final stopover before moving into the front lines, the Lieutenant tries to establish a romance between himself and Madame Kakonyi. While he is writing a letter to the lady to arrange for a meeting, Schweik unexpectedly arrives to report for duty again. Overwhelmed by the fate that pursues him in the person of Schweik, Lieutenant Lukash accepts the inevitable and sends his orderly to deliver the letter to Madame Kakonyi personally.

SCENE 6—Soprony Street

On the way Schweik meets Voditchka, an old pal, and they celebrate at a tavern. Schweik finally remembers his unfulfilled mission, and the pals leave, somewhat unsteadily, to complete it. In attempting to deliver the letter to the lady, they become embroiled in an argument with her husband, Mr. Kakonyi, out of which develops a street brawl involving the local police, Czech soldiers, and German military police. To protect Lieutenant Lukash, Schweik swallows the letter.

SCENE 7—A dugout at the front

Lieutenant Lukash and Schweik finally reach the front, a scene of vast devastation. The Lieutenant sends Schweik and a sergeant on advance patrol. They set out together but later differ as to the correct direction. Even though the sergeant's memory and the map seem to prove him right, Schweik insists that maps may be wrong.

SCENE 8—The front

Schweik and the sergeant part company, the sergeant following the map and Schweik following his inclination. He takes another road and disappears.

The Gypsy Baron

-»))*(((-

MUSIC BY: Johann Strauss II

WORLD PREMIERE: Vienna, Austria,
  October 24, 1885

LIBRETTO BY: Ignaz Schnitzer
  Libretto revised and adapted
  into English by George Mead
NEW YORK CITY OPERA PREMIERE:
  (Sung in English) November 14, 1944

CONDUCTOR: Laszlo Halasz
STAGE DIRECTOR: William Wymetal
SCENIC DESIGNER: H. A. Condell
COSTUMES*
BALLET CHOREOGRAPHER: Helen Platova

CHARACTERS (In order of appearance)	VOICE (type)	PREMIERE CAST (New York City Opera)
Czipra, Gypsy fortune teller	Mezzo	Alice Howland
Otto Kar, young Hungarian	Tenor	Thomas Hayward
Carnero, Imperial Lieutenant	Tenor	Paul Dennis
Barinkay, Hungarian landowner	Tenor	William Horne
Szupan, wealthy pig farmer	Baritone	Stanley Carlson
Arsena, Szupan's daughter	Soprano	Marguerite Piazza
Saffi, Czipra's daughter	Soprano	Polyna Stoska (debut)
Count Homonnay, Colonel of Hussars	Bass	Carlton Gauld

Solo Dancers: Ruth Harris (debut) and Tashamera (debut)
Villagers, Gypsies, Hussars, Courtiers, Soldiers, Citizens, Townfolk

SYNOPSIS OF STORY
TIME AND PLACE: Austria-Hungary, mid-19th century (1848)

*

ACT I

SCENE—A remote region of the Transylvanian
  countryside

The handsome young Sandor Barinkay returns
to his native Hungary from exile, to find his an-
cestral castle in ruins and its lands being used
as a pig farm by a wealthy ignoramus, Szupan,
and as a Gypsy encampment. Szupan would be
glad to see his daughter Arsena married to Sandor, but she is indifferent. The Gypsies, whose
friend his father had always been, swear alle-

* By Van Horn & Son.

150

giance to Sandor and acclaim him their Gypsy Baron. He is introduced to Saffi, the beautiful ward of Czipra, the Gypsy queen. She sings a wild Gypsy song, and he falls in love with her. They marry under Gypsy rites.

ACT II

SCENE—The following morning, a Gypsy encampment around the ruins of Barinkay's castle

Czipra prophesies that Sandor will find a considerable treasure, hidden in the castle by his father at the time of their banishment. He does and distributes it freely among his new friends. But a Royal Commissioner, Count Carnero, tries to call Sandor to account for consorting with a common Gypsy girl. Czipra proves that Saffi is the natural daughter of the last Pasha to rule in Hungary before the expulsion of the Turks, and so is of noble birth.

The governor of the province, Count Homonnay, arrives with recruiting officers to raise troops for an imminent war with Spain. Any man who drinks a glass of recruiting wine thereby pledges himself to serve. The Gypsies do so willingly, and the pig-breeder Szupan unwittingly. Sandor is appointed to lead the Gypsy contingent but is denounced by Carnero. The governor ignores him, however, and all march off to war.

ACT III

SCENE—A public square in Vienna

Months later, in Vienna, crowds gather to welcome the victorious soldiers. Szupan is covered with medals, which he has acquired rather than earned, but he confesses that Sandor had saved his life. The governor honors Sandor for courageous leadership, restores to him his father's wealth, and confers on him the true title of Baron. Sandor insists that his style shall be "Gypsy Baron" and anxiously looks around for Saffi. They are reunited, and gaiety prevails.

H. M. S. Pinafore

—»»·«««—

MUSIC BY: Sir Arthur S. Sullivan
WORLD PREMIERE: London, England
May 25, 1868

LIBRETTO BY: William S. Gilbert
NEW YORK CITY OPERA PREMIERE:
(Sung in English) October 15, 1961

CONDUCTOR: Felix Popper
STAGE DIRECTOR: Allen Fletcher
SCENERY and COSTUMES: Patton Campbell

CHARACTERS (In order of appearance)	VOICE (type)	PREMIERE CAST (New York City Opera)
Little Buttercup	Mezzo	Gladys Kriese
Bill Bobstay, Boatswain	Baritone	Richard Fredricks
Dick Deadeye	Baritone	Paul Ukena
Ralph Rackstraw	Tenor	Frank Porretta
Captain Corcoran	Baritone	William Chapman
Josephine	Soprano	Doris Yarick
The Rt. Hon. Sir Joseph Porter, K.C.B.	Tenor	Norman Kelley
Cousin Hebe	Mezzo	Sophia Steffan
Bob Becket, Carpenter's Mate	Bass	John Macurdy

Sailors, Relatives

SYNOPSIS OF STORY

TIME AND PLACE: Quarterdeck of H.M.S. *Pinafore*, off Portsmouth, England; 19th century

*

Some time before ACT I opens, Ralph has fallen in love with Josephine, the daughter of his commanding officer, Captain Corcoran. Likewise, Little Buttercup, a buxom peddler-woman, has fallen in love with the Captain himself. Class pride, however, stands in the way of the natural inclinations of both the Corcorans to reciprocate Ralph's and Buttercup's affections. The Captain has, in fact, been arranging a marriage between his daughter and Sir Joseph Porter, First Lord of the Admiralty, who is a social class above even the Corcorans.

ACT I

SCENE—Noon

The sailors are merrily preparing the ship for Sir Joseph's inspection. The generally happy atmosphere on deck is marred only by Little Buttercup's hints of a dark secret she is hiding, by the misanthropic grumbling of Dick Deadeye, and by the lovelorn plaints of Ralph and Josephine. Sir Joseph appears, attended by a train of ladies (his relatives, who follow him wherever he goes). He explains how he became Lord of

152

the Admiralty and examines the crew, patroniz-
ingly encouraging them to feel that they are everyone's equal, except his. Like the Captain, he
is very punctilious, demanding polite diction
among the sailors at all times.

Josephine finds him insufferable, and, when
Ralph again pleads his suit and finally threatens
suicide, she agrees to elope. The act ends with
the general rejoicing of the sailors at Ralph's
success; only Dick Deadeye croaks his warning
that their hopes will be frustrated.

ACT II

SCENE—Night

The Captain is in despair at the demoralization
of his crew and the coldness of his daughter toward Sir Joseph. Little Buttercup tries to comfort
him and prophesies a change in store. But Sir
Joseph soon appears and tells the Captain that
Josephine has thoroughly discouraged him in his
suit; he wishes to call the match off. The Captain
suggests that perhaps his daughter feels herself
inferior in social rank to Sir Joseph, and urges
him to assure her that inequality of social rank
should not be considered a barrier to marriage.
This Sir Joseph does, not realizing that his words
are as applicable to Josephine in relation to Ralph
as they are in relation to himself. He thinks that

she accepts him, whereas actually she is reaffirm-
ing her acceptance of Ralph; and they all join
in a happy song.

Meanwhile Dick Deadeye has made his way
to the Captain, and informs him of the planned
elopement of his daughter with Ralph. The Captain thereupon intercepts the elopers. When he
learns that Josephine was actually running away
to marry Ralph, he is so incensed that he cries,
"Damme!" Unfortunately, Sir Joseph and his relatives hear him and are horrified at his swearing;
Sir Joseph sends him to his cabin in disgrace.
But when Sir Joseph also learns from Ralph that
Josephine was eloping, he angrily orders Ralph
put in irons.

Little Buttercup now reveals her secret, which
solves the whole difficulty: she confesses that
many years ago she had charge of nursing and
bringing up Ralph and the Captain when they
were babies. Inadvertently, she mixed them up,
so the one who now was Ralph really should
be the Captain, and the one now the Captain
should be Ralph. This error is immediately recti-
fied. The sudden reversal in the social status of
Ralph and the Corcorans removes Sir Joseph as
a suitor for Josephine's hand and permits her
to marry Ralph and her father to marry Buttercup. Sir Joseph resigns himself to marrying
his cousin, Hebe.

153

Hansel and Gretel

-»»*«««-

MUSIC BY: Engelbert Humperdinck
WORLD PREMIERE: Weimar, Germany,
   December 23, 1893

LIBRETTO BY: Adelheld Wette
NEW YORK CITY OPERA PREMIERE:
   (Sung in English) October 14, 1953

CONDUCTOR: Thomas Schippers
STAGE DIRECTOR: Herman Geiber-Torel (debut)
SCENERY and COSTUMES: Rouben Ter-Arutunian

CHARACTERS (In order of appearance)	VOICE (type)	PREMIERE CAST (New York City Opera)
Gretel	Soprano	Laurel Hurley
Hansel	Mezzo	Frances Bible
Mother (Gertrude)	Soprano	Willabella Underwood
Father (Peter)	Baritone	Richard Wentworth
Sandman	Soprano	Teresa Gannon
Dew Fairy	Soprano	Emily Cundari (debut)
The Witch	Mezzo	Claramae Turner
Children, Angels		

SYNOPSIS OF STORY
TIME AND PLACE: Long ago, fairy tale

*

ACT I

SCENE—The house of the broom-maker

Once upon a time a poor broom-maker and his wife lived in a lonely cottage in the Harz Mountains with their little son, Hansel, and daughter, Gretel. When the story opens, the father and mother have gone to sell brooms in the neighboring villages, leaving the children at work in the house. But work is tiresome, especially when empty stomachs are clamoring for unattainable food. The children start romping about the room, and at the height of their frolic the mother enters. She scolds the children and sends them out into the forest to pick wild strawberries for supper. Later, the father returns. Missing the children, he asks after them and is horror-struck at the thought of their plight all alone after nightfall in the woods.

ACT II

SCENE—In the woods

The children roam through the woods, gradually filling their baskets with strawberries, heedless of direction and time. Evening finds them bewildered in the darkening forest, haunted, as

154

they believe, by fairies and witches. The steep, rocky bulk of the Ilsenstein, a reputed gathering place for evil spirits, looms up amid the trees. The frightened children cower beneath a spreading tree and repeat their usual bedtime prayer to the "fourteen guardian angels," after which, calmer in spirit, they fall asleep with a vision of the radiant angels floating around them.

ACT III

SCENE—The witch's home

At daybreak the children awake, refreshed by a good night's sleep. All at once they notice an object overlooked in the evening darkness—a beautiful little house built of all manner of good things to eat and giving off a most appetizing odor. This is, alas, the abode of a wicked witch, an ogress who entraps small boys and girls by her spells, pops them into her oven, and bakes them into delectable gingerbread. Hansel and Gretel approach the house and begin to break off tasty morsels from the walls; the witch appears and casts a spell over them to prevent their escape. She now shuts Hansel up in a cage and feeds him on sweets to fatten him; then she tries to entice Gretel to bend down in front of the oven so that she may be able to push her in and bake her, but Gretel pretends not to understand. When the witch herself crossly bends down to show Gretel how, the two children quickly shove her into the oven, bang the door shut, and dance around gleefully. Thereupon all the gingerbread shapes that formed the hedge around the witch's house are transformed—her spell being broken—into their rightful shapes of happy boys and girls, who thank Hansel and Gretel for their deliverance. The father and mother, who have been seeking their dear ones, burst upon the scene, and all winds up with a chorus of thanksgiving.

He Who Gets Slapped

-»»*«««-

MUSIC BY: Robert Ward
WORLD PREMIERE: New York, New York,
May 17, 1956

LIBRETTO BY: Bernard Stambler
Based on Leonid Andreyev's play
NEW YORK CITY OPERA PREMIERE: (Sung in
English) April 12, 1959

CONDUCTOR: Emerson Buckley
STAGE DIRECTOR: Michael Pollock
SCENERY and COSTUMES: Andreas Nomikos

CHARACTERS (In order of appearance)	VOICE (type)	PREMIERE CAST (New York City Opera)
Tilly	Mute	Phil Bruns (debut)
Polly	Mute	Paul Dooley (debut)
Briquet	Bass-baritone	Chester Ludgin
Count Mancini	Tenor	Norman Kelley
Zinida	Soprano	Regina Sarfaty
Pantaloon	Baritone	David Atkinson
Consuelo	Soprano	Lee Venora
Bezano	Tenor	Frank Porretta
Baron Regnard	Bass-baritone	Emile Renan
The Maestro	Mute	Will B. Able (debut)

Circus Artists, Wedding Guests

SYNOPSIS OF STORY
TIME AND PLACE: Backstage area of a small circus in Paris, 1910

*

ACT I

Tilly and Polly, clowns in Briquet's Continental Circus, are rehearsing their act when Briquet and Count Mancini enter arguing. Mancini, by threatening to remove his daughter Consuelo, the Bareback Tango Queen, from the circus, attempts to wheedle an advance on Consuelo's salary. Briquet's wife, Zinida the Lion Tamer, enters and joins the argument; finally they agree on a small advance.

While they are involved in this transaction, a stranger, aristocratic in appearance, comes in quietly by the street door. When questioned by Briquet, he expresses his wish to become a clown. Prodded by Zinida, Briquet reluctantly hires him as Pantaloon—He Who Gets Slapped. Consuelo and her partner, Bezano, enter and are introduced to Pantaloon.

Mancini reminds Consuelo of their luncheon date with Baron Regnard. When she says that she must rehearse with Bezano and cannot go,

156

he stalks outs, furious, and tells her to make her own excuses to the Baron. As Consuelo and Bezano start back toward the ring, Zinida tries in vain to get Bezano's attention.

Pantaloon tries to cover an awkward moment by asking whether the two young people are in love, but Zinida tells him to tend to his own affairs. Briquet asks Pantaloon for his real name; it is needed for the authorities. Reluctantly Pantaloon shows his credentials, which greatly impress Zinida and Briquet. Zinida tells her husband to show Pantaloon around the circus and to send Bezano in to her.

Zinida restlessly waits for Bezano. When he comes in she violently expresses her passion for him and her jealousy of Consuelo. Finally losing control, she throws herself at Bezano, but he forcibly rejects her. Bezano abruptly returns to the ring as Baron Regnard arrives for his date with Consuelo.

Zinida goes to fetch her, and the Baron, while waiting, examines a fine string of pearls. Consuelo arrives and politely tells him that she cannot join him for lunch. The Baron, irritated and disappointed, finally offers a surprise to Consuelo, who is naively pleased at the thought of a present. He places the pearls around her neck and then embraces her and pleads his love. After a struggle, during which the string of pearls is broken, Consuelo, in tears, is forced to cry out that the Baron is repellent to her and that she tolerates him only because of her father.

ACT II

The chorus of circus artists, during an intermission in their performance, sings of the splendors and excitements of the circus with its animals, freaks, acrobats, and above all, the daring tightrope walker.

Pantaloon, Briquet, and Mancini enter. The Count commends the clown for his brilliant show, but Briquet chides Pantaloon for extending his mockery to the dangerous subjects of religion, patriotism, and marriage. Pantaloon, still in the spirit of his act, extends his fantasies even further by bringing the world of the audience as well as that of the ring into the play he improvises.

As the bell rings, the chorus departs, singing once more of the pleasures of the audience. Mancini detains Pantaloon, saying—as one gentleman

to another—that he desperately needs money to buy off his latest mistress. Pantaloon takes this chance to ask about Consuelo and about Mancini's antecedents. The answers are impatient and vague, but Pantaloon is able to gather that Mancini is a fraudulent count and that Consuelo is not his daughter. As guarantee for his loan, Mancini offers his certainty that the Baron will marry Consuelo. The Baron, moved not only by an old lecher's lust but also by his desire to ally himself with a genuinely noble title, has committed himself to the marriage in a letter.

The two are interrupted by Briquet staggering out of the ring, unable to bear any longer Zinida's mad recklessness with her lions. The dead silence from the ring is broken by screams and applause. Zinida comes slowly down the ramp in a mixture of ecstasy and shock, having triumphed over her red lion but having been clawed by him. She is followed by a number of the performers, including Consuelo and Bezano. Her words are only for Bezano: all that she has been doing is for proof that her red lion really loves her, that she is capable of being loved. When Bezano, without a word, turns on his heel and goes off, her triumphant light is extinguished and she walks off as though dead.

Consuelo remains alone with Pantaloon. Saddened and puzzled by what she has just witnessed, Consuelo starts to ask whether love is always this unhappy thing that it seems to be for Zinida or that it is likely to be for her in her forthcoming marriage with the Baron. Before he can answer, she abruptly turns to playful questions. Pantaloon's response embraces both the serious and the playful. He answers her in terms of a palm-reading fantasy about her destiny, in which he warns her about the danger of marrying the Baron. When she asks about Bezano, Pantaloon grudgingly admits that she might be happy with him. He then turns to the mystery of her origin, and his fantasy becomes serious. In hypnotic tones he tells her that, like Venus, she rose from the sea and must return to the sea if she is not to be doomed. Consuelo, caught up in the fantasy, asks how she can return. Pantaloon, completely under the spell of his own imagination, says that he is the old sea god come down to carry her back—and attempts to kiss her.

This abruptly breaks the spell for Consuelo: she slaps him. At this he recalls—or realizes— that this fantasy is only another of his plays,

He Who Gets Slapped, 1969. David Atkinson and Lee Venora (courtesy Henri Dauman).

but before he can explain further he is interrupted by Zinida, who had come back from the ring and had been watching the end of this little scene.

In a violent diatribe (yet somehow tinged with sympathy), Zinida mocks Pantaloon and reveals the frustrations of his earlier attempts to reform the world about him. Consuelo, provoked by Zinida's attack, rises to his defense. Sobered by this, Zinida finally wonders only why he has continually put himself into the position of being slapped. Pantaloon, seeming to reflect on his whole life, can only reply: "Am I not Pantaloon—He Who Gets Slapped?"

ACT III

While the circus is being readied for a gala performance celebrating the forthcoming marriage of Consuelo to the Baron, Pantaloon sings a ballad symbolically expressing the fate of Consuelo and himself. The trumpets announce the entrance of the wedding procession; he abruptly ends this mood and pretends to be far gone in drunkenness. Against the background of the wedding chorus, a quintet of the major characters express their individual thoughts about this marriage: Consuelo her grief, Mancini his opportunistic triumph, Zinida her cynical prophecy of the horns that await the Baron, Briquet his disappointment at losing a star performer, and Bezano his utter despair.

Pantaloon breaks in, saying that he has arranged a little entertainment in the style of medieval court ceremonies. After a burlesqued overture, his play-within-a-play unfolds. Pantaloon takes the role of a slinking and conniving Mancini, while Tilly is an over-coy and simpering Consuelo to Polly's spiderish and lecherous Baron. The playlet farcically reveals the plots

158

and deceptions of Mancini. When the real Baron Regnard finally realizes through Pantaloon's play that Consuelo is a nameless waif and that Mancini is a fake count, he lashes out violently against Pantaloon, against Mancini, and against the whole trumpery circus—and then storms out.

Mancini confesses his frauds, entrusts Consuelo to the care of the circus folk, and departs. For a moment Consuelo is desolate, until she and Bezano realize that at last they are free to seek each other. In a tango-duet they proclaim their love and hope.

The performers jubilantly return to the ring to give a benefit performance for the Tango King and Queen. Zinida and Briquet finally give full acceptance to the wisdom as well as the clownish talents of Pantaloon, as they too go up the ramp to the ring.

Pantaloon, alone on the stage, sings to the poster picturing Consuelo: she is the Queen of Beauty for whom he is the fool, ever-loving and ever-deserving to be slapped. Tilly and Polly come to fetch him, but he tells them that he is leaving—there is nothing remaining for him here. He takes off his clown costume, revealing his street clothes underneath, and quietly departs by the street door through which he had first entered.

Help! Help! The Globolinks!

-»»*«««-

MUSIC BY: Gian Carlo Menotti

WORLD PREMIERE: Los Angeles, California, by the NEW YORK CITY OPERA* November 28, 1970 (Sung in English)

LIBRETTO BY: Gian Carlo Menotti

CONDUCTOR: Charles Wilson
PRODUCTION DEVISED and DIRECTED BY: Gian-Carlo Menotti
SCENIC DESIGNER: Ming Cho Lee
COSTUMES: Willa Kim
GLOBOLINK COSTUME BY: Alwin Nikolais

CHARACTERS (In order of appearance)	VOICE (type)	PREMIERE CAST (New York City Opera)
Tony, the school-bus driver	Baritone	Jack Bittner
Emily, a schoolgirl	Soprano	June Cooper
Dr. Stone, the Dean	Baritone	John Darrenkamp
Timothy, the janitor	Tenor	Douglas Perry
Madame Euterpova, the music teacher	Soprano	Ellen Faull
Mr. Lavender-Gas, the literature professor	Baritone	David Rae Smith
Dr. Turtlespit, the science professor	Baritone	Don Yule
Miss Penelope Newkirk, the geometry teacher	Mezzo	Beverly Evans
Globolinks		

SYNOPSIS OF STORY
TIME AND PLACE: Any time; any place

*

SCENE 1—A country road in a deserted landscape

A school bus filled with children is stalled by Globolinks, creatures from outer space. Anxiously the driver, Tony, honks his horn, which frightens them away for the moment. The radio tells the driver and children that only the sound of music will prove an effective weapon against the Globolinks. Upon asking the children, Tony

---

* This opera was not performed in regular repertory in New York. The premiere performance was given in Los Angeles.

discovers that only Emily has her violin with her. She is sent ahead to reach the school for help, playing her violin.

SCENE 2—Dean's office of St. Paul's School

Dr. Stone, the principal, worries with Timothy, the janitor, about the late-arriving children. Madame Euterpova, the music teacher, enters offering her resignation, convinced that the children aren't interested in music. She quiets down when she hears that the children are long overdue. She exits and Dr. Stone lies down, to be awakened by Globolinks. As a result of being touched by the Globolinks, Dr. Stone can utter only electronic sounds. Timothy calls the teachers for help, and Madame Euterpova organizes everyone into a musical band to ward off the Globolinks.

SCENE 3—The country road

The children wonder when Emily will return.

The Globolinks are getting bolder, but as they approach threateningly a trumpet fanfare is heard, scaring them away. There is a joyful reunion of teachers and students, but Emily is still not back. All appeal to Dr. Stone, who now has Globolink powers, and he flies off with Madame Euterpova and the children following him.

SCENE 4—The Forest of Steel

In a Forest of Steel Emily is still playing her violin. When she stops to rest, the Globolinks seize and destroy her violin. Dr. Stone arrives to reassure her, but can only say "la." As he turns into a Globolink, Emily faints. The children and the teachers arrive and dispel the Steel Forest. Madame Euterpova moralizes to the children on the need for music in the world, and they march off. A little Globolink appears to pull the curtain.

L'Heure Espagnole

⇾》》∗《《⇽

MUSIC BY: Maurice Ravel

WORLD PREMIERE: Paris, France,
May 9, 1911

LIBRETTO BY: Franc-Nohain
Prologue written by José Ruben
Spoken by Arnold Moss
NEW YORK CITY OPERA PREMIERE: (Sung in
English) October 2, 1952

CONDUCTOR: Tullio Serafin
PRODUCTION DEVISED and DIRECTED BY: José Ruben
SETS and COSTUMES: Rouben Ter-Arutunian (debut)

CHARACTERS (In order of appearance)	VOICE (type)	PREMIERE CAST (New York City Opera)
Ramiro, a muleteer	Baritone	Walter Cassel
Torquemada, a clockmaker	Tenor	Luigi Vellucci
Concepcion	Soprano	Gail Manners (debut)
Gonzalve, a poet	Tenor	David Lloyd
Don Inigo Gomez, a financier	Bass	Carlton Gauld

Note: This performance was preceded by *Bluebeard's Castle.*

SYNOPSIS OF STORY
TIME AND PLACE: Spain, 18th century

∗

SCENE—The clock shop of Torquemada

Torquemada, an absentminded clockmaker, is preparing to go on his scheduled rounds of adjusting the town clocks of Toleo when the muleteer, Ramiro, appears in the shop. Torquemada's wife, Concepcion, is annoyed when her husband asks Ramiro to wait until his return, because she always receives her admirers when Torquemada is safely away on business.

Concepcion manages to get Ramiro out of the way by having him carry one of the grandfather clocks up to her room. When Gonzalve arrives, he is hidden in one of the clocks, and Don Inigo in his turn is concealed in another clock. The unsuspecting Ramiro continues to cart the vari-

162

L'Heure Espagnole, 1969. Left to right: Spiro Malas, Nico Castel, Kenneth Riegel.

ous clocks (and their hidden contents) to Concepcion's room and back again.

Concepcion, bored with her two lovers, now turns her attention to Ramiro, leaving Gonzalve and Don Inigo to be discovered in their hiding places when Torquemada returns. Torquemada takes advantage of the situation and sells the clocks to the two "customers."

163

L'Histoire du Soldat

-»»*«(-

MUSIC BY: Igor Stravinsky

WORLD PREMIERE: Lausanne, Switzerland,
September 28, 1918

LIBRETTO BY: C. F. Ramuz
English version by Michael Flanders and
Kitty Black

NEW YORK CITY OPERA PREMIERE: (Sung in
English) October 16, 1956

CONDUCTOR: Jean Morel
STAGE DIRECTOR: Marcella Cisney
SCENERY and COSTUMES: Leo Kerz
CHOREOGRAPHY: Anna Sokolow

CHARACTERS (In order of appearance)	VOICE (type)	PREMIERE CAST (New York City Opera)
The Narrator	Spoken	Christopher Plummer (debut)
The Soldier	Dancer	James Mitchell (debut)
The Devil	Spoken	Hurd Hatfield (debut)
The Princess	Dancer	Judith Coy (debut)

Note: This opera was performed with *The Moon.*

SYNOPSIS OF STORY
TIME AND PLACE: Tragicomedy that is read, played, and danced.

*

PART I

A Soldier enters; he is bound for home on ten days' leave. He rests and plays a violin that he has taken from his knapsack. The Devil enters, disguised as an old man, and asks for the violin. When the Soldier refuses, the Devil offers to exchange it for a book, which he says can make the Soldier rich. The Devil invites the Soldier to his home for three days so that the Soldier can teach him to play the violin.

On the third day the Soldier leaves the Devil's house, continuing on his way home. When he reaches the village, he finds that none of his friends know him. His mother runs from him in fright, and his girlfriend has married. He realizes that the three days he spent with the Devil were really three years and all in the village think him dead.

The Soldier becomes rich trading in all kinds of goods. But with all his riches, he feels empty and dreams of the joys that were his long ago; he wishes that the book that brought him wealth would show him how to be happy. The Devil appears, this time in the guise of an old peddler woman. Among his goods, which are carried in

164

the Soldier's old knapsack, is the violin. But when the Soldier tries to play the violin, it has no sound. The Soldier tosses the violin away and then tears the book to pieces.

PART II

The Soldier is seen walking along a road; he has run away from all his riches. He sees a proclamation that anyone who can cure the King's daughter of her illness may marry her and receive her wealth. The Devil appears with the violin and tells the Soldier that this is the cure. Prompted by the Narrator, the Soldier enters into a card game with the Devil, in which the Soldier loses everything. Drunk with victory and wine, the Devil falls into a stupor, and the Soldier takes the violin, which he is now able to play. The Soldier cures the Princess with the music of the violin. The Devil appears and tries to retrieve the violin but is unable to. He then threatens the Soldier that if the Soldier ever crosses the frontier, he will belong to the Devil.

The Soldier and the Princess are happy together, but the Soldier wishes to see his mother once more. As he crosses the border, the Devil seizes the violin and fastens on the Soldier.

Idomeneo

→))) * (((←

MUSIC BY: Wolfgang Amadeus Mozart
(edited by Daniel Heartz)
WORLD PREMIERE: Munich, Germany,
January 29, 1781

LIBRETTO BY: Giambattista Varesco
(after Danchet)
NEW YORK CITY OPERA PREMIERE:
(Sung in Italian) March 16, 1975

CONDUCTOR: Julius Rudel
STAGE DIRECTOR: Gerald Freedman
SCENIC DESIGNER: Ming Cho Lee
COSTUMES: Theoni V. Aldredge
CHOREOGRAPHY: Thomas Andrew

CHARACTERS (In order of appearance)	VOICE (type)	PREMIERE CAST (New York City Opera)
Ilia, a Trojan Princess	Soprano	Veronica Tyler
Idamante, son of Idomeneo	Tenor	Gary Glaze
Cretans	Male and Female Voices	Patricia McCaffrey, Sharon Papian, Louis Perry, Talmage Harper
Elektra, Princess of Argos	Soprano	Maralin Niska
Idomeneo, King of Crete	Tenor	Richard Taylor
Arbace, the King's Minister	Baritone	John Lankston
High Priest	Tenor	Howard Hensel (debut)
Voice of Neptune	Bass-baritone	Irwin Densen

People of Crete, Trojan Prisoners, Sailors, Soldiers, Priests of Neptune, Dancers

SYNOPSIS OF STORY

TIME AND PLACE: The Island of Crete in mythical times, during the Trojan wars

*

ACT I

SCENE 1—Outside the castle

Ilia, a Trojan princess and now a prisoner of Idomeneo, King of Crete, is lamenting her fate. She is in love with Idomeneo's son, Idamante. As proof of his feelings for Ilia, Idamante releases the Trojan prisoners, and the Cretans and Trojans join in a celebration. The King's Minister, Arbace, informs the Prince that Idomeneo, returning from the Trojan wars, is lost in a storm at sea and feared dead.

SCENE 2—Same

Princess Elektra of Argos, who is under the protection of Idomeneo, hopes to marry Idamante. She fears that the King's death will shat-

Idomeneo, 1975

ter that hope and reveals her fierce hatred of Ilia.

SCENE 3—Same

The Cretans rush to the shore and pray to the gods to abate the storm that might destroy their king and the returning soldiers.

SCENE 4—Same

The sea and wind are calmed and Idomeneo has been miraculously saved, but only after he has made a vow to Neptune to sacrifice the first human to come within his sight. The first person to greet him is his beloved son, Idamante. In terror and remorse Idomeneo turns away from him, leaving Idamante confused and disturbed by his father's savagely spurning him.

SCENE 5—Same

The King is led into a public square and freshly robed and crowned, as the Cretans rejoice in his safe return and in the benevolence of Neptune, god of the seas.

ACT II

SCENE 1—The castle

Idomeneo confesses his fateful vow to Arbace, who advises him to marry Idamante to Elektra so that he will go with her to Argos and escape Neptune's wrath. Although Ilia expresses her newfound joy in Crete and her acceptance of Idomeneo through her love for his son, the King must sacrifice Ilia's love in order to save Idamante.

SCENE 2—Same

Elektra rejoices at her good fortune as her ladies robe her for the journey to her homeland. She is secure in the belief that Idamante, away from Ilia, will grow to love her.

SCENE 3—Same

The Cretans are gathered at the harbor to bid

167

farewell to Idamante and Elektra. Neptune, angered by the King's deception, creates another violent storm. Idomeneo offers himself as a victim, but Neptune sends a sea monster to attack and destroy the Cretans.

ACT III

SCENE 1—At the castle

Ilia, unaware of the terror at the harbor, has secluded herself in her garden mourning the loss of Idamante. He suddenly appears, and they renew their vows of love, but Idamante tells Ilia that he must attempt to destroy the monster. They are discovered by Idomeneo and Elektra. The King orders his son to leave, and Elektra, humiliated, hopes for revenge.

SCENE 2—Before the Temple of Neptune

Idomeneo, tormented at the sight of his subjects wounded and bloodied by Neptune's fury, confesses that Idamante is the innocent victim of his broken vow. The Cretans enter the temple to face the awesome judgment of the sea god. Having killed the monster, Idamante returns prepared to be sacrificed to appease Neptune's wrath. Ilia offers to substitute herself for Idamante on the bloody altar. Neptune, moved by the depth of Ilia's love, offers to pardon Idomeneo if he will surrender his crown to Idamante and Ilia and let them rule in his place. Elektra, desolate and abandoned, begs for the torments of the Furies to obliterate her grief. Idomeneo takes leave of his people, abdicating in favor of Idamante and Ilia.

The Impresario

→»*«←

MUSIC BY: Wolfgang Amadeus Mozart

LIBRETTO BY: Gottlieb Stephanie the Younger
English adaptation by Giovanni Cardelli
This adaptation dedicated to the memory of
Albert Spaulding

WORLD PREMIERE: Schönbrunn, Austria,
February 7, 1786

NEW YORK CITY OPERA PREMIERE:
(Sung in English) April 11, 1956

CONDUCTOR: Joseph Rosenstock
STAGE DIRECTOR: Vladimir Rosing
SCENIC DESIGNER: John Boyt*
COSTUMES†

CHARACTERS (In order of appearance)	VOICE (type)	PREMIERE CAST (New York City Opera)
Mr. Scruples, the old-school Impresario	Spoken	Ludwig Donath (debut)
Mr. Bluff, assistant to the Impresario	Baritone	Jack Russell
Mr. Angel, an elderly stagestruck financier	Tenor	Michael Pollock
Mme. Goldentrill, an aging opera star	Soprano	Beverly Sills
Miss Silverpeal, an aspiring opera star	Soprano	Jacquelynne Moody
Mlle. Tutu, Prima Ballerina	Spoken	Nadine Revere
Music Director	Spoken	De Lloyd Tibbs
Stage Director	Spoken	Thomas Powell

Note: This performance was preceded by *School for Wives.*

SYNOPSIS OF STORY
TIME AND PLACE: Salzburg Court Opera House, theater manager's office; 18th century

*

The Impresario, Mr. Scruples, has reluctantly agreed to become General Director of a failing and less than first-class opera company; he would prefer to be a farmer. Mr. Angel implores Scru-

---

* John Boyt's scenery for Act I, Scene 1 of *Don Pasquale* was utilized for this production.
† Unavailable.

ples to hire Mme. Goldentrill, even agreeing to provide the funds for her salary. Scruples is outraged, but before he can leave, Mme. Goldentrill arrives for her audition, for which she sings an "Ariette" to display the amazing qualities of her voice. After she leaves, Mr. Angel tells Scruples that he also wants to hire Miss Silverpeal, and he is prepared to advance the funds for her salary also. At her audition, Miss Silverpeal sings a "Rondo." Mr. Scruples then tells the company staff that he plans to try out the most modern methods of operatic production, all of which are aimed at a production of minimal cost; but these methods are met with derision by the staff, who have more grandiose ideas. Miss Silverpeal, Mr. Angel, and Mme. Goldentrill return, both women outraged that the other might be offered more than she. In a trio, each woman extols her own virtues and attacks the other, while Mr. Angel attempts to calm them. By the end, the women must be kept apart by Angel and Bluff. Angel settles the argument by making grandiose offers to each woman. Scruples then decides to retire to be a farmer and names Bluff as his successor. Bluff, preferring a stage career, engages himself as leading buffo-baritone and appoints Angel as the next Impresario. Saluting the Impresario, Bluff, Goldentrill, Silverpeal, and Angel sing of the mission of artists to serve art, the public, and more important, themselves.

L'Incoronazione di Poppea

→)))*(((←

Music by: Claudio Monteverdi
World Premiere: Venice, Italy,
  Autumn, 1642*

Libretto by: Francesco Busenello
New York City Opera Premiere:
  (Sung in Italian) March 8, 1973

Conductor: John Nelson
Production Devised and Directed by: Gerald Friedman
Scenic Designer: Lloyd Evans
Costumes: José Varona
Choreography: Thomas Andrew

CHARACTERS (In order of appearance)	VOICE (type)	PREMIERE CAST (New York City Opera)
Fortuna (Fortune)	Soprano	Faye Robinson
Virtu (Virtue)	Soprano	Pamela Hebert
Amor (Love)	Soprano	Syble Young
Ottone	Baritone	Dominic Cossa
First Soldier	Tenor	John Lankston
Second Soldier	Tenor	Jerold Siena
Poppea	Soprano	Carol Neblett
Nerone	Baritone	Alan Titus
Arnalta	Contralto	Muriel Greenspon
Ottavia	Mezzo	Frances Bible
Drusilla	Soprano	Faye Robinson
Valetto	Tenor	John Lankston
Seneca	Bass	Richard T. Gill
Pallade	Soprano	Pamela Hebert
Liberto	Bass	William Ledbetter
Damigella	Soprano	Syble Young
Lucano	Tenor	Jerold Siena
Littore	Bass	William Ledbetter

Consuls, Friends of Seneca, Tribunes, Romans

SYNOPSIS OF STORY
Time and Place: Rome, 62 A.D.

*

PROLOGUE

Fortune, Virtue, and Love dispute their power over man. Love humbles Fortune and Virtue and predicts her supremacy.

---

* Because of the early date, specific premiere performance date not available.

L'Incoronazione di Poppea, 1973. Alan Titus, Carol Nebblett, and members of the ensemble.

ACT I

SCENE 1—Ottone, the former lover of Poppea, discovers the soldiers of Nero at Poppea's door and realizes that Nero is Poppea's new lover.

SCENE 2—The soldiers awake, curse their lot under Nero, and are frightened at his approach.

SCENE 3—Poppea begs Nero not to leave; the Emperor promises that he will repudiate his wife, Ottavia, marry Poppea, and crown her Empress.

SCENE 4—Poppea sings of her happiness. Her nurse, Arnalta, warns Poppea of the dangers to follow from such a relationship.

SCENE 5—The Empress Ottavia laments her misfortune; her attendant, Drusilla, advises her not to anger the Emperor but to console herself with other lovers; but Ottavia asks the famous teacher Seneca to intercede for her with the Senate and the people. Her page, Valetto, mistrusts Seneca and threatens him.

SCENE 6—Pallade foretells Seneca's death.

SCENE 7—Nero tells Seneca of his decision to divorce Ottavia and marry Poppea; Seneca tries to dissuade him.

SCENE 8—Poppea reminds Nero of the pleasures of the previous night and denounces Seneca as her enemy and a traitor. Nero orders Seneca to kill himself.

SCENE 9—Ottone complains to Poppea about her infidelity, and she spurns him.

SCENE 10—Drusilla loves Ottone and laments his feeling for Poppea; Ottone now declares his love for Drusilla and pretends to disown Poppea.

SCENE 11—In the solitude of his villa, Seneca receives the messenger of death; his friends gather and meditate on life and death.

ACT II

SCENE 1—After Seneca's death, Nero and his friend Lucano celebrate the beauty of Poppea and the death of Seneca.

SCENE 2—Ottavia orders Ottone to kill Poppea.

SCENE 3—Ottone confides in Drusilla and asks

for her cloak as a disguise to enter Poppea's house.

SCENE 4—Poppea learns of Seneca's death and asks Love's help. Arnalta soothes Poppea to sleep; Ottone enters half ready to kill Poppea but is frightened away by Love and the watchful nurse, who sounds the alarm.

SCENE 5—Drusilla sings of her joy, anticipating her rival's death. Nero orders Drusilla tortured to force her confession. She confesses to save Ottone, but Ottone also confesses that he at-tempted the murder by order of Ottavia. Ottone and Drusilla are exiled, as is Ottavia.

SCENE 6—Nero swears to Poppea that today she will become Empress. They celebrate the removal of their enemies.

SCENE 7—Ottavia bids farewell to Rome.

SCENE 8—Arnalta boasts of her triumph in now being the confidante of an Empress, instead of a servant.

SCENE 9—Poppea is crowned.

The Inspector General

→))∗((←

MUSIC BY: Werner Egk

WORLD PREMIERE: Schwetzingen, Germany,
May 9, 1957

LIBRETTO BY: Werner Egk
Based on the play by Nikolai Gogol
NEW YORK CITY OPERA PREMIERE: (Sung in
English) October 19, 1960

CONDUCTOR: Werner Egk (debut)
STAGE DIRECTOR: William Ball
SCENIC DESIGNER: Joseph Weishar
COSTUMES: Patton Campbell

CHARACTERS (In order of appearance)	VOICE (type)	PREMIERE CAST (New York City Opera)
The Town Mayor	Baritone	Herbert Beattie
The Judge	Bass	John Macurdy
The Charity Commissioner	Baritone	Chester Ludgin
The Postmaster	Tenor	Maurice Stern
Bobtschinskij	Tenor	Michael Carolan
Dobtschinskij	Baritone	Dan Merriman
Mischka, the Mayor's servant	Tenor	Charles Broadhurst
Anna, the Mayor's wife	Mezzo	Ruth Kobart
Marja, their daughter	Soprano	Patricia Brooks
Avdotya, a servant in the Mayor's house	Mute	Joan Porter
Chlestakow, a clerk in Civil Service	Tenor	Jon Crain
Ossip, his servant	Bass-baritone	Arnold Voketaitis
A Waiter	Mute	Charles Herrick
A Young Widow	Soprano	Mary LeSawyer
The Wife of the Locksmith	Mezzo	Regina Sarfaty

SYNOPSIS OF STORY
TIME AND PLACE: Russia, middle 1800's

∗

ACT I

SCENE 1—The Mayor's house, a day in late
spring

The Mayor of a small Russian village receives
word that a government official is due to arrive
to inspect the province. The village and its official
bureaus are in such lamentable condition that
when two townsmen, Bobtschinskij and Dobt-
schinskij, arrive with the news that a mysterious

174

stranger is staying at the local inn, the Mayor and his officers are thrown into a state of panic. They plan a hasty clean-up of the town and an official visit to the stranger, whom they believe to be the Inspector General.

SCENE 2—A room in the local inn, same day

The stranger, Chlestakow, is no more than a clerk in the Civil Service, penniless and starving. The Mayor comes to greet him, offers him money to cover his expenses, invites him to take a tour of the village, and suggests that he leave the inn and stay at the Mayor's home for the remainder of his visit. Being mistaken for an official personage amuses Chlestakow, and he plays into the hands of the Mayor, accepting his money and his hospitality.

SCENE 3—The Mayor's house, later that day

Chlestakow is given his first decent meal in weeks at the local hospital and, after a tour of the village, he arrives in style at the Mayor's home. Anna and Marja, the Mayor's wife and daughter, are immediately attracted to the young rogue. Chlestakow enjoys more and more the role of Inspector, and as his improvising expands he gets drunk, passes out, and is put to bed with much ceremony.

ACT II

SCENE 1—The Mayor's house, the next morning

The town officials determine to bribe the supposed Inspector, and Chlestakow is quite eager to relieve them of their money. Two peasants rush in to complain to Chlestakow of having been beaten and robbed by the Mayor. He disposes of them quickly and then, given the opportunity, he makes love alternately to Anna and Marja. He so enjoys the advantages of being an "Inspector" that he writes a letter to a friend in St. Petersburg telling how he has exploited the stupid townspeople. His servant, Ossip, advises him to quit while he's ahead, and they determine to leave the village before his real identity becomes known.

SCENE 2—The Mayor's house, later that morning

The villagers arrive at the Mayor's house to congratulate him on the engagement of his daughter to the departed "Inspector." The Postmaster interrupts the reception with a reading of Chlestakow's letter mocking the townspeople. At the very moment that the Mayor and his officials realize how they have been gulled, a messenger arrives announcing that the real Inspector General has come and expects a thorough explanation for the dreadful condition of the village.

Jeanne D'Arc au Bucher

-»»*«(-

MUSIC BY: Arthur Honegger

WORLD PREMIERE: Basel, Switzerland,
May 12, 1938

LIBRETTO BY: Paul Claudel
English version by Dennis Arundell
NEW YORK CITY OPERA PREMIERE: (Sung in
English) October 3, 1963

CONDUCTOR: Leon Barzin (debut)
STAGE DIRECTOR: Allen Fletcher
PRODUCTION DESIGN and LIGHTING: Will Steven Armstrong
COSTUMES: (unavailable)

CHARACTERS*	VOICE (type)	PREMIERE CAST (New York City Opera)
Singers:		
The Virgin Mary	Soprano	Elizabeth Carron
A Voice } St. Margaret	Soprano	Juanita King (debut)
St. Catherine	Mezzo	Tatiana Troyanos
Chauchon (Porcus)	Tenor	Mauro Lampi (debut)
A Priest 1st Herald Clerk	Tenor	Richard Krause
2nd Herald A Priest A Voice	Bass	Ron Bottcher
A Priest	Bass	John Viorito
Actors:		
Joan	Speaking	Jacqueline Brookes (debut)
Brother Dominic	Speaking	Douglas Watson (debut)
A Herald The King of England Grinder Trusty	Speaking	Frank Converse (debut)
Mother Winebarrels	Speaking	Muriel Greenspon
The Ass The Duke of Burgundy	Speaking	David Byrd (debut)
The Usher The King of France	Speaking	Miller Lide (debut)
A Priest A Sheep Death 2nd Peasant	Speaking	John Devlin (debut)

* Not listed in order of appearance.

CHARACTERS*	VOICE (type)	PREMIERE CAST (New York City Opera)
A Sheep Guillaume de Flavy 1st Peasant	Speaking	Richard Matthews (debut)
A Sheep The Duke of Bedford The Dauphin	Speaking	Nicholas Martin (debut)
A Sheep Regnault de Chartres Perrot	Speaking	Geddeth Smith (debut)
A Sheep Jean de Luxembourg	Speaking	Terrence Scammel (debut)
1st Woman Queen Lasciviousness	Speaking	Anne Draper (debut)
2nd Woman Queen Bombast	Speaking	Patricia Hamilton (debut)
3rd Woman Queen Stupidity	Speaking	Betty Bendyk (debut)
4th Woman Queen Avarice	Speaking	Elaine Sulka (debut)

Note: This performance was preceded by *The Nightingale*.

SYNOPSIS OF STORY
TIME AND PLACE: Rouen, France; 15th century

*

Jeanne D'Arc au Bucher is a musico-dramatic poem that examines the fear, suffering, and eventual triumph of Joan's final moments on earth. The entire action of the piece is dreamlike and occurs in Joan's mind during those last seconds of earthly life.

Brother Dominic (representing St. Dominic, the founder of the Dominican order, which played a decisive part in Joan's trial and condemnation) appears to Joan at the moment of her death. He helps Joan to understand and rejoice in her martyrdom by forcing her to envisage, in reverse chronological order, the events in her life that led her to the stake.

First, Dominic shows Joan her trial as a convocation of beasts, acting only through greed and unreasoning instinct. Next, the political intrigues that led to her capture appear as an overcivilized and meaningless game of chance. Then comes the memory of the voices of her saints, Catherine and Margaret, with their promise of victory. She sees the peasants of France rejoicing at a harvest festival over the reunification of France, and the Dauphin, her king, as he marches to Rheims for his coronation. She remembers her pride at having brought this to pass. But Dominic forces her back beyond the glory to the memory of the first visitation of her saints in her beloved Lorraine. She relives the wonder, the hope and joy of the coming of spring to her countryside. At last, she returns to her childhood. Through the pure and naive faith of a childhood hymn, she joyfully realizes that she will be "the candle sweet to shed a ray at Mary's feet." Anger, bitterness, pride, and bewilderment have been stripped away. The Blessed Virgin appears to Joan and gives her the courage to endure the pain of death.

---

* Not listed in order of appearance.

Katerina Ismailova

-»»*«««-

MUSIC BY: Dimitri Shostakovich

WORLD PREMIERE: Moscow, Russia,
   January 22, 1934

LIBRETTO BY: A. Preiss and
   Dimitri Shostakovich
English translation by Julius Rudel
NEW YORK CITY OPERA PREMIERE:
   (Sung in English) March 4, 1965

CONDUCTOR: Julius Rudel
STAGE DIRECTOR: Frank Corsaro
SCENIC DESIGNER: Will Steven Armstrong
COSTUMES: Patricia Zipprodt (debut)

CHARACTERS (In order of appearance)	VOICE (type)	PREMIERE CAST (New York City Opera)
Katerina Lvovna Ismailova	Soprano	Eileen Schauler (debut)
Boris Timofeyvich Ismailov	Bass	William Chapman
Zinovy Borisovich Ismailov	Tenor	Richard Krause
Workman from the Mill	Baritone	William Ledbetter
Sergei ⎫ Work people	Tenor	Richard Cassily
⎬ employed at		
Aksinya ⎭ Ismailov's	Soprano	Sandra Darling
Coachman	Tenor	Harris Davis
Village Drunk	Tenor	Kellis Miller
Porter	Bass	Jack Bittner (debut)
Steward	Bass	Richard Park (debut)
A Workman	Tenor	Robert Kelly (debut)
Priest	Bass	Lee Cass
Police Inspector	Bass	David Smith
Old Convict	Bass	Thomas Paul
Sentry	Bass	Jack Bittner
Sonyetka, a convict	Contralto	Tatyana Troyanos
Female Convict	Soprano	Lou Ann Wyckoff
Sergeant	Baritone	William Ledbetter

Workmen, Prisoners

SYNOPSIS OF STORY
TIME AND PLACE: A provincial town in prerevolutionary Russia

*

Katerina Ismailova, 1965. Richard Cassilly, Eileen Schauler.

ACT I

SCENE 1—Courtyard of the Ismailov house
SCENE 2—Same
SCENE 3—Katerina's bedroom

Katerina Ismailova is the young wife of Zinovy Ismailov, a wealthy merchant who has been called away to a nearby mill where an accident requires his presence. Boris, Katerina's father-in-law, humiliates her by making her swear faithfulness to her husband while he is away. Several workmen, among them Sergei, who has recently been hired by the Ismailovs, tease a female servant, Aksinya. Katerina intervenes but is herself drawn by Sergei into the fracas. Boris comes upon them, and Katerina tells him that she fell over some kegs and Sergei was only trying to help her up. Later, as Katerina is preparing to go to bed, Sergei comes to her room and, on the pretext of asking for a book, enters. He makes advances to her. Katerina resists at first, but finally yields.

ACT II

SCENE 1—Courtyard of the Ismailov house

SCENE 2—Katerina's bedroom

Boris, unable to sleep, roams the courtyard. He sees Sergei leaving Katerina's bedroom. Boris grabs him, awakens the household, and calling Katerina to the window to watch, proceeds to whip Sergei and lock him in the storeroom. The old man then demands something to eat, and Katerina retaliates by putting rat poison in the mushrooms she serves him. The poison acts quickly, and as the old man is dying Katerina quickly releases Sergei from the storeroom.

A week later, Katerina and Sergei are in bed when, unexpectedly, Zinovy returns. Sergei hides, but the suspicious Zinovy confronts Katerina with evidence of her adultery. Sergei comes out of his hiding place to protect Katerina, who is being beaten. In the struggle Sergei kills Zinovy. The lovers hide the body in the cellar.

ACT III

SCENE—Courtyard of the Ismailov house

On the morning of her wedding to Sergei, Katerina is haunted by the memory of the two murders but goes off to the church. Meanwhile, the Village Drunk enters, decides to sample some wine, and breaks down the cellar door. He discovers the body and rushes off to tell the police. During the festivities after the ceremony, Katerina sees the broken cellar door; she and Sergei prepare to escape, but it is too late. The police, led by the Inspector, enter and arrest them.

SCENE—Banks of a lake on the road to Siberia

Katerina and Sergei, having been condemned, are now members of a convict train marching across the steppes. Sergei has deserted Katerina and is paying attention to the young and pretty Sonyetka, another prisoner. Sonyetka tells Sergei he must prove his love by getting her some stockings and suggests he ask his "rich merchant's wife." Pretending a passion he no longer feels, Sergei approaches Katerina and obtains the stockings, which she gladly gives him, thinking they are for Sergei's fetter-wounds. Sergei immediately gives them to Sonyetka. As the convicts prepare to resume their journey, Sonyetka flaunts her new possessions at Katerina, who, in anger and despair, pushes Sonyetka into the lake and jumps in herself.

179

Lily

→))) * (((←

MUSIC BY: Leon Kirchner
WORLD PREMIERE and NEW YORK CITY
OPERA PREMIERE: April 14, 1977
(Sung in English)

LIBRETTO BY: Leon Kirchner
Based on the Saul Bellow novel
Henderson, the Rain King

CONDUCTOR: Leon Kirchner (debut)
STAGE DIRECTOR: Tom O'Horgan
SCENIC DESIGNER: Bill Stabile (debut)
SCENIC SUPERVISOR: John J. Moore
MEDIA DESIGNER: Lynda Rodolitz
COSTUMES: Randy Barcelo
DIRECTOR for ELECTRONIC SOUND: Ivan Tcherepnin

CHARACTERS (In order of appearance)	VOICE (type)	PREMIERE CAST (New York City Opera)
Gene Henderson	Baritone	Ara Berberian
Romilayu	Tenor	George Shirley
Princess Mtalba, of the Arnewi	Soprano	Geanie Faulkner (debut)
Queen Willatale, of the Arnewi	Mezzo	Joy Blackett (debut)
Lily, Henderson's wife	Soprano	Susan Belling (debut)
Pianist		Lloyd Walser
Frances, Henderson's first wife	Mute	Victoria McCarthy
Prince Itelo, of the Arnewi	Baritone	Benjamin Matthews
Lily's mother	Mezzo	Sandra Walker
Voice on tape		Gertrude Kirchner
The Arnewi		Stanley Bates, Charles Douglass, Hubert J. Edwards, Marvin Foster, Joyce Griffen, Lee Harley, Jan Hazell, Stephanie Howard, Yvette Johnson, Jon Lavalle Jackson, Rudy Lowe, Mentha Marley III, Jasper R. McGruder, Jr., Myles McMillan, Gary Moncrieffe, Trente Morant, Glenn Roberson, Lea Scott, Dale Shields, Isaish Smalls, Vernon Spencer

SYNOPSIS OF STORY
TIME AND PLACE: Imaginary place; present time

*

A C T   I

SCENE 1—Rain forest
SCENE 2—Cocktail party
SCENE 3—Native jungle village

A C T   I I

SCENE 4—Bedroom
SCENE 5—Bedroom
SCENE 6—Bedroom
SCENE 7—Bedroom
SCENE 8—Parisian cafe
SCENE 9—Study
SCENE 10—Rain forest
SCENE 11—The letter

Gene Henderson, an American millionaire who, for all his great size and wealth, thinks of himself as a "bum," travels to an Africalike continent in his continuing quest of a philosophy of life. His second wife, Lily, appears in flashbacks and "flash forwards" from their life in America, merging past and present in her reflections.

Henderson and his native guide, Romilayu, journey to villages of the gentle Arnewi, who are known to possess the knowledge of "Grun tu molani" or "the way to live." Although Henderson cannot understand their "African" language, nor they (except for Prince Itelo) his English, he meets Queen Willatale and her younger sister, Princess Mtalba.

When Henderson defeats Itelo in a wrestling match, he is offered Mtalba as the traditional prize to the winner. He politely refuses, but to show his good will he tries to solve the village's crisis: the water supply is polluted by an invasion of frogs and the cattle are dying of thirst.

Henderson's technological know-how enables him to blow up the frogs, but the whole water supply goes too. Mortified, Henderson begs the villagers to kill him, and this seems about to happen—but a last reappearance of Lily finds her reading Henderson's latest letter in which he tells of resuming his quest, still deeper into the continent.

Lizzie Borden

-»»*«« -

MUSIC BY: Jack Beeson
WORLD PREMIERE and NEW YORK CITY
    OPERA PREMIERE: March 25, 1965
(Sung in English)

LIBRETTO BY: Kenward Elmslie

CONDUCTOR: Anton Coppola (debut)
STAGE DIRECTOR: Nikos Psacharopoulos (debut)
SCENIC DESIGNER: Peter Wexler (debut)
COSTUMES: Patton Campbell

CHARACTERS (In order of appearance)	VOICE (type)	PREMIERE CAST (New York City Opera)
Elizabeth Andrew Borden	Soprano	Brenda Lewis
Reverend Harrington	Tenor	Richard Krause
Andrew Borden	Bass-baritone	Herbert Beattie
Margret Borden	Soprano	Ann Elgar
Abigail Borden	Soprano	Ellen Faull
Capt. Jason MacFarlane	Baritone	Richard Fredricks
Children, Young People		

SYNOPSIS OF STORY
TIME AND PLACE: Fall River, Massachusetts, 1880's

*

ACT I

SCENE 1—The living room of the Borden house

During a choir rehearsal, the Reverend Harrington asks Lizzie for a donation. Her father is the richest man in town, and one day of his income would save Old Harbor Church. Lizzie advises him to speak to Abbie, her stepmother, who can persuade Mr. Borden to do as she wants. Mr. Borden enters, disrupting the rehearsal. Lizzie asks him for a formal gown. He tells her to make do with a dress from the attic. The family assembles for lunch: Andrew Borden, Abbie, Lizzie, and her younger sister, Margret.

SCENE 2—The room of Lizzie and Margret

Lizzie and Margret look at the garden. Nothing grows. Lizzie goes to warn the Reverend Harrington and Jason, Margret's sea-captain beau, not to come too early. That night Jason will ask Mr. Borden for Margret's hand.

ACT II

SCENE—The living room of the Borden house

Abbie persuades Andrew to buy her a new piano and to remove the portrait of Evangeline, his dead first wife, Lizzie's and Margret's mother. A quarrel ensues between Lizzie and Andrew, interrupted by the arrival of the Reverend Harrington and Jason. Andrew mocks Jason's proposal and tells him he can marry Lizzie, not Margret. He forbids Lizzie to see the preacher or Jason again and orders her to treat Abbie more lovingly.

ACT III

SCENE 1—The room of Lizzie and Margret

While Andrew and Abbie are out celebrating their wedding anniversary, Jason persuades Margret to elope with him. They promise to return for Lizzie, if not this voyage, then the next one. Lizzie puts on Evangeline's wedding dress, which she had intended for Margret. Entranced by her mirror image, Lizzie loses herself in fantasies that Jason will return for her. Abbie catches her by surprise and threatens to tell Andrew of Lizzie's duplicity.

SCENE 2—The living room

Lizzie sits listlessly while Jason packs Margret's belongings. She confesses how much his letters to Margret mean to her and begs him to let her keep them. Abbie sees Lizzie embracing Jason. Jason leaves; Abbie orders Lizzie to set the table and goes upstairs to nap.

The murders take place.

Lizzie Borden, 1967. Brenda Lewis (left) and Ellen Faule.

EPILOGUE

SCENE—Several years later, the living room

The Reverend Harrington returns a donation to Lizzie—the congregation has refused it, even though the jury has found Lizzie innocent. As Lizzie closes the shutters, children circle the house, mocking her.

Lost in the Stars

-»»*«(-

MUSIC BY: Kurt Weill

WORLD PREMIERE: New York, New York,
October 30, 1949

LIBRETTO BY: Maxwell Anderson
Based on Alan Paton's novel *Cry,
the Beloved Country*

NEW YORK CITY OPERA PREMIERE:
(Sung in English) April 10, 1958

CONDUCTOR: Julius Rudel
PRODUCTION CONCEIVED and STAGED BY: Jose Quintero (debut)
SCENERY and COSTUMES: Andreas Nomikos

CHARACTERS (In order of appearance)	VOICE (type)	PREMIERE CAST (New York City Opera)
Leader	Baritone	Lee Charles (debut)
Answerer	Baritone	Robert Atherton
Nita	Child	Patti Austin (debut)
Grace Kumalo	Mezzo	Rosetta Le Noire (debut)
Stephen Kumalo	Baritone	Lawrence Winters
Stationmaster	Tenor	Robert Ruddy
The Young Man	Tenor	Alexander Yancy, Jr. (debut)
The Young Woman	Soprano	Mary Louise (debut)
James Jarvis	Speaking	Nicholas Joy (debut)
Edward Jarvis	Speaking	Chris Snell (debut)
Arthur Jarvis	Speaking	John Irving (debut)
John Kumalo	Speaking	Frederick O'Neil (debut)
Paulus	Speaking	Emory Richardson (debut)
William	Speaking	Lawson Bates (debut)
Alex	Child	Frank Riley, Jr.
Foreman	Baritone	John Dennison
Mrs. Mkize	Soprano	Eva Jessye (debut)
Hlabeni	Bass	Garwood Perkins (debut)
Eland	Speaking	Conrad Bain (debut)
Linda	Soprano	Olga James (debut)
Johannes Pafuri	Speaking	Godfrey Cambridge (debut)
Matthew Kumalo	Speaking	Douglas Turner (debut)
Absalom Kumalo	Speaking	Louis Gossett (debut)
Rose	Soprano	Alyce Webb (debut)
The Other Girl	Soprano	Claretta Fabray (debut)
Irina	Mezzo	Shirley Carter (debut)
Servant	Speaking	Laurence Watson (debut)
Policeman	Tenor	William Zakariasen
White Woman	Soprano	Naomi Collier

CHARACTERS (In order of appearance)	VOICE (type)	PREMIERE CAST (New York City Opera)
White Man	Baritone	John Dennison
Burton	Speaking	Richard Bowler (debut)
The Judge	Speaking	Neil Fitzgerald

SYNOPSIS OF STORY
TIME AND PLACE: South Africa; the present

*

ACT I

NDOTSHENI—A small village in South Africa
  SCENE 1—Stephen Kumalo's home
  SCENE 2—The railroad station

JOHANNESBURG
  SCENE 3—John Kumalo's tobacco shop
  SCENE 4—The search
    (1) The factory office
    (2) Mrs. Mkize's house
    (3) Hlabeni's house
    (4) Parole office
  SCENE 5—Stephen's Shantytown lodging
  SCENE 6—A dive in Shantytown
  SCENE 7—Irina's hut in Shantytown
  SCENE 8—Kitchen in Arthur Jarvis' home
  SCENE 9—Arthur Jarvis' library
  SCENE 10—Street
  SCENE 11—Prison
  SCENE 12—Stephen's Shantytown lodging

The Reverend Stephen Kumalo, a black preacher in a small town in South Africa, worries about his son, Absalom, who is working in the mines to earn money for his education. It has been a year since the minister and his wife have heard from Absalom, and they fear he is in trouble.

Stephen agrees with his wife to go looking for Absalom in Johannesburg. At the train station Stephen meets Arthur Jarvis, a white landowner, who discusses with Stephen his own son's friendship for blacks.

In Johannesburg, Stephen is unable to find his son after searching, and agrees to return to his village with his sister's son, Alex, who will live with him.

Meanwhile, Absalom sits in a Johannesburg Shantytown nightclub listening to Linda, a singer, and pondering on a course of action. He is considering joining a group of robbers to provide for Irina and their unborn child. He joins the robbers, but in the complications that develop, Absalom fires a gun, killing a white man. A chorus at this point comments on the fears of the strong white minority and the weak black majority.

ACT II

JOHANNESBURG
  SCENE 1—John Kumalo's tobacco shop
  SCENE 2—Stephen's prayer
  SCENE 3—Arthur Jarvis' doorway
  SCENE 4—Irina's hut in Shantytown
  SCENE 5—The courtroom
  SCENE 6—Prison cell

NDOTSHENI
  SCENE 7—Stephen's chapel
  SCENE 8—Stephen Kumalo's home

Stephen is faced with a dilemma, having learned of his son's action. Alone, he argues with himself and prays. Irina also prays for Absalom and vows to stand by him regardless of the consequences.

In the courtroom the other robbers lie, but Absalom tells the truth. He is sentenced to hang, and the rest go free. A chorus sings of the broken past of these people, "Cry, the Beloved Country."

Back at the village of the Reverend Kumalo's congregation, the little boy, Alex, plays by himself while Stephen calls the congregation together to pray in this sad time.

As the time for Absalom's execution arrives, Jarvis, the father of the man who was killed, visits Stephen. He comes to the realization that the sorrow he is experiencing is a universal one that transcends skin color. Stephen, responding to this gesture, exclaims, "I have a friend."

185

Louise

→》》*《《←

MUSIC BY: Gustave Charpentier
WORLD PREMIERE: Paris, France,
February 2, 1900

LIBRETTO BY: Gustave Charpentier
NEW YORK CITY OPERA PREMIERE:
(Sung in French) October 4, 1962

CONDUCTOR: Jean Morel
STAGE DIRECTOR: Christopher West
SCENERY and COSTUMES: Gordon Micunis

CHARACTERS (In order of appearance)	VOICE (type)	PREMIERE CAST (New York City Opera)
Louise	Soprano	Arlene Saunders
Julien	Tenor	John Alexander
Mother	Mezzo	Claramae Turner
Father	Baritone	Norman Treigle
Ragpicker	Mezzo	Helen Guile
Wood Gatherer	Mezzo	Pearle Goldsmith
Noctambulist	Tenor	Frank Porretta
Milkwoman	Soprano	Miriam Burton
Ragman	Bass-baritone	Thomas Paul (debut)
Junkman	Baritone	Spiro Malas
1st Policeman	Baritone	John Smith
2nd Policeman	Baritone	James Fels
Street Urchin	Soprano	Betsy Hepburn (debut)
Street Sweeper	Mezzo	Charlotte Povia
Painter	Bass	Ron Bottcher
Sculptor	Baritone	William Metcalf
Songwriter	Tenor	Kellis Miller
Poet	Tenor	Richard Krause
1st Philosopher	Tenor	David Clatworthy (debut)
2nd Philosopher	Bass	Glenn Dowlen
Blanche	Soprano	Martha Kokolska
Marguerite	Mezzo	Helen Guile
Suzanne	Mezzo	Marlena Kleinman (debut)
Gertrude	Mezzo	Joanne Grillo (debut)
Irma	Soprano	Doris Yarick
Camille	Soprano	Bonnie Heller (debut)
Apprentice	Soprano	Betsy Hepburn
Elise	Mezzo	Beverly Evans
Madeleine	Soprano	Hanna Owen
Old Clothes Man	Tenor	Arthur Graham
Forewoman	Mezzo	Jean Kraft
King of Fools	Tenor	Frank Porretta

CHARACTERS · VOICE · PREMIERE CAST

CHARACTERS (In order of appearance)	VOICE (type)	PREMIERE CAST (New York City Opera)
Cries of Paris:		
Chair Mender	Mezzo	Joanne Grillo
Artichoke Vendor	Soprano	Doris Yarick
Bird Food Vendor	Soprano	Martha Kokolska
Carrot Vendor	Tenor	Kellis Miller
Green Peas Vendor	Tenor	Richard Krause

Street Vendors, Shop Girls, Bohemians

SYNOPSIS OF STORY
TIME AND PLACE: Paris, about 1900

*

ACT I

SCENE—Louise's home

The laws of France forbid young people to marry without the consent of their parents; it is also customary for parents to select a marriage partner for their daughter. Louise, the daughter of a Parisian working-class couple, has fallen in love with a young poet, Julien. His mode of life, however, does not appeal to her mother, who violently opposes the idea of their marriage. From the balcony of her house, Louise talks the matter over with Julien, who lives across the narrow street. Julien agrees to write to her parents once more, but in return Louise must promise to elope with him if they refuse to give their consent. Louise's mother overhears part of the conversation and berates her daughter for her liaison with a good-for-nothing artist.

The father returns from his day's work bringing with him Julien's letter, which he reads. He is kinder to Louise and more sympathetic than his wife, and when he offers to meet Julien, the mother flies into a rage and persuades her husband to forbid Louise to think further of such a marriage.

ACT II

SCENE 1—A street in Montmartre

The night prowlers and local inhabitants go about their business in the early morning hours in Montmartre: an elegantly dressed gentleman talks of the pleasures that Paris has to offer; a ragpicker denounces him as a seducer and liber-

tine; the quarter awakens and the street vendors begin their cries. Julien arrives with a group of artist friends, planning to stop Louise as she passes by on her way to work and persuade her to run away with him. The mother has escorted Louise to work this morning, so Julien waits until she has left. When Louise tells him of her parents' refusal to consent to their marriage, Julien reminds her of her promise to elope. Louise asks him for more time to think, because she knows how greatly such a defiant act would distress her father.

SCENE 2—A dressmaking factory

Louise sits in the dressmaker's workroom with the other seamstresses, who tease her about being in love. Their conversation is interrupted by Julien, who sings a serenade from the street. At first they are enchanted by his song, but they soon grow bored with him and pelt him with pennies and abuse. Louise, pleading illness, runs out of the shop and, to the amazement and amusement of her companions, rushes off with Julien.

ACT III

SCENE—A garden in Montmartre

Julien and Louise are living happily in a small house on the heights of Montmartre. Louise recalls the days when they met and fell in love and, as night falls and the city of Paris is illuminated below them, the lovers celebrate the beauty and allure of the city that has brought them together. As they go into their house, the garden is invaded by their friends among the artists and working girls, led by the elegant libertine, who have come to crown Louise as the Muse of Montmartre. The celebrations are interrupted by Louise's mother, who comes to beg Louise to return home to her dying father. The mother promises that she will make no other demands and that Louise can return to Julien as soon as the father is well. Louise agrees to go home with her.

ACT IV

SCENE—Louise's home

The father is much recovered, but he and his wife have not kept their promise to Louise. They will not permit her to return to Julien, and Louise is sad and morose. The father denounces the conduct of children whose selfishness brings unhappiness to their parents. He appeals to Louise to forget Julien and to recreate their former family happiness by being a loving daughter. But Louise is no longer a child; she can think only of Julien and her beloved Paris. This enrages her father, who curses and repudiates her, ordering her to leave his house. Louise runs out. The Father realizes what he has done and calls after her, but he is too late. He curses Paris and the effect it has had on his child.

The Love for Three Oranges

→))) * (((←

MUSIC BY: Serge Prokofiev

WORLD PREMIERE: Chicago, Illinois,
December 30, 1921

LIBRETTO BY: Serge Prokofiev
English Translation by: Victor Seroff
NEW YORK CITY OPERA PREMIERE: (Sung in
English) November 1, 1949

CONDUCTOR: Laszlo Halasz
PRODUCTION DEVISED BY: Theodore Komisarjevsky*
STAGE DIRECTOR: Vladimir Rosing (debut)*
SCENIC DESIGNER: Mstislav Doboujinsky (debut)
COSTUMES†
BALLET CHOREOGRAPHER: Charles Weidman

CHARACTERS (In order of appearance)	VOICE (type)	PREMIERE CAST (New York City Opera)
A Prologue	Spoken	John Primm (debut)
His Majesty, the King	Bass	Gean Greenwell
Pantalone, a Councilor	Baritone	John Tyers
Truffaldino, the Royal Cook	Tenor	Luigi Vellucci
Leandro, the Prime Minister	Baritone	Carlton Gauld
Her Royal Highness, the Princess Clarissa	Contralto	Margery Mayer
Smeraldina	Mezzo	Rosalind Nadell
His Royal Highness, the Prince Tartaglia	Tenor	Robert Rounseville
The Sorceress, Fata Morgana	Soprano	Ellen Faull
The Magician Celio	Bass-baritone	Lawrence Winters
The Cook	Bass	Richard Wentworth
The Princess Linetta	Contralto	Frances Lager (debut)
The Princess Nicoletta	Mezzo	Dorothy Shwan
The Princess Ninetta	Soprano	Virginia Haskins
Farferello, a devil	Bass	Nicholas Vanoff

Farcical characters, Jesters, Courtiers, Guards, Servants, Soldiers

Note: Spoken Prologue devised by Komisarjevsky after Carlo Gozzi.

---

* Vladimir Rosing took over the stage direction when Theodore Komisarjevsky became ill two weeks before the first performance, originally scheduled for October 27, 1949.

† Many of the costumes used for the original 1921 Chicago production were discovered in a warehouse. The New York City Opera used many of them for lesser characters in the 1949 production. Other costumes were executed by Kate Friedheim; masks executed by Ugi Ito and Michael Arshansky.

SYNOPSIS OF STORY
TIME AND PLACE: A Theater, Once Upon a Time

*

ACT I

SCENE 1—The bedchamber of His Royal Highness, Prince Tartaglia

The story of the opera, which is a parody on romantic plays, centers around the character of the hereditary Prince of a fairy-tale kingdom. The King's ambitious niece, Clarissa, and her lover, the villainous chancellor, Leandro, are plotting to destroy the Prince. The chancellor feeds him on romantic prose and highbrow verse, stuffing them in his food, and the Prince gets worse and worse. The doctors find his state hopeless. Suddenly the King remembers that he has heard somewhere that laughter helps the melancholic sickness from which his son is suffering. Pantalone, the state secretary, calls the royal cook, Truffaldino, who is known as a very funny man, and the King orders him to arrange a circus performance to make the Prince laugh.

SCENE 2—The circus

The performance takes place but fails to amuse the Prince, and his laughter bursts forth only when an old crone, who has come to the show uninvited, falls down during a fight with Truffaldino. Furious at being made fun of, the crone, who happens to be the witch Fata Morgana, curses the Prince, decreeing that he shall fall in love with three oranges and run three thousand miles at full speed in search of them.

ACT II

SCENE 1—The desert

In spite of the warnings of a friendly magician, Celio, the Prince, with Truffaldino, continues the search.

SCENE 2—Before the kitchen of Creonta, the Giantess

They finally reach the kitchen of the giantess Creonta, whose cook with a magic ladle guards the three oranges. The Prince manages to steal the oranges and flees to the desert.

SCENE 3—Another part of the desert

When the oranges are opened, three Princesses step out. Two die of thirst; the third, after having drunk some water, remains alive and as a matter of course is to become the Prince's bride. While the Prince goes to fetch his father, the King, Fata Morgana appears with her servant, Smeraldina, and transforms the Princess into a pigeon. Smeraldina takes the Princess' place, but the returned Prince refuses to recognize her as his bride. The King forces his son to accept her, saying, "You gave your word and the royal word cannot be broken."

SCENE 4—The royal kitchen

Truffaldino, preparing the feast for the betrothal celebration, has fallen asleep, and when Pantalone comes to discover the cause of delay in serving the banquet he finds the meat burned. Finally the King and all his court enter the kitchen to learn what is causing the delay. While they are there a pigeon flies in, and Celio, suddenly appearing, transforms the bird into the Princess Ninetta. The truth is then revealed to the King, and he punishes Leandro, Clarissa, and Smeraldina by making them kitchen sweepers. But Fata Morgana comes to their rescue and transports them to the infernal regions. The happy ending comes with the Prince marrying Princess Ninetta, with love and virtue triumphant.

Lucia di Lammermoor

→))) * (((←

MUSIC BY: Gaetano Donizetti

WORLD PREMIERE: Naples, Italy,
September 26, 1835

LIBRETTO BY: Salvatore Cammaramo
Based on Sir Walter Scott's *The Bride
of Lammermoor*

NEW YORK CITY OPERA PREMIERE: (Sung in
Italian) October 9, 1969

CONDUCTOR: Charles Wilson
PRODUCTION DEVISED and DIRECTED BY: Tito Capobianco
SCENIC DESIGNER: Marsha Louis Eck
COSTUMES: José Varona
CHOREOGRAPHY: Robert Joffrey

CHARACTERS (In order of appearance)	VOICE (type)	PREMIERE CAST (New York City Opera)
Normanno, Captain of the Guard	Tenor	Joaquin Romaguera
Lord Enrico Ashton	Baritone	Dominic Cossa
Raimondo Bidebent, tutor and confidant of Lucia	Bass	Robert Hale
Lucia, sister of Enrico	Soprano	Beverly Sills
Alisa, companion of Lucia	Mezzo	Beverly Evans
Sir Edgardo of Ravenswood	Tenor	Michele Molese
Lord Arturo Bucklaw	Tenor	David Clements

Ladies and Knights, Inhabitants of Lammermoor, Pages, Soldiers, Servants, Servants of
the Ashtons

SYNOPSIS OF STORY
TIME AND PLACE: Scotland, end of the 17th century

*

ACT I

SCENE 1—A courtyard of Ravenswood Castle

Lord Enrico Ashton, in possession of the castle
and estate of his hereditary enemy, Edgardo of
Ravenswood, now finds his own family's future
in political danger. As Normanno, the captain
of his guard, and the servants search for a rumored trespasser on the castle grounds, Enrico
appears, followed by his sister's tutor, Raimondo.
Already angry because Lucia will not agree to
marry Arturo (a marriage that could save the
family's fortune), Enrico becomes enraged when
Normanno reveals that she has been secretly

191

meeting with a stranger who had one day saved her life. When the trespasser is identified as Edgardo, Enrico ignores Raimondo's pleas and swears vengeance upon both Edgardo and Lucia.

SCENE 2—A fountain in a glade

Lucia, having received the note that Edgardo had stealthily passed to her companion, Alisa, anxiously waits for him at the fountain. She tells Alisa about the ghost of a young girl, slain long ago by the Ravenswoods, who haunts the fountain. The ghost has warned her of a tragic end to her love for Edgardo; this omen increases her fear of her brother's retribution. When Edgardo arrives, he tells her that he must go on a political mission to France but that before he leaves he wants to tell Enrico of their love and end the feud between the families. Lucia, who knows her brother will never agree, finally persuades Edgardo to overcome his pride and keep their love a secret. They pledge their faith in each other, and Lucia gives Edgardo a ring as a token of trust.

ACT II

SCENE 1—An anteroom in Ravenswood Castle

Although preparations for the marriage of Lucia and Arturo are under way, she still has not agreed to marry him. Enrico shows Lucia a letter from Edgardo (which he has forged) to prove Edgardo's faithlessness. The confused and unhappy Lucia is further coerced by the persuasions of Raimondo that it is her duty to uphold her family's honor.

SCENE 2—The Great Hall of Ravenswood

The guests have gathered to witness the uniting of the two important families. Enrico reassures Arturo that Lucia's hesitancy has been due to her long-lasting grief for her dead mother. No sooner have Arturo and Lucia signed the marriage contract than Edgardo rushes in. Edgardo accuses Lucia of being unfaithful, while the others proclaim their pity for Lucia and their regret for the parts they have played in causing her such unhappiness. Raimondo restrains Edgardo from attacking Enrico and shows him the signed contract. In the confusion, Lucia steals Enrico's dagger, concealing it from the others. Cursing Lucia, Edgardo throws at her the ring she had given him and leaves.

ACT III

SCENE 1—Wolfscrag Tower

Enrico seeks out Edgardo in Wolfscrag Tower and challenges him to a duel. The two last members of the feuding families agree to meet in the graveyard of the Ravenswoods.

SCENE 2—Great Hall of Ravenswood Castle

According to custom, the religious ceremony has taken place a few days after the signing of the marriage contract. After the ceremony, the celebration is interrupted by Raimondo's ghastly discovery that Lucia has slain her bridegroom and has lost her mind. The guests are horrified as Lucia appears, in her madness believing that Edgardo is with her and that it is their wedding day. Enrico enters to witness the pathetic scene.

SCENE 3—Tombs of the Ravenswoods

Awaiting Enrico in the graveyard of his ancestors, the distraught Edgardo thinks of Lucia as another's bride and contemplates ending his life. When he learns what has happened at the castle, he starts to go to Lucia's side but is stopped by Raimondo. He then joins his beloved in death.

Lucrezia Borgia

→))) ✳ (((←

MUSIC BY: Gaetano Donizetti

WORLD PREMIERE: Milan, Italy,
December 26, 1833

LIBRETTO BY: Felice Romani
After Victor Hugo's play *Lucrece Borgia*
NEW YORK CITY OPERA PREMIERE: (Sung in
Italian) March 18, 1976

CONDUCTOR: Julius Rudel
DEVISED and DIRECTED BY: Tito Capobianco
SCENIC DESIGNER: Henry Bardon
COSTUMES: Peter J. Hall
CHOREOGRAPHY: Thomas Andrew

CHARACTERS (In order of appearance)	VOICE (type)	PREMIERE CAST (New York City Opera)
Apostolo Gazella	Baritone	Robert Fisher
Ascanio Petrucci	Baritone	Don Yule
Maffio Orsini, a young nobleman	Mezzo	Susanne Marsee
Gubetta	Baritone	Richard McKee
Oloferno Vitellozzo	Tenor	Howard Hensel
Jeppo Liverotto	Tenor	Melvin Lowery
Gennaro	Tenor	Gaetano Scano
Lucrezia Borgia, Duchess of Ferrara	Soprano	Beverly Sills
Alfonso, Duke of Ferrara	Baritone	Richard Fredricks
Rustighello, his confidant	Tenor	Jerold Siena
Astolfo	Baritone	Alan Baker
Servant	Mute	Robert Vega
Princess Negroni	Soprano	Marie Young
Cupbearer	Mute	Ray Morrison

Noblemen, Ladies, Guards, Spies, Attendants

SYNOPSIS OF STORY
TIME AND PLACE: Venice and Ferrara, 16th-century Italy

✳

PROLOGUE

Among the revelers celebrating the eve of Grimani's departure from Venice to the court of Alfonso d'Este, Duke of Ferrara, are several gentlemen in the ambassador's retinue. Except for the young Gennaro, each of them has his own reason for loathing the Duke's wife, Lucrezia Borgia. Orsini repeats the tale of how Gennaro saved his life in battle; as they pledged to live

193

and die together, a specter appeared to prophesy that they would die at the same time—at the hand of the Borgia. He is still haunted by this thought and envies Gennaro, who has fallen asleep in the middle of the tale.

After the others leave to rejoin the festivities, Lucrezia appears, masked, and approaches the sleeping Gennaro. She is unaware of being observed by Alfonso and Rustighello. Gennaro awakens and is instantly attracted to the beautiful stranger he sees before him. He confides to her his great love for the mother he has never seen, whose name he has promised never to seek. Lucrezia is deeply touched—she alone knows that she is Gennaro's mother and for that reason has sought him out.

Orsini and the others return and, recognizing Lucrezia, denounce her for the men she has murdered: Orsini's brother, Vitellozzo's and Liverotto's uncles, Petrucci's and Gazella's cousins. Gennaro learns that the beautiful stranger is the infamous Lucrezia Borgia.

ACT I

SCENE 1—A square in Ferrara

As dawn marks the end of Gennaro's party in his house opposite the ducal palace, Alfonso tells Rustighello of the revenge he will have upon this young man Lucrezia is seeing. Gennaro and his friends plan to meet again that night at the Princess Negroni's banquet. Gennaro is suspicious of Gubetta (who is a spy), but Orsini defends him, while the others accuse Gennaro of having been bewitched by the Borgia woman. In response, Gennaro strikes the "B" from the crest on the palace, leaving the shocking word "orgia" as a final insult. Astolfo, sent to bring Gennaro to Lucrezia, is stopped by Rustighello and the Duke's men.

SCENE 2—A room in the Ducal Palace

Lucrezia demands that Alfonso punish whoever has so vilely insulted her; he encourages her anger until she makes him swear to kill the offender before her eyes. The Duke then presents his prisoner—Gennaro. When Lucrezia pleads for Gennaro's life, she is accused of trying to save her lover. Alfonso taunts her by saying that he must abide by his oath to her to kill the man who insulted her good name, but he will permit her to choose the method of his death—by the sword or by poison. He forces Lucrezia to serve the poisoned wine to the unsuspecting Gennaro, who is led to believe the Duke is freeing him. As soon as Alfonso leaves, Lucrezia tells Gennaro that he has been poisoned. He does not believe her at first, but finally swallows the antidote she gives him, and escapes.

ACT II

SCENE 1—A square in Ferrara

Orsini laughs at Gennaro's fear of the Duke, assuring him that the incident with the poison and the antidote was only a trick of Lucrezia's to make him indebted to her by believing she had saved his life. He urges Gennaro to go with him to the Princess Negroni's and promises to leave Ferrara with him at dawn. Rustighello and his men, knowing that they are heading into a trap, do not stop them.

SCENE 2—A banquet hall in the Negroni Palace

The Princess' guests are joyously toasting the various wines and their lovely hostess. Gubetta provokes a fight with Orsini so that the other guests depart, leaving only the young Venetians. Orsini resumes his toast and all but Gubetta drink. They are interrupted by the sounds of a funeral procession; when they try to leave, they find the doors locked. Lucrezia enters to announce that she has now had her revenge for their treatment of her in Venice—their wine has been poisoned and five biers await them. To her horror, she sees Gennaro and hears him declare that a sixth bier is needed, for him. Ordering the others away, she implores Gennaro to drink the remainder of the antidote she had given him. He refuses, stating that he will die with his friends after killing her. Lucrezia tries to stop him, pleading with him to take the antidote. She finally reveals her secret—that she is his mother—but it is too late. Gennaro dies in her arms.

Macbeth

-»»*«-

MUSIC BY: Giuseppe Verdi

WORLD PREMIERE: Florence, Italy,
  March 14, 1847

LIBRETTO BY: Francesco Maria Piave and
  Andrea Maffei

NEW YORK CITY OPERA PREMIERE: (Sung in
  Italian) October 24, 1957

CONDUCTOR: Arturo Basile
STAGE DIRECTOR: Margaret Webster
SETS and COSTUMES: Andreas Nomikos
CHOREOGRAPHER: Robert Joffrey

CHARACTERS (In order of appearance)	VOICE (type)	PREMIERE CAST (New York City Opera)
Macbeth	Baritone	William Chapman (debut)
Banquo	Bass	Norman Treigle
Lady Macbeth	Soprano	Irene Jordan (debut)
Macduff	Tenor	Giuseppe Gismondo
Malcolm, King's son	Tenor	Ernest McChesney
Fleance, Banquo's son	Mute	Emlyn S. Williams
Lady-in-Waiting	Mezzo	Helen Baisley
Doctor	Bass	Arthur Newman
Macbeth's Aide-de-camp	Bass	Herbert Beattie
Hecate, Goddess of the Night	Dancer	Beatrice Tompkins

Witches, Nobles, Ladies, Soldiers, Apparitions

SYNOPSIS OF STORY
TIME AND PLACE: Medieval Scotland

*

ACT I

SCENE 1—The moors

Macbeth and Banquo, generals in the army of Duncan, King of Scotland, are returning from battle. On the moors they meet a band of witch-like creatures who give them prophetic greeting. They hail Macbeth as the Thane of Cawdor and then as the future King. Challenged by Banquo, they tell him that he will never reign, but that his sons will be kings. They vanish; and immediately afterwards Duncan's messengers bring Macbeth the news that he has, in fact, been created Thane of Cawdor. Deeply troubled, he broods on the second prophecy.

SCENE 2—Macbeth's castle

Lady Macbeth is reading a letter from her husband describing these events. She determines that he shall indeed be King, even at the cost of blood. A servant brings news of the imminent arrival of Duncan. She invokes the spirits of hell to help her accomplish her design. Duncan and his thanes arrive at the castle.

SCENE 3—Same

That night the murder is accomplished, but Macbeth is filled with horror at what he has done. In the morning Macduff arrives, discovers Duncan's body, and breaks the terrible news to the other thanes.

ACT II

SCENE 1—The Royal Castle

Macbeth and his wife realize that, though they are now King and Queen, they will never be at peace while Banquo and his son, Fleance, live. Lady Macbeth knows that they must finish what has been begun.

SCENE 2—A wood near the castle

Banquo is set upon and killed, but Fleance escapes.

SCENE 3—The banquet hall of the castle

Macbeth gives a great banquet for the nobility of Scotland. The ghost of Banquo appears to him, and his terror and guilt are apparent to his guests. He decides to revisit the witches.

ACT III

SCENE—The witches' cavern

The witches summon the spirits of hell to answer Macbeth's questions. One tells him to be-

ware of Macduff; the second, to have no fear since "none of woman born can harm Macbeth"; and the third that he can never be vanquished until Birnam Wood shall move against the castle of Dunsinane. The spirits of Banquo and his descendants appear to him, crowned as Kings. The witches vanish. Lady Macbeth comes to seek him, and together they vow vengeance on Macduff.

ACT IV

SCENE 1—Countryside near the English border

The nobles of Scotland lament the fate of their country. Macduff's castle has been burned, his wife and children killed. Young Malcolm arrives at the head of an English army, and the nobles join him to march against Macbeth. Malcolm tells them to cut down boughs from Birnam forest in order to mask their approach to the castle.

SCENE 2—Macbeth's castle

Ravaged by guilt and haunted by those whom she has slain, Lady Macbeth walks in her sleep, seeking vainly to cleanse her hands of blood.

SCENE 3—Same

Macbeth prepares to make his last stand. He learns of his wife's death, and his soldiers bring the news that Birnam Wood is moving toward the castle. Desperate, he flings himself into battle. He comes face to face with Macduff; before they fight, Macduff tells him that he was not "born of woman," but was "from his mother's womb untimely ripp'd." Macbeth knows that he is doomed.

Malcolm enters with his victorious army; the royal bards and the nobility of Scotland hail Macduff as their deliverer and Malcolm as their King.

Madama Butterfly

→))) * (((←

MUSIC BY: Giacomo Puccini

WORLD PREMIERE: Milan, Italy,
February 17, 1904

LIBRETTO BY: Luigi Illica, Giuseppe
Giacosa

NEW YORK CITY OPERA PREMIERE: (Sung in
Italian) May 15, 1946

CONDUCTOR: Laszlo Halasz
STAGE DIRECTOR: Eugene S. Bryden
SCENIC DESIGNER: H. A. Condell
COSTUMES*

CHARACTERS[1] (In order of appearance)	VOICE (type)	PREMIERE CAST (New York City Opera)
Benjamin F. Pinkerton	Tenor	Eugene Conley
Goro	Tenor	Hubert Norville
Suzuki	Mezzo	Margery Mayer (debut)
Sharpless	Baritone	Ivan Petroff
Madama Butterfly (Cio-Cio-San)	Soprano	Camilla Williams (debut)
Imperial Commissioner	Bass	Arthur Newman
The Bonze	Bass	Gean Greenwell
Yamadori	Baritone	Emile Renan

Friends, Relatives, American sailors

SYNOPSIS OF STORY
TIME AND PLACE: Nagasaki, Japan, about 1900

*

ACT I

SCENE—A Japanese house, terrace, and garden
overlooking Nagasaki Harbor

Benjamin Franklin Pinkerton, lieutenant of
the U.S. Navy, is inspecting the house he has
rented from Goro, a marriage broker. Goro is
also furnishing him with a Japanese wife, Cio-
Cio-San (Madama Butterfly). Sharpless, the
American Consul, joins Pinkerton, who despite
the former's warning takes this marriage very
lightly. Cio-Cio-San appears, followed by her
friends. The Imperial Commissioner performs
the marriage in the presence of the relatives.

---

* By Kate Friedheim; additional costumes by Brooks.
[1] Role of Kate Pinkerton omitted from list of cast of premiere performance.

197

Madama Butterfly, 1946. Camilla Williams (left) and Margery Mayer.

While everybody drinks to the couple's good fortune, the Bonze, a Japanese priest, rushes on. Furious at Cio-Cio-San's abandoning her faith, he curses her. Angrily, Pinkerton orders everybody to leave. Left alone, he comforts his bride. Drying her tears, and overcome by her love for Pinkerton, she is led by him into the house.

ACT II

SCENE 1—Interior of the house, three years later

Cio-Cio-San faithfully awaits the return of her husband. The Consul enters, bringing a letter from Pinkerton. Before he can read it to her, Goro ushers in Prince Yamadori, who asks for Butterfly's hand. She refuses, considering herself still married to her American husband, and Yamadori leaves. Sharpless now reads Pinkerton's letter, which is to prepare her for the truth. Cio-

Cio-San brings in her little son, convinced that as soon as Pinkerton knows of his existence, he will return. Sharpless leaves, deeply moved. Suddenly a cannon shot is heard, announcing a ship entering the harbor. Through a spyglass, Cio-Cio-San reads the name of Pinkerton's ship. Overjoyed, she, Suzuki, and the child begin the vigil, awaiting Pinkerton's arrival through the night.

SCENE 2—Interior of the house, the next morning

Suzuki persuades Cio-Cio-San to rest. She takes the child and goes to her room. Soon Pinkerton and Sharpless enter, followed by Kate, Pinkerton's American wife. They have come to take the child into their custody. Suzuki, grief-stricken, cries bitterly. She agrees, however, to bring Cio-Cio-San the sad news, fearing the worst. Pinkerton, overcome by remorse, flees. Cio-Cio-San returns, eagerly anticipating the joy

198

of Pinkerton's return. She soon senses the truth and agrees to surrender the child, demanding only that Pinkerton return for his son. Sharpless and Kate leave. Butterfly then commits hara-kiri and in the agony of death hears Pinkerton's voice in the distance calling her name.

Note: In subsequent performances of *Madama Butterfly,* the production included three acts.

The Magic Flute

→»»*«««-

MUSIC BY: Wolfgang Amadeus Mozart

WORLD PREMIERE: Vienna, Austria,
September 30, 1791

LIBRETTO BY: Emanuel Schikander
English Translation By:
Ruth and Thomas Martin
NEW YORK CITY OPERA PREMIERE:
(Sung in English) October 13, 1966

CONDUCTOR: Julius Rudel
PRODUCTION DESIGNED AND STAGED BY: Beni Montresor (debut)
COSTUMES: Beni Montresor
CHOREOGRAPHER: Thomas Andrews

CHARACTERS (In order of appearance)	VOICE (type)	PREMIERE CAST (New York City Opera)
Tamino	Tenor	Michele Molese
First Lady	Soprano	Donna Jeffrey
Second Lady	Soprano	Sylvia Grant
Third Lady	Mezzo	Beverly Evans
Papageno	Baritone	John Reardon
Queen of the Night	Soprano	Beverly Sills
Monostatos	Tenor	Nico Castel
Pamina	Soprano	Veronica Tyler
First Spirit	Soprano	Carroll Freeman
Second Spirit	Child's voice	Stewart Fischer
Third Spirit	Child's voice	Christopher Moore
Priest	Tenor	John Lankston
Sarastro	Bass	Noel Mangin
Speaker of the Temple	Bass	Thomas Paul
Papagena	Soprano	Joan Summers
First Armored Man	Tenor	John Stamford
Second Armored Man	Bass	Edward Pierson

Servants, Priests, Slaves

SYNOPSIS OF STORY
TIME AND PLACE: In and near the Temple of Isis at Memphis, at the time of Ramses I

*

ACT I

SCENE —A rocky landscape

Tamino, a handsome young prince, is lost in the valley and is being pursued by a serpent. He cries for help, sinks to the ground unconscious, and is saved by three lovely ladies. Conscious again, Tamino meets the bird catcher, Papageno, who informs him that he is in the realm of the Queen of the Night and takes credit for killing the serpent to gain Tamino's friendship. For the lie, the three ladies return to the scene and place a lock on Papageno's lips; they show Tamino a picture of a beautiful young girl, Pamina, the daughter of the Queen of the Night. He immediately falls in love with her. He is requested by the Queen of the Night, who appears in person, to save her daughter, who has been captured and taken to Sarastro's temple. Tamino sets out to save Pamina, accompanied by Papageno and a magic flute presented to him by the three ladies.

SCENE 2—Pamina's room in Sarastro's palace

Sarastro, head of a secret and powerful Egyptian religious order, has Pamina in his power. Guarded by Monostatos, a Moorish gentleman, he threatens Pamina's life unless she will love him. Papageno wanders in and frightens Monostatos. Left alone with Pamina, Papageno assures her that a prince, who loves her, will rescue her.

SCENE 3—The three temples

Tamino is led to Sarastro's temple by three spirits. Left alone, he tries to enter three different doors but is warned away. A priest informs Tamino that Sarastro is not a villain and that Pamina is safe. In his gratitude for this information, he plays a tune on his magic flute. In her flight with Papageno, Pamina is captured and brought to Sarastro. She meets Tamino, and both are solemnly prepared to undergo the rites of initiation, which may or may not prove them worthy of each other.

SCENE 4—The City of Lights

Sarastro informs the priests of Isis and Osiris of Tamino's intent to marry Pamina. They now must prove themselves worthy of entering the Temple of Light.

ACT II

SCENE 1—Temple courtyard

Outside the temple, Tamino and Papageno undergo religious instruction. The three ladies from the Queen of the Night appear to warn them about the priests and their new adventure. The priests quickly send the ladies back to their own region.

SCENE 2—Garden in Sarastro's palace

Monostatos gloats over the lovely Pamina as she lies asleep. Just in time, the Queen of the Night intervenes. She tells her daughter that she must kill Sarastro and makes her swear it or be disowned. Monostatos returns; after hearing the plot between mother and daughter, he threatens to reveal it unless Pamina loves him. She is saved again, this time by Sarastro. Pamina begs forgiveness for her mother as Sarastro explains to her that there is no such thing as revenge in his temple and that only love binds man to man.

SCENE 3—Room in the temple

An oath of silence is placed upon Papageno and Tamino as they prepare for the ritual. This is interrupted first by Papagena, a young girl dressed as an old crone, who teases Papageno, and then by Pamina, who misinterprets Tamino's silent actions.

SCENE 4—The garden

Pamina, afraid of never seeing Tamino again, prays for his safety. Sarastro, in his most comforting tones, assures her that all will be well as Tamino is led off. Papageno has a wish granted, and the old crone now appears as a young bird girl, Papagena, with whom he exchanges sentiments.

SCENE 5—The grotto of Water and Fire

Tamino endures the tests of the four elements—fire, water, earth, and air. As he enters the grotto, Pamina runs to him. Tamino playing his magic flute, the two lovers stroll through unharmed.

201

SCENE 6—Temple of Light

Monostatos is now in league with the Queen of the Night, who has promised him Pamina. They invade Sarastro's temple, together with the three ladies. But the power of Sarastro, that of knowledge and truth, is too great for them. The villains disappear as the Temple of Isis and Osiris appears, and a chorus of triumph to the forces of good enters.

The Makropoulos Affair

-»»*«««-

MUSIC BY: Leoš Janáček

WORLD PREMIERE: Brno, Czechoslovakia,
December 18, 1926

LIBRETTO BY: Leoš Janáček
Based on the drama by Karel Capek
English translation: Norman Tucker
NEW YORK CITY OPERA PREMIERE:
(Sung in English) November 1, 1970

CONDUCTOR: Gabor Otvos
STAGE DIRECTOR: Frank Corsaro
SCENERY AND COSTUMES: Patton Campbell
FILM AND SLIDE PROJECTIONS: Gardner Compton (debut) and Emile Ardolino (debut)
KINETIC AND PHOTOGRAPHIC ENVIRONMENT: Gardner Compton

CHARACTERS (In order of appearance)	VOICE (type)	PREMIERE CAST (New York City Opera)
Vitek, a lawyer's clerk	Tenor	John Lankston
Albert Gregor	Tenor	Harry Theyard
Christa, Vitek's daughter	Mezzo	Barbara Blanchard
Emilia Marty	Soprano	Maralin Niska
Chauffeur	Baritone	David Rae Smith
Doctor Kolenaty, a lawyer	Baritone	Edward Pierson
Jaroslav Prus	Baritone	Chester Ludgin
Miss Marty's maid	Mezzo	Judith Anthony
Janek, Prus' son	Tenor	Gary Glaze
Hauk-Sendorf, an ex-diplomat	Tenor	Nico Castel

SYNOPSIS OF STORY
TIME AND PLACE: Prague, 1913

*

INTRODUCTION

Although the opera takes place in 1913, the events leading up to it began in 1587 at the court of Rudolph II of Austria. The Emperor, fearing death, ordered his Greek physician, Hieronymus Makropoulos, to provide him with an elixir of life. When the physician believed he had succeeded, the suspicious monarch insisted on its being tried first by the physician's daughter, 16-year-old Elina. She fell into a fever and appeared to be near death for weeks after taking the preparation. The physician was put to death by the enraged Rudolph, but the girl survived and secretly left Rudolph's court, taking the formula with her, a prescription for 300 additional years of life.

Elina Makropoulos developed and aged nor-

203

mally until the beginning of middle age but then never grew any older. Fearing the suspicions of those around her, she moved from place to place, changing her name, her profession, and her personality but always retaining her irresistible beauty and her intials E.M. Thus, at various times, she was known as Elsa Mueller, Eugenia Montez, Ellian MacGregor, and finally, Emilia Marty, the famous opera singer of 1913.

The events of her life as Ellian MacGregor have particular bearing on the predicament of Emilia Marty, for in that guise, in 1806, she bore an illegitimate son, Ferdinand, in the course of a love affair with the Baron Josef Prus. She did two things that altered the course of her lives: she inadvertently named the boy Ferdinand Makropoulos, and she gave the formula for immortality to the Baron. He never used it but left it hidden in his home, and now Emilia Marty (having had 300 extra years of life) must endeavor to find the formula through the heirs of Baron Prus or she will, finally, die.

The matter of gaining access to the Prus estate is complicated by the fact that a legal battle for it has been going on for more than a hundred years. A suit is being pressed against Baron Prus' legitimate descendants by Albert Gregor, 34-year-old descendant of Ferdinand, because on his deathbed the Baron had named the son of Ellian MacGregor as his heir.

ACT I

SCENE—Office of Doctor Kolenaty

The curtain rises in Prague, in the law office of Dr. Kolenaty, where Albert Gregor is about to lose his case because no valid will has been found to substantiate his claim. Emilia Marty appears and divulges to Albert and his lawyer that a valid will does exist in the Prus house (now occupied by the great grandson of the Baron Prus), in a filing cabinet marked with the year 1806. It is there that she hopes the formula will be found, together with the will. At first Kolenaty is skeptical, but he goes off to make the search. In his lawyer's absence, Emilia Marty's great grandson, Albert Gregor, bewitched by his mysterious benefactress, tries to woo her. She at first rejects him but then treats him tenderly, treatment he mistakes for passion. For one moment, she lifts her veil. Magically, her face is transformed, and Albert sees a

wizened old woman. Emilia takes advantage of his confusion to seek information about the document, but Albert appears to have none. Kolenaty returns with the will, triumphant, but with him comes Prus, congratulating Albert but still insisting that some evidence be produced that Albert's great grandfather, Ferdinand, was indeed the son of Baron Prus. Emilia Marty promises to bring that proof and leaves the office defiantly.

ACT II

SCENE—Backstage at the theater

Emilia is exhausted after a performance at the Opera. Prus, his young son Janek, and the latter's girlfriend, Christa, who longs for a career in opera, have come backstage to pay her homage. Marty is in a foul humor, and when an old man, Hauk-Sendorf, appears insisting that she is the exact duplicate of his long-lost love, Eugenia Montez, she shocks everyone by speaking Spanish to him and kissing him shamelessly. She is finally left alone with Prus, who has found not only the will but love letters from Ellian MacGregor to the Baron, as well as a baptismal certificate that records Ferdinand as "Makropoulos" rather than "Gregor." She realizes that Albert Gregor's case is thus destroyed and so now tries to deal directly with Prus for her father's formula, but Prus refuses. Albert Gregor is now useless to Emilia Marty, and she coldly rejects him. He tries to choke her and, to destroy his passion, Marty bares the scars and mutilations on her body, tokens of her past loves. He leaves and Janek, Prus' smitten son, enters, declaring his passion for her. She can use him and plots the theft of the formula from Janek's father. But the father is also in love by now and he, being the most direct route to her immortality, obtains an assignation with Emilia after she has exacted a promise that he will give her the document.

ACT III

SCENE—Emilia Marty's apartment

Prus and Marty spend a night of love in her apartment. He is horrified by her indifference; nevertheless, he gives her the document. Cataclysmic events follow. Janek, Prus' son, has com-

The Makropoulos Affair, 1970. Maralin Niska and Nico Castel.

The Makropoulos Affair, 1970. Harry Theyard and Maralin Niska.

mitted suicide; Hauk is led off to an asylum. The others, Albert Gregor, Kolenaty, Christa and her father, Vitek, and Prus converge upon Emilia Marty and demand to know the truth. She takes refuge in her bedroom, and in her absence the others examine the contents of a trunk full of letters and articles from her past. They force her from the bedroom where she had been drinking, not the elixir, but alcohol. She drunkenly unravels the Makropoulos story, proclaiming that she is Elina Makropoulos and that she is 342 years old. She faints and there appears a strange beckoning figure. The formula in hand, she accepts her mortality: "There is no joy in goodness, no joy in evil, just a vast eternal loneliness." Mysterious voices echo her sentiments. The dying Emilia Marty hands the document to Christa, enticing her with a promise of a great career and eternal life, but the terrified girl sets it on fire. With a cry of "Pater Hemon" (Our Father), Marty dies and fades back into the limbo of time.

Manon

-»»*«««-

MUSIC BY: Jules Massenet

WORLD PREMIERE: Paris, France,
January 19, 1884

LIBRETTO BY: Henri Meilhac and
Philippe Gille

NEW YORK CITY OPERA PREMIERE:
(Sung in French) March 22, 1951

CONDUCTOR: Jean Morel
STAGE DIRECTOR: José Ruben
SCENIC DESIGNER: H. A. Condell
COSTUMES: Ruth Morley (debut)
CHOREOGRAPHER: Grant Muradoff

CHARACTERS (In order of appearance)	VOICE (type)	PREMIERE CAST (New York City Opera)
Guillot de Morfontaine, Minister of Finance	Tenor	Michael Pollock
De Bretigny, a nobleman	Bass-baritone	George Jongeyans
Pousette	Soprano	Dorothy MacNeil
Javotte } actresses	Mezzo	Mary LeSawyer
Rosette	Mezzo	Edith Evans
Innkeeper	Baritone	Richard Wentworth
Lescaut, a guardsman	Baritone	Ralph Herbert
Manon, his cousin	Soprano	Ann Ayars
Chevalier des Grieux	Tenor	David Poleri
Count des Grieux	Bass	Carlton Gauld
Solo Dancers		Marina Svetlova
		Grant Muradoff

Villagers, Waiters, Police, Priest

SYNOPSIS OF STORY

TIME AND PLACE: France, early 18th century

*

ACT I

SCENE—The courtyard of an inn at Amiens

Manon, a beautiful young girl, is being sent by her parents to a convent. As she descends from the stagecoach at Amiens, she is met by her cousin, Lescaut, a soldier of doubtful character. He soon leaves her to herself and goes to

207

gamble with his fellow soldiers. Manon attracts the attention of De Bretigny, a rich nobleman, and Guillot de Morfontaine, an elderly wealthy aristocrat, who offers her the use of his carriage if she will follow him to Paris. The young Chevalier des Grieux also notices Manon. He is smitten by her youth and beauty. When he learns that she is destined for the convent, he persuades her to elope with him to Paris. Manon, finding him the most attractive of her suitors, accepts. Together they flee to Paris in Morfontaine's carriage.

ACT II

SCENE—Des Grieux's apartment in Paris

At the modest apartment, Manon and des Grieux are living together happily as lovers. Des Grieux intends to marry Manon and writes to his father for permission. In the meantime, De Bretigny has secretly made advances to Manon, promising her luxury and riches if she will leave des Grieux for him. Manon, attracted by the prospect of a life of luxury, allows des Grieux to be abducted by order of his father and becomes De Bretigny's mistress.

ACT III

SCENE 1—Cours-La-Reine, a boulevard in Paris

Le Cours-La-Reine is a promenade, the meeting place of fashionable society and the people. Manon appears in brilliant attire, courted by everyone. Morfontaine makes a new attempt to win her favor by ordering the Opera Ballet to perform for her there. But Manon, now bored with her new life, yearns for des Grieux. Learning that he has entered the Seminary of Saint Sulpice,

she decides to win him back and departs for the seminary.

SCENE 2—Seminary of St. Sulpice

At the seminary des Grieux is about to be ordained. His father, in dismay, comes to bid him goodbye and leaves with him a legacy from his mother. Manon appears, still in gala attire. At first des Grieux remains firm, but, overcome by Manon's pleading and her charm, finally succumbs and flees with her.

ACT IV

SCENE—Gambling room at Hotel Transylvanie

The demimonde gathers at the gambling hall of this establishment. Manon enters with des Grieux. Their resources have dwindled, and she persuades des Grieux to gamble in the hope of regaining their fortune. Guillot de Morfontaine, still bitter at having failed to win Manon, proposes a card game to des Grieux for high stakes. Des Grieux wins consistently. Guillot, infuriated, accuses des Grieux of cheating and calls the police. Manon is sent to prison, but des Grieux is released through the intervention of his father.

ACT V

SCENE—On a road from Paris to Le Havre

At Le Havre, Manon is to be deported as a prostitute. Des Grieux, who still loves her, tries with the help of Lescaut to rescue her. Lescaut manages to bribe the guard in charge of the women prisoners and frees her, but it is too late. Weakened by the privations of jail and the arduous journey, Manon dies in des Grieux's arms.

Manon Lescaut

-»»*«« -

MUSIC BY: Giacomo Puccini

LIBRETTO BY: Giacomo Puccini,
Ruggiero Leoncavallo, Marco Praga,
Domenico Oliva, Giulio Ricordi, Luigi Illica,
Giuseppe Giacosa

WORLD PREMIERE: Turin, Italy,
February 1, 1893

NEW YORK CITY OPERA PREMIERE:
(Sung in Italian) November 9, 1944

CONDUCTOR: Laszlo Halasz
STAGE DIRECTOR: José Ruben
SCENIC DESIGNER: Richard Rychtarik
COSTUMES*

CHARACTERS (In order of appearance)	VOICE (type)	PREMIERE CAST (New York City Opera)
Edmondo, a student	Tenor	Thomas Hayward (debut)
The Chevalier Des Grieux	Tenor	William Horne (debut)
Lescaut, Manon's brother	Baritone	John DeSurra
Innkeeper	Bass-baritone	Rudy Trautman (debut)
Geronte De Ravoir, Treasurer-General	Baritone	Ralph Telasko (debut)
Manon Lescaut	Soprano	Dorothy Kirsten
Singer	Soprano	Helen LeClaire
Dancing Master	Mute	Arthur Ulisse (debut)
Lamplighter	Tenor	Edward Visca
Captain in the Navy	Bass	Emanuel Kazarus

Students, Citizens, Courtesans, Sailors, Dancers, Police, Ladies and
Gentlemen
Solo Dancers: Dysart, Kantro (debuts)

SYNOPSIS OF STORY
TIME AND PLACE: Latter half of the 18th century; Amiens, Paris, Le Havre, Louisiana

*

ACT I

SCENE—An inn on the outskirts of Amiens

In a busy square near a small inn at Amiens,
Edmondo and a group of students are good-naturedly greeting the working girls. They urge Des
Grieux, a young seminarian, to join them; he
says he will humor them in their frivolous game

---

* Supplied by Van Horn & Son.

209

Manon Lescaut, 1974

but proceeds to show his disdain by his exaggerated romantic words. Also in the crowd is Lescaut, waiting for the coach from Arras, which is bringing his sister, Manon. The coach arrives and Des Grieux and the others watch the passengers alight. Another traveler is Geronte De Ravoir, the King's Treasurer-General, on his way to Paris. Lescaut follows Geronte into the inn, leaving his beautiful and distraught young sister outside. Des Grieux approaches her and soon learns of her unhappiness at being forced to enter the convent. Manon agrees to meet him later in the evening, and as she goes to join Lescaut in the inn, the students (who have observed Des Grieux's growing infatuation) cheerfully tease him about his professed indifference to love. The confused Des Grieux leaves, and the students continue their fun with a presentation of a play about love. During the play, the opportunistic Lescaut and the wealthy Geronte casually agree that it is a shame that a lovely young girl like Manon is to be confined in a convent. Their conversation, and Geronte's subsequent arrangement with the innkeeper for a fast carriage to be hidden

behind the inn, are overheard by Edmondo, who reveals the planned abduction to Des Grieux. Des Grieux persuades Manon to elope with him, and, aided by Edmondo, they flee in Geronte's waiting carriage. Geronte is furious, but Lescaut is unperturbed; he assures him that Manon will tire of Des Grieux when his money runs out. At that time, Geronte can pursue his "fatherly affection" for Manon, with her wily brother Lescaut to complete the family group.

ACT II

SCENE—Geronte's mansion in Paris

Manon has listened to her brother's promptings and, abandoning Des Grieux, has become Geronte's mistress. Already bored with her existence in Geronte's luxurious mansion, she asks Lescaut for news of Des Grieux. He tells her that Des Grieux has turned to gambling to make his fortune and is desperately looking for her. Lescaut is aware that his sister's growing boredom could prove dangerous to their situation, and he devises a plan. After Manon's dancing lesson, Geronte and his guests leave to wait outside for Manon to join them. Des Grieux has secretly entered the house and appears, reproaching Manon for her desertion. She soon wins him over, and they are reconciled. Geronte suddenly returns and rebukes Manon, who retaliates by taunting him about his age. After Geronte's departure, Des Grieux begs Manon to leave with him immediately. Lescaut bursts in to warn them that Geronte has denounced them to the authorities and that soldiers are on their way to arrest Manon. In spite of Des Grieux's and Lescaut's frantic pleas to hurry, Manon insists upon gathering her valuable jewels. The delay prevents her escape.

ACT III
SCENE—The port of Le Havre

Manon is being held with other prisoners in Le Havre, awaiting deportation to America. Lescaut, who has promised Des Grieux to rescue her, has bribed a guard. Des Grieux and Manon effect a reconciliation before the planned escape is discovered and Manon is led with the other deportees past a jeering crowd to board the ship. When Des Grieux realizes he cannot save Manon, he pleads with the captain, who agrees to let him sail with the ship as cabin boy.

ACT IV
SCENE—A vast plain bordering on New Orleans

The hopelessly exhausted young lovers are wandering in desertlike terrain. Des Grieux leaves the ill and thirsty Manon to go in search of water and to try to find their route. Left alone, the feverish Manon begins to hallucinate and is close to death when Des Grieux returns. While Des Grieux attempts to comfort her, Manon's strength fails and she dies in his arms.

Maria Golovin

-»»*«««-

MUSIC BY: Gian Carlo Menotti
WORLD PREMIERE: Brussels, Belgium,
    August 20, 1958

LIBRETTO BY: Gian Carlo Menotti
NEW YORK CITY OPERA PREMIERE:
    (Sung in English) March 30, 1959

CONDUCTOR: Herbert Grossman
STAGE DIRECTOR: Kirk Browning (debut)
SCENIC DESIGNER: Rouben Ter-Arutunian
COSTUMES: Ruth Morley

CHARACTERS (In order of appearance)	VOICE (type)	PREMIERE CAST (New York City Opera)
Donato	Baritone	Richard Cross (debut)
Agata	Mezzo	Regina Sarfaty
The Mother	Soprano	Patricia Neway
Dr. Zuckertanz	Tenor	Norman Kelley
Maria Golovin	Soprano	Ilona Kombrink (debut)
Trottolo	Mute	Craig Sechler (debut)
The Prisoner	Baritone	Chester Ludgin

SYNOPSIS OF STORY

TIME AND PLACE: A few years after a recent war. The entire action takes place at Donato's villa near a frontier in a European country.

*

ACT I

SCENE 1—A living room in the villa. Early spring.

Donato, who is blind, lives with his wealthy mother in an old villa. Agata, in love with Donato, and other servants share these quarters. Maria Golovin and her young son, Trottolo, also live here. Maria's husband is a prisoner of war, and she expects him to return soon; in the meantime, she has taken quarters that Donato's mother has rented to her. The mother comments on the sadness of these old surroundings for a child, but Maria feels it will be pleasant anyway. She meets Donato and is shown the bird cages he builds, as he is unable to fulfill his ambition to be an architect. Maria tells him of her painting and promises to keep him company.

SCENE 2—The same. A month later.

Donato is eager to get Agata and his mother off to church in order to be alone with Maria. They have a tender scene together, even though Agata has spoken against Maria to Donato and predicted his ultimate disappointment. Maria

212

tells him of her affectionate relationship with a young man the past summer, and Donato feels that she toyed with him the same way she is toying with Donato. She, however, declares her undying love for Donato.

ACT II

SCENE 1—The terrace of the villa. Late afternoon, midsummer.

At a prison at the bottom of the hill the alarm has been sounded. Agata and Donato speak of the possibility of a prisoner having escaped. The prisoner enters, and Agata gives him a place to hide. She also tells Donato that a letter has come to Maria from Aldo (the young friend of the summer before). She points out to Donato that Maria has other admirers. He is worried and finally convinced that Maria is unfaithful to him. A scene between Donato and his mother underlines the mutual dependence of the two upon each other. The act ends with Agata, Maria, the mother, and Donato singing together of their loneliness and their wish to recapture their youth. Donato foresees trouble and compares the three women to the three fates.

SCENE 2—The same. That night.

The little boy, Trottolo, is sent off to a costume party next door, and Maria and Donato talk. He tells her his love for her is over. Finally the reasons are revealed, and Maria has Agata come in and read the letter aloud. Maria admits to lying about who the letter was from, but only to protect Donato. He forgives her and begs her never to leave him. The prisoner enters and is about to leave, telling Donato that he has overheard the conversation and doesn't feel sorry for him any longer. He then defends himself by saying that reason has nothing to do with the human

heart. The prisoner then gives Donato a gun and runs off to escape the searchers.

ACT III

SCENE 1—The living room. Afternoon, early fall.

The mother and Zuckertanz are reading through some old music, and Maria joins them to sing too. Maria then receives word of the release of her husband. In a scene between Maria and Donato, he asks her if she will tell her husband how things are between them.

SCENE 2—The same. Evening, a week later.

The prisoners are heard singing down the hill. The mother and Maria talk of a small welcoming party for relatives and her husband. When will she be leaving? She is not sure, but the mother thinks she should leave soon. Neither of the women wishes to tell Donato this, and finally the mother asks forgiveness for being so rude. Donato and Maria meet, and she assures him she'll return to him right after the party.

SCENE 3—The same. A few hours later.

It is late at night and the mother urges Donato to go to bed, but he asks to be left alone and waits for Maria. He listens to the party music. When Maria arrives, he is bitter and accuses her of not thinking of him. She argues with him and finally tells him that this is goodbye. He refuses to let her go and calls for his mother to help him. She comes and helps him point the gun at a blank wall and fire it. He thinks he has killed Maria and goes to place a flower on her body. The mother leads him off, telling him they will leave and never come back to this house, and Maria picks up the flower and goes upstairs as she is called.

Maria Stuarda

-»»*«««-

MUSIC BY: Gaetano Donizetti

WORLD PREMIERE: Milan, Italy,
    December 30, 1835

LIBRETTO BY: Giuseppe Bardari
Based on Friedrich von Schiller's play
NEW YORK CITY PREMIERE:
    (Sung in Italian) March 7, 1972

CONDUCTOR: Charles Wilson
PRODUCTION DEVISED AND DIRECTED BY: Tito Capobianco
SCENIC DESIGNER: Ming Cho Lee
COSTUMES: José Varona

CHARACTERS (In order of appearance)	VOICE (type)	PREMIERE CAST (New York City Opera)
Court Herald	Baritone	Joseph Galiano
Elisabetta, Queen of England	Soprano	Pauline Tinsley (debut)
Talbot, Earl of Shrewsbury	Baritone	Richard Fredricks
Cecil, Lord Burghley	Bass-baritone	Michael Devlin
Roberto Dudley, Earl of Leicester	Tenor	John Stewart
Maria Stuarda, Queen of Scots	Soprano	Beverly Sills
Anna Kennedy	Contralto	Deborah Keiffer

Courtiers, Officials, Guards, Jousters, Attendants of Elizabeth and Mary

SYNOPSIS OF STORY
TIME AND PLACE: England, 16th century

*

ACT I

SCENE—Court of Elisabetta I

Elisabetta (Queen Elizabeth I) wonders whether she can in good conscience marry the Duke of Anjou, when she in fact loves Leicester. Talbot suggests that the only thing clouding her happiness is the fate of Maria Stuarda (Mary Stuart, Queen of Scots), but Cecil advises her against pity. Talbot gives Leicester a portrait and letter from Maria. Reminded of Maria's beauty by her portrait, Leicester reflects on his love for her. Elisabetta accuses Leicester of loving the Queen of Scots; hoping for clemency, he shows her the letter, which only arouses her jealousy. He asks her to grant Maria an audience and the Queen agrees, mostly with the intention of humiliating Maria.

ACT II

SCENE—Confrontation at Fotheringay Park

Maria and her companion, Anna, are enjoying

a brief walk she is allowed each day while imprisoned. She recalls happier days and is then disturbed when the arrival of Queen Elisabetta is announced. Leicester reassures her and prepares her for the meeting; they express their feelings for each other. When Elisabetta arrives, Leicester again asks for pardon, but Cecil is against it. Elisabetta comments that the prisoner is as proud as ever. Maria's pleas are answered by abuse from Elisabetta, which eventually provokes Maria to insult the Queen. Elisabetta condemns Maria to death, which dismays Leicester and Talbot but pleases Cecil. Maria herself is elated at having triumphed, if only momentarily, over the Queen.

ACT III

SCENE 1—The Sentence

Elisabetta delays signing Maria's death warrant, fearing the hostility it may cause at home and abroad, but Cecil urges her to go ahead. At Leicester's arrival and subsequent pleas for mercy, her jealousy is again aroused and she finally signs the document. Leicester finds it is too late to save Maria's life; Cecil praises the day as the most beautiful one for the English throne; and Elisabetta orders Leicester to witness the execution.

SCENE 2—The Confession

Maria is informed of her impending death and offered the services of a minister, but she refuses to hear the words of Protestant faith. She asks for Talbot (in reality a Catholic priest), who comforts her and takes her confession. Talbot gives her absolution before leading her away.

SCENE 3—The Execution

Anna and other friends of the Queen of Scots lament Maria's imminent death. When she enters in regal attire she urges them to have faith in divine justice and prays. The first of three cannon shots announcing the execution rings out. In a mood of resignation, Maria asks Cecil to tell Elisabetta she has forgiven her. Leicester comes in, which greatly disturbs Maria. She says a few words of comfort to him before the third shot is heard, then, making a final declaration of her innocence, walks to the scaffold.

The Marriage of Figaro

→))) * (((←

MUSIC BY: Wolfgang Amadeus Mozart

WORLD PREMIERE: Vienna, Austria,
   May 1, 1786

LIBRETTO BY: Lorenzo Da Ponte
English version by Ruth and Thomas Martin
NEW YORK CITY OPERA PREMIERE:
   (Sung in English) October 14, 1948

CONDUCTOR: Joseph Rosenstock (debut)
STAGE DIRECTOR: Leopold Sachse
SCENIC DESIGNER: H. A. Condell
COSTUMES*
CHOREOGRAPHY: George Balanchine

CHARACTERS (In order of appearance)	VOICE (type)	PREMIERE CAST (New York City Opera)
Figaro	Baritone	James Pease
Susanna	Soprano	Virginia MacWatters
Dr. Bartolo	Bass	Richard Wentworth
Marcellina	Mezzo	Mary Kreste
Cherubino	Mezzo	Frances Bible
Count Almaviva	Baritone	Walter Cassel
Don Basilio	Tenor	Luigi Vellucci (debut)
Countess Almaviva	Soprano	Frances Yeend
Antonio	Bass	Arthur Newman
Don Curzio	Tenor	George Vincent
Barbarina	Soprano	Dorothy MacNeil
Two Peasant Girls	Speaking	Joyce White
		Harriet Greene

Servants, Guests

SYNOPSIS OF STORY

TIME AND PLACE: The Count's castle of Aguas Frescas, near Seville, in the early 18th century

*

ACT I

SCENE—A room in the castle

Figaro, Count Almaviva's valet, and Susanna, the Countess' maid, are to be married and are preparing the room they are to occupy after the wedding. In the midst of their preparations, various characters are introduced. Dr. Bartolo and his housekeeper, Marcellina, appear; Bartolo wishes to get even with Figaro for a past debt,

---

* Executed by Kate Friedheim.

216

The Marriage of Figaro, 1977. Left to right: Catherine Malfitano, Samuel Ramey, Johanna Meier, William Justis.

while Marcellina is in love with Figaro even though she is old enough to be his mother. Cherubino, a young page, appears on the scene and confides in Susanna as to his loves, and in particular his love for the Countess. As the Count appears, Cherubino hides, and the Count flirts with Susanna. This, however, is interrupted by the music master, Don Basilio, and thus the Count must hide. Amid all this confusion, gossip from Basilio indicates Cherubino's fondness for the Countess; the Count appears, as does Cherubino, and Cherubino is inducted into the armed services as the act ends.

the Count, and the Countess is then to surprise her husband. As the preparations for the plot are taking place and Cherubino is dressing as a woman, the Count is heard approaching. In the confusion, Cherubino hides in the next room. The Count hears a noise and demands to have the door opened. As he goes for tools to open the door, Susanna changes places with Cherubino, who escapes out the window. After all the confusion, and forgiveness, the Count is still suspicious as the act ends.

ACT II

SCENE—The Countess' boudoir

The Countess, Susanna, and Figaro plot to embarrass the Count for his misbehavior with Susanna, and they write a note to the Count inviting him to meet Susanna in the garden alone. In the disguise of a woman, Cherubino is to meet

ACT III

SCENE 1—The Countess' boudoir
SCENE 2—Judicial chamber of the castle
SCENE 3—The Countess' boudoir
SCENE 4—Main stairway leading to the chapel of the castle

Marcellina, having decided to marry Figaro herself, has Don Curzio, a lawyer, inform Figaro

217

that he must marry her because of the debt he owes her. Figaro, of course, protests, stating that he needs the consent of his unknown parents, who turn out to be Marcellina and Dr. Bartolo. As the confusion carries on, preparations for a double wedding are now the order of business. Figaro is to marry Susanna and Bartolo, Marcellina. In the meantime, the Count has received the letter supposedly from Susanna to meet her in the garden. The scene ends with the rejoicing of the happy couples and the Count's meeting.

ACT IV

SCENE—The garden of the castle

At night, in the garden, there is total confusion as the women exchange costumes. Thus Susanna dresses as the Countess and the Countess dresses as Susanna. Amid all this disguise the Count is shown up as having made a fool of himself and in a noble melody begs pardon of his wronged and neglected wife. The opera ends on a note of rejoicing by everyone.

Martha

-))) * (((-

MUSIC BY: Friedrich von Flotow

WORLD PREMIERE: Vienna, Austria,
November 25, 1847

LIBRETTO BY: W. Friedrich
Adapted for the American stage
by Vicki Baum and Ann Ronell
NEW YORK CITY OPERA PREMIERE:
(Sung in English) February 22, 1944

CONDUCTOR: Laszlo Halasz
STAGE DIRECTOR: Hans Wolmut
SCENIC ADVISER and DESIGNER: Richard Rychtarik*
COSTUMES†

CHARACTERS (In order of appearance)	VOICE (type)	PREMIERE CAST (New York City Opera)
Nancy	Mezzo	Suzanne Sten (debut)
Lady Harriet	Soprano	Ethel Barrymore Colt (debut)
Lord Tristram	Bass	Stanley Carlson (debut)
Plunkett	Baritone	Robert Brink (debut)
Lionel	Tenor	Edward Kane (debut)
Sheriff	Bass	Ralph Leonard (debut)
Farmer	(unavailable)	Carl Norse (debut)
Farmer's wife	Soprano	Sally Aronovich (debut)
Three maids	Soprano	Helen LeClaire (debut)
	Soprano	Thorold Crossdale (debut)
	Mezzo	Ella Mayer (debut)
Four flunkeys	Tenors	David Osen (debut)
	and	Philip Marantz (debut)
	Baritones	Al Shapiro (debut)
		Michael Guida (debut)

Villagers, Ladies-in-Waiting

SYNOPSIS OF STORY
TIME AND PLACE: Richmond Town and County in England, 1712

*

* Scenery loaned by St. Louis Grand Opera Association.
† Miss Colt's First Act costume designed by Frank Brady. Costumes furnished by Van Horn & Son.

ACT I

SCENE 1—The Royal Garden near Richmond

Lady Harriet Durham (maid-of-honor to Queen Anne), tired of the luxury of her life and annoyed with the attentions that her cousin Sir Tristram showers upon her, holds court at the Royal Gardens. When she discovers that a Fair is being held in nearby Richmond, she and her companion, Nancy, decide to disguise themselves as country girls and go there with Sir Tristram as their escort.

SCENE 2—The Fair at Richmond

At the traditional Fair at Richmond, where farmers come to hire maids, Plunkett and Lionel, two young farmers, are looking for a maid to do the work that is needed since the death of their mother. Lionel is Plunkett's foster-brother; his father had come to the Plunkett farm as a refugee and died there, leaving his infant son nothing but a ring, which is supposed to be shown to the Queen in case of danger. The two young farmers are attracted by Harriet and Nancy and hire them. The girls take it all as a game, but when Sir Tristram finally persuades them to leave, they find they are actually bonded in service by law. The two masters drive off with them, notwithstanding Sir Tristram's protests.

ACT II

SCENE—Plunkett's farm

Plunkett and Lionel and their newly hired maids, who call themselves Martha and Julia, arrive at the farm and encounter all sorts of diffi-culties. The girls are embarrassed—they have never worked in their lives; at the same time, they fall in love with their masters—and vice versa. After Lionel and Plunkett have gone to sleep, Sir Tristram appears and helps the girls to escape.

ACT III

SCENE—The Royal Hunting Grounds

The Queen and her entourage are roaming the forests of the Royal Hunting Grounds. Harriet separates from the rest of the hunters, sadly thinking of Lionel. Yet when they meet by chance, she saves face by declaring that she has never seen him before. Lionel, realizing the game, tries to tell the truth and is arrested. At this dangerous moment he remembers his father's ring, which Plunkett hands over to the Queen.

ACT IV

SCENE—Richmond Square

Harriet has come to find Plunkett and Lionel at Richmond Square. Plunkett and Nancy tell her that Lionel, who has been freed meanwhile, refuses to talk to her. She begs Lionel's forgiveness, reveals his real rank and name (Earl of Derby), and offers him her hand. Lionel refuses in pride. Harriet realizes that she can win him only by humbling herself. With the help of the gentlemen and ladies of the court, she has a replica of the Richmond Fair built on the square, and she herself changes back into maid Martha. Now Lionel cannot resist any longer, and the opera finale unites two happy couples.

Medea

-»»*«««-

MUSIC BY: Luigi Cherubini
Revised by Vito Frazzi and Tullio Serafin
WORLD PREMIERE: Paris, France,
   March 13, 1797

LIBRETTO BY: François Benoit Hoffmann

NEW YORK CITY OPERA PREMIERE:
   (Sung in Italian) March 7, 1974

CONDUCTOR: Giuseppe Morelli
STAGE DIRECTOR: Frank Corsaro
SCENERY and COSTUMES: Lloyd Evans

CHARACTERS (In order of appearance)	VOICE (type)	PREMIERE CAST (New York City Opera)
Glauce, daughter of Creon	Soprano	Emily Derr
Two attendants of Glauce	Soprano	Diane Kehrig
	Mezzo	Puli Toro
Creon, King of Corinth	Bass	Richard T. Gill
Jason	Tenor	Dean Wilder (debut)
Children of Medea	Mute	William Ledbetter, Jr.
	Mute	Thomas Brennan
Neris, Medea's companion and the children's nurse	Mezzo	Frances Bible
Medea	Soprano	Maralin Niska
Medea's attendants	Mute	Miguel Lopez (debut)
		Michael Rubino

Corinthians, Argonauts, Warriors, Servants, Priests

SYNOPSIS OF STORY
TIME AND PLACE: Corinth, in antiquity

*

INTRODUCTION

Jason sailed on his ship, the Argo, from Thessaly to Colchis in search of the Golden Fleece. Medea, daughter of the King, fell in love with Jason and used her sorceress' powers as a descendant of the Sun God to help him secure the Golden Fleece. Later the ambitious Jason abandoned Medea and fled with the children to Corinth. There he courted Glauce, the daughter of King Creon.

ACT I

SCENE—Before the Temple of Hymen, morning
   On the eve of her wedding to Jason, Glauce

221

cannot rid herself of her great fear of Medea, although the women of her court reassure her. The Corinthians, who hate and fear Medea, want to kill her children; Creon reassures Jason that they will come to no harm. When the Argonauts enter with the Golden Fleece, Glauce is frightened; Jason vows to protect her, and Creon asks the blessings of the gods. Medea appears, determined to stop at nothing to prevent Jason from marrying Glauce, despite any punishment Creon threatens if she does not leave the city immediately. Alone with Jason, Medea reminds him of all that she has sacrificed for his love, but Jason refuses to be moved. Both blame the Golden Fleece for their misfortunes.

ACT II

SCENE—Same, early afternoon

Although the Corinthians are shouting for Medea's blood, she persuades Creon to allow her to remain in the city for one more day. Neris, the children's nurse and Medea's long-time companion, declares her loyalty to her unhappy mistress. Reviving from her exhaustion, Medea is seized with visions of vengeance concerning the children. She tricks Jason into allowing her to see their sons and sends Neris for them. She plans that they will present Glauce with a wedding present, a diadem that will burst into flame when placed upon the unsuspecting bride's head. As the procession moves into the temple, Medea watches unobserved.

ACT III

SCENE—Same, later the same day

Medea invokes the aid of the gods in her plan of revenge. When Neris brings the children to her, she pushes them away because they remind her too much of Jason. Torn between her affection for the children and the painful memories they evoke, she finally permits Neris to take them away from her and into the temple. Jason is heard lamenting over the body of Glauce, burned to death by Medea's deadly gift. Deciding now not to spare the children, Medea rushes into the temple to complete her revenge. Before Jason and the townspeople discover Medea's intentions from Neris, Medea murders the children and sets fire to the temple.

La Belle Hélène

Le Coq d'Or
Beverly Sills, Norman Treigle

Dido and Aeneas
David Holloway, Sandra Browne

Don Rodrigo
Placido Domingo

Giulio Cesare
Norman Treigle, Beverly Sills, William Ledbetter

The Love for Three Oranges

Madama Butterfly
Beverly Evans, Patricia Craig, Seymour Schwartzman

Magic Flute
John Stewart, Noel Mangin, Veronica Tyler

Monon
Beverly Sills

Mefistofele
Norman Treigle

Natalia Petrovna
John Reardon, Patricia Brooks, Muriel Costa Greenspon

The Nightingale
Patricia Brooks

Pelléas et Mélisande
Andre Jobin, Patricia Brooks

Il Ritorno d'Ulisse in Patria
Hilda Harris, Henry Price, Richard Stillwell

Der Rosenkavalier
Frances Bible

Turandot
Rachel Mathas

The Medium

→))⟩∗(((←

MUSIC BY: Gian Carlo Menotti
WORLD PREMIERE: New York, New York,
   May 8, 1946

LIBRETTO BY: Gian Carlo Menotti
NEW YORK CITY OPERA PREMIERE:
   (Sung in English) April 7, 1949

CONDUCTOR: Joseph Rosenstock
STAGE DIRECTOR: Gian Carlo Menotti
SCENIC DESIGNER: H. A. Condell
COSTUMES*

CHARACTERS (In order of appearance)	VOICE (type)	PREMIERE CAST (New York City Opera)
Monica, daughter of Madama Flora	Soprano	Evelyn Keller
Toby	Mute	Leo Coleman (debut)
Madama Flora (Baba)	Contralto	Marie Powers
Mrs. Gobineau	Soprano	Leona Scheunemann
Mr. Gobineau	Baritone	Edwin Dunning
Mrs. Nolan	Mezzo	Frances Bible

SYNOPSIS OF STORY
TIME AND PLACE: Outside a large city; today

∗

ACT I

SCENE—Madama Flora's parlor, evening

In Madama Flora's cluttered apartment the mute Toby plays in an old trunk, dressing up in odd bits of clothing. Monica, who is combing her hair, joins him, warning him of her mother's anger. Soon Baba, Monica's mother, does appear to scold them and urge them to prepare for the seance.

When the doorbell rings, Toby and Monica disappear to play their parts in the seance, and the clients enter. Baba moans during the seance and Monica, hidden, imitates a small child's voice and speaks to the visitors, who are the par-ents of a dead girl. Suddenly Baba feels something in the dark. She turns on the lights and, frightened, asks the clients to leave. Monica tries to comfort her, but she still hears the child's voice. Toby goes downstairs to investigate, but no one is there. Baba is still disturbed as Monica repeats a comforting ballad.

ACT II

SCENE—Evening, a few days later

Toby and Monica are playing and exchanging loving moments together. Baba, who has been drinking, interrupts them. She cannot forget the

---

* By Kate Friedheim.

incident of a hand touching her during the seance. She bribes and later threatens Toby into admitting that it was he who touched her, but he will not respond. Finally in a fit of temper she grabs a whip and uses it on him.

When the parents of the dead child return, Baba tries to discourage them, stating that there will be no more seances. The visitors refuse to believe that it is all a fraud, even after the gimmicks of the seance are pointed out. Baba throws their money on the table, and they are pushed out the door, still willing to believe in the seance. Now Baba drives Toby out of the house despite Monica's pleas, and she locks Monica in her room. Baba then sings of her fear of the voices and finally falls into a drunken sleep.

As she sleeps, Toby returns quietly to look in the trunk. When he finishes, the lid falls noisily and he jumps behind the puppet theater curtains. Baba awakes, terrified. She calls out, "Who's there?" and notices the curtains moving. She fires into them and Toby falls forward into the room, tangled in the curtains. She unlocks Monica's door and then kneels over Toby's body with Monica, wondering if the hand in the dark was his.

Mefistofele

→))) * (((←

MUSIC BY: Arrigo Boito
WORLD PREMIERE: Milan, Italy,
   March 5, 1868

LIBRETTO BY: Arrigo Boito
NEW YORK CITY OPERA PREMIERE:
   (Sung in Italian) September 21, 1969

CONDUCTOR: Julius Rudel
PRODUCTION DEVISED and DIRECTED BY: Tito Capobianco
SCENIC DESIGNER: David Mitchell (debut)
COSTUMES: Hal George (debut)
CHOREOGRAPHER: Robert Joffrey

CHARACTERS (In order of appearance)	VOICE (type)	PREMIERE CAST (New York City Opera)
Mefistofele	Bass	Norman Treigle
Faust	Tenor	Robert Nagy
Wagner	Tenor	John Lankston
Margherita	Soprano	Carol Neblett
Marta	Contralto	Beverly Evans
Elena	Soprano	Carol Neblett
Pantalis	Contralto	Mary Cross Lueders
Nereo	Tenor	John Lankston

Angels, Penitents, Peasants, Hunters, Students,
Townspeople, Nobles, Soldiers, Witches, Greek Men
and Women

SYNOPSIS OF STORY

TIME AND PLACE: Heaven, Germany, and Greece; medieval and ancient times

*

PROLOGUE

As heavenly choirs sing praises of the Creator, the discordant figure of Mefistofele appears to mock them. He feels that Man has become too weak to be worth tempting, so he eagerly accepts the challenge to lure even the devout scholar Faust to sin.

ACT I

SCENE 1—Easter

As Faust and his pupil Wagner wander through the rejoicing Easter crowds, Faust is troubled by the constant presence of a mysterious friar. Wagner tries to allay his fears, assuring him that there is nothing menacing in the friar's

225

appearance, but when they leave, the gray figure follows.

SCENE 2—Faust's studio

Alone in his study, the aging scholar's contemplation of nature's goodness inspires him to read his Bible. A sudden outcry discloses the friar hidden in a corner, who then identifies himself as the Spirit of Denial. In return for Mefistofele's promise to show him the one perfect moment of happiness that he seeks, Faust agrees to surrender his soul.

ACT II

SCENE 1—Marta's garden

Hoping to find contentment through romantic love, Faust (transformed into a youthful cavalier) courts the innocent country girl Margherita while Mefistofele diverts the attention of her companion Marta. So that they can later meet alone, Faust gives Margherita a supposedly harmless sleeping potion (supplied by Mefistofele) for her mother.

SCENE 2—Witches' Sabbath

Mefistofele leads Faust to a jagged mountain peak, where he witnesses the ritual of the Witches' Sabbath, a scene of demonic revelry and adulation of the Prince of Darkness. Amid the chaos created by Mefistofele, an apparition of Margherita in chains alarms Faust.

SCENE 3—Prison

Margherita, dazed and frightened, lies imprisoned for the murder of her mother and of the child she bore Faust. At first she does not recognize Faust when he tries to help her escape, but her mind clears and she then listens as he urges her to flee with him. When Mefistofele appears, she turns away from them both. Her dying pleas to Heaven for forgiveness are answered, and Faust must depart alone with Mefistofele.

ACT III

SCENE—Classical Sabbath

Faust is transported to a setting of classical enchantment presided over by the legendary symbol of beauty, Helen of Troy. Faust believes he will at last find, through Elena's love, the happiness of a perfect life.

EPILOGUE

Faust has once again grown old, yet has failed to find perfection in either the real or the ideal world. As Mefistofele waits anxiously to claim his soul, Faust finally sees a vision of the perfect life. As he prays fervently for salvation, the heavenly choirs aid him in the ultimate struggle for his soul.

Die Meistersinger

→»*«←

MUSIC BY: Richard Wagner
WORLD PREMIERE: Munich, Germany,
  June 21, 1868

LIBRETTO BY: Richard Wagner
NEW YORK CITY OPERA PREMIERE:
  (Sung in German) October 13, 1950

CONDUCTOR: Joseph Rosenstock
STAGE DIRECTOR: Otto Erhardt (debut)
SCENIC DESIGNER: H. A. Condell
ARTISTIC COUNSELOR: Friedrich Schorr (debut)
BALLET CHOREOGRAPHER: Charles Weidman
COSTUMES*

CHARACTERS (In order of appearance)	VOICE (type)	PREMIERE CAST (New York City Opera)
Eva, Pogner's daughter	Soprano	Frances Yeend
Magdalena, Eva's nurse	Mezzo	Margery Mayer
Walter Von Stolzing, a young knight	Tenor	Hans Beirer
David, apprentice to Sachs	Tenor	David Lloyd (debut)
Veit Pogner, Goldsmith	Bass	Oscar Natzka
Sixtus Beckmesser, Town Clerk	Bass-baritone	Emile Renan
Kunz Vogelgesang, Furrier	Tenor	Nino Luciano
Konrad Nachtigall, Tinsmith	Bass	Arthur Newman
Fritz Kothner, Baker	Bass	Richard Wentworth
Hermann Ortel, Soap Boiler	Bass	Thomas Powell
Balthazar Zorn, Pewterer	Tenor	Sumner Crockett (debut)
Augustin Moser, Tailor	Tenor	Nathaniel Sprinzena
Ulrich Eisslinger, Grocer	Tenor	Luigi Vellucci
Hans Foltz, Coppersmith	Bass	George Jongeyans
Hans Schwarz, Stocking Weaver	Bass	Luis Pichardo (debut)
Hans Sachs, Cobbler	Bass	James Pease
Night Watchman	Bass	Lawrence Winters

Citizens of Nuremberg, Apprentices

SYNOPSIS OF STORY
TIME AND PLACE: Nuremberg, 16th century

*

---

* The costumes, designed for a 1938 Chicago production of *Die Meistersinger,* were loaned by the Chicago Civic Opera. James Pease's costumes, however, were loaned by Friedrich Schorr.

Die Meistersinger, 1975. Left to right: Norman Bailey, Johanna Meier, John Alexander, and members of the ensemble.

ACT I

SCENE—Interior of St. Catherine's Church

The young knight Walter tries to attract the attention of Eva, daughter of the Mastersinger Pogner, who, accompanied by her nurse, Magdalena, is among the worshippers. After the congregation has left, Walter learns from Eva that her father has promised her hand as prize to the Mastersinger who wins the singing contest to be held the following day. Walter, anxious to compete, remains and is briefed by David, Magdalena's admirer, in the rules of the Mastersingers.

The Mastersingers assemble, among them Beckmesser, an elderly bachelor and a candidate for Eva's hand. Pogner officially announces the prize. Walter attempts to demonstrate his talents to the assembly. He fails completely in the estimation of the pedantic masters, convincing only Hans Sachs, the dean and greatest of the Masters, that he is a true poet.

ACT II

SCENE—Street, the houses of Sachs and Pogner in the foreground

Sachs is approached by Eva, who wishes to learn how Walter fared. Sachs shrewdly makes her believe that he shares the general opinion, and Eva leaves angrily. Although the middle-aged Sachs, a widower, loves Eva, he now decides to foster the young people's romance. Walter appears and, in desperation because of his failure, persuades Eva to flee with him. Beckmesser arrives to serenade Eva, and Sachs, by singing and hammering loudly, completely upsets his song, a ruse calculated to hinder the lovers' flight. David, awakened by Beckmesser's singing, thinks the serenade is meant for Magdalena, who has appeared at Eva's window, and gives Beckmesser a sound beating. A general melee ensues, finally dispersed by the nightwatchman's horn. Sachs pushes Walter into his house, and Eva into hers.

ACT III

SCENE 1—Sachs' workroom

Walter enters, and Sachs encourages him to compose a master-song under his guidance. Walter puts into words a dream he had during the night, improvising the melody, while Sachs writes down the poem. Then both leave to change into festival dress. Beckmesser enters, finds the poem on the table, and puts it in his pocket. Sachs returns and presents the angry Beckmesser with the poem. Beckmesser leaves, overjoyed, thinking that it is by Sachs and planning to use it as his contest song. Eva enters, and later Walter.

She now realizes Sachs' generous plan. Sachs "baptizes" the new master-song, and the party leaves cheerfully for the Festival Meadow.

SCENE 2—The Festival Meadow

The guilds arrive in splendor. Beckmesser is the first contestant and fails miserably in his attempt to sing the stolen song, distorting the words and music. Sachs calls a witness to testify, and Walter, singing the song correctly, thus proves his authorship. He wins easily and receives his Mastersingership, and with it, Eva's hand.

The Merry Widow

-»)»*«(«-

MUSIC BY: Franz Lehár
WORLD PREMIERE: New York, New York,
   October 21, 1907

LIBRETTO BY: Adrian Ross
NEW YORK CITY OPERA PREMIERE:
   (Sung in English) October 27, 1957

CONDUCTOR: Franz Allers
STAGE DIRECTOR: Glen Jordan
SCENIC DESIGNER: George Jenkins (debut)
COSTUMES: (unavailable)
CHOREOGRAPHY: Robert Joffrey

CHARACTERS (In order of appearance)	VOICE (type)	PREMIERE CAST (New York City Opera)
Raoul de St. Brioche	Baritone	John Reardon
Natalie, wife of Baron Popoff	Soprano	Peggy Bonini
Mme. Khadja	Soprano	Helen Baisley
Mme. Novikovich	Soprano	Lu Leonard
Vicomte Camille de Jolidon	Tenor	William Lewis
Admiral Khadja	Bass-baritone	Arthur Newman
Marquis de Cascada	Baritone	Herbert Beattie
General Novikovich	Bass	Richard Wentworth
Mme. Sonia Sodoya (the widow)	Soprano	Beverly Sills
Prince Danilo	Tenor	Robert Rounseville
Lo-Lo	Soprano	Naomi Collier
Solo Dancers	Dancers	Beatrice Tompkins
		Dianne Consoer
		Gerald Arpino
Baron Popoff	Speaking	Hiram Sherman
Nish	Actor	Coley Worth
King	Baritone	George Del Monte

Note: The last performance of the New York City Opera in the old City Center Theater was that of *The Merry Widow* on November 1, 1965. Julius Rudel was on stage as an extra in the final scene, and the company and audience sang "Auld Lang Syne."

SYNOPSIS OF STORY
TIME AND PLACE: Paris; late 19th century

*

PROLOGUE*

SCENE—Baron Popoff's study

The Baron is bemoaning his country's bankrupt condition. If only Prince Danilo would return and rekindle his romance with the wealthy widow Mme. Sonia Sodoya!

ACT I

SCENE—The reception room in the Marsovian Embassy, Paris

Baron Popoff is hosting a party for his countrymen and Parisian society to celebrate the birthday of Marsovia's Prince. Everyone is awaiting the arrival of the lovely and wealthy widow Sonia Sodoya. She has inherited a fortune and because of this is doubly attractive to all the men except the French nobleman Camille de Jolidon. He would rather continue his affair with Natalie, Baron Popoff's wife. The Baron is oblivious to his wife's caprice—he is too concerned that Sonia's money not fall into foreign hands. She must marry the dashing Marsovian Prince Danilo.

When Sonia arrives, she is flattered by the attention she receives but sees it merely as an attempt to win her money. She invites everyone to her house the following day for a truly Marsovian party and goes off for some champagne.

Danilo is late in arriving. He has been at Maxim's dancing with the famous Can-Can girls to relieve the boredom of embassy life.

Sonia returns and hears someone snoring. She discovers Danilo, who has fallen asleep, and laughs. He is embarrassed and says he regrets not having married her years earlier as he had wanted to. But as she wasn't of noble blood then, his family would have objected. Since she is wealthy, doesn't that make a difference? No, it doesn't. He will never marry her, he says, and goes off, leaving her alone to wonder if he is the man of her dreams.

Natalie, meanwhile, has devised a masterful plan: Camille should marry Sonia. In this way she, Natalie, will not have to worry about a scandal should she continue her affair with Camille. Camille protests, but when ladies' choice is announced, Natalie proposes him as Sonia's partner.

---

* Only the early production included a Prologue.

Danilo, in the meantime, has found plenty of girls to fulfill the other men's dancing desires; but only by buying the dance himself for 10,000 francs is he able to stop their advances upon Sonia. Camille is prepared to pay the price, but the now jealous Natalie stops him. Left alone with Sonia, Danilo sweeps her into his arms to the refrain of a waltz.

ACT II

SCENE—Grounds of Sonia's house, near Paris

The Marsovians are singing and dancing their native songs. She recalls to them the childhood legend of the forest nymph, Vilja, and all join in her refrain. While applauding, Natalie drops her fan.

As the guests go into the house for dinner, Danilo enters. Sonia accuses him of avoiding her, but he says he is employing a kind of military strategy. They sing a duet about the kind of game love can become. Sonia goes to join her guests, and Danilo discovers Natalie's fan. He reads, "I love you," Camille's message to Natalie, and decides to use the fan to test his prowess with the embassy officials' wives. They are indeed delighted, although their husbands are quite upset. Danilo tells the men they must learn to handle women.

Danilo is alone when Sonia reenters. She takes the fan, reads the message, and thanks Danilo for such a nice present. They begin to dance, and Sonia drops the fan. She and Danilo waltz off as Natalie and Camille enter. Natalie is desperate to find her fan. Suddenly they both see the fan Sonia has dropped, and before anything else can happen, Natalie writes on it, "To my husband from his faithful wife." Camille is upset until she agrees to have a last tête-à-tête with him in the garden pavilion.

Popoff enters, having arranged an appointment with Prince Danilo concerning his marrying Sonia. The appointment is to take place in the pavilion, but Nish sees that Natalie is there with Camille. The Baron is impatient for the meeting to begin and peers through the keyhole. He is shocked to see his wife, but Nish quickly exchanges her for Sonia. The Baron demands that the door be opened, and Sonia and Camille slip out. Sonia decides to play the game to its fullest and announces that she will marry Camille. Popoff is despondent: Sonia's money will now go to a Parisian; Marsovia will fall. Natalie is deeply hurt. Camille had no idea, and objects. But Sonia silences him. Danilo can't stand it. He tells Sonia she is like any common woman, ready to have the first man who comes along. He rushes off to Maxim's. Sonia exults! She knows he is hers.

ACT III

SCENE—Maxim's restaurant, Paris

Sonia rents Maxim's for the evening so she can see the "real" Danilo. He is there with the Can-Can girls, as are Popoff and Nish.

Danilo is upset when he sees Sonia there. She tells him it would be nice for them to go and have some supper in a separate room. Maybe they could confess their . . . but she breaks off. Pride has the better of them both; and yet in the famous waltz they decide to forget such pride and confess their love. Popoff and the others return, delighted that Sonia will marry Danilo after all. Nish brings in a fan he has found in the pavilion, and when Natalie claims it as hers, Popoff demands to see it. He reads, "To my husband from his faithful wife" and forgets his suspicions. Everyone joins Sonia as she warns men studying women to beware.

The Merry Wives of Windsor

-»»∗«««-

MUSIC BY: Otto Nicolai

WORLD PREMIERE: Berlin, Germany,
   March 9, 1849

LIBRETTO BY: Hermann Salomon Mosenthal
English version by Josef Blatt
NEW YORK CITY OPERA PREMIERE:
   (Sung in English) March 31, 1955

CONDUCTOR: Joseph Rosenstock
STAGE DIRECTOR: Vladimir Rosing
SCENIC DESIGNER: John Boyt*
COSTUMES: John Boyt*
CHOREOGRAPHER: John Butler

CHARACTERS (In order of appearance)	VOICE (type)	PREMIERE CAST (New York City Opera)
Mistress Ford	Soprano	Phyllis Curtin
Mistress Page	Mezzo	Edith Evans
Mr. Ford	Baritone	William Shriner
Mr. Page	Bass	Leon Lishner
Slender	Tenor	Michael Pollock
Dr. Caius	Bass	John Reardon
Fenton	Tenor	Jon Crain
Sir John Falstaff	Bass	William Wilderman
Host	Tenor	Thomas Powell
Citizen	Tenor	Charles Kuestner
Anne Page	Soprano	Peggy Bonini
	Villagers	

SYNOPSIS OF STORY

TIME AND PLACE: England, during the reign of King Henry IV

∗

ACT I

SCENE 1—Outside Mr. Ford's house

In the courtyard between the houses of Mistress Ford (Alice) and Mistress Page (Meg), the two ladies discover that they have received identical crude love letters from Sir John Falstaff, a rotund, middle-aged knight. They decide to get even with him and make plans to teach him a lesson. Meg's husband is concerned about a suitable marriage for his daughter, Anne. Two suitors, Slender, a rich but timid and foolish man, who

---

* John Boyt's sets and costumes for his 1954 production of *Falstaff* were utilized.

The Merry Wives of Windsor, 1955.

is the choice of Page, and the bumbling Dr. Caius, who is Mistress Page's preference as a son-in-law, appear with Page and Ford. When the penniless Fenton, who is Anne's favorite, comes to ask her father for her hand, he is rudely rejected—but not discouraged.

SCENE 2—Mr. Ford's house

Alice and Meg send an anonymous letter to Ford telling him of Alice's rendezvous. Meg hides, and Alice admits Sir John. Almost immediately, Meg announces that Ford is returning home, and Falstaff, in an attempt to hide, is persuaded to be stuffed into a laundry basket, which is soon thrown into the river. The women's plan works perfectly. When Ford does return, he brings his neighbors with him and angrily searches for his wife's lover, but finds no one.

ACT II

SCENE 1—Tavern

At the Garter Inn, Ford in disguise pretends to seek Sir John's help in gaining favor with Mistress Ford. He discovers that Sir John had been at the Ford house the previous day and that he has been invited back again that afternoon.

SCENE 2—Mr. Ford's house

In a garden, Anne's two unwanted suitors, Slender and Caius, unknown to each other, plan to meet her during her daily walk, but they are forced to hide when Fenton arrives with Anne. The two lovers reaffirm their affection, unaware that they are being watched.

Back in the Ford house, shortly after Alice has received Sir John, Meg reports the unexpected approach of Alice's husband. This time the two women quickly disguise the knight as an old woman—a sorceress who is a relative of Alice's maid. Ford, who has forbidden the old sorceress to enter his house, takes out his anger on "her" and beats the "old woman" mercilessly, driving "her" away. Then he searches unsuccessfully for Sir John Falstaff.

234

ACT III

SCENE 1—Outside Mr. Ford's house

In the courtyard again, Alice and Meg have told their husbands about Sir John's identical letters, his visits, and his punishments. Ford is forgiven for his jealousy, and the two couples decide to play one more trick on the knight. There is to be a masquerade in Windsor Forest, and the wives send word to Falstaff that they will meet him there if he appears as the legendary hunter, Herne. Later, Mistress Page, alone with Anne, tells her that she is to wear a red costume so that Dr. Caius will be able to recognize her and to elope with her. Anne's father has a similar idea and informs her that she will wear a green costume so that Slender can find her and run off with her. Anne has a mind of her own and decides to give the costumes to the two suitors so that she can steal away with Fenton.

SCENE 2—Forest of Windsor

The townspeople are disguised as spirits of the forest and are waiting for Sir John. They hide. Falstaff appears dressed as Herne the Hunter, with large antlers on his head. Alice and Meg meet him as they have promised, but when the ghosts come noisily out of hiding, the women run away, leaving the terrified Sir John to face his tormentors alone. He tries in vain to hide, but he is pinched, stabbed, and mocked until he repents. Falstaff swears never again to indulge in amorous pursuits, the masqueraders are revealed, and the opera ends on a note of laughter and merriment.

A Midsummer Night's Dream

-»»*«««-

MUSIC BY: Benjamin Britten

WORLD PREMIERE: Aldeburgh, England,
June 11, 1960

LIBRETTO BY: Benjamin Britten and
Peter Pears
Adapted from William Shakespeare
NEW YORK CITY OPERA PREMIERE:
(Sung in English) April 25, 1963

CONDUCTOR: Julius Rudel
STAGE DIRECTOR: William Ball
PRODUCTION DESIGNED BY: Robert Fletcher
COSTUMES*

CHARACTERS (In order of appearance)	VOICE (type)	PREMIERE CAST (New York City Opera)
Oberon, King of the Fairies	Tenor	William McDonald (debut)
Tytania, Queen of the Fairies	Soprano	Nadja Witkowska
Puck	Speaking	Julian Miller (debut)
Theseus, Duke of Athens	Bass	Arnold Voketaitis
Hippolyta, Queen of the Amazons, betrothed to Theseus	Contralto	Tatiana Troyanos (debut)
Lysander	Tenor	Charles Hindsley (debut)
Demetrius, in love with Hermia	Baritone	David Clatworthy
Hermia, in love with Lysander	Mezzo	Marlena Kleinman
Helena, in love with Demetrius	Soprano	Marguerite Willauer
Bottom, a Weaver	Bass	Spiro Malas
Quince, a Carpenter	Bass	John Fiorito
Flute, a Bellows Mender	Tenor	Richard Krause
Snug, a Joiner	Bass	Richard Wentworth
Snout, a Tinker	Tenor	Howard Fried
Starveling, a Tailor	Baritone	David Smith
Fairies		

Note: Boys Choir from Epiphany Church trained by Mildred Hohner (debut).

SYNOPSIS OF STORY
TIME AND PLACE: The palace of Theseus and the wood; imaginary times

*

---

* Executed by Grace Costumes, Inc.

ACT I

SCENE—The wood, deepening twilight

It is dusk. The fairies and Puck appear in the wood and witness a violent quarrel between their leaders, Oberon and Tytania, over the disposition of Tytania's young page. When she refuses to yield to his wish and surrender the boy, Oberon plots to enchant Tytania in her sleep so that she will fall in love with the first vile creature she sees upon awakening.

Lysander and Hermia appear attempting to escape Hermia's unwanted suitor Demetrius, who presently enters followed by Helena, his own unwelcome admirer. Oberon, who overhears their talk while invisible, vows that Demetrius shall love Helena before the pair leave the wood, and Puck is dispatched with the love potion.

A band of Athenian workingmen arrive to plan a play they hope to present at Theseus' wedding. Hermia and Lysander return and presently fall asleep. Puck, mistaking Lysander for Demetrius, puts the love potion in his eyes, so that when he is awakened by Helena he immediately pursues her, leaving a bewildered Hermia.

Tytania returns and is sung to sleep, and Oberon then bewitches her with the magic herb.

A Midsummer Night's Dream, 1963. Left to right: Nadia Witkowska, William McDonald, Kellis Miller.

ACT II

SCENE—The wood

Later that night, the Athenian men return to rehearse their play. Puck impishly transforms Bottom's head into that of an ass, which frightens off his fellow actors. Tytania awakens at the din and falls instantly in love with Bottom.

Hermia and Demetrius reenter, and Oberon, realizing Puck's mistake, anoints Demetrius' eyes in an attempt to correct the error. The confusion, however, is redoubled, for Demetrius on awakening first sees Helena and immediately loves *her.*

Puck, by leading the lovers on a wild goose chase through the wood, exhausts them, and they fall asleep. Carefully arranged in correct pairs by Puck, he re-enchants Lysander and leaves the lovers asleep.

ACT III

SCENE—The wood, early next morning

Oberon, having stolen Tytania's page during the night, removes the spell from her, and they are reunited.

The four lovers awaken, now properly paired, and depart happily for Athens. Bottom once again rejoins his fellows, and they set out to perform their play before the Duke and his bride, Hippolyta.

The scene changes to Theseus' palace, where the lovers are pardoned and all are entertained by the workingmen's play. The mortals retire to bed. The fairies bless the three happy couples, leaving Puck to bid us farewell.

Mignon

-->»*«<--

MUSIC BY: Ambroise Thomas

WORLD PREMIERE: Paris, France,
  November 17, 1866

LIBRETTO BY: Michel Carré and
  Jules Barbier
Based on Goethe's *Wilhelm Meister*
NEW YORK CITY OPERA PREMIERE:
  (Sung in French) September 25, 1956

CONDUCTOR: Jean Morel
STAGE DIRECTOR: Marcella Cisney (debut)
SCENIC DESIGNER: Leo Kerz
COSTUMES: Leo Van Witsen
CHOREOGRAPHER: Anna Sokolow

CHARACTERS (In order of appearance)	VOICE (type)	PREMIERE CAST (New York City Opera)
Lothario	Bass	Emile Markow
Gypsy Dancer		Raimonda Orselli (debut)
Philine	Soprano	Beverly Sills
Laertes	Baritone	Donald Gramm
Giarno	Bass	Richard Wentworth
Mignon	Mezzo	Frances Bible
Wilhelm Meister	Tenor	Richard Verreau (debut)
Frederick	Tenor	Frank Porretta (debut)
Antonio	Spoken	Mark Elyn

Gypsies, Actors, Actresses, Townspeople

SYNOPSIS OF STORY
TIME AND PLACE: Italy and Germany, 18th century

*

ACT I

SCENE—Courtyard of a German inn

Mignon is a strange little creature, stolen in childhood from her home in Italy and made to dance for bread by a band of wandering Gypsies. We meet her in the court of an inn in Germany, where a band of actors are lodging. She is rescued from a beating by a wealthy traveler, Wilhelm Meister, who catches the roving eye of the leading lady, Philine, to the dismay of her two admirers, the leading man, Laertes, and a young noble, Frederick. The flirtation disturbs Mignon, too, for she has formed an immediate attachment to her rescuer, who is the only person ever to have shown her kindness or concern.

238

ACT II

SCENE 1—Boudoir in the castle
SCENE 2—(a) Garden of the castle near a lake
         (b) Garden outside the castle ball-
            room

Philine is ensconced in the castle, preparing for her performance as "Titania" in *A Midsummer Night's Dream* and coquetting with her suitors. Mignon had persuaded Wilhelm to let her dress in a manservant's livery and travel with him, but now he ignores her completely in his fascination with the charming actress. In her despair and loneliness, hearing the applause of Philine's triumph, she wildly wishes the castle would burst into flames. She is overheard by old Lothario, who in his muddled mind thinks to please her and sets the building afire. Wilhelm saves Mignon from perishing in the flames and takes her to Italy to recuperate.

ACT III

SCENE—A palace in Italy

Lothario gradually recovers his memory as he finds himself in his own palace, and Mignon is not only reassured that Wilhelm really loves her, not Philine, but finds her long-lost home and father in a happy finale.

The Mikado

-»»*«« -

MUSIC BY: Arthur Sullivan
WORLD PREMIERE: London, England,
  March 14, 1885

LIBRETTO BY: William S. Gilbert
NEW YORK CITY OPERA PREMIERE:
  (Sung in English) October 1, 1959

CONDUCTOR: Robert Irving (debut)
STAGE DIRECTOR: Dorothy Raedler (debut)
SCENERY and LIGHTING: Donald Oenslager
COSTUMES: Patton Campbell

CHARACTERS (In order of appearance)	VOICE (type)	PREMIERE CAST (New York City Opera)
Nanki-Poo, son of the Mikado of Japan, disguised as a wandering minstrel	Tenor	Frank Porretta
Pish-Tush, a Noble Lord	Baritone	Robert Kearns (debut)
Pooh-Bah, Lord High Everything Else	Baritone	Herbert Beattie
Ko-Ko, Lord High Executioner of Titipu	Tenor	Norman Kelley
Yum-Yum ⎱ Three sisters, wards	Soprano	Barbara Meister (debut)
Pitti-Sing ⎰ of Ko-Ko	Soprano	Nancy Dussault
Peep-Bo	Mezzo	Sophia Steffan
Katisha, an elderly Lady, in love with Nanki-Poo	Contralto	Claramae Turner
The Mikado of Japan	Bass	George Gaynes

Chorus of Schoolgirls, Nobles, and Guards

SYNOPSIS OF STORY

TIME AND PLACE: The official residence of Ko-Ko, in the town of Titipu; legendary times

*

ACT I

In the courtyard of the Lord High Executioner's palace, several Japanese gentlemen are passing the time of day. Suddenly, Nanki-Poo, a handsome young man, enters. He claims he is a wandering minstrel, looking for Yum-Yum, ward of Ko-Ko, the tailor. He declares he has long loved Yum-Yum and wishes to renew his suit because Ko-Ko, to whom Yum-Yum is betrothed, is to be beheaded for the capital crime of flirting.

A group of nobles enter. Ko-Ko, now reprieved, is with them and reveals that he has been raised to the exalted office of Lord High Executioner. He anticipates his marriage and dis-

240

cusses plans for the festivities to follow with Pooh-Bah, who is Lord High Everything Else. Yum-Yum and her two friends come in, giggling like schoolgirls.

When Nanki-Poo is introduced to Ko-Ko, he apologizes for being in love with Yum-Yum, but Ko-Ko isn't angry. He is pleased that someone agrees with his choice.

Nanki-Poo and Yum-Yum are at last alone, and she confesses that she does not love her guardian to whom she is engaged to be married. Nanki-Poo also confesses to Yum-Yum that he is really the son of his Majesty, the Mikado, in disguise because he does not wish to marry Katisha, an elderly lady at court who has claimed his hand in marriage. Under the Mikado's law, he will have to marry her or die.

A message has come from the Mikado saying that if someone isn't executed in the near future, the position of Lord High Executioner will be abolished. Ko-Ko, who holds this position, has no desire to kill anyone and is in despair until he learns that Nanki-Poo is about to take his own life because of his hopeless love. Ko-Ko suggests that as long as Nanki-Poo wishes to die, he will execute him and thus appease the Mikado. Nanki-Poo agrees but insists that he be allowed to marry Yum-Yum and live with her for a month. They all accept this arrangement.

But Katisha stalks in, recognizes Nanki-Poo, and claims him. She announces that he is the son of the Mikado but is ignored because everyone is too excited over the forthcoming wedding.

ACT II

In Ko-Ko's garden, Yum-Yum is being readied for her wedding. The happy moment is interrupted by Ko-Ko, who has just learned that the law requires Nanki-Poo's widow to be buried alive with him when he is executed. An atmosphere of gloom descends on the gathering.

However, Ko-Ko has a suggestion. He will get a fake certificate of execution from Pooh-Bah and give this to the Mikado. All goes as planned until Katisha points out that if the certificate is correct, it is the Mikado's son who has been executed.

The Mikado says that he is not really angry over what has happened but the law requires that Ko-Ko and all involved be punished. When Ko-Ko asks Nanki-Poo to help him straighten out the tangled affair, Nanki-Poo suggests that if Ko-Ko can win the heart of Katisha, Nanki-Poo will be free from the difficult situation.

Ko-Ko is successful in his suit and is accepted by Katisha. As soon as she marries Ko-Ko, Nanki-Poo is free to appear with Yum-Yum, and he presents her to his father, the Mikado, as his daughter-in-law-elect.

Miss Havisham's Fire

Being an Investigation into the Unusual and Violent Death of Aurelia Havisham on the Seventeenth of April in the Year Eighteen Hundred and Sixty

→))) * (((←

MUSIC BY: Dominick Argento
WORLD PREMIERE and NEW YORK CITY
   OPERA PREMIERE: March 22, 1979 (Sung
   in English)

LIBRETTO after DICKENS BY:
   John Olon-Scrymgeour

CONDUCTOR: Julius Rudel
STAGE DIRECTOR: H. Wesley Balk (debut)
SCENERY and COSTUMES: John Conklin
CHOREOGRAPHY: Dorothy Frank Danner (debut)

CHARACTERS*	VOICE (type)	PREMIERE CAST (New York City Opera)
Aurelia Havisham,		
an elderly, eccentric recluse,	Soprano	Rita Shane
also seen as a young woman of 1810	Soprano	Gianna Rolandi
Estella Drummle, nee Havisham,		
a beautiful young woman,	Mezzo	Susanne Marsee
also seen as a young girl of 1846	Soprano	Lorna Wallach
Phillip Pirrip, known as Pip,		
a handsome young man,	Baritone	Alan Titus
also seen as a young boy of 1846	Boy soprano	Robert Sapolsky
Grace-Helen Broome, called Nanny,		
former governess to Miss Havisham,	Mezzo	Elaine Bonazzi
also seen as a young woman of 1810	Soprano	Martha Sheil
Jaggers, Miss Havisham's legal counsel	Baritone	Richard Cross
The Examiner, officiating at the inquest	Baritone	Ralph Bassett
Bently Drummle, man about town	Tenor	John Lankston
Old Orlick,		
drunken and demented caretaker of		
Satis House,	Baritone	Paul Ukena
also seen as a young man of 1810	Tenor	James Brewer
Pumblechook, uncle to Pip	Baritone	William Ledbetter
The relatives of Miss Havisham		
Sarah Pocket	Mezzo	Rosemarie Freni

---

* Not in order of appearance.

CHARACTERS*	VOICE (type)	PREMIERE CAST (New York City Opera)
Camilla Pocket	Soprano	Martha Thigpen
Georgiana Pocket	Mezzo	Kathleen Hegierski
Raymond Pocket	Tenor	Jonathan Green
The reflections of Miss Havisham	Mutes	Laura Harth
		Judith-Mari Jarosz
		Zola Long
Guests at the Assembly Ball	Sopranos,	Robert Brubaker
	Tenors,	James Brewer
	Baritones	Lee Bellaver
		Sally Lambert
		Jean Rawn
First Maid	Soprano	Gwenlynn Little
Second Maid	Mezzo	Eunice Hill

Note: The final performance of the Spring Season, April 29, 1979, of *Miss Havisham's Fire* was conducted by Julius Rudel. Following the performance, the company, the audience, the Opera Guild, and invited guests joined on stage to honor Julius Rudel's years of service as General Director.

SYNOPSIS OF STORY

TIME AND PLACE: Satis House, its garden and environs, Essex, England; 19th century

*

PROLOGUE: The Fire, 1860

In the dark, deserted garden of Satis House, Pip recalls his first meeting with Estella fourteen years earlier, when they were children, then imagines a scene fifty years ago: the evening of Miss Havisham's engagement. The romantic vision vanishes abruptly when screams are heard from the mansion. A figure enveloped in flames appears at the window—it is Miss Havisham. Pip rushes in to try to save her.

ACT I: The Ashes

SCENE 1—The Inquest Begins

At the inquest on Miss Havisham's death, 1860, the Examiner takes testimony from the four over-emotional relatives and from her imperturbable attorney, Jaggers. Grace-Helen Broome (Nanny) tells how her mistress became a recluse.

SCENE 2—Miss Havisham's Wedding Day, 1810

The bride-to-be is giddy with happiness in a room filled with preparations for the wedding

and wedding journey. When a letter from her fiancé arrives, all joy dies and the curtains are drawn, the clocks broken. Miss Havisham will never leave her room again.

SCENE 3—At the Inquest

Nanny wildly accuses them all of guilt in her mistress' death, but she is not taken seriously. However, Sarah Pocket, one of the relatives, more directly accuses Estella, Miss Havisham's adopted daughter, claiming to have overheard a quarrel between them.

SCENE 4—The Quarrel in the Room of Mirrors, 1860

Estella returns to Satis House after the failure of her marriage to the insolent Bently Drummle and blames Miss Havisham's teachings for the wretched results. Having reared Estella to be her instrument of vengeance—to break men's hearts—the old woman is enraged that her scheme has failed, leaving Estella the injured party. They quarrel. Pip loudly protests as the scene vanishes.

* Not in order of appearance.

243

Miss Havisham's Fire, 1979. Left to right: Lorna Wallach, Rita Shane.

SCENE 5—At the Inquest

The relatives quarrel among themselves and with Jaggers, who reminds them of the danger of invective and innuendo. Their own ambitions to inherit might be construed as a possible motive. They deny the charge. Jaggers takes the witness chair.

SCENE 6—Miss Havisham's Birthday Party, 1847

As young Pip pushes Miss Havisham's wheel-chair about the room, she commands her syco-phantic relatives to lay her corpse, when she has died, on the very table where the wedding cake still stands, encrusted in cobwebs and crawling with insects—it will complete the ruined room. Slyly, she implies that each relative will be her principal heir. Curtly dismissing them, she winks at Jaggers and says: "We fooled them again." She draws Pip's attention to the charms of Es-tella, though he needs no reminding. They sing together a folk tune Pip has taught them till Miss Havisham naps.

SCENE 7—At the Inquest

The relatives are dismayed by Jaggers' revela-tion and renew their charges against Estella. Pip asks to be allowed to testify. He was the last to see Miss Havisham before her death and can exonerate Estella.

SCENE 8—The Introduction to Satis House, 1846

It is Pip's first visit to Satis House. He tells how he was absorbed into the household as a "model with a mechanical heart for her to prac-tice on." He at last broke away and made his own life, but she summoned him back, "to forgive her." The others protest—what had she done that needed to be forgiven? Pip recounts the early days, when he was under the spell of both Miss Havisham and Estella and led to believe he had great expectations—the wealth of the old woman and the love of the beautiful girl. He throws the company into confusion as he weepingly con-fesses that even now, knowing the cruel hoax played on him, he loves Estella still. The Exam-iner calls a recess.

244

ACT II: The Embers

SCENE 9—The Recess. A confrontation between Estella and Pip in the garden.

Even now, after her failed marriage, Estella holds out no hope to Pip—they both have been chilled and made inhuman. Shockingly, she cries out that Miss Havisham deserved to die and "to die in flames!" as the bell summons them back to the inquest.

SCENE 10—At the Inquest

Raymond Pocket relates how Estella first encountered Bentley Drummle.

SCENE 11—The Assembly Ball, 1859

As dancers disperse, Estella and Bentley are discovered, gazing at one another. Pip is forced to introduce them. Dancing and a joyous chorus intervene before the two are seen again; it is obvious that they are mutually attracted, each in a cold way. At the end of a rather stormy scene, Estella leaves with Bentley, deserting Pip.

SCENE 12—At the Inquest. A Surprise Witness

To everyone's surprise, Old Orlick demands a hearing. The others protest that he is drunk or mad, but the Examiner permits him to testify.

SCENE 13—Remorse in the Garden, 1860

Orlick vows that Miss Havisham came into the garden for the first time in fifty years, met Pip, asked his forgiveness, and tried to justify her treatment of Estella, who left her after their quarrel. She goes into the house, leaving Pip alone as at the beginning of the Prologue. The scene ends as before, the woman enveloped in flames, Pip trying to wrap her in the curtains.

SCENE 14—At the Inquest

Orlick dementedly claims that it is he who killed his mistress and that she loved him. Nanny soothes him and takes him away. The Examiner adjourns the inquest for want of conclusive evidence and calls them all victims of Miss Havisham's sick fancy. Estella and Pip, left alone except for Nanny, sorrowfully agree to remain friends—but apart. They go. Nanny weeps for her mistress. Bitterly she demands to know "Who will speak for *her,* who ever looked into *her* heart?" As her words echo through Satis House, the scene vanishes.

EPILOGUE: Miss Havisham's Wedding Night, 1846

The old Miss Havisham, her mind wandering back and forth in time, relives her wedding night and the events that followed; she invokes the imaginary presence of her false lover, denounces him, and reveals the reason for her madness. Finally, as morning arrives, she calls for young Estella; when the child enters, they sit together by the fireplace. Miss Havisham says "Now let us drink our tea, and I will tell you all about men."

Miss Julie

-»»*«««-

MUSIC BY: Ned Rorem

LIBRETTO BY: Kenward Elmslie

WORLD PREMIERE AND NEW YORK CITY
OPERA PREMIERE: November 4, 1965 (Sung
in English)

CONDUCTOR: Robert Zeller (debut)
STAGE DIRECTOR: Nikos Psacharopoulous
SCENERY and LIGHTING: Will Steven Armstrong
COSTUMES: Patton Campbell
CHOREOGRAPHY: Thomas Andrew

CHARACTERS (In order of appearance)	VOICE (type)	PREMIERE CAST (New York City Opera)
Christine	Mezzo	Elaine Bonazzi (debut)
Wildcat Boy	Soprano	Betsy Hepburn
Niels	Tenor	Richard Krause
Miss Julie	Soprano	Marguerite Willauer
John	Bass-baritone	Donald Gramm
A young couple	Soprano	Joan Summers
	Tenor	Nico Castel

Revelers, Farmhands, Servants

SYNOPSIS OF STORY

TIME AND PLACE: A country estate in Sweden; 1880's

*

ACT I

SCENE—Midsummer eve

Farmhands disguised as animals interrupt the reveries of Christine, the cook. Accompanying the revelers, the Count's daughter, Miss Julie, commands her fiancé, Niels, to kiss her boot. He breaks off their engagement.

In the kitchen, John, the Count's valet, and Christine, his betrothed, gossip about Miss Julie's desperate mood. Miss Julie joins them and insists that John dance with her. They flirt in French while Christine pretends to sleep. Miss Julie, after Christine has gone to bed, describes a recurrent nightmare: trapped on a pillar, she feels she is falling to the ground, only to find herself still trapped on the pillar. John tells her his dream of capturing a golden egg, always beyond his reach in the top branches of a tree. He confesses he has loved her ever since as a boy he saw her stroll in a white lace dress through the rose garden.

The revelers approach. John leads Miss Julie to his room, where they hide. The revelers taunt them from the kitchen.

ACT II

SCENE—Dawn

The revelers stumble out of the kitchen into the dawn. John tells Miss Julie his plan of escape: to run away with her to Lake Como, where he can run a hotel and make his fortune—if she advances him the necessary capital. She tells him that she has no money of her own. After a violent quarrel, dazed by wine and fatigue, she asks him what to do. He orders her to get dressed for the trip and to find money somehow.

Christine enters and, while getting John ready for church, realizes he has slept with Miss Julie. She threatens to quit the Count's employ. Miss Julie returns with money stolen from her father's desk. When she insists on taking her canary on the trip, John snatches it from her and kills it. After denouncing him hysterically, she turns to Christine for help and tries to persuade her to go with them to Lake Como. Christine leaves for church. Miss Julie picks up John's razor and holds it against her wrist. A bell rings, and John shrinks into servility. The Count has returned. Miss Julie walks into the garden to kill herself.

The Moon

-»»∗«« -

MUSIC BY: Carl Orff

WORLD PREMIERE: Munich, Germany,
   February 5, 1939

LIBRETTO BY: Carl Orff
English translation by Maria Massey
NEW YORK CITY OPERA PREMIERE and
   UNITED STATES PREMIERE: (Sung in English)
   October 16, 1956

CONDUCTOR: Joseph Rosenstock
STAGED and CHOREOGRAPHED BY: Maria Massey
SCENIC DESIGNER: Leo Kerz
COSTUMES: Leo Van Witsen

CHARACTERS (In order of appearance)	VOICE (type)	PREMIERE CAST (New York City Opera)
The Narrator	Tenor	Norman Kelley
1st Fellow	Baritone	Donald Gramm
2nd Fellow	Bass-baritone	Richard Wentworth
3rd Fellow	Tenor	Michael Pollock
4th Fellow	Bass	Joshua Hecht
Peasant	Baritone	Bernard Green
Mayor	Tenor	Gregory Miller
Innkeeper	Baritone	Thomas Powell
Mayor	Baritone	Jack Moore (debut)
Peasant		Don Wayne
1st Card Player		Robert Atherton
2nd Card Player		George Del Monte
3rd Card Player		Don Wayne
1st Dice Player		Thomas Powell
2nd Dice Player	Tenors, Baritones, and Basses	DeLloyd Tibbs
3rd Dice Player		Robert Ruddy
1st Bowler		John Lick
2nd Bowler		John Person
1st Drinker		Edson Hoel
2nd Drinker		William Nahm
3rd Drinker		William O'Leary
4th Drinker		Tom Plank
Girl	Soprano	Mary LeSawyer
Boy	Tenor	Tom Plank
St. Peter	Bass	Norman Treigle

Note: This performance was preceded by *L'Histoire du Soldat* (Stravinsky).

SYNOPSIS OF STORY
TIME AND PLACE: Space, anytime

*

Two Scenes

Out of a moonless, starless land four fellows go forth to see the world. They come to a place where a luminous globe, hanging from an oak-tree, brightens the night. They learn its name: the Moon! They steal the Moon and take it home to their own dark country. They are received with joy, while the people from whom the Moon has been stolen curse their mayor for his negligence.

For the rest of their lives the four fellows tend the Moon, keep it clean and bright, and are paid by the community for this service. On his death-bed each of the four asks to have one quarter of the Moon put into his coffin.

In the burial vault, the dead fellows rise from their coffins, paste the Moon together, and hang it up. Its light wakes the other dead, who begin to drink, gamble, carouse, and fight. The noise of their brawling brings St. Peter down from the sky. At first the dead are afraid of St. Peter, but he appears jovial and encourages them to go on drinking. Gradually, he lulls them back to sleep, then takes down the Moon, carries it away, and finally hangs it in the sky. The living on earth see the moon in the sky and stare at it in amazement.

The Most Important Man

→))) * (((←

MUSIC BY: Gian Carlo Menotti
WORLD PREMIERE and NEW YORK CITY
  OPERA PREMIERE: March 7, 1971 (Sung in
  English)

LIBRETTO BY: Gian Carlo Menotti

CONDUCTOR: Christopher Keene
STAGE DIRECTOR: Gian Carlo Menotti
SCENIC DESIGNER: Oliver Smith
COSTUMES: Frank Thompson (debut)

CHARACTERS (In order of appearance)	VOICE (type)	PREMIERE CAST (New York City Opera)
Toime Ukamba	Baritone	Eugene Holmes
Dr. Otto Arnek, a distinguished scientist	Tenor	Harry Theyard
Leona, his wife	Mezzo	Beverly Wolff
Eric Rupert, his assistant	Baritone	Richard Stilwell
Cora, Dr. Arnek's daughter	Soprano	Joanna Bruno (debut)
Professor Clement	Tenor	John Lankston
Professor Risselberg	Tenor	Joaquin Romaguera
Professor Bolental	Baritone	Thomas Jamerson
Professor Hisselman	Baritone	William Ledbetter
Professor Grippel	Bass	Don Yule
The Undersecretary of State	Bass	Jack Bittner
Mrs. Agebda Akawasi, a native leader	Soprano	Delores Jones (debut)

Servants, Natives, Soldiers

SYNOPSIS OF STORY

TIME AND PLACE: The present; an African "white state"

*

ACT I

SCENE 1—Dr. Arnek's laboratory
SCENE 2—The same, next morning
SCENE 3—Dr. Arnek's living room
SCENE 4—The same, a week later
SCENE 5—Dr. Arnek's laboratory

Dr. Arnek, a distinguished scientist, has retreated to a forest laboratory to develop an experiment which, if brought to completion, will revolutionize human society and make the country that possesses the formula the most powerful in the world.

One night Arnek, his wife, Leona, and his assistant, Eric, surprise a young black thief in the laboratory. The thief turns out to be Toime Ukamba, a former assistant of Arnek's who had fled the country some years earlier. Alone with Toime, Arnek tells him that his assistants have all abandoned him over the years, convinced that he is mad. He persuades Toime to stay and work with him on his current project.

Arnek's daughter, Cora, an aspiring actress, returns home. Leona complains bitterly to her and to Arnek of the scandal occasioned by the black Toime's residence in their house. Cora falls in love with Toime, who resists her advances for a time but finally succumbs.

ACT II

SCENE 1—A conference room in the nation's capital, two years later
SCENE 2—Dr. Arnek's living room, the next day
SCENE 3—The same, some days later
SCENE 4—The same, a few days later

After two years of work Arnek presents his theory to a group of scientists and politicians, who unanimously acknowledge the brilliance and significance of his scientific achievement. To their astonishment, Arnek then announces that it was not he who made the actual discovery, but rather his unknown assistant Toime, whom he then introduces to them. The mistrust of the scientists arouses Toime's hostility; he refuses to turn over his formula to the government unless certain unspecified conditions are met.

The scientists prevail upon Leona to influence Arnek, warning her that the country will not tolerate the spectacle of a black man dictating policy to the government of a white nation.

Mrs. Akawasi, a native leader, comes to the house to warn Toime that, by disturbing their lives and traditions, he is alienating the blacks as well as the whites. She tells him that he can expect no support from the people of his own race. Toime orders her from the house.

In spite of Leona's efforts to persuade him, Arnek refuses to betray Toime by taking credit for the discovery. He is deeply shocked, however, when Leona tells him that Cora and Toime are having an affair. Arnek confronts Toime with this information and demands to know why Toime had not confided in him. Toime accuses Arnek of objecting to the affair for reasons of prejudice; Arnek insists that he is disturbed only by Toime's betrayal of his trust. In a rage, Toime denounces him as a hypocrite and bigot. Horrified by the violence of Toime's reaction, Arnek authorizes Eric to remove the formula from the safe.

ACT III

SCENE 1—Dr. Arnek's laboratory, evening of the same day
SCENE 2—A swamplike area on the outskirts of the city

While removing the formula from the safe in the laboratory, Eric is caught by Toime and, in the ensuing struggle, killed. Although the house is heavily guarded, Cora and Toime escape but are pursued by soldiers. They camp for the night on the outskirts of a city, and an exhausted Toime instructs Cora to burn the papers containing the formula. As she does so, they are surrounded by the soldiers. Arnek, who has come with them, pleads with Toime to save himself. Although he fires his gun into the air, Toime is shot by the soldiers and dies in Arnek's arms.

Natalia Petrovna

-»»*«««-

MUSIC BY: Lee Hoiby

WORLD PREMIERE and NEW YORK CITY
  OPERA PREMIERE: October 8, 1964 (Sung in
  English)

Commissioned by Julius Rudel for New York
  City Opera

LIBRETTO BY: William Ball

CONDUCTOR: Julius Rudel
DIRECTOR: William Ball
SCENERY AND LIGHTING: Howard Bay
COSTUMES: Patton Campbell

CHARACTERS (In order of appearance)	VOICE (type)	PREMIERE CAST (New York City Opera)
Lisavetta	Soprano	Patricia Brooks
Anna Semyonovna	Mezzo	Muriel Greenspon
Doctor	Tenor	Jack Harrold
Natalia Petrovna Isaleva	Soprano	Maria Dornya (debut)
Mikhail Mikhailovitch Rakitin	Bass-baritone	Richard Cross
Vera Alexandrovna	Soprano	Sandra Darling (debut)
Alexei Alexeivitch Belaev	Baritone	John Reardon
Arkady Sergeitch Isalev	Tenor	John McCollum
Bolisov	Tenor	Richard Krause
Kolia	Mute	Anthony Rudel (debut)
Servants		

SYNOPSIS OF STORY
TIME AND PLACE: The Isalev estate in central Russia, 1850, midsummer

*

ACT I

SCENE 1—Late one morning

A month has passed since the arrival of Belaev, the young summer tutor to Kolia, the son of Arkady and Natalia Petrovna Isalev. Rakitin, who has loved Natalia for five years, has just returned to the Isalev estate from Moscow; he notes in Natalia an unusual nervousness. Her sheltered existence and strict self-imposed morality make it impossible for her to reciprocate Rakitin's advances and prevent her from realizing that her unusual melancholy and gaiety are due to her awakening love for the young tutor, Belaev.

SCENE 2—The following afternoon

Vera, Natalia's young niece and ward, has be-

252

come increasingly friendly with Belaev but has failed to recognize in this adolescent attraction the first stirrings of love. Natalia jealously suspects a love affair between Vera and Belaev and tricks her niece into admitting her love for the tutor. For the girl's own good, Natalia forbids Vera to see Belaev alone, but in doing this she recognizes the fact of her own infatuation.

ACT II

SCENE 1—A few moments later

During Kolia's birthday party, Rakitin, who has guessed Natalia's love for Belaev, advocates Belaev's dismissal as the only honorable solution to Natalia's dilemma. Natalia hesitates, but Rakitin takes the matter into his own hands and informs Belaev that his continuing presence is a cause of pain to Vera. Belaev decides to leave the household, but before departing he begs Vera's forgiveness. Vera realizes that her aunt has her confidence, and in an agony of hurt pride she forces Natalia to admit her love to the unsus-

pecting tutor. Belaev responds to her declaration with exuberance and passion, but they are discovered by the jealous Rakitin, who berates and denounces Natalia.

Meanwhile an old family friend, Doctor Ignaty Illyich, has taken advantage of the party festivity to propose to Lisavetta, an attendant of Natalia's mother-in-law.

SCENE 2—The following morning

The following morning, because of the intervention of Natalia's mother-in-law, Rakitin is forced to admit his love for Natalia to her husband, Arkady, and declares that he also will leave the estate.

Vera accepts the marriage proposal of Bolisov, a local landowner. Rakitin and Belaev are gone, Vera will soon be leaving, and the Doctor and Lisavetta will soon be married. Natalia is left alone, forced to face a future with her aging husband, filled only with the routine, rural life of the provincial estate.

Naughty Marietta

→》》∗《《←

MUSIC BY: Victor Herbert

NEW BOOK and ADDITIONAL LYRICS
BY: Frederick S. Roffman
Based on the 1910 original of Rida Johnson Young

WORLD PREMIERE: New York, New York, October 24, 1910

NEW YORK CITY OPERA PREMIERE: (Sung in English) August 31, 1978

CONDUCTOR: John Mauceri
STAGE DIRECTOR: Gerald Freedman
MUSICAL NUMBERS STAGED BY: Graciela Daniele (debut)
SCENIC DESIGNER: Oliver Smith
COSTUMES: Patricia Zipprodt
PRODUCTION CONCEIVED BY: Frederick S. Roffman

CHARACTERS*	VOICE (type)	PREMIERE CAST (New York City Opera)
Marietta d'Altena	Soprano	Gianna Rolandi
Captain Richard Warrington of Kentucky	Tenor	Jacque Trussel
Etienne Grandet	Baritone	Alan Titus
Adah Le Clercq, his quadroon mistress	Mezzo	Joanna Simon
Private Silas Slick of the Rangers	Baritone	Russ Thacker (debut)
Acting Governor Grandet, Etienne's father	Baritone	James Billings
Florenze, his secretary	Actor	Brooks Morton (debut)
Sergeant Harry Blake of the Rangers	Bass-baritone	Don Yule
Rudolfo	Baritone	Harlan Foss
Pierre La Farge, envoy from Napoleon	Bass-baritone	Richard McKee
Pirates	Chorus	Dan Kingman
		James Sergi
Sister Domenique	Chorus	Rita Metzger
Casquette Girls	Chorus	Patricia Price
		Sally Lambert
		Lee Bellaver
Ranger	Chorus	Herbert Hunsberger

* Not listed in order of appearance.

CHARACTERS*	VOICE (type)	PREMIERE CAST (New York City Opera)
Town Crier	Chorus	Edward Vaughan
Flower girls	Chorus	Susan Delery-Whedon
		Sally Lambert
Flower vendor	Chorus	George Bohachevsky
Bird vendor	Chorus	Louis Perry
Fruit vendor	Chorus	Robert Brubaker
Sugarcane vendor	Chorus	Harris Davis
Citizens	Chorus	Leslie Luxemburg
		Lila Herbert
		Marie Young
		Jean Rawn
Vendor	Chorus	Robert Brubaker
Men	Chorus	James Brewer
		Louis Perry
		Herbert Hunsberger
		Edward Vaughan
Thomas Bailey	Chorus	James Sergi
Giovanni	Dancer	José Bourbon
Gambler	Chorus	Don Carlo
Pierre	Chorus	Kenn Dovel
Robillard	Chorus	Herbert Hunsberger
Plauche	Chorus	James Brewer
Beaurivage	Chorus	Harris Davis
Majordomo	Chorus	Glenn Rowen
Spanish dancer	Dancer	Esperanza Galan
Quadroons	Chorus	Sharon Claveau
		Rosalie Tisch
		Rita Metzger
		Marie Young
		Madeleine Soyke
		Lila Herbert
French girls	Chorus	Susan Delery-Whedon
		Sally Lambert
		Jean Rawn
		Myrna Reynolds
Bordenave	Chorus	James Sergi
Durand	Chorus	Louis Perry
La Fourche	Chorus	Dan Kingman
San Domingo ladies	Dancers	Toni-Ann Gardella
		Candace Itow
		Rebeka Pradera

SYNOPSIS OF STORY

TIME AND PLACE: New Orleans, Louisiana; about 1780

*

---

* Not listed in order of appearance.

ACT I

SCENE 1—Barataria, the island hideout of privateers, at the mouth of the Mississippi River

SCENE 2—The main square in New Orleans

SCENE 3—Rudolfo's theatre; a week or two later

ACT II

SCENE —The Jeunesse Dorée Club in New Orleans

Marietta d'Altena, a Neapolitan who had run away from her native city to escape having to marry a man she did not love, has come to New Orleans with a group of French "Casket Girls," sent out to provide wives for Louisiana planters. Marriage has not yet caught up with her; however, the tramp of marching soldiers' feet resounds, and Capt. Richard Warrington (Captain Dick) meets her in his search for the notorious pirate, Bras Pique.

Capt. Dick makes friends (at first only platonic) with Marietta. The Lieutenant-Governor's son, Etienne Grandet, is in love with Marietta, even though the quadroon slave, Adah, loves him. To rid her of this affection, Etienne puts her up for auction. Capt. Dick bids highest for her, in order to set the slave girl free. The gesture is misinterpreted by Marietta, who believes he wants the girl for his own purposes. In a jealous rage, she accepts Etienne's marriage proposal.

At this point, Capt. Dick realizes that he loves Marietta, but it seems too late now to conquer her. The grateful Adah clears the way for him by revealing that Etienne is the pirate Bras Pique. The Lieutenant-Governor refuses to order his own son's arrest, but Etienne is just as effectively removed by having to leave New Orleans, permitting Capt. Dick and Marietta to express their love for each other.

256

The Nightingale

-))) * (((-

Music by: Igor Stravinsky

World Premiere: Paris, France,
May 26, 1914

Libretto by: Igor Stravinsky and
Serge Mitousoff
after Hans Christian Andersen's fairy tale
English translation by Robert Craft
New York City Opera Premiere:
(Sung in English) October 3, 1963

Conductor: Walter Susskind
Stage Director: Bliss Hebert (debut)
Sets and Costumes: Gordon Micunis
Choreography: Thomas Andrew

CHARACTERS (In order of appearance)	VOICE (type)	PREMIERE CAST (New York City Opera)
Fisherman	Tenor	Arthur Graham
Nightingale	Soprano	Patricia Brooks
Cook	Soprano	Elisabeth Carron
Chamberlain	Bass	Thomas Paul
Bonze	Bass	John Fiorito
Emperor	Baritone	Donald Gramm
Mechanical nightingale	Dancer	Rochelle Zide
Three Japanese Envoys	Tenor	Richard Krause
	Baritone	Ron Bottcher
	Tenor	Kellis Miller
Death	Contralto	Jean Kraft

Note: This opera was performed with *Jeanne d'Arc au Bucher.*

SYNOPSIS OF STORY
TIME AND PLACE: Ancient China

*

ACT I

SCENE—A nocturnal forest near the sea

The Fisherman (narrator) sets the scene, describing the heavenly spirit throwing its nets into the seas, catching fish, and transforming these fish into birds. The Fisherman is enchanted each night by the voice of the Nightingale, which now appears, singing of the beauty of the Palace Garden. The Cook, Chamberlain, and Bonze enter,

257

searching for the Nightingale; the Emperor has heard of the beauty of this marvelous creature's voice. Only the little Cook knows the voice—the other courtiers mistake the moo of a cow and the croaking of frogs for the Nightingale's song. At last the Nightingale reveals itself and accepts an invitation to sing for the Emperor. All are astounded by the dull appearance of the bird but condescend to take it to the Palace.

The Fisherman tells how this heavenly voice brought tears to the rulers of the world, tears which became the stars in the sky.

ACT II

SCENE—Court of the Emperor of China

During the entr'acte the chorus calls for lights and bells, anticipating the entrance of the Nightingale. The entire Court enters in an elaborate procession, ushering in the festivities planned for the Emperor. The Nightingale sings for the Emperor and brings tears to his eyes. When asked what it wishes for a reward, the Nightingale replies that the Emperor's tears are more than enough reward. The Japanese Ambassadors are announced; they bring a gift—an exotic mechanical nightingale which when wound up sings a single, perfect tune. During the performance, the real Nightingale disappears; the Emperor thenceforth banishes it for such insolence and orders the mechanical bird placed in his bedchamber.

By the shore, the Fisherman foretells that Death will hide the stars in darkness but that the heavenly voice will conquer Death and set the stars free.

ACT III

SCENE—The Emperor's bedchamber

Many years have passed. The Emperor, tormented by specters, lies on his deathbed. The mechanical nightingale has long since become so worn that it can be played only once a year. In his delirium the Emperor calls for music. Quietly the real Nightingale enters, singing of the beauty of the garden with its weeping roses. Death is deeply moved and agrees to return the precious crown and sword if only the Nightingale will continue its song. The Nightingale soothes the Emperor with a lullaby; the Emperor insists on making the bird the highest personage in his realm. The Nightingale again declares that the Emperor's tears are ample reward and promises to return and sing to him each night. In a solemn procession the courtiers approach what they believe to be the deathbed. When the bedcurtains are opened, the Emperor is revealed, alive and healthy, sitting in full regalia and welcoming the day.

The night is ended with the new sun; the Fisherman begs us to rejoice with the singing birds, for they are the voice of the heavenly spirit.

Nine Rivers from Jordan

-»»∗«««-

MUSIC BY: Hugo Weisgall   LIBRETTO BY: Denis Johnston
WORLD PREMIERE AND NEW YORK CITY
  OPERA PREMIERE: October 9, 1968 (Sung in
  English)

CONDUCTOR: Gustav Meier (debut)
STAGE DIRECTOR: Vlado Habunek (debut)
SCENERY and LIGHTING: Will Steven Armstrong
COSTUMES: Jane Greenwood (debut)
CHOREOGRAPHY: Maria Grandy

CHARACTERS (In order of appearance)	VOICE (type)	PREMIERE CAST (New York City Opera)
Lt. Jean l'Aiglon	Tenor	William Brown (debut)
Father Matteo Angelino	Baritone	William Ledbetter
Sgt. Abe Goldberg	Bass-baritone	Joshua Hecht
Maj. Mark Lyon	Tenor	John Lankston
Capt. Rev. Lucius Bull	Bass	Will Roy
Lance Corp. Don Hanwell	Baritone	Julian Patrick
Leader of the Bedouins	Baritone	Don Yule
Muezzin	Tenor	Joaquin Romaguera
The Salt Woman	Soprano	Eileen Schauler
Andy, the Highlander	Tenor	John Stewart
Copperhead Kelly	Tenor	Paul Huddleston
Little Jim Clap	Baritone	Kellis Miller
Peeper Johnny	Bass	Raymond Gibbs
Tom Tosser	Tenor	Nico Castel
Simple Simon	Baritone	Raymond Papay
Sgt. Pete Fisher	Bass	Michael Devlin
Phil	Tenor	Leo Goeke
Jim Gunner	Bass	Dan Kingman
Taddeo ⎤	Tenor	Anthony Darius
Bartolomeo ⎬ Italian P.O.W.'s	Tenor	Ronald Bentley
Giuda ⎦	Bass	Don Henderson
Italians	Tenor	Joseph Galiano
	Bass	Douglas Hunniken
	Tenor	Karl Patrick Krause
Woman's Voice on Radio	Mezzo	Kay Creed
Otto Suder	Tenor	David Clements
The Pietà	Soprano	Eileen Schauler

259

CHARACTERS | VOICE | PREMIERE CAST
(In order of appearance) | (type) | (New York City Opera)

CHARACTERS (In order of appearance)	VOICE (type)	PREMIERE CAST (New York City Opera)
The Woman D.P.	Soprano	Eileen Schauler
The Dead Man	Tenor	Joaquin Romaguera
Italian Women	Soprano	Lila Herbert
	Mezzo	Arlene Adler

Displaced Persons, Soldiers, Workers

SYNOPSIS OF STORY
TIME AND PLACE: World War II, 1942–1945; Europe, The Jordan, The Libyan Desert

*

PROLOGUE

Brenner Pass: May, 1945. A ragged column of Displaced Persons of many nationalities is trudging past a bombed-out cemetery. Four Allied officers, members of a War Graves unit, are in a truck driven by Master Sergeant Abe Goldberg. Their attention is caught by a British soldier sitting beside a newly dug grave. His replies are enigmatic when they question him about the name on the dogtags that hang on the marker— Hanwell, D. R., Lance Corporal, the Buffs, Rationalist. Goldberg, attracted by the name, comes across to speak to the Englishman. He knew such a man in the Middle East. In fact, he suspects that this is Hanwell. Why is he sitting beside his own grave? All the man will say is that he is both dead and not dead—with which apparent nonsense Goldberg has little patience. His friend was always a bit difficult, even back in Palestine, where they used to truck gypsum from the headwaters of the Dead Sea to the Allied airfields at Lydda and Aqir. So from the Brenner, we cut back to—

ACT I

SCENE 1—The River Jordan

It is 1942, and Abe and Don R. Hanwell are bargaining with a party of Bedouins over the price of gypsum. As they load their truck, Goldberg expresses his regard for Palestine, to which Hanwell replies sardonically, Why should men fight to keep a strip of sand and scrub from Rommel? There is no meaning to this war, or even

to life itself. Abe goes off to see The Jordan. Surprised, Don hears the voice of a woman— an image of the first Eve, here appearing as a Pillar of Salt. She prophesies that Hanwell will find a meaning before the end of his journey, which will come after he has crossed his ninth river; and she urges him on his skeptical way to find a pearl of innocence that his parents lost after they had gone forth from Eden. She warns him, however, never to carry a weapon, as a man must die by what he carries. Don asks how he will know when he has crossed his last river. "By the Dove," she says.

SCENE 2—The Nile

It is Christmas Eve in the same year. A victory has been won at Alamein. Twelve soldiers—nine of Montgomery's Eighth Army and three Italian prisoners are in pursuit of the Afrika Korps. Don, now a Dispatch Rider, arrives from the wilderness, escorting a captured German officer, Otto Suder. As his companions doze off to the strains of "Lili Marlene" on the radio, the Corporal and the Nazi drift into a conversation about the merits and demerits of the war, at the close of which Don cynically allows his prisoner to escape. Why not? It will be all the same in the end. He falls asleep.

ACT II

Act II describes the progress of Don's odyssey from the desert, up the spine of Italy, through Rome and southern France, over the Sangro, the Tiber, the Seine, and the Meuse, and into the land of the Rhine and the Danube. Still in search of the gift for which the first Eve has sent him, he meets with Copperhead—one of the twelve of the desert—and with his friend Abe, who warns him that sooner or later he will be forced to give up this act of never carrying a gun. From here the Pietà of Saint Peter's (Michelangelo's celebrated figure of the second Eve) leads him to a forest, where he finds himself face to face with Otto Suder standing guard outside a concentration camp. Inside he will find a meaning for the war, but Suder refuses to allow him to look inside. However, the German is presently overpowered by the twelve companions, who break open the doors and let loose all the horrors of the day and age. This is the Knowledge of Good and Evil that Don has been tempted to find for himself—the situation is followed by a dreamlike witches' Sabbath which takes the form of a mock trial. "The Dead" is the prosecutor, while Abe Goldberg defends the helmet and tunic of Suder that hang empty in the dock. The fault, if any, is not the fault of one, but of Everyman. At this point, the Pietà intervenes to say that the answer lies in atonement. If some real Suder can be found and slaughtered, the Almighty might be persuaded to absolve mankind from its collective guilt; but not otherwise. Don, as the one responsible for the escape of this image of Evil, is invested with this task and sent forth to cross his last river, armed with a hand grenade that is plucked like an apple from a tree and placed in his unresisting hand by the second Eve.

ACT III

SCENE—The River Inn

On the Brenner Pass in May, 1945, just as the war is ending, Hanwell arrives with his guide, Copperhead—the Judas of the twelve—who is leading him on to this inevitable fate. Here they meet with the last Eve—a woman with quite a different message. She urges Don to throw away his weapon before it is too late. As Don refuses, he finds himself confronted by Suder, disguised in British battle dress, whose desperate wish now is that all should go down together in a common holocaust. The crowd of D.P.'s, thinking that he is their liberator, hail him as such, but before Don can use the bomb the third Eve gently takes it from his hand and brings it to Suder, in whose grasp it explodes. When the dust has settled in the ruined cemetery, the voice of God can be heard from a hilltop speaking through Copperhead. It tells the survivor to go about his business and to leave matters of guilt or innocence to Heaven where they belong. To this instruction Don satirically replies by committing the body of his enemy to the ground and hanging his own dogtags on the marker. If God and Copperhead are one, then it matters little what is the name of the deceased, or who has atoned for what. At this point we are back with the arrival of Goldberg and the Graves Commission, and the opera ends with the fulfillment of a promise about a Dove in a shape that could hardly have been expected.

Oedipus Rex

→))) ✳ (((←

MUSIC BY: Igor Stravinsky

WORLD PREMIERE: Paris, France
May 30, 1927

LIBRETTO BY: Jean Cocteau
English translation of narration by:
e. e. cummings

NEW YORK CITY OPERA PREMIERE: (Sung in Latin; narration spoken in English) September 24, 1959

CONDUCTOR: Leopold Stokowski (debut)
PRODUCTION DESIGNED and DIRECTED BY: Paul Sylbert
COSTUMES: Paul Sylbert

CHARACTERS (In order of appearance)	VOICE (type)	PREMIERE CAST (New York City Opera)
Narrator	Speaking	Wesley Addy (debut)*
Oedipus	Tenor	Richard Cassilly
Creon	Bass-baritone	Arnold Voketaitis
Tiresias	Bass	Joshua Hecht
Jocasta	Mezzo	Claramae Turner
The Messenger	Bass-baritone	John Macurdy
The Shepherd	Tenor	Grant Williams
	Citizens, Soldiers	

Note: This opera was performed with *Carmina Burana.*

SYNOPSIS OF STORY
TIME AND PLACE: Thebes, in classical times

✳

PREFACE

Laius, King of Thebes, is warned by an oracle that he will be killed by his own son. Therefore, he and Jocasta, his wife, leave their young son, Oedipus, to die on a mountainside. However, Oedipus is rescued and becomes the adopted son of Polybus, King of Corinth. Oedipus also receives a prophesy: he will kill his father and marry his mother. Thinking Polybus his true father, he flees Corinth; on his way to Thebes he kills an old man (Laius) and solves the riddle of the Sphinx, which is plaguing Thebes. Because of this triumph, he is crowned King of Thebes

---

* Replaced Jason Robards, Jr., who was indisposed.

262

Oedipus Rex, 1959

and marries Jocasta, who bears him four children.

The narrator introduces the tragedy.

ACT I

The populace of Thebes laments the raging plague and implores Oedipus to give them aid. Oedipus, who is by now a master of oratory, assures them that he—the brilliant Oedipus—will save them. Creon, the brother of Jocasta, returns from having consulted the oracle. The oracle demands that Laius' murderer, who is hiding in Thebes, be discovered and punished. Oedipus swears to discover and drive out the assassin.

The populace awaits Tiresias, the seer. He arrives and refuses to prophesy further; he realizes that Oedipus is a plaything of the gods. This silence angers Oedipus, who accuses Creon of desiring the throne for himself and Tiresias of being his accomplice. Angered by Oedipus' unjust attitude, Tiresias speaks: "The assassin of the King is a King." Oedipus, at his most elequent, reminds the Thebans that he had saved them from the Sphinx and therefore they had made him king. He again swears to solve the new riddle. Jocasta enters, attracted by the dispute of the princes.

ACT II

Jocasta calms the princes and shames them for raising their voices in a stricken city. She proves that oracles lie by citing that an oracle had predicted that Laius would perish by the hand of her son, whereas Laius was murdered instead by thieves at the crossing of three roads from Daulis and Delphis. These words horrify Oedipus. He remembers how, arriving from Corinth before encountering the Sphinx, he killed an old man where three roads met.

A messenger, announcing the death of King Polybus of Corinth, reveals to Oedipus that he was only the adopted son of Polybus. The messenger had found Oedipus as a child, cast out on a mountainside. He gave the child to a shepherd, who revived him. Jocasta realizes that Oedipus is her son. (The prophecy is fulfilled—Oedipus, the son of Laius and Jocasta, has killed his father and married his mother.) She flees. Unable to accept the complete truth, Oedipus believes that Jocasta is ashamed of his humble birth, but he learns his true origin from the shepherd and the messenger. Now he sees the light.

The messenger announces the death of Jocasta. The chorus assists his narrative: Jocasta has hanged herself, and Oedipus, in horror and degradation, has plucked out his eyes with her golden pin. As he wanders sightless into exile, the populace bids farewell to the king: "—we loved you!"

The Old Maid and the Thief

-»»*«« -

MUSIC BY: Gian Carlo Menotti
WORLD PREMIERE: NBC Radio Broadcast
  April 22, 1939
STAGE PREMIERE: Philadelphia, Pennsylvania,
  February 11, 1941

LIBRETTO BY: Gian Carlo Menotti
NEW YORK CITY OPERA PREMIERE:
  (Sung in English) April 8, 1948

CONDUCTOR: Thomas P. Martin
STAGE DIRECTOR: Gian Carlo Menotti (debut)
SCENIC DESIGNER: H. A. Condell
COSTUMES*

CHARACTERS (In order of appearance)	VOICE (type)	PREMIERE CAST (New York City Opera)
Miss Todd	Contralto	Marie Powers (debut)
Miss Pinkerton	Soprano	Ellen Faull
Laetitia	Soprano	Virginia MacWatters
Bob	Baritone	Norman Young

Note: This opera was performed with *Amelia Goes to the Ball.*

SYNOPSIS OF STORY
TIME AND PLACE: Small town in the United States; the present

*

SCENE 1—Miss Todd's house, late afternoon

Miss Todd and Miss Pinkerton exchange gossip over their teacups. Each discloses that, years ago, a man wrecked her life. Knocks are heard at the back door. Laetitia announces a man to see Miss Todd. Miss Pinkerton leaves. The man proves to be a tramp, yet such an attractive one that he is invited to stay overnight.

SCENE 2—Miss Todd's house, next morning

Miss Todd and Laetitia cannot bear the thought of Bob's leaving. They decide to ask him to remain a week. To the neighbors it can be explained that he is Miss Todd's cousin. But how to persuade him to stay? Laetitia suggests that a good breakfast will be the most convincing argument possible.

---

* By Kate Friedheim; additional costumes by Stivanello.

SCENE 3—Same

Laetitia arrives with breakfast. Bob agrees to stay but warns her that he will be a cousin—nothing more—since he hates women.

SCENE 4—A street, a few minutes later

Miss Pinkerton excitedly informs Miss Todd that a notorious desperado has escaped from the county jail of Timberville and has been seen in the neighborhood. She describes him as "tall and burly, black hair and curly, light complexion, Southern inflection, and altogether handsome."

SCENE 5—Miss Todd's house, a few minutes later

Miss Todd relays the news to Laetitia. Both women are convinced that Bob is the escaped criminal. Goodness gracious! He might rob and murder them in their beds. Yet—he has such lovely eyes. They decide to let him stay. But for his contentment (and their safety), they must keep him liberally supplied with money. There being no alternative, they decide to rob the neighbors.

SCENE 6—Miss Todd's house, a week later

For days, remarks Laetitia, Miss Todd has been committing robberies in Bob's behalf and has been making languid eyes at him. Bob accepts money with entrancing smiles, yet shows no affection for her. Laetitia reveals that she, too, has lost her heart to him.

SCENE 7—Miss Todd's house, a little later

According to Miss Pinkerton, the thief is still hiding in the neighborhood. Many houses have been mysteriously robbed. The town must ask for police protection.

SCENE 8—Miss Todd's house, a few days later

Bob voices his philosophy that "a man born in a house is a bird born in a cage." Laetitia discovers him packing, begs him to stay, and learns that he longs for "just something to drink."

SCENE 9—Same

Laetitia and Miss Todd confer. How to avert the imminent catastrophe? Miss Todd, a leader in a temperance movement, cannot buy liquor publicly. Laetitia suggests that they rob the liquor store and rationalizes such conduct by pointing out that "sinning against a sin can be no sin."

SCENE 10—In front of the liquor store, 2 A.M.

The two women break through a window, fill their basket with gin bottles (so noisily that they rouse the storekeeper from his sleep upstairs), and flee helter-skelter through the town.

SCENE 11—Miss Todd's house, the next morning

Miss Pinkerton reports that last night's robbery of the liquor store has thrown the town into an uproar. A famous detective has been hired. Every house will be searched. As Miss Todd struggles to conceal her alarm, Bob's voice, wavering in a drunken song, floats down from upstairs, arousing Miss Pinkerton's suspicions. When Miss Pinkerton leaves, Laetitia and Miss Todd decide that Bob must be warned.

SCENE 12—Same

The two women rouse Bob from a drunken stupor to warn him that the police are closing in. His puzzlement leads to the disclosure that he is not a hunted criminal—just an honest beggar, a "lost, wind-tossed leaf." Miss Todd romantically urges him to flee to France with her. He prosaically refuses. Infuriated, she declares she will call the police, accuse him of heinous crimes, and see him sent to prison.

SCENE 13—Same

Laetitia sees her opportunity for romance. She persuades Bob that Miss Todd has unlimited influence with the local authorities and that "it would be a pity for one so young to be electrocuted." His only hope of freedom lies in flight—and it might as well be with her, in Miss Todd's car. Bob is forced to agree. But since he must assume the role of thief, he may as well really become one. So he and the unscrupulous Laetitia plunder the house of all its valuables before taking flight.

SCENE 14—Miss Todd's house, a few minutes later

A brief picture of Miss Todd's tragicomic return to her empty house.

Orpheus in the Underworld

→))) * (((←

MUSIC BY: Jacques Offenbach

WORLD PREMIERE: Paris, France,
October 21, 1858

LIBRETTO BY: Ludwig Halévy and
Hector Crémieux in French;
Eric Bentley in English

NEW YORK CITY OPERA PREMIERE:
(Sung in English) September 20, 1956

CONDUCTOR: Erich Leinsdorf (debut)
STAGED and DESIGNED BY: Leo Kerz (debut)
COSTUMES: Leo Van Witsen (debut)
CHOREOGRAPHER: Anna Sokolow (debut)

CHARACTERS (In order of appearance)	VOICE (type)	PREMIERE CAST (New York City Opera)
Eurydice	Soprano	Sylvia Stahlman (debut)
Orpheus	Tenor	Jon Crain
Pluto (Aristeus—earthly form of Pluto)	Tenor	Norman Kelley
Mars	Baritone	Joshua Hecht
Miss P. Opinion	Actress	Paula Lawrence (debut)
Venus	Soprano	Marquita Moll
Jupiter	Actor	Hiram Sherman (debut)
Mercury	Tenor	Michael Pollock
Juno	Mezzo	Irene Kramarich
Diana	Soprano	Beverly Bower
Cupid	Soprano	Jacquelynne Moody
Minerva	Mezzo	Mignon Dunn
John Styx	Tenor	Richard Humphrey (debut)

Shepherds, Gods and Goddesses, Infernal Spirits, Policemen

SYNOPSIS OF STORY

TIME AND PLACE: Mythological times, updated; Athens, Olympus, and Hades

*

ACT I

SCENE—A field in Thebes

The Goddess of Public Opinion appears to explain that she is living in the guise of a Vestal Virgin named Miss P. Opinion and that although she is a new Goddess, her powers exceed those of any of the old Gods.

Eurydice appears carrying flowers for her lover, the shepherd Aristeus, Pluto's earthly

268

character. She is seen by Orpheus, her husband, who believes her to be his mistress, Chloe. Both are indignant at discovering the other's infidelity. Orpheus hints that he has taken measures to end the affair, and Eurydice runs off to warn her lover. Aristeus enters as a mountaineer but hints that this is only a disguise. Eurydice rushes in to warn him that Orpheus has laid wolf-traps, but he doesn't listen to her. As she follows him, her foot is caught in one of the traps set out by Orpheus. Aristeus then reveals that he is really Pluto, King of the Underworld; he tells Eurydice she is dying, and she goes to Hades with him. Orpheus is overjoyed on learning of Eurydice's death and is about to rush off to be with Chloe when Miss P. Opinion appears. She insists that he accompany her to Olympus to seek the aid of Jupiter, King of the Gods.

ACT II

SCENE—Mount Olympus

The Gods and Goddesses recount the sex life of Olympian society. Because of the existence of Miss P. Opinion, they complain that they have had to conceal their activities. The news that Eurydice has been carried off by Pluto reaches Olympus, and Jupiter sends a messenger to find out the truth. Pluto appears, but he denies that he has Eurydice. The Olympians grow restive and complain about their boring diet of nectar and ambrosia. They are on the verge of revolution when Miss P. Opinion appears, dragging a reluctant Orpheus with her. She demands that Jupiter take action and direct Pluto to return Eurydice to Orpheus. Jupiter agrees to take responsibility

for the case and, along with all the Gods and Goddesses, goes to the Underworld of Hades.

ACT III

SCENE—A chamber in Hades

Eurydice is being kept prisoner, guarded by the devilish John Styx, who keeps threatening to make love to her. Though she is willing, he never carries out his threats. When Jupiter arrives in Hades, he demands that Eurydice be produced, but Pluto refuses. Jupiter then disguises himself as a bee and passes through the keyhole of Eurydice's cell. They are intrigued by each other, and Jupiter, forgetting his promise, plots with Eurydice to help her escape from Hades by taking her back to Olympus.

ACT IV

SCENE—The Underworld

At a fancy dress ball in the Underworld, Eurydice appears in the guise of a Bacchante. When she and Jupiter attempt to escape, they are stopped by Pluto. Miss P. Opinion and a reluctant Orpheus appear, and she demands that Eurydice be returned to her husband. Jupiter agrees to return Eurydice, but only on the condition that, on the journey out of Hades, Orpheus not turn around to look at his wife. Jupiter is about to throw his thunderbolts and force Orpheus to look back, when Miss P. Opinion steps in to reveal her status as a Goddess. She insists that Eurydice return to Greece with Orpheus. Jupiter protests that she is changing mythology; Orpheus has to look back and lose Eurydice. But the new Goddess of Public Opinion insists, and Eurydice returns to earth.

Pagliacci

-»»*«««-

MUSIC BY: Ruggiero Leoncavallo
WORLD PREMIERE: Milan, Italy,
    May 21, 1892

LIBRETTO BY: Ruggiero Leoncavallo
NEW YORK CITY OPERA PREMIERE:
    (Sung in Italian) May 5, 1944

CONDUCTOR: Laszlo Halasz
STAGE DIRECTOR: Hans Wolmut
SCENIC DESIGNER: Richard Rychtarik
COSTUMES*

CHARACTERS (In order of appearance)	VOICE (type)	PREMIERE CAST (New York City Opera)
Tonio	Baritone	John DeSurra
Nedda	Soprano	Norina Greco (debut)
Canio	Tenor	Norbert Ardelli
Beppe	Tenor	Henry Cordy
Silvio	Baritone	Edwardo Rael
Villagers, Children		

Note: This opera was performed with *Cavalleria Rusticana.*

SYNOPSIS OF STORY

TIME AND PLACE: A southern Italian village, Montalto; late 19th century, during the Feast of the Assumption

*

A troupe of comedians headed by Canio travels into town. Canio addresses the crowd of villagers, inviting them to the performance that evening. He presents his wife, Nedda, who plays Columbine; Tonio, who plays the clown, Taddeo; and Beppe, the Harlequin. The peasants disperse. Only Nedda stays behind, while Canio joins the peasants in the tavern. Tonio, who is secretly in love with Nedda, approaches her and first begs, then demands, her love. Nedda, who despises him, grabs a whip and lashes him. The infuriated Tonio threatens revenge. Silvio, a young peasant with whom Nedda once had a love affair, appears and entreats her to leave the troupe and flee with him. Nedda, who respects but does not love Canio, who is brutal and insanely jealous, promises to meet Silvio after the performance and elope. During their passionate parting embrace, Canio, led on by Tonio, surprises the two. Silvio rushes away, and Canio, not familiar with the

---

* Supplied by Van Horn & Son.

270

pathways, cannot catch him. In his first rage he is about to kill Nedda, but Tonio slyly persuades him to wait until the performance, when the lover surely will appear and betray himself. That evening the villagers assemble for the performance. At first things go well. Nedda, as Columbine, is visited by Harlequin. According to the script, Canio, the "Pagliaccio," appears. Barely able to stay in his role as jealous husband, he demands the name of his wife's lover. Nedda, at first trying to play her part, refuses jokingly, and when she realizes that Canio is in earnest, she boldly defies him. Beside himself, he stabs her. Silvio, who has been in the audience, rushes forward and is stabbed by Canio, who dismisses the horrified audience with the words: "The comedy is ended."

The Passion of Jonathan Wade

→))) * (((←

MUSIC BY: Carlisle Floyd
WORLD PREMIERE and NEW YORK CITY
  OPERA PREMIERE: October 11, 1962 (Sung
  in English)

LIBRETTO BY: Carlisle Floyd

CONDUCTOR: Julius Rudel
STAGE DIRECTOR: Allen Fletcher
SCENIC DESIGNER: Will Steven Armstrong
COSTUMES: Ruth Morley

CHARACTERS (In order of appearance)	VOICE (type)	PREMIERE CAST (New York City Opera)
Judge Brooks Townsend	Bass-baritone	Norman Treigle
Celia Townsend, his daughter	Soprano	Phyllis Curtin
Young Girl	Girl voice	Linda Newman
Young Boy	Boy voice	Jeffrey Meyer (debut)
Confederate Soldier	Baritone	Richard Fredricks
Lt. Patrick	Tenor	Harry Theyard
Col. Jonathan Wade	Baritone	Theodor Uppman
Four Young Boys	Boy voices	Vaughn Fubler (debut)
		Ainsley Sigmond (debut)
		Robert Hawkins (debut)
		Mal Scott (debut)
Nicey	Soprano	Miriam Burton
J. Tertius Riddle	Bass	Paul Ukena
Lucas Wardlaw	Tenor	Frank Porretta
Ely Pratt	Tenor	Norman Kelley
Amy Pratt	Soprano	Patricia Brooks
Union Soldier	Bass-baritone	Ron Bottcher
Rector	Bass	Thomas Paul
Union Leaguer	Tenor	Arthur Graham
A Senator	Bass	Eugene Brice
Judge Bell	Baritone	Andrew Frierson
1st Carpetbagger	Tenor	Arthur Graham
2nd Carpetbagger	Bass-baritone	David Smith
Driver	Boy voice	Mal Scott

People of Columbia, Confederate and Union Soldiers, Party Guests, Ku Klux Klansmen, Sandhillers

SYNOPSIS OF STORY
TIME AND PLACE: Columbia, South Carolina; May, 1865

*

ACT I

SCENE 1—A public square

A group of people are waiting for the return of Confederate soldiers who are coming from the North with the Union occupation forces. The Confederate soldiers appear and are reunited with their families. They are followed by the Union troops headed by Colonel Jonathan Wade. Judge Brooks Townsend introduces himself and greets Jonathan. He introduces Wade to his daughter, Celia, who coldly refuses to acknowledge the introduction.

EPISODE—A street

A quartet of Negro boys dance and sing of their newfound freedom. In somber counterpoint to their jubilation is a maimed Confederate soldier who has returned to his desolated home.

SCENE 2—Drawing room in the home of Judge Brooks Townsend

Jonathan is a guest of the Townsends. Left alone with the silent, still-veiled Celia, he provokes her into conversation and she denounces him bitterly, prompting him to angrily describe to her his experiences with war and his passionate hatred of it. Celia is stirred and chastened by his fervor, and they each in turn apologize for their outbursts. Jonathan leaves and Celia sings wonderingly at first and later exultantly of the stranger who has come into her life.

EPISODE—A street

As J. Tertius Riddle, a pardon-broker, is flamboyantly describing the merits of obtaining a pardon from the President, he is interrupted by Lucas Wardlaw and his cronies, who taunt him on his attempts to sell pardons. Riddle, undaunted, approaches Townsend and is sternly rebuked for his greed.

SCENE 3—The drawing room of Townsend's home; spring, 1866

A party is in progress in the Townsend drawing room. Nicey, the colored maid, announces the arrival of Ely Pratt and his wife, Amy. They enter, and Ely tells Townsend of his work with the Freedmen's Bureau. Ely, to illustrate his point of assisting Negroes to obtain an education, asks Nicey if she wouldn't like to avail herself of their services. Nicey good-naturedly rebuffs him, and the party guests applaud her. Ely turns on them furiously, saying that they, the Southerners, will be taught the war's lessons by the North. The party guests shout their defiance at him as the curtain falls.

ACT II

SCENE 1—Army of Occupation headquarters

Jonathan is administering the oath, reinstating them as citizens, to a group of tenant farmers. Lucas, who has watched the proceedings, scorns the taking of the oath and complains of having no Negro servants and of being unable to keep Negro laborers on his farm. Jonathan, exasperated and angered by Lucas, threatens him and Lucas exits. Patrick, Jonathan's aide, enters with an order from Washington. As Jonathan reads the order with evident consternation, Ely enters and Jonathan tells him that he has been commanded to remove Townsend as District Judge. He pleads with Ely to intercede on Townsend's behalf, but Ely refuses. Ely then exhorts Jonathan to forget his allegiance to Lincoln and to join the Radical Party in their efforts to raise the status of the Negro and thereby hold political power for a hundred years. Jonathan rejects his urging, refusing to condone the methods and aims of the party, and Ely obliquely threatens Jonathan with the loss of his command. As he exits, Jonathan sends a message appealing the order. Celia appears and announces that she has come to take the oath even though it means risking the disapproval of her family and her friends. She declares her belief in Jonathan and, moved, he tells her he loves her. As they are embracing, Lucas reappears; when he teases Jonathan about his feeling for Celia, Jonathan knocks him down. Lucas threatens Jonathan by asking him if he knows of the Ku Klux Klan.

EPISODE—A street

A Union Leaguer is proclaiming to a group of colored people that plantations will be divided and that they each will be given forty acres and a mule. J. Tertius Riddle reappears, this time selling bogus certificates to credulous Negroes.

SCENE 2—Headquarters building; October 1869

Patrick enters with the response to Jonathan's appeal. Jonathan, disconsolate, tells his aide that he has been denied and asks Patrick to bring Townsend to his office. Townsend enters with Celia, and Jonathan tells him of the order and of his efforts to have it countermanded. Townsend retains his poise until Jonathan tells him that he will be replaced by a Negro judge. Townsend, his pride attacked, lashes out; when Jonathan refuses to agree with him that his honor has been impugned, Townsend turns on Jonathan, accusing him of betrayal and saying that he is never to see Celia again. Jonathan asks Celia to marry him, and she pleads with her father not to make her choose between him and Jonathan. He is implacable, and Celia remains with Jonathan as Townsend disowns her and exits. When he has gone, Jonathan calls in Nicey, and Patrick appears with the rector, who marries Jonathan and Celia. When the couple are alone once more, they listen to Nicey and her friends who are huddled outside singing to them. Suddenly intruding into the song are the distant sounds of the Ku Klux Klan. The Negroes grow silent and then scream and run as the Klansmen rush on stage. Jonathan, alarmed, calls Patrick to pursue the Klansmen and then returns to comfort Celia.

ACT III

SCENE 1—The Wade home, four years later

Celia is rocking her child as Jonathan enters, followed by Amy and by Ely, who is arguing

with Jonathan over the political motives of the Union League. Ely warns Jonathan that his lack of cooperation with the reigning political party may cost him his job and then maliciously suggests that his lack of cooperation may be due to his Southern wife. Celia angrily tells Pratt of her ostracism for four years and demands that he leave them alone. She exits, followed by Jonathan. Ely, frustrated in his efforts to sway Jonathan, tells his wife that he must devise a scheme to force Jonathan out of the Army. He seizes on the idea of confiscation of Townsend's household goods to satisfy a tax assessment as a means of coercing Jonathan into insubordination, and he calls Patrick in to help him carry out his plans. Patrick, loyal to Jonathan, at first refuses but weakens when Ely threatens him by questioning his loyalty. Ely instructs Patrick to watch for the order commanding Jonathan to take possession of Townsend's property.

EPISODE—Outside the State Capitol

Two carpetbaggers question a group of colored senators whom they have bribed to pass bills. A distinguished colored man rebukes them and, when asked by a carpetbagger to identify himself, reveals himself to be Judge James Bell, the man who has replaced Townsend.

SCENE 2—The Wade home

Jonathan says goodbye to Bell, who is resigning his appointment as judge in protest over the corruption in the state capital. Patrick brings in Ely's order, which has been sent from Washington, and notes Jonathan's anger at reading it. Jonathan calls Celia in and tells her that he refuses to execute the order and therefore must decide whether or not he can continue to live with himself if he remains in the Army. Jonathan struggles with his conscience, and finally announces his decision to desert. Celia attempts to console him, and he tells her his plans for escape.

EPISODE—A public gathering

Townsend, addressing a group of people, reveals that the order to confiscate his household goods has been carried out, and he swears vengeance against the tyrants from the North. Celia listens, alarmed, realizing that somebody else has known of the order and has executed it.

SCENE 3—The Wade home

Jonathan, sensing a trap after hearing Celia's news, sends Nicey for their driver so that they may leave immediately. As they are packing, Patrick appears with three Klansmen who were discovered lighting a cross on Jonathan's lawn. The Klansmen are ordered to unmask, and Lucas is revealed under the last hood. He laughs at Jonathan's astonishment and warns him that his men are coming to rescue him and that their orders are to kill Jonathan on sight. Jonathan commands the Klansmen to be locked up, and as they exit, Nicey reappears with the driver. As the driver takes their baggage, Nicey, the child, and Celia follow him to the carriage while Jonathan changes his clothes. In the distance once again is heard the sound of the Ku Klux Klan. Jonathan reappears on stage; as he hurries out to the carriage he is shot and staggers back into the room. Celia rushes in, followed by Patrick, Nicey, and the child. Immediately the room fills with Union soldiers led in by Ely and Ku Klux Klansmen captured by the soldiers. Jonathan dies in Celia's arms, and the Klansmen and soldiers immediately begin to accuse each other of his murder. At the peak of their argument, Celia screams that they are all murderers and commands them to leave. When they have gone, she says goodnight to her child and, left alone with the body of Jonathan, she mourns the fact that there was no other time in which they might have lived their lives.

Pelléas et Mélisande

→))∗(((←

MUSIC BY: Claude Debussy

WORLD PREMIERE: Paris, France,
April 30, 1902

LIBRETTO: Based on text by Maurice
Maeterlinck

NEW YORK CITY OPERA PREMIERE:
(Sung in French) March 25, 1948

CONDUCTOR: Jean Morel
PRODUCTION DESIGNER and STAGE DIRECTOR: Theodore Komisarjevsky
COSTUMES: H. A. Condell

CHARACTERS (In order of appearance)	VOICE (type)	PREMIERE CAST (New York City Opera)
Golaud	Baritone	Carlton Gauld
Mélisande	Soprano	Maggie Teyte (debut)
Geneviève	Mezzo	Mary Kreste
Arkel	Bass	Norman Scott
Pelléas	Tenor	Fernand Martel (debut)*
Yniold	Soprano	Virginia Haskins
A physician	Bass	Arthur Newman
Six Serving Women		

SYNOPSIS OF STORY
TIME AND PLACE: Legendary kingdom, Allemonde, in the Middle Ages

∗

ACT I

SCENE 1—A forest

The action of the opera centers around the castle of Arkel, King of Allemonde, who lives with his daughter-in-law, Geneviève, and her sons by two marriages, Golaud and the younger Pelléas. At the opening of the opera, Mélisande is discovered in a forest by Golaud; she will tell nothing of her past but agrees to go with him to the castle of his grandfather.

SCENE 2—In the castle

Geneviève reads a long letter from Golaud to Pelléas asking his half brother to signal whether or not he will be welcome with his new bride, Mélisande. Arkel agrees to receive his grandson.

* Theodor Uppman was originally to have replaced French tenor Jacques Jansen, who was also indisposed.

276

SCENE 3—In a garden by the castle

Pelléas and Mélisande meet. Mélisande is saddened to hear that he plans to depart.

SCENE 4—A well in the park

Pelléas and Mélisande sit by a well. Mélisande accidentally drops her wedding ring into the water.

SCENE 5—Golaud's room in the castle

Golaud, upon noticing the absence of the ring, insists that Mélisande search for it at once, suggesting that Pelléas would be glad to accompany her.

SCENE 6—A cavern by the sea

They search for the ring in a gloomy cavern.

ACT II

SCENE 7—Outside the tower

Pelléas discovers Mélisande combing her hair at a tower window. As she leans over, her hair envelops him; he will not let it go, and they are discovered by Golaud, who chides them for their strange behavior.

SCENE 8—Underground vaults of the castle

Golaud warns Pelléas that he must try to avoid Mélisande.

SCENE 9—In front of the castle

Golaud questions his son by his first marriage, Yniold, as to the actions of Pelléas and Mélisande. The child's descriptions increase the anxiety of Golaud's suspicious and tortured mind.

SCENE 10—In front of the castle

Pelléas tells Mélisande that he must go away, and they agree to meet that evening for the last time at the well.

ACT III

SCENE 11—A room in the castle

Arkel comforts Mélisande. Golaud enters and in a frenzied fit cruelly seizes her by the hair, inflicting great pain upon her.

SCENE 12—A well in the park

Pelléas and Mélisande meet. Pelléas bids her farewell, as they acknowledge their love for each other. Golaud approaches silently; though hearing him, they embrace passionately while Golaud with drawn sword rushes upon them, killing Pelléas.

SCENE 13—The bedroom of Mélisande

Mélisande, though uninjured, lies upon her deathbed. Golaud questions her about her love for Pelléas; she replies that it was not a guilty love. Mélisande dies—Golaud has gained no satisfaction for his tortured mind.

Pirates of Penzance

-»»*«««-

MUSIC BY: Sir Arthur Sullivan
WORLD PREMIERE: New York, New York,
    December 31, 1879

LIBRETTO BY: William S. Gilbert
NEW YORK CITY OPERA PREMIERE:
    (Sung in English) May 12, 1946

CONDUCTOR: Julius Rudel
STAGE DIRECTOR: Eugene S. Bryden
SCENIC DESIGNER: H. A. Condell
COSTUMES*
BALLET CHOREOGRAPHER: Igor Schwezoff

CHARACTERS (In order of appearance)		VOICE (type)	PREMIERE CAST (New York City Opera)
Samuel		Tenor	Hubert Norville
Ruth		Mezzo	Catherine Judah (debut)
The Pirate King		Bass	Gean Greenwell
Frederick		Baritone	John Hamill
General Edith	Daughters	Soprano	Susan Griska
Stanley's Kate	of Major-	Mezzo	Leonore Parker
Major Mabel	General	Soprano	Virginia MacWatters (debut)
Daughter Isabel[1]	Stanley	Mezzo	Mary Polynack (debut)
Major-General Stanley		Baritone	John Dudley
Sergeant of Police		Baritone	Emile Renan

Chorus of Pirates, Police, and General Stanley's Wards

SYNOPSIS OF STORY
TIME AND PLACE: England, 19th century

*

ACT I

SCENE—A rocky shore on the coast of Cornwall

Frederick, an apprentice in a band of pirates, is celebrating his twenty-first birthday with them. He has been freed from his indentures and has won full piratehood. But Frederick is not happy with this change, and Ruth, maid of all work, explains why.

It was Ruth who made the error. She did not hear clearly the instructions given to her by Frederick's father. He had requested that she appren-

---

* By Kate Friedheim; additional costumes by Brooks.
[1] Daughter Isabel was added to the New York City Opera production.

278

tice Frederick to a pilot, but she thought he said to a pirate. This is the cause of the present predicament.

Now the error must be corrected. Frederick on this his twenty-first birthday is to return to the world of honest men, and he believes it his duty to exterminate his beloved pirates. He pleads with the pirates to leave their evil trade and become honest men with him, but they refuse.

Ruth wants to leave with Frederick and suggests that they marry. He rejects this idea, mainly because of the difference in their ages.

Just then, a group of young maidens appears. Frederick sees beautiful young ladies for the first time and pleads with them to have pity on him in his predicament. One of them, Mabel, volunteers to sacrifice her future for him.

The pirates see this as a chance to marry, and each seizes one of the maidens. However, when their father, Major-General Stanley, enters, he arouses the sympathy of the pirates by claiming also to be an orphan. He persuades them to release his daughters, and they depart in peace. Only poor Ruth remains behind.

ACT II

SCENE—A ruined chapel on General Stanley's estate

General Stanley had purchased an estate in-cluding the family tombs, to which he and all his daughters have come. He confesses to Frederick and Mabel that he is really not an orphan as he had claimed to win the sympathy of the pirates.

Frederick is proposing to Mabel but is interrupted by policemen, who are to exterminate the pirates. However, the assignment does not appeal to them, and they are reluctant to look for the pirates.

Ruth and the Pirate King arrive to announce distressing news. They maintain that Frederick is not yet twenty-one years of age because he was born in leap year and is therefore still apprenticed to the pirates.

Being a slave of duty, Frederick resumes his indentures, tells the pirates that General Stanley is not really an orphan, and leaves his beloved Mabel. The policemen hide until the pirates appear and attempt to capture them. The police are quickly overcome by the pirates and, in order to save themselves, display and wave small Union Jack flags. The pirates recognize their allegiance to Queen Victoria and release the policemen.

Ruth has another announcement. She reveals that the pirates are really noblemen who have gone wrong and thus secures their pardon. General Stanley announces that they are forgiven and invites them to resume their ranks and marry his daughters.

Porgy and Bess

-»»*«««-

MUSIC BY: George Gershwin

WORLD PREMIERE: Boston, Massachusetts
September 30, 1935

LIBRETTO BY: DuBose Heyward
LYRICS BY: DuBose Heyward and Ira Gershwin
NEW YORK CITY OPERA PREMIERE:
(Sung in English) March 31, 1962

CONDUCTOR: Julius Rudel
STAGE DIRECTOR: William Ball
SCENIC DESIGNER: Stephen O. Saxe (debut)
COSTUMES: Stanley Simmons (debut)

CHARACTERS (In order of appearance)	VOICE (type)	PREMIERE CAST (New York City Opera)
Clara	Soprano	Gwendolyn Walters (debut)
Mingo	Tenor	Harold Pierson (debut)
Sportin' Life	Tenor	Rawn Spearman (debut)
Serena	Soprano	Barbara Webb (debut)
Jake	Baritone	Irving Barnes (debut)
Robbins	Tenor	Ned Wright (debut)
Jim	Baritone	Scott Gibson (debut)
Peter	Tenor	Joseph Crawford
Lily	Mezzo	Edna Ricks (debut)
Maria	Contralto	Carol Brice
Porgy	Bass-baritone	Lawrence Winters
Crown	Baritone	James Randolph (debut)
Annie	Mezzo	Alyce Webb
Bess	Soprano	Leesa Foster (debut)
Policemen	Speaking roles	Glenn Dowlen / James Fels
Detective	Baritone	Richard Fredricks
Undertaker	Baritone	Wanza King (debut)
Frazier	Baritone	Eugene Brice (debut)
Strawberry Girl	Mezzo	Doreese Duguan (debut)
Nelson	Tenor	Arthur Williams (debut)
Crabman	Tenor	Clyde Turner (debut)
Coroner	Speaking role	Richard Krause
Police Sergeant	Speaking role	Norman Grogan

Residents of Catfish Row, Fishermen, Children, and Stevedores

280

SYNOPSIS OF STORY
TIME AND PLACE: Charleston, South Carolina; 1920's

*

ACT I

SCENE—Catfish Row, a summer evening

It is a lazy summer evening as Clara, a fisherman's wife, sings a lullaby to her baby. Soon it will be time for the nightly dice game. Robbins, a stevedore, joins the gamblers in spite of the protests of his wife, Serena, and the crapshooters begin to "roll the bones." Porgy, a crippled beggar who makes his rounds in a little cart drawn by a goat, enters the game. So does Crown, a stevedore who is accompanied by his woman, Bess. Another player is Sportin' Life, a dope peddler from New York, who has come South to sell "happy dust" (cocaine) along the waterfront.

Crown is drunk and roisterous, and a sniff of Sportin' Life's "happy dust" drives him amuck. He quarrels with Robbins over a throw of the dice and kills him. The game breaks up hurriedly, and the tenants of Catfish Row hasten indoors as a police whistle blows. Crown makes for the palmetto jungles of Kittiwah Island across the bay to hide out. Bess seeks shelter, but the neighbors slam their doors in her face. Sportin' Life begs her to come with him to New York, but she spurns him to find refuge in Porgy's poor hovel.

It is night. Robbins' corpse lies shrouded and the neighbors file past, each contributing a mite to the saucer that holds the burial fund. A detective enters and warns Serena that unless her husband is buried next day his body will be turned over to medical students. The undertaker agrees to bury Robbins although the money collected only reached eighteen dollars.

It is morning some weeks later. Porgy, now settled down comfortably with Bess as his housekeeper, explains his philosophy of life to his neighbors. He has "plenty of nothin'," but nothin's plenty for him as long as he has his gal, his song, and heaven the whole day long. Sportin' Life tempts Bess with "happy dust," and Porgy warns him to keep away. Bess is reluctant to join the annual picnic of the "Repent Ye Saith the Lord" lodge, but Porgy persuades her to go with Maria as her escort. A happy procession forms, and the neighbors depart for Kittiwah Island, leaving Porgy alone.

ACT II

SCENE 1—Kittiwah Island, evening, the same day

Sportin' Life tries hard to turn the innocent picnic into an orgy. He skeptically reviews the Bible stories of David and Goliath, Jonah and the whale, and Moses and Pharaoh's daughter. The steamboat siren sounds, and the picnickers depart for the mainland. Bess is last to leave. Crown springs out of hiding and seizes her. She tells him that she now belongs to Porgy, but he roars with laughter and carried her, yielding, into the thicket.

SCENE 2—Catfish Row, before dawn, a week later

The fishermen, led by Clara's husband, Jake, depart for the Blackfish Bank. Bess is delirious, and Porgy is distraught. Serena prays for her, tells Porgy that she will soon be well again. The afternoon passes, and Bess emerges from her fever to consciousness. She is full of shame and fear that Crown will return to snatch her away again, but Porgy soothes her and promises to protect her. Suddenly the tranquility of the afternoon is broken by the sharp peal of the hurricane bell, the wind rises, and the shutters rattle and bang in the gathering storm.

The neighbors huddle together for shelter in Serena's room. There is a sudden knocking at the door, and Crown breaks into the room. He has swum all the way from Kittiwah through the hurricane and demands that Bess return to him. In a sudden lull in the storm, Clara looks out the window and shrieks that her husband's boat has capsized in the river. She hands her baby to Bess and rushes out. Crown follows her.

It is night, and the storm has blown itself out.

Bess nurses Clara's baby, and Porgy sits watching at the window. Crown stealthily enters and creeps over to Porgy's door. The crippled beggar springs out at him, seizes the knife in Crown's hand, and twists it into his body. Now, he cries exultantly, Bess has her man.

Next morning the neighbors remove the traces of last night's struggle. A group of white men enter—the detective, the coroner, a policeman—and doors and shutters are closed on them. The coroner explains that he is Porgy's friend, and his room is pointed out. Porgy admits that he knew Crown and is taken away as a witness to identify the body. Sportin' Life tells Bess that her man has gone for good. Now is the time for her to come to New York and enjoy life with him. He forces a dose of "happy dust" into her hand, and she succumbs.

A week goes by and Porgy returns home. As he is about to enter his room, he sees a buzzard, bird of ill omen, hovering above his window and drives it away. Sadly, the neighbors tell him that Bess has gone with Sportin' Life to New York. Porgy calls for his goatcart and leaves on the long journey north in search of his lost Bess.

Prince Igor

-»»*«««-

MUSIC BY: Alexander Borodin
(Completed by Alexander Glazunov and
Nikolai Rimsky-Korsakov)
WORLD PREMIERE: St. Petersburg, Russia,
November 4, 1890

LIBRETTO BY: Alexander Borodin and
Vladimir Vasilevich Stassov
English Translation By: Robert K. Evans
NEW YORK CITY OPERA PREMIERE:
(Sung in English) February 27, 1969

CONDUCTOR: Julius Rudel
STAGE DIRECTOR: Frank Corsaro
SETS, COSTUMES and LIGHTING: Will Steven Armstrong
CHOREOGRAPHY: Ron Sequoio (debut)

CHARACTERS (In order of appearance)	VOICE (type)	PREMIERE CAST (New York City Opera)
Eroshka, a Russian Army deserter	Tenor	Jack DeLon
Skula, a Russian Army deserter	Bass	Jack Bittner
Vladimir Jaroslavich, Prince Galitzky, brother of Jaroslavna	Bass	Roy Samuelsen
Igor Sviatoslavich, Prince of Poutivle	Baritone	Julian Patrick
Vladimir Igorevitch, Igor's son by his first marriage	Tenor	John Stewart
Jaroslavna, Igor's second wife	Soprano	Maralin Niska
Jaroslavna's nurse	Soprano	Beverly Evans
Polovtsian maiden	Soprano	Patricia Wise
Kontchakovna, Khan Kontchak's daughter	Mezzo	Joy Davidson (debut)
Polovtsian Chief	Dancer	Edward Villella (debut)
Ovlour, Igor's Polovtsian servant	Tenor	John Lankston
Kontchak, Polovtsian Khan	Bass	William Chapman
Favorite Slave Dancer		Katharyn Horne (debut)

Citizens, Soldiers, Prisoners, Dancers

SYNOPSIS OF STORY
TIME AND PLACE: Russia, 1185; Poutivle and the camp of the Polovtsians

*

283

Prince Igor, 1969

ACT I

SCENE—The public square of Poutivle

Prince Igor, who is going to war against the invading Polovtsians, enters the square with his son, Vladimir. As the troops are about to depart, everyone is dismayed by an eclipse of the sun. They believe it to be an evil omen, and two soldiers, Eroshka and Skula, decide to desert. Igor's wife, Jaroslavna, enters and begs him not to go. He gently reminds her that it is his duty as a ruler and leaves her in the care of her brother, Prince Galitzky.

ACT II

SCENE 1—The courtyard of Galitzky's palace

Prince Galitzky is trying to sway the people from their loyalty to Igor with lavish hospitality and gifts. In return, Galitzky is flattered by the whole court. A young girl has been abducted for Galitzky; he scorns a group of maidens begging him to restore her to them and to her family.

In a mock ceremony, Galitzky's drunken companions crown him in place of the absent Igor.

SCENE 2—A private chamber in Igor's palace

Jaroslavna mourns her husband's absence. The women of her court tell her of Galitzky's vile deeds, and when he enters, she threatens him with exile. Galitzky mocks her, claiming that Igor is dead, and implies that he himself is now master. After Galitzky leaves, news comes to Jaroslavna that Igor has lost a battle and been taken captive by the Polovtsians. Too late, a delegation of nobles warns that the city is in danger and offers to defend it; as they speak, flames break out in the city, which has already been taken by surprise.

ACT III

SCENE—The Polovtsian camp

Prince Igor and Vladimir are prisoners. Igor has given his word to Khan Kontchak that neither he nor his men will attempt to escape. A chorus of young girls is singing, and the Khan's beautiful daughter, Kontchakovna, joins them. Vladimir serenades her, and they confess their mutual love. Ovlour, a Polovtsian convert to Christianity, offers Igor a means of escape, but Igor reminds him of his pledge to the Khan. Meanwhile, Vladimir, spurred to action by his father's grief, breaks his word to the Khan and attempts to escape. While Igor is being entertained by Polovtsian songs and dances, the Khan has the body of the apprehended Vladimir brought in as a warning to Igor.

ACT IV

SCENE 1—Outside the Polovtsian camp

Distraught over his son's murder, Igor also decides to ignore his promise to Kontchak and escape.

SCENE 2—The public square of Poutivle

Jaroslavna sings a lament, and the populace of Poutivle bemoans the devastation of their city. Jaroslavna's grief turns to joy as she sees her husband returning, and they are reunited. Eroshka and Skula, who have been enjoying the favor of Galitzky during Igor's absence, skillfully allay the wrath of the populace and save their own lives. The opera ends amid general rejoicing over Igor's return.

The Prisoner

→))) * (((←

MUSIC BY: Luigi Dallapiccola

WORLD PREMIERE: Turin, Italy on radio—
December 1, 1949
Florence, Italy, First Stage Presentation—
May 20, 1950

LIBRETTO BY: Luigi Dallapiccola
English translation and text: Harold Heiberg
NEW YORK CITY OPERA PREMIERE:
(Sung in English) September 29, 1960

CONDUCTOR: Leopold Stokowski
STAGE DIRECTOR: Christopher West (debut)
SCENERY, COSTUMES, and LIGHTING: Donald Oenslager

CHARACTERS (In order of appearance)	VOICE (type)	PREMIERE CAST (New York City Opera)
The Mother	Soprano	Anne McKnight
The Prisoner	Bass-baritone	Norman Treigle
The Jailer	Tenor	Richard Cassilly
The Priests	Tenor	Maurice Stern
	Baritone	John Macurdy
The Inquisitor	Tenor	Richard Cassilly

Note: This performance followed Monteverdi's *Orfeo.*

SYNOPSIS OF STORY

TIME AND PLACE: A horrible cell, the dungeons of Saragossa, Spain; second half of the 16th
century

*

PROLOGUE
(Before a black curtain)

The Mother sings to her Son of a vision that she has nightly. She sees a deep cavern with a shadowy figure approaching from the rear. She believes it to be King Philip, returned from the grave with his claim to be the ruler of the earth. Suddenly, before she awakens, the specter is re-placed by a death's head. The Mother cries out to her beloved Son.

FIRST SCENE

The Son is telling his Mother of his loneli-ness in the darkness of the cell. He has suffered tortures beyond description. He has been in deep despair until the Jailer speaks to him and he is once again able to pray. The Mother believes that she will not see her Son again.

SECOND SCENE

The Jailer comes to the cell with a lighted lamp and urges the Prisoner to have hope, to keep his hold on life. He describes the uprising that is taking place throughout many cities in Flanders. The beggars are fighting for liberty. King Philip and the Duke of Alba are leading their troops against the beggars.

THIRD SCENE

The Prisoner is praying for guidance and deliverance. Two priests appear and discuss the fate of the prisoners. The Prisoner does not speak to them. He continues to pray for help.

FOURTH SCENE

The Prisoner is jubilant at the prospect of being released from his suffering. He believes that his prayers have been answered and that he will be free to roam the countryside. The Grand Inquisitor does not understand the Prisoner's jubilation at his sentence. The Prisoner repeats "Liberty."

I Puritani

-»»*«(-

MUSIC BY: Vincenzo Bellini
WORLD PREMIERE: Paris, France,
    January 25, 1835

LIBRETTO BY: Carlo Pepoli
NEW YORK CITY OPERA PREMIERE;
    (Sung in Italian) February 21, 1974

CONDUCTOR: Julius Rudel
PRODUCTION DEVISED and DIRECTED BY: Tito Capobianco
SCENERY and COSTUMES: Carl Toms (debut)

CHARACTERS (In order of appearance)	VOICE (type)	PREMIERE CAST (New York City Opera)
Sir Riccardo Forth (Sir Richard)	Baritone	Richard Fredricks
Sir Bruno Roberton, his confidant	Tenor	Jerold Siena
Elvira, daughter of Lord Walton	Soprano	Beverly Sills
Enrichetta (Henrietta), widow of Charles I	Mezzo	Diane Curry
Sir Giorgio (George) Walton, Elvira's uncle	Bass	Richard T. Gill
Lord Gualtier Walton, Puritan Governor-General	Bass	Samuel Ramey
Lord Arturo Talbot, Cavalier, loyal to the Stuarts (Lord Arthur)	Tenor	Enrico Di Giuseppe

Puritans, Ladies, Soldiers, Nobles, Men and Women of the Fortress

SYNOPSIS OF STORY
TIME AND PLACE: Plymouth, England; 1650's

*

ACT I

SCENE 1—Outside Lord Walton's fortified castle

Cromwell's supporters, the Puritans, are fighting the Cavaliers, royalists loyal to the executed Stuart King, Charles I. The Puritan Governor-General, Lord Walton, holds the king's widow, Henrietta, prisoner in his fortified castle near Plymouth. Although he has arranged for his daughter, Elvira, to marry a fellow Puritan, Sir Richard Forth, she is in love with one of the enemy, the Cavalier, Lord Arthur Talbot. Sir Richard expresses his anger at Elvira's rejection to his confidant, Sir Bruno Roberton.

SCENE 2—Elvira's apartments in the castle

Elvira, afraid that she will not be permitted to marry Lord Arthur, waits in her rooms for her father's decision. Her uncle, Sir George Walton, brings the happy news that he has finally persuaded her father to give in to her wishes.

288

SCENE 3—A large hall in the castle

Preparations are being made for the wedding when Lord Walton receives instructions to send Henrietta to London. Despite his pending marriage to Elvira, Lord Arthur hopes to save the woman he still regards as his Queen from the same fate as her husband. When Elvira leaves her bridal veil with Henrietta, Arthur persuades her to use the veil as a disguise to escape with him. Their flight is blocked by the arrival of the jealous Sir Richard. But, discovering that it is Henrietta in the veil, he helps them to escape since he realizes that Arthur's departure will mean that his rival's marriage to Elvira will not take place. Their escape becomes known and Elvira, thinking she has been deserted, goes mad, while everyone denounces Arthur.

ACT II

SCENE—The Puritan castle

Sir George announces that death has been decreed for the fugitive Lord Arthur for his part in the Queen's escape. He describes the distressing effect of madness upon his niece Elvira. Her pathetic behavior when she appears bears witness to his words. Both Sir George and the rejected Sir Richard try to console her, and Richard is moved to agree to Arthur's safe return if he comes alone and unarmed. They fail to reach Elvira's demented mind. They swear to fight faithfully together against the Cavaliers.

ACT III

SCENE—Outside the castle

Arthur, hunted by the Puritan soldiers, secretly returns to the castle grounds, hoping to see Elvira once more before he leaves England forever. He hears her voice, and when he serenades her she appears. As he explains why he had to abandon her on their wedding day, Elvira begins to understand and her sanity slowly returns. Their joy in being together is short-lived: her madness is brought back by the sound of drums. Her cries for help bring the soldiers, who recognize Lord Arthur. Knowing that Arthur's death will surely mean Elvira's own demise, Sir George and Sir Richard try to prevent his capture. A messenger arrives with the news that the Puritans have defeated the Stuart forces and that Cromwell has pardoned all prisoners held by the Puritans. Elvira once again regains her senses when she hears this, and the lovers are united.

The Rape of Lucretia

–»»*«««–

MUSIC BY: Benjamin Britten

WORLD PREMIERE: Glyndebourne, England,
    July 12, 1946

LIBRETTO BY: Ronald Duncan
After Andre Obey's play *Le Voil de Lucrece*
NEW YORK CITY OPERA PREMIERE:
    (Sung in English) October 23, 1958

CONDUCTOR: Julius Rudel
STAGE DIRECTOR: John Daggett Howell (debut)
SCENERY and COSTUMES: Andreas Nomikos

CHARACTERS (In order of appearance)	VOICE (type)	PREMIERE CAST (New York City Opera)
Male Chorus	Tenor	David Lloyd
Female Chorus	Soprano	Brenda Lewis
Collatinus	Bass	Joshua Hecht
Junius	Baritone	Emile Renan
Tarquinius	Baritone	William Chapman
Lucretia	Contralto	Frances Bible
Bianca	Mezzo	Ruth Kobart
Lucia	Soprano	Lee Venora

SYNOPSIS OF STORY
TIME AND PLACE: Rome, 500 B.C.

*

ACT I

SCENE 1—The army camp

Rome is ruled by the Etruscan upstart Tarquinius. The officers are discussing the outcome of their bet of the night before when they rode home unannounced to see what their wives were doing in their absence. Only Lucretia, Collatinus' wife, was at home. The others, not excluding Junius' Patricia, were all found in one compromising situation or another.

Tarquinius and Junius quarrel over this and start to fight but are separated by Collatinus.

Junius rushes angrily from the tent. The idea of revenge fills his mind.

Collatinus follows Junius to reason with him and persuade him to take a less directly personal view of the situation. Junius leaves Tarquinius alone, after suggesting that to prove Lucretia chaste is something even the Prince will not attempt.

SCENE 2—Lucretia's house

Lucretia and her two female companions are spinning. The women prepare for bed.

290

A loud knock announces that Tarquinius has arrived. Lucretia's two companions remark on the strangeness of a visit so late from the Prince, whose palace lies only across the city. Lucretia cannot refuse the Prince the hospitality he is asking for.

ACT II

SCENE 1—Lucretia's bedroom

Lucretia is asleep. Tarquinius enters the room, goes to the bed, bends over Lucretia to wake her, as he had planned, with a kiss.

Lucretia wakes. She pleads for mercy, but Tarquinius insists that her resistance is diminishing. Lucretia again pleads with Tarquinius to leave, but he pulls the covers from her bed and threatens her with his sword. He beats out the candle with his sword.

SCENE 2—Lucretia's house

Lucia and Bianca discuss whether it was Tarquinius they heard gallop out of the courtyard earlier in the morning. Lucretia enters, but her usually quiet behavior gives way to something like hysteria. She orders Lucia to send a messenger to Collatinus telling him to come home.

Collatinus and Junius arrive. Lucretia, dressed in mourning, tells of her tragedy. Collatinus attempts to comfort and sustain his wife, affirming that they must never again be parted. Lucretia is overcome by what has happened to her and stabs herself.

Regina

-»»*«««-

MUSIC BY: Marc Blitzstein

WORLD PREMIERE: Boston, Massachusetts,
October 11, 1949

LIBRETTO BY: Marc Blitzstein, based on
the play *The Little Foxes* by Lillian Hellman

NEW YORK CITY OPERA PREMIERE:
(Sung in English) April 2, 1953

CONDUCTOR: Julius Rudel
STAGE DIRECTOR: Robert Lewis
SCENIC DESIGNER: Horace Armistead*
COSTUMES: Aline Bernstein*

CHARACTERS (In order of appearance)	VOICE (type)	PREMIERE CAST (New York City Opera)
Addie, the cook	Contralto	Lucretia West (debut)
Cal, the butler	Baritone	Lawrence Winters
Belle, the maid	Soprano	Margaret Tynes
Alexandra Giddens (Zan), daughter of Regina and Horace Giddens	Soprano	Priscilla Gillette (debut)
Regina Giddens	Soprano	Brenda Lewis
Birdie Hubbard	Soprano	Ellen Faull
Oscar Hubbard, Birdie's husband	Baritone	Emile Renan
Leo Hubbard, their son	Tenor	Michael Pollock
William Marshall	Tenor	Lloyd Thomas Leech
Ben Hubbard	Bass	Leon Lishner (debut)
Horace Giddens, Regina's husband	Bass	William Wilderman (debut)
Manders	Tenor	Charles Kuestner
Jazz	Tenor	William Dillard (debut)
Bagtry	Baritone	Russell Goodwin
Band:		
Banjo	Musicians	Bernard Addison
Clarinet		Eddie Barefield
Trombone		Theodore Donnelly
Drums		Sticks Evans
Pianist		Lucy Brown
Violinist		Eugene Bergen

Townspeople, Field Workers

SYNOPSIS OF STORY
TIME AND PLACE: Alabama; 1900

*

---

* Sets and costumes from the original production by Cheryl Crawford.

292

PROLOGUE

SCENE—The veranda of the Giddens' home

It is late morning in spring. A number of people are gathered on the veranda of the Giddens' house in Bowden, Alabama. Spiritual and ragtime singing can be heard. The pleasant scene is interrupted by the appearance of Regina Giddens, who dispels the friendly atmosphere.

ACT I

SCENE—The living room of the Giddens' home, the same evening

William Marshall, a financier from the North, is the guest of honor at a party given by Regina. Other members of the Giddens family are present—Regina's two brothers, Ben and Oscar Hubbard; Oscar's wife, Birdie, and his son, Leo; and Alexandra, Regina's daughter. With the exception of Alexandra, the members of the family are unpleasant to each other. After Regina has completed the business deal with Marshall, he leaves the party and the family becomes involved in feuding over the possession of the family money now in the hands of Regina's husband, Horace Giddens. Horace is in the hospital, ill with heart trouble. Regina sends Alexandra to bring him home. She is also plotting to marry Alexandra to Leo in order to keep the money in the family.

ACT II

SCENE 1—The living room, a week later

Another ball to entertain Marshall is being planned by Regina. When Horace and Alexandra arrive home from the hospital, there is a pretense of reconciliation, at which Regina urges Horace to put his signature on the deal she has arranged with Marshall. Horace will not consent to the deal. Meanwhile, Leo, at Oscar's insistence, has stolen bonds from his uncle's bank, where he works.

SCENE 2—Same

At the ball, the townspeople are guests but demonstrate their hatred of the Hubbards. Horace is in a wheelchair. He tells his bank manager to bring him his safe deposit box the next morning; he intends to change his will. Leo returns with the stolen bonds and gives them to Ben, who can now tell Marshall the deal is settled. Regina becomes so angry at Horace, because he will not agree to the deal, that she tells him she hopes he dies.

ACT III

SCENE—The living room, the next afternoon

Horace, Alexandra, Addie, and Birdie are kept indoors because of rain. They are enjoying a quiet afternoon with wine and cookies until Regina appears. Horace shows her the empty safe deposit box. Although he knows Leo has stolen the bonds, he insists he will say he lent them to the brothers. Regina wants Horace to die and taunts him until he has a heart attack. She stands by refusing to give him any aid. After he collapses, she calls for help to carry him upstairs.

When Ben, Oscar, and Leo come into the room and see the empty box, they know the theft has been discovered. Regina tells them she knows, too, and threatens them with exposure and jail unless she gets a larger share of the money. They have no choice and must agree, now that Horace has died.

Finally, Alexandra becomes aware of the whole situation and what her mother has done. She tells Regina she knows what has happened and that she has decided to go away.

Rigoletto

-»»*«««-

MUSIC BY: Giuseppe Verdi
WORLD PREMIERE: Venice, Italy,
   March 11, 1851

LIBRETTO BY: Francesco Maria Piave
NEW YORK CITY OPERA PREMIERE:
   (Sung in Italian) May 9, 1946

CONDUCTOR: Laszlo Halasz
STAGE DIRECTOR: Leopold Sachse
SCENIC DESIGNER: Richard Rychtarik
BALLET CHOREOGRAPHER: Igor Schwezoff
COSTUMES*

CHARACTERS (In order of appearance)	VOICE (type)	PREMIERE CAST (New York City Opera)
The Duke of Mantua	Tenor	Eugene Conley
Borsa, a courtier	Tenor	Nathaniel Sprinzena
Countess Ceprano	Mezzo	Susan Griska
Rigoletto	Baritone	Ivan Petroff (debut)
Marullo	Baritone	Arthur Newman
Count Ceprano	Baritone	Emile Renan
Count Monterone	Bass	Grant Garnell
Sparafucile	Bass	James Pease (debut)
Gilda	Soprano	Rosemarie Brancato
Giovanna	Mezzo	Mary Kreste
A Page	Mezzo	Lenore Parker
Maddalena	Contralto	Rosalind Nadell

Courtiers and their ladies

SYNOPSIS OF STORY
TIME AND PLACE: Mantua in the 16th century

*

ACT I

SCENE 1—Court of the Duke of Mantua

The amours and intrigues of the Duke of Mantua have begun to antagonize the courtiers and guests assembled at a party at the Duke's palace. Rigoletto, the Duke's hunchback jester, mocks the courtiers and ridicules Count Monterone, who has come to denounce the Duke for seducing his daughter. Monterone turns in a rage

---

* Executed by Kate Friedheim.

294

and places a curse on both the Duke and Rigoletto.

SCENE 2—Rigoletto's house and street nearby

On the street near his house, Rigoletto is accosted by an assassin, Sparafucile, who offers his services. Rigoletto then comments bitterly on how his own life is as offensive to him as the man he has just met, and broods about the curse of Monterone. As he enters his garden, Rigoletto is greeted by his beloved daughter, Gilda, whose existence he has successfully hidden from the world he hates. Hearing a noise outside, Rigoletto goes to investigate, and the Duke (disguised as a student) slips into the garden with the aid of Giovanna, Gilda's nurse. Gilda recognizes him as the young man who has been so attentive to her at church. Fearing her father's return, Gilda persuades the Duke to leave; giving her a false name, the Duke departs. The courtiers trick Rigoletto into helping them abduct Gilda (whom they believe to be his mistress) by telling him that it is Ceprano's wife they are kidnapping. When Rigoletto discovers what he has done, he recalls Monterone's curse.

ACT II

SCENE—A room in the Ducal Palace

The courtiers inform the Duke that Rigoletto's "mistress" is now in the palace. The Duke, realizing her true identity, rushes off to where she is being held. Rigoletto enters, bemoaning the loss of his daughter. He pretends to ignore the taunts of the courtiers in the hope of finding out what they have done with Gilda. When he learns that she is in the palace, he demands, then begs that they return her to him and reveals that she is his daughter. The men are unmoved and bar his way to the Duke's quarters. Gilda enters in tears and confesses her shame to Rigoletto, who orders the courtiers to leave them alone. In spite of Gilda's protestations, Rigoletto swears vengeance upon the Duke.

ACT III

SCENE—Sparafucile's inn on the outskirts of Mantua

The Duke has come to Sparafucile's inn by the river, where he is being entertained by the assassin's sister, Maddalena. Rigoletto and Gilda watch the scene from outside. Rigoletto tells Gilda to go to Verona, where he will join her, adding that she must dress as a man for safety on her journey. After she leaves, he arranges with Sparafucile to kill the Duke and leave his body in a sack outside the door at midnight. However, Gilda, still in love with the Duke, returns to the inn. When she overhears Maddalena persuading Sparafucile to spare the Duke's life and kill in his place anyone else who arrives at the inn, she decides to sacrifice her own life. Later, as Rigoletto drags the sack toward the river, gloating over his revenge, he hears the voice of the Duke. Tearing open the sack, he discovers the body of the dying Gilda. The curse of Monterone has been fulfilled.

Il Ritorno D'Ulisse in Patria

→»»*«««

MUSIC BY: Claudio Monteverdi
Realized and Orchestrated by
  Raymond Leppard
WORLD PREMIERE: Venice, Italy, February 1641
First modern staging took place in Paris, France,
  May 16, 1925

LIBRETTO BY: Giacomo Badoaro
NEW YORK CITY OPERA PREMIERE:
  (Sung in Italian) February 29, 1976

CONDUCTOR: Mario Bernardi
STAGE DIRECTOR: Ian Strasfogel
SCENIC DESIGNER: Douglas W. Schmidt
COSTUMES: Jane Greenwood

CHARACTERS (In order of appearance)	VOICE (type)	PREMIERE CAST (New York City Opera)
L'Umana Fragilita	Mezzo	Alice Shields (debut)
Il Tempo	Bass-baritone	Irwin Densen
La Fortuna	Mezzo	Diane Curry
Amore	Soprano	Rose Wildes
Penelope	Mezzo	Frederica Von Stade (debut)
Ericlea, Ulisse's old nurse	Mezzo	Sandra Walker
Nettuno	Bass	Ara Berberian
Giove	Tenor	David Griffith
Ulisse	Baritone	Richard Stilwell
Minerva	Mezzo	Hilda Harris
Melanto, Penelope's servant	Mezzo	Kathleen Hegierski
Eurimaco, Antinoo's servant	Tenor	Howard Hensel
Eumete, a shepherd	Tenor	David Lloyd
Iro, a gluttonous beggar	Tenor	Nico Castel
Telemaco, Ulisse's son	Tenor	Henry Price
Antinoo	Bass	Will Roy
Pisandro	Tenor	John Lankston
Amfinomo	Tenor	Melvin Lowery

Nymphs, Sailors, and Suitors

SYNOPSIS OF STORY

TIME AND PLACE: A dramatic setting of the final part of the *Odyssey*, which recounts Ulysses'
return to his homeland

*

PROLOGUE

SCENE—The Heavens

Human Frailty bemoans her weakness, tormented by the lame deity Time, the willful changes of Fortune, and the all-conquering power of Love.

ACT I

SCENE 1—Penelope's bedchamber

Penelope, Ulysses' faithful wife, laments her twenty years' separation from her husband. She is pitied by Ulysses' old nurse, Ericlea.

SCENE 2—The coast of Ithaca

A raging storm forces a Phaeacian boat to shore. Neptune appears and angrily accuses the Phaeacians of violating his wishes by helping Ulysses to return home. Jove hears his complaints sympathetically and allows him to wreak his revenge on the Phaeacians. They set sail again, leaving Ulysses on shore, only to have Neptune transform their ship into a rock. Ulysses awakens, alone and angered by the apparent treachery of the Phaeacians. He prays to the gods to avenge his wrath.

The scene is transformed into verdant countryside as Minerva appears in the disguise of a shepherd boy. Ulysses is overjoyed to learn that he has landed in Ithaca, his home. Minerva then reveals herself to Ulysses and tells him that his wife, Penelope, has remained faithful. Minerva instructs her nymphs to conceal the treasures Ulysses has brought back with him, transforms him into an aged beggar, and tells him to seek out the shepherd Eumete, his faithful follower.

ACT II

SCENE 1—Penelope's bedchanber

Melanto, maid to Penelope, and Eurimaco, a servant of one of Penelope's suitors, declare their love for each other and curse the fact that the joy of their love is overcast by Penelope's mourning for Ulysses. As Penelope arrives, Melanto tries to persuade her to yield to the wooers, but Penelope responds that she who has known the pain of love once can never love again.

SCENE 2—Eumete's hut

Eumete, the shepherd, complains of the treachery now dominant in the court. He is interrupted by the gluttonous beggar, Iro, and drives him off. Ulysses, disguised as an old beggar, tells a joyful Eumete of the imminent return of his old master.

SCENE 3—A rocky pass

Minerva brings Telemachus, Ulysses' son, back to Ithaca. The shepherd and the old beggar tell him of Ulysses' return. After Telemachus sends Eumete off to the palace with the good news, the beggar vanishes and reappears in the form of Ulysses. Father and son rejoice at their reunion.

SCENE 4—The banquet hall

Antinoo, Amfinomo, and Pisandro, three of the insolent princes who have terrorized the Ithacan court for the past years as they wooed Penelope, call upon her to forget her husband and to declare love for one of them. Suddenly, Eumete appears, announces the arrival of Telemachus, and suggests that Ulysses may also soon appear. Enraged by the news, the suitors plot to murder Telemachus. The sudden appearance of an eagle, an omen of doom, causes them to decide to offer great gifts to Penelope so that she may finally choose among them.

SCENE 5—Entrance hall of the palace

Home at last, the transformed Ulysses enters the palace. Minerva promises him a glorious triumph in battle against the suitors. Eumete enters to report that the suitors were terrified at the mention of Ulysses' name.

SCENE 6—A room in the palace

Telemachus tells Penelope of having met the beautiful Helen of Troy, who indicated that Ulysses would return. Penelope prays that this is true.

ACT III

SCENE 1—Main hall of the palace

The suitors object when Eumete brings the

old beggar (Ulysses) to the throne room. Iro picks a fight with the old man. In the ensuing wrestling match, Ulysses triumphs. The suitors present Penelope with their rich gifts, and she commands Melanto to fetch the bow of Ulysses. Whoever can bend the bow will become her husband and the successor to Ulysses' throne. When the suitors fail, the aged beggar asks for his chance. He bends the bow and slays the wooers.

Iro mourns for the suitors and their magnificent feasts. He vows to kill himself because he can no longer find support for his parasitical ways.

SCENE 2—Penelope's bedchanber

Eumete and Telemachus try unsuccessfully to persuade the doubting Penelope that it was actually Ulysses who triumphed over the suitors. Ericlea considers whether or not she should reveal her secret to Penelope. She has recognized the wound that Ulysses had at one time suffered from a wild boar.

Eumete and Telemachus urge Penelope to give up her disbelief. Ulysses enters the room. Penelope, fearful after the twenty years' absence, believes that a strange power has given someone the means of assuming Ulysses' form. Ericlea then ends her silence and tells her secret. When Ulysses describes to Penelope how she covered her bed—a secret he alone knows—she finally believes he has returned.

Roberto Devereux

-»»*«««-

MUSIC BY: Gaetano Donizetti

WORLD PREMIERE: Naples, Italy,
October 29, 1837

LIBRETTO BY: Salvatore Cammarano
Based on François Ancelot's play
Elisabeth d'Angleterre
NEW YORK CITY OPERA PREMIERE:
(Sung in Italian) October 15, 1970

CONDUCTOR: Julius Rudel
PRODUCTION DEVISED and DIRECTED BY: Tito Capobianco
SCENIC DESIGNER: Ming Cho Lee
COSTUMES: José Varona

CHARACTERS (In order of appearance)	VOICE (type)	PREMIERE CAST (New York City Opera)
Sara, Duchess of Nottingham	Mezzo	Beverly Wolff
Queen Elizabeth	Soprano	Beverly Sills
Lord Cecil	Tenor	John Lankston
Page	Bass	Jack Bittner
Sir Walter Raleigh	Bass	David Rae Smith
Roberto Devereux, Earl of Essex	Tenor	Placido Domingo
Duke of Nottingham	Baritone	Louis Quilico
A servant of Nottingham	Bass	Don Yule

Lords and Ladies of the Court, Attendants, Servants, and Guards

SYNOPSIS OF STORY
TIME AND PLACE: England, 1601

*

ACT I

SCENE 1—Reception chamber in Westminster Palace

Sitting apart from the other Ladies of Queen Elizabeth's court, Sara, Duchess of Nottingham, tries in vain to hide her tears. With a false smile she attempts to blame her unhappiness on the tragic love story she is reading. Queen Elizabeth enters, anxious about the imminent return from Ireland of the Earl of Essex, Robert Devereux, to face charges of treason. She confides in Sara that she is fearful that Devereux has betrayed not only Elizabeth the Queen, but also Elizabeth, the woman. As Queen she could pardon his treason, but she hints that she would do so only if he has been faithful in his love for her.

The Queen again refuses to give in to the demands of Lord Cecil and her Royal Council that she proclaim Devereux's guilt, saying that she requires more proof. The page's announcement of the Earl of Essex's arrival causes different reac-

"The Tudor Queens." Beverly Sills as (left to right) Elizabeth in *Roberto Devereux,* 1970, *Maria Stuarda,* 1972, and *Anna Bolena,* 1973.

tions in the angry Lords, the worried Queen, and the distraught Sara.

Elizabeth dismisses the others as Robert enters and kneels before her. He denies that he has plotted against her and asks why she has ordered him executed. Declaring that it is by her order alone that he remains free, the Queen reminds him of the ring he wears, which she has long ago given him as a pledge of her protection. She reminisces about the happy past when Devereux's love made each day seem like a dream, a dream that has since dissolved. Devereux's continued silence, when it is obvious that she wants only a reassurance of his love for her to forgive him anything, arouses Elizabeth's suspicions. Thinking that the Queen has discovered his and Sara's secret, Devereux traps himself in answering her further questions. He realizes, despite his subsequent denials, that Elizabeth now knows that he does indeed love another. Vowing to herself to destroy both Devereux and her unknown rival, the Queen angrily departs.

The entrance of the Duke of Nottingham (Sara's husband) interrupts Devereux's thoughts.

When his offer of help is rejected, Nottingham remarks that his wife has also turned from him, sitting alone in her rooms, weeping as she embroiders a blue sash. Lord Cecil summons Nottingham to the Council, and the Duke leaves, swearing to defend Devereux against his enemies.

SCENE 2—Sara's rooms in the Palace of Nottingham

Sara is thinking of the danger facing Devereux when he suddenly appears. She answers his angry accusations of betrayal by explaining that, after the death of her father, she was forced by the Queen to marry Nottingham. She begs Devereux to save himself, to remember the ring and its promise of the Queen's protection, but he casts off the ring, saying that he would rather die for Sara's love than turn to the Queen. Sara finally convinces him that their love is hopeless and that he must escape, to save his life and her honor. As they bid a sorrowful final farewell, Sara gives Devereux the blue sash as a remembrance of their love.

ACT II

SCENE—Great Hall of Westminster

Lord Cecil enters to announce to Queen Elizabeth and her Court, who have waited anxiously throughout the night to learn of Devereux's fate, that the Royal Council has reached its decision—death. Elizabeth dismisses the Court as Sir Walter Raleigh arrives to report Devereux's capture, showing the Queen the sash they discovered while searching him. Bearing the execution decree that he has so passionately fought against, Nottingham pleads with the Queen not to sign the order but to pardon Devereux. Elizabeth refuses to listen, proclaiming that she now has proof of his guilt. Enraged, Elizabeth turns to Devereux as the guards lead him in. At the sight of the blue sash she holds, Devereux realizes he is doomed—by the vengeance of a betrayed Queen and of a husband faced with evidence of his own wife's betrayal. Elizabeth, believing it is her dishonor he is avenging, prevents Nottingham from drawing his sword against Devereux, declaring that he is already condemned. When Devereux refuses to name Elizabeth's rival in return for his life, the Queen summons the Court and signs the order for his beheading.

ACT III

SCENE 1—Sara's private rooms

Nottingham returns home to find Sara with a letter from Devereux urging her to rush to the Queen with the ring. Ignoring Sara's tearful protestations of innocence, the vengeful Nottingham orders her kept a prisoner until Devereux's death.

SCENE 2—Tower of London

Alone in his cell, Devereux awaits his execution, hoping that he will receive word that Sara has reached the Queen and saved him from the block. He does not fear death, but wants to die at the hands of Nottingham and save Sara's honor.

SCENE 3—Reception chamber of Westminster

Surrounded by her Court, Queen Elizabeth awaits the hour of Devereux's execution. She has sent Raleigh to bring Sara to her, wanting the solace of her friendship. Although prepared, even at this late moment, to pardon Devereux if he should send her the ring, the Queen is told by Lord Cecil that Devereux had no message for her.

The disheveled Sara rushes in with Devereux's ring; she asks no mercy for herself, only that Devereux's life be spared. The Queen immediately orders the Lords to bring Devereux to her—but it is too late. In her anguish, Elizabeth turns her vengeance upon Sara, who took Devereux's love, and Nottingham, who allowed him to die.

Der Rosenkavalier

-))⁕(((-

MUSIC BY: Richard Strauss
WORLD PREMIERE: Dresden, Germany,
    January 26, 1911

LIBRETTO BY: Hugo von Hofmannsthal
NEW YORK CITY OPERA PREMIERE:
    (Sung in German) October 6, 1949

CONDUCTOR: Joseph Rosenstock
STAGE DIRECTOR: Leopold Sachse
SCENIC DESIGNER: H. A. Condell
COSTUMES*

CHARACTERS (In order of appearance)	VOICE (type)	PREMIERE CAST (New York City Opera)
Octavian	Mezzo	Frances Bible
The Marschallin	Soprano	Maria Reining
Baron Ochs	Bass	Lorenzo Alvary (debut)
Majordomo of Marschallin	Tenor	Thomas Powell
Notary	Bass	Arthur Newman
A milliner	Soprano	Dorothy MacNeil
Animal vendor	Tenor	Michael Pollock (debut)
Valzacchi	Tenor	Luigi Vellucci
Annina	Contralto	Rosalind Nadell
Hairdresser	Mute	Michael Arshansky
Three Orphans	Soprano	Basel Landia (debut)
	Mezzo	Mary LeSawyer
	Contralto	Lorraine Farnsworth (debut)
A singer	Tenor	Rudolf Petrak
Marianne	Soprano	Leona Scheunemann
Majordomo of Von Faninal	Tenor	Richard Wright (debut)
Herr von Faninal	Baritone	Richard Wentworth
Sophie	Soprano	Virginia Haskins
Innkeeper	Tenor	Nathaniel Sprinzena
Police Commissioner	Bass	Arthur Newman
Leopold	Mute	Alan Winston

Footmen, Couriers, Waiters, Guests, Musicians, Children

Note: Character of Mohamet (mute role) added to the program on November 15.

SYNOPSIS OF STORY
TIME AND PLACE: Vienna, mid-18th century during the reign of Maria Theresa

⁕

---

* By Kate Friedheim.

302

ACT I

SCENE—The boudoir of the Princess von Werdenberg (the Marschallin)

During their passionate love scene, the Marschallin and her young lover, Octavian, are first interrupted by a little blackamoor with the Princess' breakfast tray, and then by the boorish Baron Ochs who is trying to bolster his depleted finances by marrying Sophie, the daughter of the "nouveau riche" von Faninal. The engagement to Sophie doesn't stop the Baron from making overt advances to Octavian, who has disguised himself as the maid, "Mariandl," in order to facilitate his escape from the Marschallin's boudoir. Baron Ochs is looking for a Rosebearer to present a silver rose to Sophie as a symbol of his love. In a mischievous mood the Marschallin proposes Octavian as the Rosebearer. Ochs notices the resemblance between the portrait of Octavian and "Mariandl." Various favor-seekers and members of the Princess' household arrive for the "levee," disrupting the morning routine. Valzacchi and his "niece," Annina, two Italians of many talents and shady character, manage to attach themselves to the retinue of Ochs, promising to find the elusive "Mariandl."

The Marschallin, prompted perhaps by her liaison with a younger lover, muses on the relentlessness of time. When Octavian returns, he finds her in a melancholy state of mind, and even his ardent protestations of love cannot alter her mood. Whatever his intentions now, her young lover will, one day, leave her for a younger and prettier woman.

ACT II

SCENE—The main hall in von Faninal's house

Great excitement prevails as Octavian arrives bearing the traditional silver rose for Sophie.

During their short conversation the two young people are drawn to each other, and only the appearance of Ochs prevents them from declaring their love. Sophie is appalled by the gross manners and the appearance of her future bridegroom. While Ochs and Faninal retire to finalize their financial arrangements, Octavian promises to save Sophie from a marriage to Ochs. Valzacchi and Annina surprise the lovers and summon Ochs. During the dispute that follows, Octavian slightly wounds Ochs. This produces a gigantic turmoil in von Faninal's house. Octavian manages to bribe Valzacchi and Annina, changing their allegiance; he plans to maneuver Ochs into such a compromising situation that he will become unacceptable to Sophie. To accomplish this, Annina brings Ochs a note, letting him know that "Mariandl" (Octavian himself) will be delighted to meet the Baron the following evening for an intimate rendezvous.

ACT III

SCENE—A tavern on the outskirts of Vienna

In a disreputable tavern Ochs meets "Mariandl." During their tête-à-tête, various "ghosts" (all in the employ of Valzacchi) and Annina—as the supposedly abandoned wife of Ochs—appear, causing a scandal which in turn brings the police onto the scene. Von Faninal, summoned by Octavian, witnesses the outrageous behavior of his future son-in-law, as does the Princess, who has been brought there by Ochs' lackey, Leopold. The entire masquerade is unveiled, and Ochs is forced to give up his dreams of wealth and of a pretty young bride. At the same time the Marschallin realizes that her premonition of losing her young lover to another has come true. The Marschallin generously gives her blessing to the couple and leaves with von Faninal as Octavian and Sophie declare their love.

The Saint of Bleecker Street

-»»*«««-

MUSIC BY: Gian Carlo Menotti
WORLD PREMIERE: New York, New York,
    December 27, 1954

LIBRETTO BY: Gian Carlo Menotti
NEW YORK CITY OPERA PREMIERE:
    (Sung in English) March 18, 1965

CONDUCTOR: Vincent La Selva (debut)
STAGE DIRECTOR: Gian Carlo Menotti
SETS and COSTUME DESIGNER: Robert Randolph (debut)

CHARACTERS (In order of appearance)	VOICE (type)	PREMIERE CAST (New York City Opera)
Assunta	Mezzo	Muriel Greenspon
Carmela	Soprano	Mary Jennings
Maria Corona	Soprano	Anita Darian
Her dumb son	Mute	Clyde Ventura (debut)
Don Marco	Bass	Thomas Paul
Annina	Soprano	Joan Sena
Michele	Tenor	Enrico Di Giuseppe (debut)
Desideria	Mezzo	Beverly Wolff
Salvatore	Baritone	David Smith
Concettina	Speaking	Wendy Morris
A young man	Tenor	Anthony Safina
Woman	Soprano	Anthea deForest
Bartender	Bass	Don Henderson
First guest	Tenor	Richard Krause
Second guest	Baritone	William Ledbetter

Neighbors, Friends, Wedding Guests

SYNOPSIS OF STORY
TIME AND PLACE: New York City, mid-20th century

*

ACT I

SCENE 1—A cold-water flat on Bleecker Street;
    a Good Friday afternoon

The neighbors are gathering, praying, outside the door of the room where Annina lies in a trance. They believe that by touching them she can cure them of their illnesses. Two women fall to quarreling, and the ensemble is growing noisy when Don Marco, the parish priest, comes from

304

The Saint of Bleecker Street, 1976

Annina's room. No one, he warns, is to touch the stigmata that may be expected to appear on her hands. Deathly pale, Annina is carried in and placed in an armchair. Barely conscious, she relives the Crucifixion in a powerful aria, "Oh sweet Jesus, spare me this agony." At the end, exhausted, she unclenches her fists, revealing the bleeding stigmata. The neighbors, disregarding Don Marco's warning, struggle to be the first to touch the stigmata and be cured.

In the midst of the confusion, the door is flung open and Annina's brother Michele makes an angry entrance. He orders the neighbors out. He savagely tells Don Marco that it is a doctor, not a priest, that Annina needs. They argue, but in the end the priest departs and Michele slams the door behind him.

SCENE 2—A vacant lot on Mulberry Street, San Gennaro Day

Several months have passed. The neighbors are preparing for a parade in honor of the Festival of San Gennaro. Assunta sings an Italian lullaby, "Canta Ninna, Canta Nanna," to her baby. As she sits on her doorstep, the neighbors gossip. For the festival, Carmela and Annina dress little Concettina as an angel. When the neighbors ask Annina if she is appearing in the parade, she realizes that her brother will not allow it. When they have gone, she and Carmela have a touching scene in which Carmela blushingly admits that she has promised to marry Salvatore in the spring. She will not become a nun with Annina, as they had planned. Annina sweetly congratulates her and asks her to promise to come to the ceremony when she herself enters the nunnery.

Assunta joins them. Maria Corona rushes in, saying that the Sons of Gennaro have vowed to take Annina to the procession by force if Michele tries to stop them. Michele comes in at this point, and brother and sister sing a dramatic duet, "Oh, dear Michele." He argues with her about her supposed visions, her sainthood, and her belief that the church is her vocation. But he cannot shake her faith. They cling to each other lovingly

all the same. The procession starts, singing "Ve-
glia su di noi" ("Watch over us"). A band of
young Sons of Gennaro appear, demanding their
"little saint." While four of them overpower
Michele and chain him by the wrists to a
fence, the others carry Annina off on their
shoulders to join the procession. The street
grows dark. The music dies away. Desideria,
the siren, comes from her house. She compassion-
ately releases Michele, takes him in her arms,
and presses her lips to his in a sultry kiss as
the curtain falls.

ACT II

SCENE—An Italian restaurant, the following
    May

The wedding of Carmela and Salvatore is in
full swing. The guests improvise toasts, "There
never was such a pair." Annina instructs the
groom to be kind to his pretty bride, and all
go into the banquet room for the wedding feast.
Only the bartender remains behind. Desideria
enters sullenly. She insists that he call Michele.
When Michele comes, she works herself into a
towering rage because she has not been invited
to the wedding and demands that Michele take
her into the banquet room with him. He refuses.
She goes on to complain of his devotion to Annina, always Annina, which comes between
them, and in the end, with a shrug of despair,
he leads her to the entrance of the banquet room.
Don Marco blocks their way, and Michele is
about to come to blows with him when the guests
come pouring out. Michele turns on them. "I
know that you all hate me," he begins, and in
a magnificent aria he tries to explain himself as
an Italian who wishes to be a true American
yet retain the best of his Italian heritage. This
breaks up the party. Everyone goes home except
Michele, Annina, and Desideria. Again Desideria
taunts Michele, and this time she accuses him
of being in love with his sister. This is too much.
He shouts at her to be quiet. "You love her!
You love her!" she retorts. He snatches a knife
from the bar and plunges it into her. She falls
to the floor, dying. Annina takes Desideria's head
to her bosom and prays with her. Michele runs

into the street to escape the police. Desideria
dies in Annina's arms, weakly repeating Annina's
prayer. A policeman enters as the curtain
falls.

ACT III

SCENE—A subway station, a few months
    later

The priest brings Michele to meet Annina at
Maria Corona's newsstand, warning him that
Annina is very ill. Annina tells Michele that her
dearest wish is to become a nun before she dies.
Michele again loses his temper and churlishly
refuses his permission, though she says she believes that her prayers will save him. He curses
her, but she defies him. "This is good-bye!" she
cries. He dashes away, and she falls senseless
to the ground.

SCENE 2—The cold-water flat, several months
    later

Annina sits in the armchair in her apartment,
deadly weak. Carmela, Assunta, and others kneel
in prayer. Angelic voices have assured Annina
that today she will become a nun, but the message
from Don Marco's superior giving permission
has not been received. Agitatedly, she worries
because she has no white dress and veil for the
ceremony, and Carmela, weeping, promises to
lend her her wedding outfit. The message finally
arrives. In a transport of joy, Annina asks to
be left alone to pray and sings her final aria,
imploring Death to delay long enough for her
to take the veil. She walks weakly from the room
with Carmela. The priest, in an aside, tells those
nearest the door to watch out for Michele, who
has been seen in the neighborhood. He is to be
kept out if he tries to enter. The ceremony then
is solemnly conducted. Annina, all in white, tot-
ters in weakly. She prostrates herself on the floor,
her arms in the form of a cross, as the priest
intones the words. When he proclaims, to triumphant music, that she is now Sister Angela and
that Annina is dead to the world, a nun covers
her with a black veil. At this moment, Michele
breaks in and implores Annina for the last time

to listen to him. She kneels, silent and unresponsive. He watches, frustrated, as she staggers toward the priest to receive the ring of Christ. All kneel. The ceremony concludes. At the end, she falls lifeless to the floor, and Don Marco presses on her finger the ring that signifies that she is the bride of the Church. Michele's heartbroken sobs sound over a triumphant chorale as the curtain falls.

Salome

-»»*«««-

MUSIC BY: Richard Strauss

WORLD PREMIERE: Dresden, Germany,
December 9, 1905

LIBRETTO BY: Richard Strauss
Based on play by Oscar Wilde
NEW YORK CITY OPERA PREMIERE:
(Sung in German) April 16, 1947

CONDUCTOR: Laszlo Halasz
STAGE DIRECTOR: Leopold Sachse
SCENIC DESIGNER: H. A. Condell
COSTUMES*

CHARACTERS (In order of appearance)	VOICE (type)	PREMIERE CAST (New York City Opera)
Narraboth	Tenor	William Horne
The Page	Contralto	Rosalind Nadell
First soldier	Bass	Manfred Hecht
Second soldier	Bass	Arthur Newman
Jochanaan[1]	Baritone	Ralph Herbert
Cappadocian	Bass	Edwin Dunning
Salome	Soprano	Brenda Lewis
A slave	Tenor	Frank Mandile (debut)
Herod	Tenor	Fredrick Jagel (debut)
Herodias	Mezzo	Terese Gerson (debut)
First Jew	Tenor	Nathaniel Sprinzena
Second Jew	Tenor	Frank Murray
Third Jew	Baritone	Grant Garnell
Fourth Jew	Tenor	Allan Stewart
Fifth Jew	Bass	Paul Dennis
First Nazarene	Tenor	Desire Ligeti
Second Nazarene	Bass	Lawrence Harwood

Soldiers, Guests of Herod, Slaves

SYNOPSIS OF STORY
TIME AND PLACE: Judea, circa A.D. 30

*

SCENE—A great terrace at the Palace of Herod

It is a moonlit night. Narraboth and his sol-diers are guarding the entrance to Herod's ban-quet hall. Narraboth, madly in love with Salome, is warned by the Page of impending doom. From

---

* By Kate Friedheim; additional costumes by Stivanello.
[1] First heard as voice from cistern; figure appears later.

the cistern the voice of the imprisoned Jochanaan is heard prophesying the coming of a greater one than he.

Salome, wearied by the banquet guests and the glances of Herod, comes onto the terrace. When she hears the mysterious voice of the prophet, she entreats Narraboth to break the commands of her master and bring Jochanaan to her.

The prisoner appears and denounces Herodias, wife of Herod and mother of Salome. The girl desires to possess this man, but he rejects her; she becomes more insistent in her passionate outbursts, driving Narraboth to suicide. The prophet finally returns to the cistern, condemning Salome.

Herod, Herodias, and the guests come out on the terrace. Herod fears impending danger. Fascinated by Salome, he begs her to dance for him. Herodias, however, forbids it. With lust for Salome consuming him, Herod offers her anything she wants, even half his kingdom, if she will but dance for her King. The girl agrees and performs the Dance of the Seven Veils. This finished, Salome demands as her reward that a silver charger be brought her bearing the head of Jochanaan. Herod is horrified and in vain attempts to dissuade Salome, who is applauded by Herodias. At length Salome's demand is fulfilled. The head is brought in, and Salome sings triumphantly to the decapitated Jochanaan, who no longer can refuse her kisses. Herod, thoroughly revolted, orders his guards to crush Salome beneath their shields.

The Scarf

—»»*««—

MUSIC BY: Lee Hoiby

WORLD PREMIERE: Spoleto, Italy,
June 20, 1958

LIBRETTO BY: Harry Duncan
Based on a story by Chekhov
NEW YORK CITY OPERA and UNITED STATES
PREMIERE: (Sung in English) April 5, 1959

CONDUCTOR: Russell Stanger (debut)
STAGE DIRECTOR: Kirk Browning
SCENERY and COSTUMES: Rouben Ter-Arutunian

CHARACTERS (In order of appearance)	VOICE (type)	PREMIERE CAST (New York City Opera)
Miriam	Soprano	Patricia Neway
Reuel, her husband	Tenor	John Druary
The Postman	Baritone	Richard Cross

Note: This opera was performed with *The Devil and Daniel Webster*.

SYNOPSIS OF STORY

TIME AND PLACE: The kitchen, serving in winter also as the bedroom, of an isolated farmhouse;
a blizzardy February night

*

Miriam sits at a spinning wheel, a long scarf of scarlet wool in her lap. Reuel, her husband, sits on the bed watching her. She is young; he is old. It is snowing, and he pleads with her to come to bed, but she remains impassive. She hears a postman coming and reminds Reuel that postmen are well paid. Her husband accuses her of casting an evil spell on the night, on the postman (who is lost), and on their marriage. He recounts the number of men who have stayed the night in their house and suggests her having had affairs with all of them. He calls her a witch, she discounts everything he is saying, and he predicts a judgment on her soul. The postman arrives and asks a chance to get warm. She gives

him tea and rouses Reuel to help him bring in the mailbags. She asks Reuel then to go out and stable the horse, which he does. She tells the postman of her youth and how she grew up on this farm. Her father has been dead two years, and Reuel lived on the neighboring farm. Reuel returns from the barn and goes back to bed in a surly mood. She again recalls her past, but Reuel finally speaks briefly of her father's poor management of the farm. The postman also speaks of his work and the tiresomeness of it all. Miriam sings a song that is a kind of reminiscence, and finally Reuel breaks in to wake the postman to remind him of the work he has to do. Miriam wants him to rest, but finally the

310

postman agrees that it is time to go. Reuel goes to get the horse, and the postman sings lovingly to Miriam, but they separate when Reuel returns to announce that the storm has let up. As the postman leaves, Miriam takes the scarf and puts it around his neck. When the two men leave, she calls on the evil spirits Lucifer, Satan, and Bael and offers her soul to them if they will bring the postman back to her. She takes a small packet of feathers from beneath the spinning wheel, a votive light from beneath the picture of the Virgin Mary, and a piece of chalk. She draws a circle on the floor, asks the red scarf to bring him back to her, and falls to the floor. Reuel bursts into the room with the red scarf around his neck to stare in horror at Miriam on the floor. She blocks his way to the door, and as he comes toward her she strangles him with the scarf. She opens the door and calls for the postman to come back as the curtain falls.

The School for Wives

→))) * (((←

MUSIC BY: Rolf Liebermann

WORLD PREMIERE: Louisville, Kentucky,
    December 3, 1955

LIBRETTO BY: Heinrich Strobel
English adaptation by: Elizabeth Montague
NEW YORK CITY OPERA PREMIERE:
    (Sung in English) April 11, 1956

CONDUCTOR: Joseph Rosenstock
STAGE DIRECTOR: Moritz Bombard (debut)
SCENERY and COSTUMES: Wolfgang Roth (debut)

CHARACTERS (In order of appearance)	VOICE (type)	PREMIERE CAST (New York City Opera)
Poquelin (Alain, Henry)[1]	Baritone	John Reardon
Arnolphe	Baritone	William Pickett (debut)
Horace	Tenor	Jon Crain
Georgette	Contralto	Mignon Dunn
Agnes	Soprano	Peggy Bonini
Oronte	Bass	Joshua Hecht
	Servants	

Note: This opera was performed with *The Impresario.*

SYNOPSIS OF STORY
TIME AND PLACE: France, 17th century

*

An elderly gentleman, Arnolphe, has brought a very young and radiantly beautiful girl, Agnes, to his house to marry her. For many years he has been her benefactor and has given her all that a girl could ask.

No sooner has Agnes come to his house than, with the help of friendly servants, she makes the acquaintance of Horace, a handsome youth. It so happens that Horace meets Arnolphe and, not knowing of his relationship to Agnes, tells him of his plan to liberate Agnes from her tyrannical benefactor and win her for himself. Thus informed of the dangerous competition, Arnolphe tries to succeed through force, and the outlook for the young couple is anything but bright. True to comic opera tradition, however, there is the deus ex machina in form of the fathers of the young couple, who, having been away for

---

[1] Poqueline (Molière, the author) sits on stage, makes comments on the play, and assumes various other roles.

312

many years, have planned the marriage all along and now appear in order to bring the glad news to the youngsters.

Arnolphe saves face by joining all present in singing the moral "Voulez-vous donnez de l'es- prit a une sotte, enfermez la," which, being really no moral at all, adds just the right touch of farce that characterizes the tongue-in-cheek attitude of the libretto.

The Servant of Two Masters

-»»*«-

MUSIC BY: Vittorio Giannini
WORLD PREMIERE AND NEW YORK CITY
  OPERA PREMIERE: March 9, 1967 (Sung in
  English)

LIBRETTO BY: Bernard Stambler

After the play by Carlo Goldoni

CONDUCTOR: Julius Rudel
STAGE DIRECTOR: Tito Capobianco
SETS and COSTUMES: Robert Fletcher

CHARACTERS*	VOICE (type)	PREMIERE CAST (New York City Opera)
Silvio, Lombardi's son	Bass-baritone	Charles Hindsley
Clarissa, Pantalone's daughter	Soprano	Donna Jeffrey
Pantalone, a Venetian merchant	Bass-baritone	Michael Devlin
Lombardi, a lawyer	Bass-baritone	David Smith
Brighella, an innkeeper	Tenor	Nico Castel
Smeraldina, chambermaid of Clarissa	Soprano	Patricia Brooks
Truffaldino, servant of Beatrice, and then also of Florindo	Bass	Raymond Myers (debut)
Beatrice, a lady of Turin, disguised as her brother, Federigo Rasponi	Soprano	Eileen Schauler
Florindo, her sweetheart	Tenor	Frank Porretta

SYNOPSIS OF STORY
TIME AND PLACE: Venice, mid-18th century

*

ACT I

SCENE 1—Pantalone's house, morning

Clarissa and Silvio are plighting their troth. The two fathers are present and also, as witnesses, Clarissa's maid, Smeraldina, and the innkeeper, Brighella. After the clauses of the marriage contract have been confirmed, Pantalone offers a toast in memory of Federigo Rasponi. Clarissa had been contracted in marriage to him; the re-

_____
* Not in order of appearance.

314

port, recently come, of Federigo's death in Torino had released her from marrying a man she
had never seen.

As they are drinking the toast, Truffaldino enters and stands agape. Having just arrived at
Pantalone's door with his master, he is astonished
at hearing that master, Federigo Rasponi, saluted
in a toast.

Federigo enters and in a lordly way accepts
introductions to the stunned assemblage. He
makes his demands: for money, as Pantalone's
business associate; and for Clarissa's hand.

Consternation turns to turmoil. In an elaborate
fugue, Clarissa, Silvio, and Lombardi converge
upon Pantalone to cajole, reproach, appeal, re-
vile—to prevent him from fulfilling the contract
with Federigo. At the same time, apart from the
others, Brighella, who has recognized the newcomer as Federigo's sister, Beatrice, learns the
motive for her disguise: only with a man's freedom of action can she hope to find her lover,
Florindo Aretusi, who had fled Torino after
wounding her brother in a duel.

Pantalone caps the protesting storm by shouting that the contract with Federigo will be fulfilled.

SCENE 2—Piazza before Brighella's inn, noon
    of the same day

Truffaldino, waiting for his master, grows hun-
grier by the moment. He is struck by the great
law of Nature which decrees that men are born
either with money or with an appetite. Upon
these meditations enter a young gentleman (we
soon learn that this is Florindo Aretusi) and an
overburdened porter. Florindo asks Truffaldino
to carry his bags into the inn in return for a
meal; liking his silent and willing behavior, Florindo offers to take him on as servant and sends
him to pick up the mail.

Before Truffaldino can decide what to do, Beatrice-Federigo enters—and also sends Truffaldino after the mail. At this point all that
Truffaldino wants is just one good meal—but
then the great idea dawns. Why not two jobs,
two masters? If he can carry it off, think of the
splendors of two salaries, two dinners every evening, and perhaps other desirables in double!
Even if he can get away with it for no more
than a day, his name will live forever in the annals
of servantdom.

At this moment Smeraldina enters. She fits
perfectly into his prospects—that is, if she can
measure up to his newly elevated standards. He
puts her through a little catechism, but all her
responses are flippant or evasive. Finally she tells
him that she came only to deliver a purse of
money for his master, throws it to him, and runs
off.

SCENE 3—Pantalone's garden, afternoon of the
    same day

Clarissa is in tears, Pantalone is regretful but
determined: she must live up to his word and
marry Federigo. Beatrice-Federigo enters and,
seeing Clarissa's tears, asks for a moment alone
with her. Failing to persuade Clarissa that this
marriage is equally undesired by both of them,
Beatrice finally reveals that she is a woman. But
she reminds Clarissa how powerless she herself
had been to get anywhere in a man's world and
obtains Clarissa's promise to keep the secret until
Florindo has been found.

Pantalone enters to find them in a friendly
embrace: the wedding, he decides, must take
place immediately. Before this can be straight-
ened out, Lombardi and Silvio enter. Silvio wants
only his bride; Lombardi asserts that by law the
second contract supersedes the first. Pantalone
will hear none of this; for him, honor is higher
than the law. But love is yet higher than honor—
and he had seen Clarissa in Federigo's embrace.
In agony to reveal all but bound by her word
to Beatrice, Clarissa must admit that her father
has told the truth. Silvio violently attacks Clarissa with words and Beatrice-Federigo with his
sword. The servants push the two interlopers out,
and the two tearful women can only hope that
finding Florindo soon will put an end to their
problems.

ACT II

SCENE 1—Interior of Brighella's inn, evening
    of the same day.

Truffaldino, who never managed to get to the
post office, fails to persuade Florindo that it is
time for dinner. Florindo himself goes after the
mail. Beatrice enters, despondent over not hearing from her lover, and tells Truffaldino to have
dinner served.

Brighella says that because of the lateness of the hour there is barely enough for the gentleman; Truffaldino will be lucky to get some fragments for his own dinner.

Florindo comes in, hunger awakened by his walk, and requests dinner. Truffaldino's ensuing task calls upon his highest talents at being servant of two masters. From the kitchen he fetches the first trayful of courses for Florindo's dinner. His faith in the tiny appetite of gentlemen is sustained: after he has fetched the second tray to Florindo, a slight rearrangement of the first tray makes it servable to Beatrice. And so through the entire meal, with everything kept in good order by three signal bells of recognizably different tones and timbres.

In the midst of this feat of serving, Smeraldina comes with a letter from Pantalone. Truffaldino seizes this occasion for a more elaborate catechism and proposal. This time Smeraldina cooperates perfectly. They find themselves soulmates, and dream of a future in which, both of them weary of being servants, they soar to an idyllic livelihood—a shop of delightful delicacies. But the awakening comes in the midst of the dream: Smeraldina is bound as servant for six more years; they have no way of getting the capital needed for their enterprise.

SCENE 2—The same, next morning

Florindo has decided to return to Torino and has told Truffaldino to be ready to leave immediately. Beatrice decides to transfer her search to Naples, and so informs Truffaldino.

Florindo sees Beatrice's luggage at the door and recognizes a case and a portrait. Under his intense questioning, Truffaldino first flounders and then invents a story: the luggage, the case—these things belonged to the dead master of his friend. In his grief Florindo is barely able to get to his room.

Beatrice comes in and recognizes Florindo's luggage and portrait. This time Truffaldino is quicker with the story about Pasquale. Heartbroken, Beatrice goes to her room. A moment later she comes out, with uplifted dagger, for a last look at the luggage, the only surviving token of her lover. Florindo, with his dagger uplifted, comes out of his room at the same moment. As they turn, they see each other and rush into an embrace.

In the midst of their joy they discover the dual role of Truffaldino. Called to account, he is taken aback but not shamefaced. Life provides opportunities but does not insure that all will pan out. The two cannot really reproach him; he has, after all, brought them together. He takes advantage of their good will to ask their help toward the dream he shares with Smeraldina.

While Beatrice-Federigo has gone to transform herself into woman, Pantalone enters, with Clarissa and Smeraldina, to fetch Federigo to his wedding. Lombardi enters with notice of a lawsuit against Pantalone, and Silvio comes with a challenge to Federigo of a duel to the death. Beatrice's entrance with Florindo clears up all these contentions. Pantalone willingly releases Smeraldina; Beatrice, with some byplay about "Pasquale," bestows the bag of money upon the young shopkeepers-to-be.

The two fathers depart to prepare for a triple wedding. Truffaldino, in the mode of *commedia dell'arte,* addresses the audience directly—asking them to remember for themselves, as in the concluding sextet of the opera, the gleaming and redeeming gifts of love.

Show Boat

-»»*«««-

MUSIC BY: Jerome Kern

WORLD PREMIERE: New York, New York,
December 27, 1927

LIBRETTO BY: Oscar Hammerstein II
from the novel by Edna Ferber

NEW YORK CITY OPERA PREMIERE:
(Sung in English) April 8, 1954

CONDUCTOR: Julius Rudel
STAGE DIRECTOR: William Hammerstein
SCENIC DESIGNER: Howard Bay
COSTUMES: John Boyt

CHARACTERS*	VOICE (type)	PREMIERE CAST (New York City Opera)
Queenie	Mezzo	Lucretia West
Parthy Ann Hawks	Actress	Marjorie Gateson
Captain Andy	Actor	Stanley Carlson
Ellie	Soprano	Diana Drake
Frank	Actor-dancer	Jack Albertson
Steve	Actor	Robert Gallagher
Gaylord Ravenal	Tenor	Robert Rounseville
Magnolia	Soprano	Laurel Hurley
Joe	Bass-baritone	Bill Smith
Julie	Soprano	Helena Bliss
Jim	Tenor	Michael Pollock
Windy McClain	Baritone	Arthur Newman
Guitar player	Nonsinging	Charles Kuestner
Piano player	Nonsinging	Milton Lyon

SYNOPSIS OF STORY

TIME AND PLACE: Along the Mississippi River and in Chicago, late 1800's and early 1900's

*

_____
* Not in order of appearance.

317

ACT I

Captain Andy Hawks' show boat the *Cotton Blossom* has arrived at the levee in Natchez on the Mississippi. Julie, the leading lady, is accused of being a Negress, and according to the laws of Mississippi she and her husband, Steve, are prohibited from playing on the stage of the *Cotton Blossom*. Andy puts his daughter, Magnolia, on the stage as leading lady and offers the juvenile lead to Gaylord Ravenal, a river gambler. They fall in love and soon become the stars of the river towns. In the last scene, they are married over the objections of her mother, Parthy, who disapproves of Ravenal.

ACT II

Ravenal and Magnolia have left the *Cotton Blossom* and live in Chicago, where he is a prosperous gambler. His luck leaves him, and he deserts Magnolia and their little girl, Kim, in the belief that they will be better off without him. Magnolia finds a job singing at the Trocadero and eventually becomes a Broadway star. In the final scene, Andy has found Ravenal and invites him to visit the *Cotton Blossom*, where he arranges a reconciliation with Magnolia and Kim, who is now grown up and has also achieved success on the stage.

The Silent Woman

-»»*«««-

MUSIC BY: Richard Strauss

WORLD PREMIERE: Dresden, Germany,
June 24, 1935

LIBRETTO BY: Stefan Zweig
Adapted from Ben Jonson's *The Silent Woman*
Translation by: Herbert Bedford
AMERICAN and NEW YORK CITY OPERA
    PREMIERE: (Sung in English) October 7, 1958

CONDUCTOR: Peter Herman Adler
STAGE DIRECTOR: Margaret Webster
SCENERY and COSTUMES: Andreas Nomikos

CHARACTERS (In order of appearance)	VOICE (type)	PREMIERE CAST (New York City Opera)
A Housekeeper	Contralto	Ruth Kobart
Cutbeard, a barber	Baritone	Paul Ukena
Sir Morosus Blunt	Bass	Herbert Beattie
Henry, his nephew	Tenor	John Alexander
Vanuzzi	Bass	Arnold Voketaitis (debut)
Morbio	Baritone	Arthur Newman
Farfallo A company of singers	Bass	Joshua Hecht
Isotta	Soprano	Jacquelynne Moody
Carlotta	Mezzo	Regina Sarfaty (debut)
Aminta	Soprano	Joan Carroll
Other members of the company of singers	Tenors and Bass-baritones	Edson Hoel, John Dennison, William Zakariasen, Peter Sliker, George Del Monte, Marshall Stone (debut)
	Neighbors	

SYNOPSIS OF STORY

TIME AND PLACE: A house near London; about 1760

*

ACT I

SCENE—A room in Sir Morosus Blunt's home

Sir Morosus Blunt is a retired admiral but a miser. He lives alone but for an old housekeeper, who has strong hopes of becoming Lady Blunt. He has a terror of noise of any kind, since years ago his eardrums were shattered in a naval battle. His barber tries to persuade him to marry a silent woman who will comfort his loneliness and

319

The Silent Woman, 1958

promises that he will find such a phenomenal creature.

Henry, Morosus' nephew and ward, arrives unexpectedly after a long absence. He has become an opera singer, and with him are Maestro Vanuzzi and the rest of the company, one of whom is Aminta, his wife. Enraged by all this, Morosus disinherits his nephew and commands the barber to bring him, the very next morning, a silent woman.

ACT II

SCENE—Same

The barber concocts a plan to teach Morosus a lesson and retrieve Henry's fortune. The troupe is to impersonate the various characters necessary to the plot. The next morning, he brings three girls to Morosus, who of course chooses the silent one, Aminta in disguise. A "parson" and a "notary" arrive to perform the supposed marriage ceremony, which is interrupted by the noisy entrance of alleged sailors to salute their

old admiral. But when Aminta and Morosus are left alone, she is genuinely touched by his kindness and evident need for companionship.

She forces herself to play the trick that has been planned. She screams at him, smashes the furniture, and terrifies him with noise and clamor. Henry arrives and "rescues" his uncle, as arranged. He promises to obtain for him an immediate divorce from this dreadful woman. Having got Morosus off to bed, he settles down with Aminta to "guard the door" all night.

ACT III

SCENE—Same

Next morning, chaos reigns supreme. Presently a judge and two lawyers arrive with the barber and various "witnesses" to hear the divorce case. The confusion and contradictions of the proceedings reduce Morosus to utter despair, until the actors cast off their disguises and reveal the trick. Morosus, a sadder and wiser man, is finally reconciled to his nephew and his ex-silent wife.

Six Characters in Search of an Author

->)))*(((<-

MUSIC BY: Hugo Weisgall
WORLD PREMIERE and NEW YORK CITY
  OPERA PREMIERE: April 26, 1959
(Sung in English)

LIBRETTO BY: Denis Johnston
From the play by Luigi Pirandello

CONDUCTOR: Sylvan Levin (debut)
STAGE DIRECTOR: William Ball (debut)
SCENERY, COSTUMES and LIGHTING: Gary Smith (debut)

CHARACTERS (In order of appearance)	VOICE (type)	PREMIERE CAST (New York City Opera)
The Accompanist	Baritone	Craig Timberlake (debut)
The Stage Manager	Bass	Arnold Voketaitis
The Mezzo	Mezzo	Regina Sarfaty
The Tenore Buffo	Tenor	Grant Williams
The Prompter	Soprano	Anita Darian (debut)
The Basso Cantante	Bass	John Macurdy
The Director	Tenor	Ernest McChesney
The Wardrobe Mistress	Contralto	Elizabeth Mannion
The Coloratura	Soprano	Beverly Sills
The Characters:		
The Father	Baritone	Paul Ukena
The Stepdaughter	Soprano	Adelaide Bishop
The Mother	Mezzo	Patricia Neway
The Son	Baritone	Robert Trehy (debut)
Madame Pace	Contralto	Ruth Kobart
The Boy	Mute	Marc Sullivan (debut)
The Child	Mute	Barbara Becker
The Chorus, The Seven Deadly Sins		
Pride	Soprano	Mary LeSawyer
Envy	Soprano	Jennie Andrea
Sloth	Contralto	Lou Rodgers
Lust	Contralto	Rita Metzger (debut)
Anger	Tenor	William Saxon
Avarice	Baritone	George Del Monte
Gluttony	Bass	Peter Sliker
Another Tenor	Tenor	Anthony Balestrieri (debut)

    Actors, Carpenters, Electricians, Ushers, Front-Office Men, Actresses, Cleaning Women, Seamstresses, Secretaries

Six Characters in Search of an Author, 1959. Left to right: Beverly Sills, Grant Williams, Ernest McChesnoy.

SYNOPSIS OF STORY
TIME AND PLACE: The bare stage of an opera house during a rehearsal

*

ACT I

As the cast and the director rehearse a new opera, six characters appear suddenly—a family consisting of a father, a mother, two small children, a son, and a stepdaughter. It is apparent that these people, although a family, are in deep discord. However, they convince the rehearsing cast that they are also a cast, but in search of an author who can finish their drama for them. A substitution of the play in rehearsal for this new play is proposed to the group and accepted. The family problems are soon evident—the son despises his father, and the other three children are illegitimate.

ACT II

As this new rehearsal proceeds, arguments develop around the concept that the six characters be allowed to play themselves. Members of the company take exception to this, and the director points out the legal regulations covering performances in this opera house. However, the rehearsal proceeds, and when Madame Pace appears, all too abruptly, the cast is amazed. The father points out the values of theatrical means, and Madame Pace continues to perform, much to the amusement of the cast. Finally she leaves, insulted. Now the stepdaughter insists that taking off her dress will be an important aspect of her

322

performance, but the director forbids such an action in his theater. She settles on revealing one bare arm. As discord develops over these points of rehearsal, the curtain is closed, much to the chagrin of the director. He insists that he was only speaking with the prompter.

ACT III

The disruptive rehearsal continues, with the son and mother arguing over the proper setting for the next scene. After a chorus run-through, the argument is finally resolved by the director's stating that excessive scenery is not possible. A garden scene is decided on, and as the stepdaughter sings, the scenic change is made. The son, who has never agreed that this play should be given at all, is urged to begin the scene, but in a fit of temper he slaps his mother. The cast is horrified and several leave, threatening again a complete halt in the rehearsal. But this is not the end of the unusual turn of events, as the children are missing. The son, rushing to the fountain, finds the little girl drowned by the small boy, who is now discovered behind a tree. As she is carried offstage, the boy appears with a gun and, despite the pleas of those around him, shoots himself. There is a blackout. The cast is hysterical by this time, and when the lights come on again the six characters are gone. Perhaps this was only something in the director's mind, suggest members of the chorus. Angered, he declares an end to the rehearsal, and the cast leave, singing the first piece they were originally rehearsing.

As the director attempts to sort out the events of the day, the six characters suddenly appear far upstage, as in a funeral. The director, not seeing them, only hears the laughter of the daughter as she runs across the stage. He inquires who is there, but the puzzle remains. He resigns himself to not finding answers and leaves. The stage is again bare and empty, and the piece is ended.

Street Scene

-»>*«<-

MUSIC BY: Kurt Weill

WORLD PREMIERE: New York, New York,
January 9, 1947

BOOK BY: Elmer Rice
LYRICS BY: Langston Hughes

NEW YORK CITY OPERA PREMIERE:
(Sung in English) April 2, 1959

CONDUCTOR: Samuel Krachmalnik
STAGE DIRECTOR: Herbert Machiz (debut)
SCENERY and COSTUMES: Paul Sylbert
CHOREOGRAPHY: Herbert Machiz (debut) and Richard Tone (debut)

CHARACTERS* (In order of appearance)	VOICE (type)	PREMIERE CAST (New York City Opera)
Abraham Kaplan	Tenor	Howard Fried
Greta Fiorentino	Soprano	Dolores Mari
Caro Olsen	Bass	Arnold Voketaitis
Emma Jones	Mezzo	Ruth Kobart
Olga Olsen	Contralto	Beatrice Krebs
Shirley Kaplan	Speaking	Florence Anglin (debut)
Mrs. Davis	Soprano	Mary Louise
Henry Davis	Baritone	Andrew Frierson
Willie Maurrant	Child	Michael Mann (debut)
Anna Maurrant	Soprano	Elisabeth Carron
Sam Kaplan	Tenor	David Poleri
Daniel Buchanan	Tenor	Keith Kaldenberg
Frank Maurrant	Baritone	William Chapman
George Jones	Baritone	Arthur Newman
Steve Sankey	Baritone	Arthur Storch (debut)
Lippo Fiorentino	Tenor	Jack DeLon
Jennie Hildebrand	Mezzo	Nancy Dussault (debut)
2nd Graduate	Soprano	Fiddle Virocola (debut)
3rd Graduate	Mezzo	Jennie Andrea
Mrs. Hildebrand	Mezzo	Elizabeth Mannion
Charlie Hildebrand	Child	Richard Clemence (debut)
Mary Hildebrand	Child	Lynn Taussig
Grace Davis	Child	Sharon Williams (debut)
Rose Maurrant	Soprano	Helena Scott
Harry Easter	Baritone	Scott Merrill (debut)
Mae Jones	Dancer	Sondra Lee (debut)
Dick McGann	Dancer	Richard Tone (debut)

* The character of Joan was added to the program on April 19.

324

Street Scene, 1959

CHARACTERS* (In order of appearance)	VOICE (type)	PREMIERE CAST (New York City Opera)
Vincent Jones	Dancer	Albert Lewis (debut)
Dr. Wilson	Baritone	John Macurdy (debut)
Officer Murphy	Baritone	Dan Merriman (debut)
City Marshal	Bass	George Del Monte
Fred Cullen	Tenor	William Zachariasen
First Nursemaid	Mezzo	Mary LeSawyer
Second Nursemaid	Soprano	Greta Wolff

Policemen, Milkman, Old Clothes Man, Music Pupil, Intern, Ambulance Driver, Married Couple, Passersby, Neighbors, Children

SYNOPSIS OF STORY
TIME AND PLACE: A sidewalk in New York City, 20th century

*

---

* The character of Joan was added to the program on April 19.

ACT I

SCENE—An evening in June

It is a hot evening in front of a New York tenement. Abraham Kaplan, Lippo Fiorentino, Emma Jones, and the janitor's wife, Mrs. Olsen, are talking about their neighbor, Mrs. Maurrant, who is carrying on with Sankey, the milk collector. The subject is changed when Mrs. Maurrant appears. Her husband, Frank Maurrant, enters and tells his wife that he has to go out of town on business. He is anxious about his daughter, Rose, and berates his wife for not keeping track of her. He storms upstairs, and Steve Sankey appears. He goes off to the drugstore, and Mrs. Maurrant goes in the same direction, ostensibly to look for her son, Willie. The ladies gossip about the flagrant affair.

Maurrant returns, and soon an argument begins concerning the efficacy of organized charity. It grows almost into a physical fight, with Shirley Kaplan trying to drag her father away and Mrs. Maurrant urging her husband to quit. As the neighbors drift off, Rose Maurrant appears. Her father returns from the saloon and berates her. Rose and Sam, Abraham Kaplan's son, have a tender scene that shows her warm regard for him and his love for her.

ACT II

SCENE 1—The following morning

At daybreak the tenement slowly comes to life.

The neighbors argue and talk. Maurrant is ready to go to work, but before he goes he threatens his wife. Later Mrs. Maurrant explains to Rose that she has tried to be a good wife but must have someone to talk with. Rose asks her to be more discreet. Amid the general activity, Sankey appears nonchalantly and is invited up to Mrs. Maurrant's apartment. Frank Maurrant suddenly appears. Sam Kaplan tries to stop him and yells a warning to Mrs. Maurrant. There are two shots and a heavy thud. Sankey tries to get out the window, is dragged back by Maurrant, and another shot is heard. In the confusion Maurrant escapes. Rose comes back in time to see her mother being carried away in an ambulance.

SCENE 2—Afternoon of the same day

As the neighbors discuss the tragedy, shots ring out again and Maurrant is brought in. Rose goes to her father, and Maurrant pleads with the police to let him have a moment with her. He tries to explain to her that he was out of his head when he shot her mother and Sankey. Sam and Rose are left behind as the police take Maurrant away. Sam begs Rose to go away with him, but Rose realizes how young they are and how tied down they would be if they married now. She tries to explain to him that good-bye now needn't be forever. Shirley brings her suitcase, and Rose goes off as a couple appear to rent the apartment. The neighbors pick up the broken thread of their conversation.

Summer and Smoke

–»»∗«« –

MUSIC BY: Lee Hoiby

WORLD PREMIERE: St. Paul, Minnesota,
June 19, 1971

LIBRETTO BY: Lanford Wilson
Based on the play by Tennessee Williams
NEW YORK CITY OPERA PREMIERE:
(Sung in English) March 19, 1972

CONDUCTOR: Julius Rudel
STAGE DIRECTOR: Frank Corsaro
SCENERY and COSTUMES: Lloyd Evans

CHARACTERS (In order of appearance)	VOICE (type)	PREMIERE CAST (New York City Opera)
Alma, as a child	Spoken	Riley Kellogg (debut)
John, as a child	Spoken	Colin Duffy
Alma Winemiller	Soprano	Mary Beth Peil (debut)
The Rev. Winemiller, her father	Bass-baritone	J. B. Davis
Mrs. Winemiller, her mother	Spoken	Zoya Leporska (debut)
John Buchanan, Jr.	Baritone	John Reardon
Dr. Buchanan, his father	Bass-baritone	David Rae Smith
Rosa Gonzales	Mezzo	Mary Cross Lueders
Papa Gonzales, her father	Spoken	James Cade (debut)
Nellie Ewell	Soprano	Barbara Shuttleworth
Mrs. Bassett	Mezzo	Judith Anthony
Roger Doremus	Tenor	John Lankston
Rosemary	Soprano	Deborah Keiffer
Vernon	Baritone	Karl Patrick Krause
Archie Kramer	Baritone	Alan Titus (debut)
Townspeople		

SYNOPSIS OF STORY
TIME AND PLACE: Glorious Hill, Mississippi; 1910

∗

PROLOGUE

Alma Winemiller, a minister's daughter, and John Buchanan, a doctor's son, both age 10, meet by the statue of an angel.

ACT I

SCENE 1—Alma and John, now adult, meet in the park. He has become a doctor. Her manner is reserved, and she shows a nervous disposi-

Summer and Smoke, 1972. Karl Patrick Krause, John Reardon, Mary Beth Peil.

tion. He teases her about her "nervous" heart.

SCENE 2—Alma is giving a singing lesson to Nellie, a young friend. Mrs. Winemiller comes in with a hat she has stolen. She mocks Alma for being in love with John.

SCENE 3—At a poetry reading in Alma's house, Mrs. Bassett, Rosemary, Vernon, and Roger are bickering. John, the guest of honor, can take no more and leaves. The eccentric Mrs. Winemiller appears in utter disarray, and the meeting comes to an end.

SCENE 4—Unable to sleep, Alma goes to see Dr. Buchanan and finds John with Rosa Gonzales, a Mexican dancer. Rosa leaves, and John gives Alma a sedative. He promises to take her riding in his car.

SCENE 5—At the Moon Lake Casino, Alma tries to persuade John to reform. He invites her to the "room upstairs." She rushes off in dismay.

SCENE 6—As Alma arrives at the rectory, she sees John joined by Rosa.

ACT II

SCENE 7—Roger is paying court to Alma, who is more interested in the party going on in John's house. Alone again, Alma calls Dr. Buchanan in a nearby town. The doctor returns and, in a fight with Rosa's drunken father, is shot.

SCENE 8—While the Rev. Winemiller prays over Dr. Buchanan, John and Alma argue over her having called the doctor back; he then taunts her about her ideas of love. The scene ends with a procession of mourners.

SCENE 9—Several months pass. Alma wanders around her home in a unkempt manner and is scolded by her father for her strange behavior. A marching band is heard, honoring John for having completed his father's work.

SCENE 10—Nellie, on vacation from school, visits John at the office and flirts with him.

SCENE 11—Nellie presents Alma with a Christmas present "from Nellie and John."

SCENE 12—Alma, in confusion, goes to John and confesses her love. But it is too late, and Nellie comes in, proudly showing off her engagement ring.

EPILOGUE

In the park, Alma meets a traveling salesman. As they leave, she hears the echo of children's voices near the angel.

Suor Angelica

->))*(((-

MUSIC BY: Giacomo Puccini
WORLD PREMIERE: New York, New York,
   December 14, 1918

LIBRETTO BY: Giovacchino Forzano
NEW YORK CITY OPERA PREMIERE:
   (Sung in Italian) October 5, 1961

CONDUCTOR: Julius Rudel
STAGE DIRECTOR: Christopher West
SCENERY and COSTUMES: Rouben Ter-Arutunian

CHARACTERS (In order of appearance)	VOICE (type)	PREMIERE CAST (New York City Opera)
Le Due Converse	Soprano	Mary LeSawyer
	Mezzo	Beverly Evans (debut)
Suor Angelica	Soprano	Maria DiGerlando
La Suora Zelatrice	Mezzo	Eunice Alberts
La Maestra Delle Novizie	Contralto	Sophia Steffan
Suor Genovieffa	Soprano	Martha Kokolska
Suor Dolcina	Mezzo	Charlotte Povia
La Cercatrice	Mezzo	Debria Brown
Le Altre Suore*	Sopranos	Sandra Barnette
	and	Lynda Jordan
	Mezzos	Leonore Lanzillotti
		Elizabeth Schwering
Le Due Novizie	Mezzo	Joan Owen (debut)
	Soprano	Nancy Roy (debut)
La Badessa	Mezzo	Gladys Kriese (debut)
La Zia Principessa, her aunt	Mezzo	Claramae Turner

Note: This performance was presented with *Gianni Schicchi* and *Il Tabarro*, as part of *Il Trittico.*

SYNOPSIS OF STORY
TIME AND PLACE: A convent in Italy; 17th century

*

The nuns of a convent are enjoying their recreation. Among them is Suor Angelica. Several years ago she had taken the veil in penitence for an illegitimate love affair, for which she had

---

* Le Altre Suore added to program on October 15.

330

been disowned by her rich and noble family. She longs to hear news of her son, whom she had been forced to abandon. The Princess, her aunt, arrives. Unforgiving, she reiterates Angelica's guilt and reveals that the child has died from illness. Left alone, Angelica longs to die. She takes poison, then prays for forgiveness to the Blessed Virgin. While she suffers the agony of death, the Blessed Virgin miraculously appears and opens her arms to Angelica in forgiveness for her mortal sin.

Susannah

-»»»*«««-

MUSIC BY: Carlisle Floyd
WORLD PREMIERE: Tallahassee, Florida,
February 24, 1955

LIBRETTO BY: Carlisle Floyd
NEW YORK CITY OPERA PREMIERE:
(Sung in English) September 27, 1956

CONDUCTOR: Erich Leinsdorf
STAGED and DESIGNED BY: Leo Kerz
MEN'S COSTUMES: Leo Van Witsen
WOMEN'S COSTUMES: Courtesy of the School of Music, Florida State University
CHOREOGRAPHER: Anna Sokolow

CHARACTERS (In order of appearance)	VOICE (type)	PREMIERE CAST (New York City Opera)
Mrs. Gleaton	Soprano	Sarah Fleming
Mrs. Ott	Contralto	Mignon Dunn
Mrs. Hays	Soprano	Olivia Bonelli (debut)
Mrs. McLean	Mezzo	Irene Kramarich
Elder McLean	Baritone	Arthur Newman
Olin Blitch, an evangelist	Bass-baritone	Norman Treigle
Elder Hays	Tenor	John Druary
Elder Ott	Bass	Joshua Hecht
Elder Gleaton	Tenor	Gregory Millar (debut)
Susannah Polk	Soprano	Phyllis Curtin
Little Bat McLean	Tenor	Ed Thomas (debut)
Sam Polk, Susannah's brother	Tenor	Jon Crain
Churchgoers		

SYNOPSIS OF STORY

TIME AND PLACE: New Hope Valley, Tennessee; the present

*

ACT I

SCENE 1—Yard of New Hope Church

At a square dance in the church, Susannah is seen dancing while the women gossip about her attractiveness to men and remark that she must be evil. Olin Blitch, an evangelical preacher, enters the dance; after a while, he too seeks to join Susannah's circle.

SCENE 2—The front of the Polk farm

Susannah is accompanied to the Polk farmhouse by Little Bat; he apparently worships Sus-

Susannah, 1958. Norman Treigle, Phyllis Curtin (courtesy Eugene Cook).

annah, but he is mentally weak and is frightened off by Sam Polk.

SCENE 3—A woods close to the Polk place

The Elders discover Susannah bathing in a creek that they want to use as a baptismal font. Because of lust and the guilt accompanying this emotion, the Elders brand Susannah as evil and set out to announce their discovery to the valley people and to the visiting evangelist, Olin Blitch.

SCENE 4—Same as Scene 1

At a supper in the churchyard, rumor, elaboration, and lies are spread about, and Susannah becomes an outcast.

SCENE 5—Front porch of the Polk house

Little Bat comes to the Polk farmhouse to tell Susannah that the Elders had seen her bathing and to admit that, under pressure of his parents

and Olin Blitch, he lied and claimed that he had been intimate with her.

ACT II

SCENE 1—Front porch of the Polk house

Sam, who must leave for the night to collect game from his traps, persuades Susannah to attend the revival meeting that night.

SCENE 2—Interior of New Hope Church

At the revival meeting, Susannah is called upon by Blitch to confess and repent, but she refuses and runs from the meeting.

SCENE 3—Front porch of the Polk house

Blitch, convinced of Susannah's guilt, follows her home and tries to obtain a confession from her. When he fails, he succumbs to his own lust for her. Susannah, exhausted and broken, is seduced by him.

333

SCENE 4—Interior of New Hope Church

Blitch, who has discovered Susannah's innocence, becomes a man bereft of spiritual support and terrified by his image of a vengeful God. He summons the Elders and their wives and, in Susannah's presence, attempts to convince them of her innocence. They leave, remaining implacable and unbelieving, and Blitch, pitiable and anguished, throws himself upon Susannah's mercy, which she denies.

SCENE 5—Front porch of the Polk house

Sam extracts the story of the seduction from Susannah. Enraged, he leaves the house and shoots and kills Blitch at the creek where he is baptizing. The people of the valley come after Susannah, menacing her and warning her to leave the valley. They are met by her wild and derisive laughter, and when they advance upon her she threatens them with a gun. Little Bat, who sneaks in after the others leave, is cajoled by Susannah into embracing her. As he does, she slaps him viciously, and she is left alone in her self-imposed exile.

Il Tabarro

→»∗«←

MUSIC BY: Giacomo Puccini
WORLD PREMIERE: New York, New York,
   December 14, 1918

LIBRETTO BY: Giuseppe Adami
NEW YORK CITY OPERA PREMIERE:
   (Sung in Italian) October 5, 1961

CONDUCTOR: Julius Rudel
STAGE DIRECTOR: Christopher West
SCENERY and COSTUMES: Rouben Ter-Arutunian

CHARACTERS (In order of appearance)	VOICE (type)	PREMIERE CAST (New York City Opera)
Giorgetta, Michele's wife	Soprano	Arlene Saunders (debut)
Michele, the owner of the barge	Baritone	William Chapman
Luigi, a stevedore	Tenor	John Alexander
Tinca, a stevedore	Tenor	Maurice Stern
Talpa, a stevedore	Bass	John Macurdy
A song vendor	Tenor	Harry Theyard
Frugola, Talpa's wife	Mezzo	Claramae Turner
Two lovers	Tenor	Maurice Stern
	Soprano	Martha Kokolska (debut)

Stevedores, Midinettes, Organ Grinder

Note: This performance was presented with *Suor Angelica* and *Gianni Schicchi* as part of *Il Trittico.*

SYNOPSIS OF STORY
TIME AND PLACE: Paris; beginning of the 20th century

∗

Michele's barge is anchored to the dock on a bank of the Seine. Michele is overseeing the unloading of the barge by the stevedores. Giorgetta asks him to offer them some wine; he agrees and attempts to embrace her, but she draws away. The young stevedore Luigi tells the passing organ grinder to play a waltz. Giorgetta first dances with the drunken Tinca, but then she slips into Luigi's arms and abandons herself to the waltz. Michele returns, and the dancing stops. He calls Giorgetta back to the barge, and she replies "soon." The song vendor sings a romanza of the unhappy Mimi, and Mimi's theme from *La Bohème* is cleverly woven into the refrain. Frugola comes to fetch Talpa. They are both content with their modest life and dream of the little house they want but will never have. Tinca and Luigi complain bitterly of their hard life; it is the reason for Tinca's drinking. Giorgetta is also sick of her life on the barge and longs for the Paris suburb where she spent her youth. When everyone leaves, Luigi arranges a rendezvous with

Il Tabarro

Giorgetta. Fearing that Michele might surprise them, they arrange that Giorgetta will light a match when the coast is clear. Michele then comes on deck and reminds Giorgetta of the good times that they have spent together and of the child that they have lost. He begs her for a little love and tenderness, but she is impatient and, pleading tiredness, goes below deck. "You whore," he mutters after her. He drapes his cloak around himself and remains on deck to see Giorgetta still awake in the cabin and apparently waiting for something. For whom? Who is her lover? In an agonized monologue Michele tries to guess his identity and swears a terrible revenge. He then relaxes and strikes a match to light his pipe, unwittingly giving the signal. As Luigi comes onto the barge, Michele attacks him and seizes him by the throat. Michele forces a confession from Luigi before strangling him. From the cabin Giorgetta calls and then comes on deck. Michele hides the body under his cloak. Suddenly frightened by his manner, Giorgetta asks him to warm her under his cloak as he used to do. As she comes to him, he throws open the cloak with a terrible cry and lets the body fall at her feet.

Tale for a Deaf Ear

-»»*«««-

MUSIC BY: Mark Bucci
WORLD PREMIERE: Berkshire Music Center,
  Massachusetts, August 5, 1957

LIBRETTO BY: Mark Bucci
NEW YORK CITY OPERA PREMIERE:
  (Sung in English) April 6, 1958

CONDUCTOR: Arnold Gamson (debut)
STAGE DIRECTOR: Michael Pollock
SETS and COSTUMES: Paul Sylbert (debut)

CHARACTERS (In order of appearance)	VOICE (type)	PREMIERE CAST (New York City Opera)
Laura Gates	Soprano	Patricia Neway
Tracy Gates	Baritone	William Chapman
The Woman	Soprano	Beverly Bower
The Girl	Soprano	Lee Venora (debut)
The Soldier	Tenor	Richard Cassilly
The Doctor	Speaking	Arthur Newman

Note: This opera was performed with *Trouble in Tahiti.*

SYNOPSIS OF STORY
TIME AND PLACE: The Gates' living room; a winter Sunday afternoon, the present time

*

Laura and Tracy Gates are sitting in their home, reading the papers; he makes himself a drink, which begins an argument about alcoholism. In the heat of the discussion, Tracy falls to the floor, apparently dead. An unseen chorus tells of Old Hypraemius the Mariner, who gave life back to repentant souls, and a new scene reveals a Florentine noblewoman of 1500 asking that the child in her arms be restored to life. The child is given life, and the scene changes to show a 15-year-old Scottish girl asking that her cow, which has been killed by lightning, be revived—and it is. Another scene shows a soldier grieving for his brother's premature death on the battlefield, and the brother is revived. The scene again shifts to the living room of Laura and Tracy, and Tracy revives. Laura is thankful and tender, but Tracy renews the argument. Finally the fight reaches the point of physical violence it had reached the first time, and again Tracy falls down, apparently dead. The doctor arrives and pronounces death from coronary thrombosis; to Laura's apparently incoherent words, the doctor responds by giving her a sedative. The chorus again sings the opening lines of the "death of love."

The Taming of the Shrew

—》》*《《—

MUSIC BY: Vittorio Giannini

WORLD PREMIERE: Cincinnati, Ohio,
January 31, 1953

LIBRETTO BY: Dorothy Fee
Freely adapted from Shakespeare
NEW YORK CITY OPERA PREMIERE:
(Sung in English) April 13, 1958

CONDUCTOR: Peter Hermann Adler
STAGE DIRECTOR: Margaret Webster
SCENIC DESIGNER: Watson Barratt (debut)
COSTUMES: (unavailable)

CHARACTERS (In order of appearance)	VOICE (type)	PREMIERE CAST (New York City Opera)
Lucentio	Tenor	John Alexander
Tranio, his servant	Baritone	Paul Ukena (debut)
Baptista, a wealthy gentleman	Bass	Chester Watson (debut)
Katharina, his elder daughter	Soprano	Phyllis Curtin
Bianca, his younger daughter	Soprano	Sonia Stolin (debut)
Gremio } suitors to Bianca	Tenor	Grant Williams (debut)
Hortensio	Baritone	Walter Farrell (debut)
Biondello, servant to Lucentio	Bass	John Gillaspy (debut)
Petruchio	Baritone	Walter Cassel
Grumio } his servants	Tenor	Keith Kaldenberg
Curtis	Bass	George Del Monte
A tailor	Tenor	John Wheeler
Vincentio, father of Lucentio	Bass	Arthur Newman
A pedant, masquerading as Vincentio	Tenor	Jack DeLon

Servants of Baptista and Petruchio, Maids of Katharina, Citizens

SYNOPSIS OF STORY
TIME AND PLACE: Padua, 16th century

*

ACT I

SCENE—A street in Padua, outside Baptista's house

Lucentio and his servant, Tranio, discuss Lucentio's arrival in the city and his determination to pursue knowledge. Katharina and Bianca, their father, Baptista, and Bianca's suitors Gremio and Hortensio discuss the possibilities of marriage. Baptista is determined to have Katharina married first, but her willful nature makes this difficult. Lucentio and Tranio decide that the way to attract Bianca is to serve as her tutor, so they exchange clothes and then reveal the plan to Biondello, Lucentio's other servant. Petruchio enters to visit his "dearest friend Hortensio." He announces that his father has died and left him wealthy and he wishes to marry. Gremio and Hortensio tell him of Katharina, and he is interested. They all present themselves to Baptista—Petruchio for Katharina, Gremio presenting Lucentio as a young scholar to tutor Bianca, and Hortensio disguised as a musician come to tutor her also. The father states the dowry he will leave to Katharina, and Petruchio urges that the marriage contract be drawn. Tranio and Gremio vie with each other to out-offer their hand to Bianca, but the father remains undecided. They are interrupted by Katharina driving Hortensio out of the house with a broken lute around his neck. Petruchio is curious to meet Katharina, and Baptista goes into the house to bring her out. They immediately spar verbally for advantage but, despite her protestations, Petruchio is determined to marry her, and Baptista gives them his blessing.

ACT II

SCENE 1—The garden of Baptista's house on the afternoon before the wedding

Hortensio and Lucentio are arguing over who should give Bianca her first lesson—music or Latin. Petruchio enters, wearing ragged clothes, and asks to see Katharina. She is disgusted with his outfit and declares she will not marry him.

Her father, however, says that she will. When they exit, Lucentio tells Bianca of his love for her and his desire to plot a quick marriage.

SCENE 2—The garden on the day of the wedding

Katharina is heard making wedding preparations. Bianca and Lucentio come into the garden and disappear lovingly in a nook. It is discovered that Petruchio is late for the wedding, but a letter is produced explaining that he was detained by business. He asks that Katharina meet him at the church, and after much hesitation on Baptista's part everyone goes to the church.

ACT III

SCENE—A room in Petruchio's house, a few days after the wedding

The servants speak of the mad-house atmosphere. They agree that Petruchio is more of a shrew than she. The newlyweds enter, and Petruchio finds fault with the tailor's work on Katharina's hat and dress and demands that it be redone. She, however, is satisfied, but he will have none of it. When the food is brought, he won't let her eat it and says it is unfit to be consumed. She is famished and ready to eat anything. Lucentio and Bianca arrive and announce their secret marriage; on their heels are both fathers. After a series of mistaken identities are cleared up, all is forgiven and Katharina declares her happiness with Petruchio and he with her.

The Tempest

→))) * (((←

MUSIC BY: Frank Martin

WORLD PREMIERE: Vienna, Austria,
June 17, 1956

LIBRETTO BY: Frank Martin
Adapted from the play by William
Shakespeare

AMERICAN PREMIERE and NEW YORK CITY
OPERA PREMIERE: (Sung in English*) October
11, 1956

CONDUCTOR: Erich Leinsdorf
PRODUCED and DIRECTED BY: Leo Kerz and Erich Leinsdorf
STAGE DESIGNER: Leo Kerz
COSTUMES: Leo Von Witsen
CHOREOGRAPHY: Anna Sokolow

CHARACTERS (In order of appearance)	VOICE (type)	PREMIERE CAST (New York City Opera)
Boatswain	Tenor	John Druary
Alonso, King of Naples	Bass	Joshua Hecht
Antonio, brother of Prospero	Tenor	Gregory Millar
Gonzalo, a counselor	Baritone	Donald Gramm
Sebastian, brother of Alonso	Bass-baritone	Richard Wentworth
Miranda, daughter of Prospero	Soprano	Priscilla Gillette
Prospero, Duke of Milan	Bass-baritone	Kenneth Smith (debut)
Caliban, a savage slave	Baritone	Richard Humphrey
Ariel, an airy spirit	Dancer	Raimonda Orselli
Ferdinand, son of Alonso	Tenor	Richard Cassilly
Adrian, a Lord	Tenor	Rudolf Petrak
Trinculo, a jester	Tenor	Michael Pollock
Stephano, a drunken butler	Baritone	Cornell MacNeil
Master of a ship	Baritone	Arthur Newman

Ariel's voices: Sylvia Stahlman, Mary LeSawyer, Sarah Fleming, Pat
MacDonald, Shirley Winston, Helen Baisley, Mignon Dunn, Cleo
Fry, Eudice Charney, Edson Hoel, Frank Porretta, John Pearson,
John Druary, William O'Leary, Emile Markow, Tom Plank, Mark
Elyn

SYNOPSIS OF STORY
TIME AND PLACE: A fairy tale, legendary times

*

---

* Identity of source of English translation unavailable.

Prospero and his daughter, Miranda, live on a desert island. The only other inhabitants are Caliban, a strange, disfigured creature resembling a gorilla, and Ariel, a sprite who has been imprisoned for twelve years in the rift of a pine tree, from which Prospero sets him free. One day Prospero sees a ship off the island and raises a tempest to wreck it. By this means, his brother Antonio, Prince Ferdinand, Alonso, the King of Naples, and others aboard are brought to the island. Now, it must be known that Prospero was once Duke of Milan, but his brother Antonio, aided by Alonso, usurped the throne and set Prospero and Miranda adrift in a small boat, which was wind-driven to the desert island. The outcome is that Ferdinand and Miranda fall in love, Antonio asks forgiveness of his brother, Prospero is restored to his dukedom, and the entire party is escorted by Ariel's magical ship back to Naples.

The Tender Land

-»»*«««-

MUSIC BY: Aaron Copland
WORLD PREMIERE and NEW YORK CITY
  OPERA PREMIERE: April 1, 1954 (Sung in
  English)

LIBRETTO BY: Horace Everett

CONDUCTOR: Thomas Schippers
STAGE DIRECTOR: Jerome Robbins (debut)
SCENIC DESIGNER: Oliver Smith (debut)
COSTUMES: John Boyt
CHOREOGRAPHER: John Butler

CHARACTERS (In order of appearance)	VOICE (type)	PREMIERE CAST (New York City Opera)
Beth	Child soprano	Adele Newton (debut)
Ma Moss	Contralto	Jean Handzlik (debut)
Mr. Splinters, postman	Tenor	Michael Pollock
Laurie Moss	Soprano	Rosemary Carlos (debut)
Top, a drifter	Baritone	Andrew Gainey
Martin, a drifter	Tenor	Jon Crain
Grandpa Moss	Bass	Norman Treigle
Mrs. Splinters	Mezzo	Mary Kreste
Mrs. Jenks	Soprano	Teresa Gannon
Mr. Jenks	Baritone	Thomas Powell

Guests at the Party, Square Dancers

SYNOPSIS OF STORY
TIME AND PLACE: Midwest farm; June, during the 1930's

*

ACT I

SCENE—The day before graduation, late afternoon

The isolated world of a rural family turns around the graduation of its elder daughter. Yet she is unsure of her place in that world. It is invaded by a threat and then an actuality of two outsiders, who excite in the girl dreams of a larger life. The boys are accepted into the community as harvesters.

ACT II

SCENE 1—That evening

At a party on the eve of graduation, one of the drifters falls in love with the girl. The match

342

is discovered by the grandpa, and the boys are ordered away. The boy and girl plan to elope at daybreak, but the boy, attacked by fears of responsibility abetted by forebodings of his companion, flees.

SCENE 2—Later that night

The girl's anticipation of fulfillment turns to despair when she finds the boys gone. She is consoled by her family, who remind her of gradua-tion and the pattern of her life. But she realizes that the time has come to break that pattern and assert her own being.

SCENE 3—Graduation Day, dawn

Though accepting, the mother does not recog-nize the woman her daughter has become. As the girl goes to find her own life, the mother turns to her younger daughter, knowing that one responsibility has ended and another begun.

Tosca

→))) * (((←

MUSIC BY: Giacomo Puccini

WORLD PREMIERE: Rome, Italy,
   January 14, 1900

LIBRETTO BY: Luigi Illica and
   Giuseppe Giacosa
Based on a drama by V. Sardou
NEW YORK CITY OPERA PREMIERE:
   (Sung in Italian) February 21, 1944

CONDUCTOR: Laszlo Halasz (debut)
STAGE DIRECTOR: Hans Wolmut (debut)
SCENIC DESIGNER and ADVISOR: Richard Rychtarik (debut)*
COSTUMES†

CHARACTERS (In order of appearance)	VOICE (type)	PREMIERE CAST (New York City Opera)
A Sacristan[1]	Baritone	Emile Renan (debut)
Cesare Angelotti	Baritone	Sidor Belarsky (debut)
Mario Cavaradossi	Tenor	Mario Berini (debut)
Floria Tosca	Soprano	Dusolina Giannini (debut)
Baron Scarpia	Baritone	George Czaplicki (debut)
Spoletta	Tenor	Hubert Norville (debut)
Sciarrone	Baritone	Emanuel Kazaras (debut)
Voice of a Shepherd Boy	Child	[2]
Gaoler	Baritone	Alexander Lorber (debut)

Executioner, Cardinal, Judge, Scribe, Officer, Sergeant, Soldiers, Police Agents, Ladies,
Nobles, Citizens, Artisans, Choirboys, Priests

SYNOPSIS OF STORY
TIME AND PLACE: Rome; June, 1800

*

ACT I

SCENE—Interior of church

In the church of Sant'Andrea della Valle in
Rome, Cesare Angelotti, a political prisoner who
has escaped from Castel Sant'Angelo, takes refuge, hiding in the chapel of the Marchesa Attavanti. Mario Cavaradossi, a painter, enters and

---

* Sets were loaned by the St. Louis Grand Opera Association.
† Supplied by Van Horn & Son.
[1] In premiere performance, Sacristan preceded Angelotti.
[2] Performer not identified in premiere performance.

begins work on a painting of Mary Magdalen. A blonde beauty who had come to pray had been his model. Angelotti emerges from the chapel and joyfully recognizes in Cavaradossi a sympathizer with his political faith, the Republican cause. He is forced to hide again when Tosca, the famous singer and beloved of Mario, enters. She invites Mario to meet her that evening after her performance. As she is about to leave, she sees the blonde Magdalen in the portrait, and her jealousy is aroused. Mario convinces her that his model was an unknown worshipper. The lovers part affectionately. Angelotti reenters. The blonde beauty is his sister, the Marchesa Attavanti, who had been hiding women's clothes and provisions for her brother behind the altar. A cannon shot is heard; Angelotti's flight has been discovered. Cavaradossi now offers his help, and both men leave together so that Angelotti may hide in Mario's country villa. The sacristan enters with great news: Bonaparte and the Republican forces have been crushed. While the choirboys excitedly prepare for the "Te Deum," Baron Scarpia and his police agents appear. They have traced the fugitive to the church. Scarpia now finds another clue—the fan bearing the Attavanti crest, which Angelotti has dropped. Tosca returns to tell Mario that she cannot join him that evening, as she must sing in the victory celebration; she is perturbed not to find him there. Scarpia, who has long desired her, sees his opportunity to arouse her jealousy and through her discover the fugitive's hideout. He shows her the fan of the Marchesa Attavanti. Consumed with jealousy, she leaves. Scarpia orders his spies to follow her and gloats over the impending realization of his double goal: Cavaradossi on the gallows, and Tosca in his arms.

ACT II

SCENE—Scarpia's study in the Farnese Palace

That evening Scarpia is dining in his apartment. He knows Tosca is in the palace for the celebration and sends her a note asking to see her. The police agent, Spoletta, reports that he followed Tosca to Cavaradossi, who is now brought in. Scarpia orders the painter to reveal Angelotti's hiding place, but he refuses. Tosca enters in great anxiety as Cavaradossi is led away to the torture chamber. She skillfully evades Scarpia's questions. However, when she hears her lover's cries from the adjoining room, her spirit breaks and she reveals Angelotti's hiding place. Cavaradossi is brought in. Sciarrone, a policeman, arrives with the news that Bonaparte and the Republican army have triumphed at Marengo. Cavaradossi, beside himself with joy, predicts Scarpia's downfall. The latter, in a fury, orders him to be executed, and he is taken out. Tosca now knows the manner of man she is dealing with and asks his price for releasing Cavaradossi. Scarpia reveals his passion; the price is herself. Tosca, horrified, pleads with him in vain. Spoletta arrives with the news that as they approached Angelotti, he killed himself. Scarpia explains that he cannot pardon Mario openly; the painter will have to go through a mock execution. He gives Spoletta orders to that effect, although couched in such a way that Spoletta divines Scarpia's real intentions. Tosca then demands a safe-conduct for herself and her lover to leave Rome and permission to take him the news herself. Scarpia complies. While he is writing the safe-conduct, she notices a knife on the supper table. She picks it up and stabs him.

ACT III

SCENE—Citadel of Sant'Angelo

At dawn the next morning Cavaradossi is led onto the platform. Tosca appears, excitedly showing a safe-conduct, and explains that Scarpia is dead and that the execution will be only a sham. The soldiers enter and carry out the execution. After they have retired, Tosca calls and bids Mario to rise. When he remains motionless, she discovers that he is dead. Spoletta and Sciarrone rush in, seeking Tosca for the murder of Scarpia. Before they can reach her, she throws herself off the parapet.

Die Tote Stadt

-»»*«««-

MUSIC BY: Erich Wolfgang Korngold

WORLD PREMIERE: Hamburg and Cologne, Germany (simultaneously), December 4, 1920

LIBRETTO BY: Paul Schott
After G. Rodenbach's *Bruges-la-morte*
NEW YORK CITY OPERA PREMIERE: (Sung in German) April 2, 1975

CONDUCTOR: Imre Pallo
PRODUCTION CONCEIVED BY: Frank Corsaro and Ronald Chase
DIRECTED BY: Frank Corsaro
FILMS and PROJECTIONS BY: Ronald Chase*
SCENIC DESIGNER: Joan Larkey
COSTUMES: Theoni V. Aldredge
CHOREOGRAPHY: Thomas Andrew, Zoya Leporska

CHARACTERS (In order of appearance)	VOICE (type)	PREMIERE CAST (New York City Opera)
Brigitta, Paul's housekeeper	Mezzo	Diane Curry
Frank, Paul's close friend	Baritone	Charles Roe
Paul	Tenor	John Alexander
Marietta	Soprano	Carol Neblett
Victorin	Tenor	John Lankston
Count Albert	Tenor	Jerold Siena
Juliette	Soprano	Rose Wildes
Lucienne	Mezzo	Puli Toro
Fritz	Baritone	Dominic Cossa
Gaston	Tenor	Dennis Seetoo

SYNOPSIS OF STORY
TIME AND PLACE: Bruges, Belgium; early 20th century

*

The atmosphere of Bruges (the dead city)— the mystic peace of its churches and bells, its weather-worn Gothic facades, its stagnant waterways and abandoned canals—permeates the thoughts of the living with remembrances of the past.

---

* *Die Tote Stadt Films:* Marietta, played by Kristen Milward
Paul, played by Richard Easton
The Players: Michael Beck, Anthony Daniels, Celia Fox, Rita Giovannini, Nicolas Grace, Allen Hunter, Francis Ward-Smith, Gwen Whitby, Philip York

Die Tote Stadt, 1975. John Alexander and Carol Neblett.

ACT I

Paul, whose cherished wife, Marie, has been dead for many years, devotes his life to her memory, sorrowfully worshipping at the shrine to her that he has created. Here, surrounded by relics that include her portrait and locks of her long hair, he loses himself in the past. He tells his friend, Frank, about a woman he has met who resembles Marie in every detail. Marietta, a dancer with an itinerant opera troupe, enters. Paul begins to believe that she is a reincarnation of his dead wife and soon transfers to her the emotions he feels for Marie. Marietta's seductive dancing attracts him, but he becomes repelled by her behavior when he thinks of the purity of Marie. He asks her to leave, and she does. In a dazed mood, he now hears Marie's voice urging him to be aware of and to understand what is happening. Two men appear and escort him on a journey through Bruges.

It is night. Paul, torn with jealousy, waits for Marietta. When Brigitta passes by with a group of nuns on the way to the cathedral, he discovers that his faithful housekeeper has deserted him because of Marietta. Paul argues with Frank, who has become one of Marietta's lovers. Horrified and angered by the sacrilegious revelry of Marietta and her companions, which mocks his belief in the resurrection of the dead, Paul bitterly reveals that he loved in her only her resemblance to his beloved Marie. Her vanity wounded, Marietta challenges the dead woman's hold on Paul, passionately seducing him once again. To make her triumph complete, she insists that they spend this night at his house—Marie's home.

ACT II

After their night of love, Marietta roams through Paul's house. Paul returns, to discover her in Marie's special room. He angrily rebukes her and orders her to go. Marietta ridicules Paul's false piety and remorse and attempts to distract him from the sounds of a religious procession passing by. She denounces his hypocrisy and superstition when Paul defends his belief in love and faith. Paul imagines the procession advancing upon him, threatening him. When Marietta rejects his efforts to remake her into his idea of purity, Paul curses her. She defiantly takes the locks of Marie's hair and begins to dance. Enraged, Paul seizes her and strangles her with the hair.

Paul awakens with a start as Marietta returns for the parasol she had forgotten when she left—just moments before. Paul ignores her hint that she might stay, and, with a shrug, she leaves. He now understands—he will leave Bruges, the dead city, and all that it represents.

La Traviata

→))) * (((←

MUSIC BY: Giuseppe Verdi

WORLD PREMIERE: Venice, Italy,
  March 6, 1853

LIBRETTO BY: Francesco Maria Piave
Based on a play by Alexandre Dumas
NEW YORK CITY OPERA PREMIERE:
  (Sung in Italian) May 8, 1944

CONDUCTOR: Wolfgang Martin
STAGE DIRECTOR: José Ruben
SCENIC ADVISOR: Richard Rychtarik
COSTUMES*

CHARACTERS (In order of appearance)	VOICE (type)	PREMIERE CAST (New York City Opera)
Violetta Valery	Soprano	Dorothy Kirsten (debut)
Flora Bervoix	Mezzo	Marjorie King (debut)
Marquis D'Obigny	Bass	Edward Visca (debut)
Baron Douphol	Baritone	Hamilton Benz
Doctor Grenville	Bass	Ralph Leonard
Gaston de Letorieres	Tenor	Henry Cordy
Alfredo Germont	Tenor	John Hamill (debut)
Annina	Mezzo	Nina Sanya (debut)
Giorgio Germont	Baritone	Mack Harrell (debut)
Solo Dancers		Pilar Gomez
		Giovanni Rozzino

Guests of Violetta and Flora, Gypsies, Servants

SYNOPSIS OF STORY
TIME AND PLACE: Paris and vicinity, about 1700†

*

ACT I

SCENE—The terrace of Violetta's mansion

The curtain rises on the elegant home of Violetta, a charming belle of Parisian demimonde society. A brilliant party is in progress. Among Violetta's guests is Alfredo Germont, a young gentleman of distinguished family, who meets her for the first time. The strains of a brilliant waltz are heard, and the guests disperse to dance.

---

* Supplied by Van Horn & Son.
† Setting is usually about the year 1840, although some productions make the year 1700.

La Traviata, 1966. Dominic Cossa and Patricia Brooks.

and he fears that the scandal aroused by Alfredo's relationship with Violetta will have a ruinous effect upon his daughter's future life. Violetta is persuaded by the urgency of his request and writes Alfredo a letter, bidding him goodbye forever. Alfredo unexpectedly enters and jealously asks to whom she is writing. She replies that the letter is to him but that he must wait until later to read it. She assures him of her undying love and leaves. Alfredo is alone for a short time when a messenger brings to him Violetta's farewell letter. His desperate outburst is softened by his father's pledges. But he will not agree to forget about her and, finding an invitation from Flora to Violetta for the same night, rushes to Flora's party after her.

ACT III

SCENE—The ballroom of Flora's mansion

Flora is giving a large party at her home. As part of an improvised entertainment, the ladies dress as Gypsies and read fortunes, while the gentlemen dress as toreadors and sing a song about a bullfighter who, in order to win the hand of his lady-love, kills five bulls in one day. (In this performance the ballet enacts the story of the bullfighter in pantomime during the toreador's song.)

Flora learns that Violetta has left Alfredo and that she will appear at the party accompanied by Baron Douphol, who has long sought favor with her.

When Alfredo arrives he is challenged by the furiously jealous Baron Douphol to gamble with him. Alfredo wins large sums of money. When the guests are called in to supper, Violetta sends a message to Alfredo, asking him to meet her alone. She begs him to leave the party, saying that he is in great danger. Alfredo answers that he will leave if Violetta will go with him. When she refuses, he accuses her of loving the Baron, and she says that she does, although it is untrue. Alfredo, in a violent rage, throws the money he has won at her feet, calling upon the guests to witness that he has paid back all the money he owed her. Alfredo's father appears and sternly reproves his son for his cruel and unjustified behavior. The act closes in a large ensemble during which each of the principal characters expresses his own thoughts.

Violetta remains alone, suffering from a sudden attack of illness, which she tries to hide. Alfredo comes to her and declares his love. She tells him that he must love her only as a friend, but when she realizes his sincerity she admits her love for him and determines to give up her frivolous life and go with Alfredo to live in the country. The guests depart, and the act closes with Violetta's singing of the brilliant coloratura aria, "Sempre Libera," in which she expresses the new feelings aroused in her by her love.

ACT II

SCENE—A villa near Paris

In a country house Alfredo and Violetta are leading an idyllic life. Alfredo learns that Violetta has decided to sell her home in Paris in order to secure money to finance the life they are living. Conscience-stricken, he leaves for Paris to see whether he can obtain this money. After his departure, his father, Giorgio Germont, calls on Violetta. He demands that she give up his son because his daughter is engaged to be married,

ACT IV

SCENE—Violetta's bedroom

Violetta is dangerously ill, in the last stages of consumption. Her maid, Annina, watches near the bed where she sleeps. Dr. Grenville arrives. While Annina is absent for a moment, Violetta reads a letter form Giorgio Germont, announcing Alfredo's return. He knows the truth now and realizes the sacrifice Violetta has made for him. Alfredo arrives and rushes to Violetta, and once more they renew their vows of love. In spite of her great happiness at having Alfredo again, Violetta's life is ebbing, and to the horror of the remorseful Giorgio Germont, she dies in the arms of the brokenhearted Alfredo.

The Trial

-»»*«««-

MUSIC BY: Gottfried Von Einem

LIBRETTO BY: Boris Blacher and
Heinz Von Cramer
After the novel by Franz Kafka
English translation by Ruth and Thomas Martin

WORLD PREMIERE: Salzburg, Austria,
August 17, 1953

AMERICAN and NEW YORK CITY OPERA
PREMIERE: (Sung in English) October 22, 1953

CONDUCTOR: Joseph Rosenstock
PRODUCTION DEVISED and EXECUTED BY: Otto Preminger
SCENIC DESIGNER and COSTUMES: Rouben Ter-Arutunian

CHARACTERS (In order of appearance)	VOICE (type)	PREMIERE CAST (New York City Opera)
Joseph K.	Tenor	John Druary
Franz	Bass	Norman Treigle
Willem	Baritone	Emile Renan
The Inspector	Baritone	Lawrence Winters
Frau Grubach	Mezzo	Edith Evans
Fraulein Burstner	Soprano	Phyllis Curtin
A passerby	Baritone	Lawrence Winters
Son of the Janitor (a young lad)	Tenor	Luigi Vellucci
Investigating Magistrate	Bass	William Wilderman
Wife of the Court Attendant	Soprano	Phyllis Curtin
A student	Tenor	Michael Pollock
Court Attendant	Baritone	Emile Renan
The Whipper	Bass	William Wilderman
Albert K. (Joseph K.'s uncle)	Bass	Leon Lishner
Leni	Soprano	Phyllis Curtin
The Lawyer Huld	Baritone	Ralph Herbert
The Chief Recorder of the Court	Bass	William Starling
Manufacturer	Tenor	Luigi Vellucci
Three Gentlemen	Tenor	Luigi Vellucci
	Baritone	Richard Torigi
	Bass	Arthur Newman
Assistant Manager	Tenor	Michael Pollock
A hunchback girl	Soprano	Teresa Gannon
Titorelli	Tenor	Jon Crain

SYNOPSIS OF STORY
TIME AND PLACE: A European country; 1919

*

352

ACT I

SCENE 1—"The Arrest"

One morning, bank manager Joseph K. awakens and rings for Anna, the chambermaid, to bring his breakfast. Instead, Franz and Willem enter the room. They inform him that he is under arrest, order him to dress immediately, and escort him to the Inspector, who is waiting in the adjoining room. The Inspector also tells him that he is under arrest but that, even so, he can continue to practice his profession.

SCENE 2—"Fraulein Burstner"

The same evening, Joseph K. apologizes to his landlady for the inconvenience of the morning. He awaits Fraulein Burstner in her room and tries to explain the circumstances of his arrest and the disturbance of her room. Suddenly someone knocks, and the startled Fraulein Burstner begs him to leave. A passionate embrace follows and K. leaves hastily.

SCENE 3—"The Summons"

It is night. In the street a soldier walks back and forth in front of K.'s house. K. sees him and believes he is under guard, but the soldier suddenly departs with a servant girl who has brought beer for him. K. heaves a sigh of relief. A passerby pauses and addresses K. On Sunday there is to be a hearing in the action against K. Such hearings are to be held regularly, although not every Sunday. It is understood that K. will appear in person. With a short bow, the passerby disappears into the darkness. A young fellow leans against the wall. K., suddenly aware of him, is startled; however, it is only the janitor's son. K. mutters that he is being haunted.

SCENE 4—"The First Investigation"

In an attic loft sit the preliminary court and some spectators. The investigating magistrate is angry because K. has arrived an hour late. K. protests against superficial charges and a prejudiced public. He appeals for the rights of all others in the same position and challenges the system for its persecution of innocent victims and its corruption. He is interrupted by a cry. A student has embraced the wife of a court attendant. The

hearing is adjourned, and K. speaks to the attendant's wife. She complains about the situation in the court and what she must do so that her husband can keep his job. She promises to do what she can for K., claiming to have influence with the investigating magistrate. But K. does not believe that her connections are to any high-ranking court official. She would go away with him, but K. realizes that she belongs to those people he must fight. However, before she is able to approach the investigating magistrate, the student comes and drags her away on orders of the magistrate. The court attendant enters and describes to K. how, if only he were free, he would smash the student. The investigating magistrate and jury return, and the public resume their seats. K. sees that all the observers are wearing badges and realizes that they are officials who have come on orders. He leaves, cursing the hearings.

ACT II

SCENE 5—"The Whipper"

A moan is heard from a tent in the street. K. opens the flap and finds Willem and Franz, the two men who had entered his bedroom the first morning, and also the Whipper, who must flog them because of K.'s alleged complaint. They beg K. to say a good word for them, but the Whipper pushes them back. It becomes dark. The passerby whom he encountered in the third scene reappears, stops, and, turning to K., tells him that he is ordered to come at once to the office of the court. This is to be the final summons. K. is warned that it is not wise to arouse the wrath of the higher powers.

SCENE 6—"The Lawyer"

Joseph K., together with his uncle, Albert, visits the Lawyer Huld to ask him to act as his defending counsel. The lawyer introduces to them the court recorder, who happens to be in his house. While the lawyer discusses matters with the uncle, K. leaves the room and joins Leni, the lawyer's nurse. K. speaks only of his coming trial, but Leni, ignoring his words, tries to make him think less of the trial and more of her and sits on his lap and kisses him. He returns her embrace. The lawyer, annoyed by

K.'s behavior, remarks that while it is a difficult case, he will not give up.

SCENE 7—"The Manufacturer"

In the office of the bank, Joseph K., bank manager, leans on his writing desk. He is now unable to work any more, for the trial has become an obsession. The manufacturer enters the office and advises K. to visit the painter Titorelli, who has influence with the court, and to seek his advice. As K. is about to leave the bank, three men who have been waiting a long time press him to stay. The assistant manager appears and, sizing up the situation, takes the reins into his own hands.

SCENE 8—"The Painter"

K. pushes his way into the studio of the painter through a group of noisy girls. Titorelli offers his assistance. He tells K. that there are three possibilities: complete acquittal (which, he admits, has never happened), ostensible acquittal, and postponement. He describes each to K., telling him to weigh each point but warning him to make his decision quickly. K. leaves undecided.

SCENE 9—"In the Cathedral"

In a dark cathedral, a priest calls to Joseph K. He is the prison chaplain. The priest tells K. that he foresees a bad ending, that K. is believed to be guilty. K. objects. All of this is prejudice against him. How could he be declared guilty? The priest warns K. not to rely so much on others, particularly on women. K. hopes the priest will help him, but he only tells K. how to leave the cathedral. The priest disappears into the darkness. Two men join K., his executioners.

The Triumph of St. Joan

-»»*«««-

MUSIC BY: Norman Dello Joio
WORLD PREMIERE: New York, New York,
  December 5, 1951

LIBRETTO BY: Norman Dello Joio
NEW YORK CITY OPERA PREMIERE:
  (Sung in English) April 16, 1959

CONDUCTOR: Herbert Grossman
STAGE DIRECTOR: José Quintero
SCENERY and LIGHTING: David Hays (debut)
COSTUMES: Ruth Morley

CHARACTERS (In order of appearance)	VOICE (type)	PREMIERE CAST (New York City Opera)
Kind Inquisitor	Bass	Arnold Voketaitis
Stern Inquisitor	Tenor	Jack DeLon
Inquisitors	Tenor	Grant Williams
	Tenor	Keith Kaldenberg
	Tenor	Harry Theyard
	Bass	John Macurdy
	Tenor	Dan Merriman
	Bass-baritone	Arthur Newman
An English Sentry	Tenor	Frank Porretta
Friar Julien, Joan's confessor	Bass-baritone	Chester Watson
Pierre Cauchon, Bishop of Beauvais Beauvais	Baritone	Mack Harrell
The Jailer	Baritone	Chester Ludgin
Saint Joan	Soprano	Lee Venora
Joan's Voices (heard offstage)	Soprano and Mezzo voices	Jacqueline Moody Regina Sarfaty Sharon Williams

Note: This performance was followed by *The Medium.*

SYNOPSIS OF STORY
TIME AND PLACE: Rouen, France; 1431

*

SCENE 1—A parapet of the fortress at Rouen
  An English soldier expresses his wish that the imprisoned Joan of Arc would give in to the inquisitors and allow him to return to his love in England. Friar Julien tells him that, weary as she is, she still hopes for deliverance.

355

SCENE 2—A corridor of the fortress

Friar Julien encounters Pierre Cauchon, who leaves him in no doubt that Joan is foredoomed. Cauchon instructs the friar again to offer her woman's dress for her appearance before the inquisitors in token of submission to their wishes.

SCENE 3—Joan's cell

Her drunken jailer tries to seize and kiss Joan, and she fights him off. Only Friar Julien's timely arrival saves her. In a scene of combined tenderness and bitterness, he tries to save her soul as instructed by Cauchon. He is obviously touched by her sincerity and humility. He places the dress in her cell as he leaves for the trial chamber. In a soliloquy, she admits she is tempted to put it on. But rather than betray her guiding Voices, she resists the temptation.

SCENE 4—The trial chamber

Joan faces the inquisitors with dignity as they seek to entrap her. Again and again her simple honesty confounds the questioners. Faced finally with the threat of the stake, she shrinks from the sight of the executioner and in a moment of weakness recants. But her Voices speak to her, unheard by all save herself. She gathers her strength and holds out the dress to Cauchon in refusal. As she does so, the chains fall miraculously from her hands. Nevertheless, she is condemned to be burned.

SCENE 5—A square in Rouen

In a quick change of scene, she is led by the executioner to the stake, and the people surround her. Clad in a white robe, clutching to her breast a crucifix made of twigs, she sings her last farewell, "O pray for me!" A woman in the crowd shrieks, "We are burning a saint," and the people, in a panic, run away, leaving Cauchon to see that justice is done before he, too, slowly walks off.

Troilus and Cressida

-)))*(((-

MUSIC BY: Sir William Walton

WORLD PREMIERE: London, England,
   December 3, 1954

LIBRETTO BY: Christopher Hassall
Based on Greek legend as interpreted
   by Boccaccio and Chaucer
NEW YORK CITY OPERA PREMIERE:
   (Sung in English) October 21, 1955

CONDUCTOR: Joseph Rosenstock
STAGE DIRECTOR: Margaret Webster (debut)
SCENIC DESIGNER: John Boyt
COSTUMES*

CHARACTERS (In order of appearance)	VOICE (type)	PREMIERE CAST (New York City Opera)
Calkas, High Priest of Pallas	Bass	Yi-Kwei Sze (debut)
Antenor, Captain of Trojan Spears	Baritone	Richard Torigi
Troilus, Prince of Troy	Tenor	Jon Crain
Cressida, daughter of Calkas	Soprano	Phyllis Curtin
Pandarus, brother of Calkas	Tenor	Norman Kelley
Evadne, her servant	Mezzo	Gloria Lane
Horaste, friend of Pandarus	Baritone	John Reardon
First Lady	Soprano	Mary LeSawyer
Second Lady	Mezzo	Margery MacKay
Third Lady	Soprano	Peggy Bonini
Fourth Lady	Mezzo	Edith Evans
Diomede, Prince of Argos	Baritone	Lawrence Winters

Priests and Priestesses, Soldiers, Citizens, Slaves

SYNOPSIS OF STORY
TIME AND PLACE: Troy, 12th century B.C.

*

ACT I

SCENE—Before the Temple of Pallas

Troy has been besieged by the Greek army for almost ten years. Calkas, the High Priest, despairing of a Trojan victory, decides to desert to the Greeks, leaving in Troy his daughter, Cressida. Troilus, son of King Priam, loves Cressida, but she dares not acknowledge her love for him.

---

* Executed by Manhattan Costume Co., Inc.

357

ACT II

SCENE—Room in Pandarus' house

Pandarus undertakes to bring the young lovers together and secures from Cressida her red scarf as a token for Troilus. He arranges for them to meet after a supper party at his house. But at dawn the Greek Prince Diomede arrives with an escort to effect an exchange of prisoners—the Trojan Captain Antenor is to be sent back in exchange for Cressida. The lovers are forced to part, swearing fidelity, and Troilus returns the scarf as a symbol of their vow.

ACT III

SCENE—The Greek camp overlooking Troy

For ten weeks Cressida hears nothing from Troilus. She does not know that her maid, Evadne, has burned his messages. At last she yields to her father's insistence that she become Diomede's queen and to her own awakening feeling for the Greek warrior. Troilus arrives to ransom Cressida on the eve of her marriage and sees Diomede wearing the favor. He claims Cressida as his own. She is ordered by Diomede to renounce Troilus but cannot do so. Troilus assaults Diomede but is stabbed in the back by Calkas. Cressida's traitor-father is returned to Troy, and Cressida cheats her Greek captors by taking her own life.

Troilus and Cressida, 1955. Left to right: Jon Crain, Norman Kelley, Phyllis Curtin.

Trouble in Tahiti

–)))*(((–

MUSIC BY: Leonard Bernstein
WORLD PREMIERE: Waltham, Massachusetts,
  June 12, 1952

LIBRETTO BY: Leonard Bernstein
NEW YORK CITY OPERA PREMIERE:
  (Sung in English) April 6, 1958

CONDUCTOR: Leonard Bernstein (debut)
STAGE DIRECTOR: Michael Pollock
SETS and COSTUMES: Andreas Nomikos

CHARACTERS (In order of appearance)	VOICE (type)	PREMIERE CAST (New York City Opera)
Trio	Soprano	Naomi Collier
	Tenor	William Metcalf (debut)
	Baritone	Stanley Kolk (debut)
Dinah	Mezzo	Beverly Wolff (debut)
Sam	Bass-baritone	David Atkinson (debut)

Note: This opera was performed with *Tale for a Deaf Ear.*

SYNOPSIS OF STORY
TIME AND PLACE: An American city, 1950's

*

SCENE 1—Sam and Dinah's house

The scene is an American suburban home of the 1950's; a cheerful singing television commercial accompanies Dinah and Sam, who are at breakfast. It is not a happy scene, as the two squabble although they long to have a greater understanding. At the end of the scene, Sam goes to work.

SCENE 2—Sam's office

In his office, Sam is unhappy about his marriage, but when the phone rings he proceeds to handle a business deal with strength and knowledge—quite unlike his manner at home.

SCENE 3—The psychiatrist's office

Meanwhile Dinah visits her psychiatrist, and the audience sees contrasting views of Dinah and Sam in their day's activities.

SCENE 4—A street in the city

At lunch time the couple bump into each other but escape with many excuses, and both sing of their wish for happiness. The TV commercial chorus ironically comments further on the pleasures of suburbia.

SCENE 5—The gym

That afternoon Sam is at the handball court, where he is a great success.

359

SCENE 6—The hat shop

Dinah visits a women's shop, where she tells of seeing a movie, *Trouble in Tahiti*. She becomes more and more involved in telling the story, only to realize to her embarrassment that it serves as a fill-up for her own frustration. She rushes out and hurries home to prepare dinner for Sam.

SCENE 7—Sam and Dinah's house

After dinner, as they sit by the fireplace with coffee, Sam and Dinah recount their loneliness and inability to establish meaningful contact. Interpolated with this sad scene is the television chorus singing of the "Island Magic" of the movie Dinah has seen earlier.

Troubled Island

-»»*«(-

MUSIC BY: William Grant Still

LIBRETTO BY: Langston Hughes

WORLD PREMIERE and NEW YORK CITY
OPERA PREMIERE: March 31, 1949 (Sung in
English)

CONDUCTOR: Laszlo Halasz
STAGE DIRECTOR: Eugene Bryden
SCENIC DESIGNER: H. A. Condell
COSTUMES*
CHOREOGRAPHY: George Balanchine
Special Haitian dance choreography: Jean Destine (debut)

CHARACTERS (In order of appearance)	VOICE (type)	PREMIERE CAST (New York City Opera)
Celeste, a slave mother	Mezzo	Muriel O'Malley
Popo, a slave	Tenor	Nathaniel Sprinzena
Azelia, wife of Dessalines	Contralto	Marie Powers
Dessalines, slave leader	Baritone	Robert Weede
Martel, an old man	Bass	Oscar Natzka
Vuval, a mulatto	Tenor	Richard Charles (debut)
Stenio, Vuval's cousin	Baritone	Arthur Newman
Papaloi, a voodoo priest	Baritone	Robert McFerrin (debut)
Mamaloi, a voodoo priestess	Soprano	Ruth Stewart
Claire, the mulatto Empress	Soprano	Helena Bliss (debut)
1st Servant	Soprano	Dorothy MacNeil
2nd Servant	Mezzo	Frances Bible
3rd Servant	Mezzo	Rosalind Nadel
The Steward	Baritone	Edwin Dunning
The Chamberlain	Bass	Richard Wentworth
The Fisherman	Baritone	Edwin Dunning
The Mango Vendor	Mezzo	Frances Bible
The Melon Vendor	Soprano	Mary LeSawyer

Slaves, Voodoo Attendants, Servants, Guests, Courtiers, Market Women, Fishermen, Peasants, Soldiers, Dancers, Drummers, Ragamuffins, Boys

SYNOPSIS OF STORY
TIME AND PLACE: The Island of Haiti, the Napoleonic Era

*

---

* By Kate Friedheim.

ACT I

SCENE—In front of an abandoned sugar mill

Led by Jean Jacques Dessalines, the Haitian slaves revolt against their French masters. Azelia, Dessalines' wife, stands by his side in all his dangerous enterprises.

ACT II

SCENE 1—The Cabinet of State in the palace of the Emperor; several years later

As Haiti's new Emperor, Dessalines lives in splendor with the lovely mulatto Empress, Claire. Azelia is cast off, though she comes to warn him of his danger when she finds that he is resented by those who wish to supplant him: those whom he forces to work for the good of the nation. These people plot against him, assisted by his mistress, the Empress Claire, who secretly loves the traitor, Vuval.

SCENE 2—The banquet terrace, immediately following

The sumptuous banquet of state, with entertainment by the court ballet, is interrupted by the throbbing of voodoo drums—insistent throbbing that presages ill for Dessalines. Dessalines goes to quell the uprising.

ACT III

SCENE—A quay in a fishing village, the next day

In a distant marketplace he meets his traitorous general, Stenio, and is at the point of winning a duel with him when Vuval shoots him in the back. His body is left in the square to be robbed by ragamuffins and wept over by Azelia. She, now crazed by her harrowing experiences, alone remains faithful to her husband—that broken Dessalines who once had all Haiti at his feet, who once cast her aside for the unfaithful Claire.

Il Trovatore

-»»*«(«-

MUSIC BY: Giuseppe Verdi
WORLD PREMIERE: Rome, Italy,
   January 19, 1853

LIBRETTO BY: Salvatore Cammarano
NEW YORK CITY OPERA PREMIERE:
   (Sung in Italian) April 4, 1956

CONDUCTOR: Julius Rudel
STAGE DIRECTOR: Otto Erhardt
SCENIC DESIGNER: Lester Polakof (debut)
COSTUMES: (unavailable)

CHARACTERS (In order of appearance)	VOICE (type)	PREMIERE CAST (New York City Opera)
Ferrando	Bass	Norman Treigle
Inez	Mezzo	Margery MacKay
Leonora	Soprano	Ellen Faull
Count di Luna	Baritone	Aldo Protti
Manrico	Tenor	Piero Miranda Ferraro
Azucena	Mezzo	Irene Kramarich
Old Gypsy	Tenor	Thomas Powell
Messenger	Tenor	DeLoyd Tibbs
Ruiz	Tenor	Michael Pollock

Soldiers, Gypsies, Nuns, Guards, Monks

SYNOPSIS OF STORY
TIME AND PLACE: Spain, 15th century

*

ACT I—The Duel (Il Duello)

Ferrando, Captain of the Guards, relates to his companions on night watch the tragedy that happened before the opera begins. It is not Azucena but her mother, who, about 15 years earlier, had been accused of having put an evil spell on the younger of Count di Luna's two little sons. For this alleged deed she was condemned to be burned to death. On the pyre, before the flames engulfed her, she beseeched her daughter, who was standing in the crowd with her own little son in her arms, to avenge her. The young Azucena, obeying her mother, kidnapped di Luna's younger boy from his cradle in order to burn him as her mother had been burned. As the Gypsy attempted to carry out her mother's dying wish, the horror of the deed, in addition to the pitiful cries of the child, confused and unnerved her. In that moment of half-crazed hallucination, she heard her mother's final screams and mistakenly threw her own son into the flames. She then raised the abducted son of the Count as her own, giving him the name of Manrico. He grew up to become a leader of revolutionary forces, a troubador, and the rival in both love and war of the young Count di Luna. The object of their love is the beautiful and noble Leonora. The two enemies duel; Manrico obeys an inexplicable impulse to spare the Count's life.

ACT II—The Gypsy (La Gitana)

Manrico is recovering from wounds inflicted by di Luna and his soldiers when he learns that Leonora, thinking him dead, has decided to enter a convent. He rushes off to prevent this. Di Luna, who also knows of Leonora's intention, almost succeeds in abducting her but is stopped in time by Manrico and his soldiers. Manrico takes Leonora with him to Castellor, a castle that he must defend against di Luna and his forces.

ACT III—The Son of the Gypsy (Il Figlio della Zingara)

The day before the final assault on Castellor, a wandering Gypsy is captured in di Luna's camp. Ferrando recognizes her as the woman who burned di Luna's supposed brother, and Azucena is condemned to die as her mother did.

ACT IV—The Judgment (Il Supplizio)

After Castellor has been taken by di Luna, Manrico is thrown into the same dungeon with the woman he believes to be his mother. Leonora, to save his life, offers herself to di Luna, who thereupon agrees to release Manrico. However, Leonora has secretly taken poison and dies. In his fury di Luna orders the immediate execution of Manrico. He learns too late that he has just killed his own brother—Azucena's mother has been avenged.

Turandot

-»»*«««-

MUSIC BY: Giacomo Puccini
Last duet and final scene were
    completed by Franco Alfano
WORLD PREMIERE: Milan, Italy,
    April 25, 1926

LIBRETTO BY: Giuseppe Adami and
    Renato Simoni

NEW YORK CITY OPERA PREMIERE:
    (Sung in Italian) April 6, 1950

CONDUCTOR: Laszlo Halasz
STAGE DIRECTOR: Vladimir Rosing
SCENIC DESIGNER and COSTUMES: H. A. Condell

CHARACTERS (In order of appearance)	VOICE (type)	PREMIERE CAST (New York City Opera)
Mandarin	Baritone	Arthur Newman
Liu	Soprano	Dorothy MacNeil
Prince Calaf	Tenor	Giulio Gari
Timur	Bass	Richard Wentworth
Turandot	Soprano	Dragica Martinis (debut)
Ping	Baritone	Lawrence Winters
Pang	Tenor	Luigi Vellucci
Pong	Tenor	Nathaniel Sprinzena
Emperor	Bass	Edwin Dunning

Soldiers, Executioners, Loyal Subjects, Servants

SYNOPSIS OF STORY
TIME AND PLACE: The Celestial City of Peking in legendary times

*

ACT I

SCENE—Square in front of the palace

In legendary China, there lived a princess by the name of Turandot. Her beauty attracted many suitors, but anyone seeking to marry the princess had to answer three riddles. The imperial mandarin announces that the Prince of Persia has failed to answer the riddles and therefore must die. In the crowd awaiting the execution, a young girl, Liu, and the exiled king of the Tartars, Timur, recognize the old man's son, Calaf. The Prince of Persia is led to his doom. Calaf is incensed by the cruelty of Turandot, but his anger turns to love when he sees the princess appear on the balcony of her palace. In vain Timur and Liu try to persuade Calaf not to seek the hand of Turandot. In vain the three ministers, Ping, Pang, and Pong, warn the young prince not to enter the palace. Calaf strikes the fatal gong, and with the word "Turandot" on his lips he rushes into the palace.

learn his name by dawn, she will be his; otherwise he will gladly face death.

ACT II

SCENE 1—The Ministers' Pavilion

Ping, Pang, and Pong bemoan their cruel destiny; they long for peace and quiet and a way out of the clutches of the bloodthirsty Turandot. Their thoughts are interrupted by the trumpets and drums heralding the arrival of a new suitor to solve the riddles.

SCENE 2—The Imperial Court

The aged emperor begs Calaf to reconsider, but Calaf stands firm. Turandot enters. Before posing the riddles, she reveals the reason for her cruel behavior. She is avenging the death of her ancestor, Princess Lu-o-ling, who took her own life rather than submit to a conquering prince. Then she poses the riddles. Calaf answers them with ease—Turandot's pride is broken. The emperor insists that the law of the land must be followed. Now it is up to Calaf to show mercy. He does not wish to possess her against her will; she must of her own accord become his wife. He in turn poses one riddle: If Turandot cannot

ACT III

SCENE 1—The palace garden

In the garden Calaf awaits the new day. By imperial decree no one is to sleep in Peking that night until the stranger's identity is revealed. Ping, Pang, and Pong try to persuade Calaf to leave the city. They promise him riches and love—all unsuccessfully. Then an angry mob tortures Timur and Liu. Liu confesses she alone knows the name of the unknown prince, but before they can drag the secret out of her she takes her own life. Turandot confronts Calaf alone. She admits she has fallen in love with him and begs him to reveal his name. Now the prince puts his love to the ultimate test. He tells her he is Calaf, the son of Timur.

SCENE 2—The Imperial Court

As the people gather around the emperor, the triumphant Turandot announces that she knows the identity of the unknown prince. His name is Love, and so, as in all fairytales, Turandot and Calaf live happily ever after.

The Turk in Italy

→》》＊《《←

MUSIC BY: Gioachino Rossini

WORLD PREMIERE: Milan, Italy,
   August 14, 1814

LIBRETTO BY: Felice Romani
English translation by: Andrew Porter
NEW YORK CITY OPERA PREMIERE:
   (Sung in English) September 24, 1978

CONDUCTOR: Julius Rudel
DEVISED and DIRECTED BY: Tito Capobianco
SETS and COSTUMES: John Conklin
CHOREOGRAPHY: Gigi Denda

CHARACTERS (In order of appearance)	VOICE (type)	PREMIERE CAST (New York City Opera)
Punchinellos	Actors	Gary J. Dietrich
		Ronald Kelley
		Paul Kosopod
		John Henry Thomas
Zaida, a Gypsy	Mezzo	Susanne Marsee
Albazar, a Gypsy, and friend of Zaida	Tenor	Jonathan Green
Prosdocimo, a friend of Don Geronio	Baritone	Alan Titus
Donna Fiorilla, wife of Don Geronio	Soprano	Beverly Sills
Selim, a Turkish Pasha	Baritone	Donald Gramm
Don Narciso, Donna Fiorilla's admirer and companion	Tenor	Henry Price
Don Geronio	Baritone	James Billings

Gypsies, Turks, Fiorilla's Friends, Masqueraders

SYNOPSIS OF STORY
TIME AND PLACE: Naples, Italy; 18th century

＊

ACT I

SCENE 1—The shore near Naples

On the shore, Gypsies are encamped. Prosdocimo, a poet, has a libretto to write and racks his brains for a novel subject—something less hackneyed than the triangle plot he might base on his friends Don Geronio, a much put-upon husband, Donna Fiorilla, Geronio's flighty young wife, and Don Narciso, Fiorilla's *cavaliere ser-*

367

The Turk in Italy, 1978 (courtesy Sally Cooney).

vente or steady admirer and companion. The sight of the Gypsies gives him the idea for a picturesque opening chorus—but what should happen next? As a start, he goes off to prime the Gypsies, with the result that they are able to read Geronio's palm with uncanny accuracy. Fate comes to the poet's aid when he learns that among these Gypsies is the Caucasian maiden Zaida, once cruelly abandoned by the Pasha Selim, whom she still loves, whom she yearns to find again. A truly operatic plight!

Fiorilla arrives, intent on capturing some new heart—and the one she quickly captures is that of an amorous Turk who has landed in Italy to sample the delights of that country. They go off arm in arm. Narciso, who is distressed by Fiorilla's absence, Geronio, who is even more distressed since he has seen her with the Turk, and the poet, who is delighted at this turn of events, gather on the shore. When the poet learns that the Turk is none other than the Pasha Selim himself, loved by Zaida, he has all the necessary ingredients for a lively operatic intrigue. Narciso

and Geronio are less delighted at the roles the poet intends to assign to them.

SCENE 2—The terrace of Don Geronio's house

A tête-à-tête between Fiorilla and Selim becomes a trio at Geronio's arrival, and a quartet at Narciso's. Selim thinks it best to leave and arranges to meet Fiorilla later, by the sea. The poet gives Geronio some good advice: He must be firm with his wife. But in a subsequent confrontation, Geronio's firmness quickly falters.

SCENE 3—The shore

Selim is waiting for Fiorilla, and to pass the time he invites a passing Gypsy to tell his fortune. The Gypsy, of course, is Zaida—and the poet (as he tells us) has planned this recognition scene, which quickly becomes a scene of tender reconciliation. Narciso laments his faithless Fiorilla—who then arrives, amid a company of revelers, disguised as the High Priestess of Love. The ever-

368

susceptible Selim approaches the lovely Priestess, and Fiorilla throws off her disguise. In the traditional andante of surprise, Fiorilla and Zaida both reproach the fickle Selim. Then the two ladies come to blows over him.

ACT II

SCENE 1—A tavern

The poet tries to pour some liquid courage into Geronio and eavesdrops approvingly as Geronio defiantly resists Selim's proposals to buy—or if necessary, abduct—Fiorilla from him. Fiorilla and her companions enter, singing the praises of Love. She has summoned Zaida and Selim, and now she orders the Turk to choose between herself and her rival. But Zaida retires from the contest. Nevertheless, it takes all Fiorilla's wiles to extract from Selim a promise of eternal love.

The poet tells Geronio that an abduction has been planned, to take place during a masquerade that night. But he has thought of a way to foil it. Zaida will attend dressed exactly like Fiorilla, and so Selim will go off with her. And Geronio must attend dressed like Selim, and thus claim his wife. Narciso has overhead the plot; he resolves to attend, also disguised as Selim.

SCENE 2—A ballroom

When Geronio goes to the party, he sees, apparently, two Fiorillas with two Selims. Selim is beside Zaida, believing her to be Fiorilla; Fiorilla herself has joined Narciso, believing him to be Selim. When Geronio is unable to recognize his own wife, he loses his temper, and the party breaks up in confusion.

SCENE 3—Outside Don Geronio's house

Selim has decided to take Zaida back to Turkey. The poet advises Geronio to cure his wife's caprices by serving her with a formal deed of separation. When Fiorilla arrives in search of Selim, she learns that he has returned to Zaida; then she is handed Geronio's deed of separation. All seems lost: her fair-weather friends desert her, and Geronio's doors are barred against her. To the poet's satisfaction, she expresses her grief in a full-scale aria.

SCENE 4—The shore

But a comic opera needs a happy ending. Back on the shore, Geronio and a now penitent Fiorilla are reunited. All is forgiven, and Zaida and Selim embark for Turkey.

The Turn of the Screw

–»»∗«« –

MUSIC BY: Benjamin Britten

WORLD PREMIERE: Venice, Italy,
   September 14, 1954

LIBRETTO BY: Myfanwy Piper
After the story by Henry James
NEW YORK CITY OPERA PREMIERE:
   (Sung in English) March 25, 1962

CONDUCTOR: Julius Rudel
STAGE DIRECTOR: Allen Fletcher
SCENIC DESIGNER: Jac Venza (debut)
COSTUMES: Alvin Colt (debut)

CHARACTERS* (In order of appearance)	VOICE (type)	PREMIERE CAST (New York City Opera)
The Prologue	Tenor	Richard Krause
The Governess	Soprano	Patricia Neway
Miles ⎱ young children	Child	Bruce Zahariades (debut)
Flora ⎰ in her charge	Child	Michele Fahr
Mrs. Grose, the housekeeper	Soprano	Janice Martin (debut)
Quint, a former manservant	Tenor	Richard Cassilly
Miss Jessel, a former governess	Mezzo	Jean Kraft

SYNOPSIS OF STORY

TIME AND PLACE: In and around Bly, a country house in the east of England; the middle of the
19th century

∗

ACT I

PROLOGUE

SCENE 1—The Journey
SCENE 2—The Welcome
SCENE 3—The Letter
SCENE 4—The Park
SCENE 5—The Window
SCENE 6—The Lesson
SCENE 7—The Lake
SCENE 8—At Night

A young governess is hired to care for two orphaned children at Bly, a lonely English country house. The children's handsome guardian explains the one condition of her employment: that she not bother him or contact him in any way. Full of purpose, the governess is happily welcomed to Bly by the children, Miles and Flora, and the housekeeper, Mrs. Grose.

A letter arrives announcing that Miles has been dismissed from school. Shortly thereafter, the governess is frightened by a stranger. After seeing

---

* Role of The Guardian was not listed in the original cast.

The Turn of the Screw, 1962

him a second time, she describes him to Mrs. Grose; the frightened housekeeper identifies him as Peter Quint, a former valet who had worked his evil ways not only upon little Miles but on the governess' predecessor, Miss Jessel. Both Quint and Miss Jessel are now dead. The governess concludes that the spirit of Quint has come for Miles and determines to protect the child.

During his Latin lesson, the boy repeats the word "malo" (which has the double meaning of "bad" or "I would rather be"), as if under a spell. Later at the lake, while Flora is reciting her geography lesson, the figure of Miss Jessel appears. The governess begins to feel that the children's souls have been hopelessly seduced, a feeling confirmed by Miles' own confession of guilt.

ACT II

SCENE 1—Colloquy and Soliloquy
SCENE 2—The Bells
SCENE 3—Miss Jessel
SCENE 4—The Classroom

SCENE 5—Quint
SCENE 6—The Piano
SCENE 7—Flora
SCENE 8—Miles

In the spirit world, Quint and Miss Jessel renew their determination to enslave the souls of the children. The governess, beset with fear, searches for a way out of the labyrinth in which she has found herself. On the way to church, Mrs. Grose suggests that the children's guardian be notified, but the governess refuses to do so. When Miles virtually challenges her to destroy the ghosts, the governess flees from the churchyard, deciding to leave Bly and the children forever.

Still at Bly, the governess is confronted by Miss Jessel in the children's schoolroom. This confrontation causes her to break her promise, and she writes at last to her employer. Quint, however, persuades the young boy to steal the letter before it can be sent. The housekeeper takes Flora away from Bly and the influence of Miss Jessel, and the governess remains to struggle with Quint for the boy.

371

La Vida Breve

-»»*«««-

MUSIC BY: Manuel de Falla
WORLD PREMIERE: Nice, France,
   April 1, 1913

LIBRETTO BY: Carlos Fernandes-Shaw
NEW YORK CITY OPERA PREMIERE:
   (Sung in Spanish) October 16, 1957

CONDUCTOR: José Iturbi (debut)
STAGE DIRECTOR: Jean Dalrymple (debut)
SCENIC DESIGNER: Manual Muntanola (debut)
COSTUMES: Peggy Clark
CHOREOGRAPHER: Carola Goya (debut) and Matteo

CHARACTERS (In order of appearance)	VOICE (type)	PREMIERE CAST (New York City Opera)
The Grandmother	Mezzo	Mignon Dunn
Salud	Soprano	Consuelo Rubio (debut)
Paco	Tenor	Richard Cassilly
Uncle Sarvaor	Baritone	Richard Wentworth
The Singer	Baritone	Hernan Pelayo (debut)
Carmela	Soprano	Jacqueline Moody
Manuel, her brother	Baritone	John Reardon
Worker in the forge	Tenor	Paul Huddleston
1st Vendor	Soprano	Naomi Collier
2nd Vendor	Mezzo	Helen Baisley
3rd Vendor	Soprano	Cleo Fry
4th Vendor	Tenor	David Williams
Solo Dancers		Carola Goya
		Matteo

Blacksmiths, Guests at Feast

Note: This production was performed with *El Amor Brujo.*

SYNOPSIS OF STORY
TIME AND PLACE: Granada; 1907

*

ACT I

SCENE—An inner court of a Gypsy house

Salud, a young Gypsy girl, is passionately in love with Paco, who constantly declares his undying devotion to her although he is engaged to a wealthy young girl of his own class. Salud, disturbed because he is late for a rendezvous with

Note: Scenery was loaned by Teatro Liceo, Barcelona, Spain.

372

her one evening, tells her Grandmother that should she lose Paco's love, the pain would be too terrible for her to bear and death would be her only refuge. The Grandmother warns her of loving too greatly, but when Paco arrives her own fears are calmed. However, while Paco once more assures Salud that their love will last forever, her Uncle Sarvaor comes home enraged by the news he has heard of Paco's approaching wedding. He would attempt to kill Paco if it were not for the Grandmother's pleas that Salud be left to her dreams just a little longer.

to the place where the bride and groom and wedding guests are happily celebrating. At first Salud is able to delude herself into believing that Manuel, the bride's brother, is the groom. Later, she and her Uncle make their way into the midst of the merrymakers, and she pleads to know the truth. Paco callously denies even knowing her, and when Salud tries to remind him of their love, he cries out that she lies and must be sent away. Knowing the truth at last, the pain is too terrible for her to bear; true to her prophesy, she dies at his feet, his name upon her lips.

ACT II

SCENE—An alley in Granada

On Paco's wedding day, the Uncle takes Salud

A Village Romeo and Juliet

-»»*«««-

MUSIC BY: Frederick Delius

WORLD PREMIERE: Berlin, Germany,
   February 21, 1907

LIBRETTO BY: Frederick Delius
After a novel by Gottfried Keller
NEW YORK CITY OPERA PREMIERE:
   (Sung in English) October 6, 1973

CONDUCTOR: Mario Bernardi
STAGE DIRECTOR: Frank Corsaro
PRODUCTION CONCEIVED BY: Frank Corsaro and Ronald Chase
COSTUMES: Theoni V. Aldredge
FILMS and PROJECTIONS: Ronald Chase (debut)

CHARACTERS (In order of appearance)	VOICE (type)	PREMIERE CAST (New York City Opera)
Manz, a rich farmer	Baritone	Thomas Jamerson
Marti, a rich farmer	Baritone	Richard T. Gill
Sali, son of Manz (as a child)	Boy Soprano	Colin Duffy
Vreli, Marti's daughter (as a child)	Soprano	June Angela
Dark Fiddler	Baritone	David Holloway
Sali	Tenor	John Stewart
Vreli	Soprano	Patricia Wells
Pastry woman	Soprano	Rose Wildes
Wheel of Fortune woman	Soprano	Judith Lynn (debut)
Cheap Jewelry woman	Contralto	Margaret Yauger
Doll and Puppet man	Tenor	Erik Townsend
Fruit man	Bass-baritone	Irwin Densen
Knickknack man	Baritone	David Ronson
First woman	Soprano	Diane Kehrig
First man	Baritone	William Ledbetter
Second man	Baritone	Don Yule
Second woman	Soprano	Arlene Adler
Third woman	Contralto	Beverly Evans
Slim Girl	Soprano	Margaret Yauger
Wild girl	Contralto	Rose Wildes
Poor horn player	Tenor	Erik Townsend
Hunchbacked bass fiddle player	Bass	James Billings
First barge man	Baritone	Thomas Jamerson
Second barge man	Baritone	William Ledbetter
Third barge man	Tenor	David Griffith

Vagabonds, Peasants, Barge Men

374

SYNOPSIS OF STORY
TIME AND PLACE: Seldwyla, Switzerland; middle of the 19th century

*

ACT I

SCENE 1—A field

Manz and Marti, rivals for a strip of wild land that lies between their fields, are both plowing. When the other is not looking, each takes an extra furrow from the wasteland. Sali and Vreli bring their parents' midday meals and later rejoin the two fathers as they eat together. The Dark Fiddler is heard in the distance. Marti recognizes him as the true owner of the wild land, but being illegitimate, the Fiddler has no legal right to it. The discussion about the sale of the land erupts into a quarrel, and the two fathers furiously forbid their children to play together.

SCENE 2—Six years later

Sali approaches Vreli's house, which has fallen into disrepair during the six years since he last saw it. Both his and Vreli's parents have been involved in bitter lawsuits over the ownership of the wild land. As Vreli appears, Sali stops her and they talk dejectedly about the situation. Sali hopes that all may yet end well if only they do not lose each other, and they plan to meet that evening in the wild land.

SCENE 3—A poppy field, that evening

Sali and Vreli are enjoying each other's company when they hear the playing of the Dark Fiddler. He reminds them that they have played on his land and suggests, now that they are all beggars, that they come with him and share his vagabond existence. They refuse and talk happily of their childhood days. Marti discovers the lovers and is dragging Veli away when Sali fells him with a blow.

SCENE 4—Marti's house

Sali's blow has damaged Marti's mind, and he is taken away to a sanatorium. Now Vreli sits alone with her few remaining possessions. As Sali comes to say goodbye, Vreli tells him that she too must leave, for the house has been sold. They sit together in front of the fire and fall asleep in each other's arms. They dream they are being married, but as dawn breaks they awake. Together they leave the house to share one day of happiness.

ACT II

SCENE 5—A Fair

Sali and Vreli join in the gaiety of the Fair until they are recognized. They buy everything that attracts them but suddenly notice that they are being watched curiously by the crowd. Self-consciously they leave the Fair and set out for The Paradise Garden, a country house near the river that is now used as an inn.

A Village Romeo and Juliet, 1973. Patricia Wells and John Stewart.

SCENE 6—The Paradise Garden

The Dark Fiddler and his friends, the vagabonds, sit around a table in the Paradise Garden. The Fiddler is telling them of the origin of the strife between Marti and Manz. As he is finishing, Vreli and Sali enter. The Fiddler urges them again to join him and his friends and take to the open road. The two lovers decide that their only way out is to drift down the river like the bargemen whose voices they hear, except that they can never return. They get into the boat.

The Voice of Ariadne

$\rightarrow\!\!\rangle\!\!\rangle * \langle\!\langle\!\leftarrow$

MUSIC BY: Thea Musgrave

WORLD PREMIERE: Aldeburgh, Scotland,
  June 11, 1974

LIBRETTO BY: Amalia Elguera
Based on *The Last of the Valerii* by Henry James
NEW YORK CITY OPERA PREMIERE:
  (Sung in English) September 30, 1977

CONDUCTOR: Thea Musgrave (debut)
STAGE DIRECTOR: Colin Graham (debut)
SETS and COSTUMES: Carl Toms

CHARACTERS (In order of appearance)	VOICE (type)	PREMIERE CAST (New York City Opera)
Gualtiero, the Count's gardener	Bass-baritone	Richard T. Gill
Giovanni, a servant	Tenor	Melvin Lowery
Marchesa Bianca Bianchi	Mezzo	Sandra Walker
Mrs. Tracy, an American	Mezzo	Frances Bible
Baldovino, a friend of the Count	Baritone	David Griffith
The Countess, Marco's American wife	Soprano	Cynthia Clarey (debut)
Mr. Lamb, her godfather	Baritone	Thomas Jamerson
Count Marco Valerio	Baritone	David Holloway
The voice of Ariadne	Soprano	the voice of Joan Davies

SYNOPSIS OF STORY
TIME AND PLACE: Rome, 1870

*

ACT I

SCENE 1—Garden of the Count's villa

On a summer night old Gualtiero, the gardener, and the young manservant, Giovanni, wait for their master and the guests of his young American wife, the Countess. Their young and exuberant mistress has summoned friends to celebrate the unearthing of an ancient statue of a goddess, legendary to generations of the Valerii Counts. The Countess arrives with her guests. When the Count appears, ill at ease with his wife and friends, the group hears Gualtiero tell the statue's enthralling legend:

"Who finds her and who wakes her from her
  sleep
Shall find the happiness she keepeth in her keep."

The guests conjecture about the identity of the goddess. But as the gardener leaves they uncover only an empty pedestal, bearing not a divine inscription, but the name of the mythical woman

377

Ariadne. Disappointed, the Countess and her guests leave, while the Count remains alone with the pedestal to observe it in the moonlight. Turning to leave, he hears a distant plangent voice:

> "It is I who call,
> Ariadne.
> . . . Theseus,
> Return and find me."

SCENE 2—Salon of the Count's villa

The Countess bids her guests goodnight and worries about her growing estrangement from her husband. The Count, brooding and impatient, refers to the legend of Theseus and Ariadne. Left on Naxos by her impatient lover, the desperate Ariadne forever awaits his return. As he thinks about her, he hears Ariadne's voice calling him by the name of Theseus.

ACT II

SCENE—A garden in the Pincio, Rome. Some days later.

In a secluded part of a public park, Gualtiero meets the Marchesa Bianca Bianchi, who questions him about a rumored rift between the Count and Countess. Gualtiero declares that the Count has fallen forever in love with Ariadne, whose voice he hears calling him. Bianca, selfishly happy for any estrangement between the Count and Countess, mocks the old man's story. He, shocked by her sacrilege, persuades her to meet him in the garden that evening to witness the Count's obsession. Baldovino enters and confides to Bianca his infatuation with Mrs. Tracy. Mrs. Tracy arrives and turns a deaf ear to his protestations. The Countess enters, looking for the Count. Playing the Iago, Bianca offers advice to the Countess. As the others leave, a sudden terror seizes the Countess. Left in the same situation as Ariadne, she invokes the memory of the love she once shared with her husband.

ACT III

SCENE 1—An antechamber of the Count's villa, the same evening

The Count confronts Gualtiero, who tells him

that the gods demand from him a personal commitment and sacrifice—"From your own hand, a drop of noble blood"—in order that he may finally find Ariadne. The Count dismisses him angrily, then voices his disillusion: He yearns for the warm relationship with Ariadne that he has not known with his wife. Giovanni rushes in to announce that the Countess, absent since early morning, has been found dazed and wandering in the streets. When she enters, the Count brushes aside her distress until she begs him to give up his infatuation with the invisible Ariadne. His refusal gives credence to Bianca's claim that the Count is in love with another woman. Her accusation inspires his contempt, and he rushes from her. Mr. Lamb appears and, witnessing her desperation, consoles her:

> "There is a love
> That asks for nothing, nothing
> Except the loved one's joy."

In advising her to love the Count by allowing him to love freely, Mr. Lamb implies his own secret love for the Countess. Comprehending the substance but not the sentiment of his words, the Countess sadly thanks him for his counsel.

SCENE 2—Garden of the Count's villa

In the evening, Count Valerio invokes the ancient gods and, in an act of sacrifice, draws his own blood. Mr. Lamb comes upon the scene and, appalled by the extremes to which the Count's obsession has carried him, reprimands him. Bianca enters the garden to keep her appointment with Gualtiero, and Baldovino and Mrs. Tracy happen by as well. Enraged by this concerted interruption, the Count repulses them all. The confusion is abruptly silenced by a voice audible to everyone. In the Count's ears the voice of Ariadne and the new voice vie, the former finally fading beneath the clarity of the latter. The Count realizes that in his wife he has found his Ariadne. Her selfless devotion and his newly awakened love for her meet in a glance, and they rush to each other's arms. The others, absorbed by their own thoughts, drift away, and the two lovers sing of the hope and freedom they have won.

La Voix Humaine
(The Voice)

-»»*«««-

MUSIC BY: Francis Poulenc

WORLD PREMIERE: Paris, France,
February 6, 1959

LIBRETTO: Text by Jean Cocteau
English translation by Joseph Machlis
NEW YORK CITY OPERA PREMIERE:
(Sung in English) April 22, 1977

CONDUCTOR: Imre Pallo
STAGE DIRECTOR: Frank Corsaro
SCENERY and COSTUMES: Lloyd Evans

CHARACTERS (In order of appearance)	VOICE (type)	PREMIERE CAST (New York City Opera)
The Woman	Soprano	Maralin Niska

Note: *La Voix Humaine* was performed as part of a trilogy, with *The Impresario* and *L'Histoire du Soldat.*

SYNOPSIS OF STORY
TIME AND PLACE: An apartment; the present

*

A distraught woman is speaking on the telephone with her lover, who has left her. The woman, under the influence of alcohol, is carrying on an emotional conversation with periodic and dramatic pauses to listen, but she becomes more and more hysterical and eventually is overcome and falls across the bed.

La Voix Humaine, 1977. Maralin Niska.

Werther

-»»*«<

MUSIC BY: Jules Massenet

WORLD PREMIERE: Vienna, Austria,
February 16, 1892

LIBRETTO BY: Edouard Blau,
Paul Milliet, Georges Hartman
Based on a novel by Goethe

NEW YORK CITY OPERA PREMIERE:
(Sung in French) October 2, 1947

CONDUCTOR: Jean Morel
STAGE DIRECTOR: Leopold Sachse
SCENIC DESIGNER: H. A. Condell
COSTUMES*

CHARACTERS (In order of appearance)	VOICE (type)	PREMIERE CAST (New York City Opera)
The Bailli (Bailiff)	Baritone	Gean Greenwell
Johann	Baritone	Arthur Newman
Schmidt	Tenor	Nathaniel Sprinzena
Sophie	Soprano	Virginia Haskins
Werther	Tenor	Eugene Conley
Charlotte	Mezzo	Winifred Heidt
Bruehlma	Bass-baritone	John Bailey
Kaitcher	Soprano	Lenore Portnoy
Albert	Baritone	Norman Young
Villagers, Children		

SYNOPSIS OF STORY
TIME AND PLACE: Western Germany, in the late 1700's

*

ACT I

SCENE—In front of the Bailli's house

The action takes place in a small town where Werther, a young man of poetic gifts and a dreamy temperament, meets the daughter of the Bailli and falls in love with her. Charlotte, however, is no longer free. Her mother upon her deathbed had exacted from her a promise that she would marry Albert. Werther, heartbroken, runs off in despair.

ACT II

SCENE—A square in Wetzlar

Three months later, as the community convenes in church to celebrate the fiftieth anniver-

---

* By Kate Friedheim; additional costumes by Stivanello.

sary of the pastor's marriage, Werther enters, highly disturbed; he cannot bear the surrounding happiness. He declares his burning love to Charlotte and his decision to leave. Charlotte asks him to return at Christmas time. Sophie, her younger sister, vainly tries to get him to remain, and Albert, learning of Werther's sudden departure, realizes the poet's deep passion for his wife.

ACT III

SCENE 1—A room in the Bailli's house

On Christmas Eve, as Charlotte reads letters from Werther, she is disturbed by his image. Werther returns prematurely. Nostalgic feelings overwhelm him at the sight of the house, with its happy memories of Charlotte. He reads her

---

* Some productions present this scene as Act IV.

his translation of a poem by Ossian. Charlotte yields for a moment and then, becoming strong, rejects him. Werther departs emotionally shaken. Albert returns. A messenger brings a letter from Werther asking Albert to lend him his pistols under the pretext of leaving for a long trip. Albert orders Charlotte to give the pistols to the messenger. Charlotte, realizing Werther's true intentions, rushes out to find him.

SCENE 2—A room in Werther's home*

It is early Christmas morning. Werther lies dying in his room. Charlotte enters full of apprehension. After a few tender moments, Werther dies in Charlotte's arms as the voices of Sophie and the children are heard singing the Christmas carols that they were practicing in the first act.

The Wings of the Dove

->»»*«<-

MUSIC BY: Douglas Moore
WORLD PREMIERE and NEW YORK CITY
  OPERA PREMIERE: October 12, 1961
  (Sung in English) Commissioned by Julius
  Rudel for the New York City Opera

LIBRETTO BY: Ethan Ayer
Based upon the novel by
  Henry James

CONDUCTOR: Julius Rudel
STAGE DIRECTOR: Christopher West
SCENIC DESIGNER: Donald Oenslager
COSTUMES: Patton Campbell
CHOREOGRAPHER: Robert Joffrey

CHARACTERS (In order of appearance)	VOICE (type)	PREMIERE CAST (New York City Opera)
Homer Croy, Kate Croy's father	Baritone	Paul Ukena
Steffens, a servant	Baritone	Richard Fredricks
Kate Croy	Mezzo	Regina Sarfaty
Miles Dunster	Baritone	John Reardon
Aunt Maud Lowder, Kate's aunt	Contralto	Martha Lipton
Lord Mark	Tenor	Norman Kelley
Milly Theale	Soprano	Dorothy Coulter (debut)
Susan Stringham, her companion	Soprano	Mary LeSawyer
Lecturer at the National Gallery	Tenor	Maurice Stern
Giuliano, Majordomo at the Palazzo Leporelli	Baritone	Fredric Milstein
Venetian Players in the "Janus Ballet"		
Janus		Gerald Arpino
		Paul Sutherland
The Seasons:		
Goddess of Spring		Françoise Martinet
Her Attendants		Rita Bradley (debut)
		Mary Ellen Jackson
Goddess of Winter		Brunilda Ruiz
Her Attendants		Suzanne Hammons (debut)
		Marie Paquet
Warriors		James DeBolt (debut)
		James Howell (debut)
		Nels Jorgenson
		Lawrence Rhodes
		John Wilson

The Wings of the Dove, 1961. Dorothy Coulter (left) and Regina Sarfaty.

SYNOPSIS OF STORY
TIME AND PLACE: London and Venice; 1902

*

ACT I

SCENE 1—London. Parlor of Maud Lowder at Lancaster Gate

Homer Croy, Kate's gambling father, enters to get needed funds from his daughter, who lives with her wealthy aunt. He flouts her objections and finally is given the money. Miles Dunster, a journalist, arrives to see Kate, but he is considered ineligible for her hand by Aunt Maud Lowder. He is invited to stay for dinner by both Kate and Aunt Maud, but he declines. Aunt Maud has made it clear to him that he is someone she would like to "count on" but he is not to entertain ideas of marriage to Kate.

SCENE 2—The same, several weeks later

The parlor is now in readiness for a party honoring Milly Theale, a beautiful, frail American heiress who is touring Europe. Lord Mark, an eligible suitor for Kate's hand, remarks on the similarity between Milly and a portrait of a Renaissance woman on an easel in the room. When Milly arrives, the similarity is apparent. She is asked to sing by Aunt Maud and does so, fainting at the conclusion of her recital. Miles is also present and helps her recover. They had met previously in America. Lord Mark also has been attracted to Milly and would like to marry her, but she is not interested. Kate expresses her concern for Miles' attraction to Milly, but she sees it also as an advantage—a convenient third party who will make meetings possible for her and Miles.

SCENE 3—Several weeks later; a room in the National Gallery

Milly and Susan, her traveling companion, meet Kate, and Milly proposes that she go to Italy as her guest. Miles arrives and is included in the invitation. Milly and Susan leave, and Kate points out to Miles the advantages of their being together in Italy. She also points out that Miles can marry Milly and that when she dies he will be wealthy, thus enabling Kate and Miles to marry. Miles is shocked at this, but Kate promises herself to him if he will go. He accepts her offer.

ACT II

SCENE 4—Later that month; courtyard and balcony of the Palazzo Leporelli, Venice

Milly and Miles are entertained by a group of players as consolation for Kate's departure to London. The players perform a dance based upon the Janus theme of mythology—the god with two heads. Miles leaves with a promise from Milly to visit him the next afternoon. After he has gone, Lord Mark steps out from behind a pillar and urges Milly to join him in a gondola ride. She begs to be excused, but before he leaves he tells her that Miles and Kate are lovers, and the news leaves Milly stricken.

SCENE 5—Several weeks later; Milly's apartment in the Palazzo Leporelli

Milly is ill and surrounded by flowers, Susan, and a Sister of Mercy. Milly has "turned her face to the wall" during her illness. Miles arrives, and he and Milly exchange affectionate concern in wishing for each other's happiness. Milly feels that she has come between him and Kate and asks him to send no more flowers.

SCENE 6—Several weeks later; parlor of Maud Lowder in London

Kate is reading a letter from Susan telling of Milly's death. Kate's father arrives to tell her of Miles' inheritance from Milly. Aunt Maud is also informed of this turn of events, and then Miles enters. He tells Kate of his inheritance but says that he won't accept it and marry her too. She must decide if she will marry him under these conditions. She then asks if he loves her, and finally he say he does not. She wilts, and he leaves as she calls for her Aunt Maud. She comes in to comfort Kate by putting Milly's shawl around her, but Kate shrinks from it, and Aunt Maud assures her that "You'll be all right by tomorrow."

Wozzeck

→))) ✳ (((←

MUSIC BY: Alban Berg

WORLD PREMIERE: Berlin, Germany,
December 14, 1925

LIBRETTO BY: Alban Berg
Based on the drama by:
George Buechner
English translation by: Eric Blackall
NEW YORK CITY OPERA PREMIERE:
(Sung in English) April 3, 1952

CONDUCTOR: Joseph Rosenstock
STAGE DIRECTOR: Theodore Komisarjevsky
SCENERY and COSTUMES: Mstislav Doboujinsky

CHARACTERS (In order of appearance)	VOICE (type)	PREMIERE CAST (New York City Opera)
The Captain	Tenor	Luigi Vellucci
Wozzeck, a soldier	Baritone	Marko Rothmuller
Marie, a seamstress	Soprano	Patricia Neway
The child of Wozzeck and Marie	Soprano	Linda Oram (debut)
The Doctor	Bass	Ralph Herbert
Andres, a soldier	Tenor	David Lloyd
Margaret, a waitress	Mezzo	Edith Evans
The Drum Major	Tenor	Howard Vandenburg (debut)
First Workman	Bass	Arthur Newman
Second Workman	Tenor	Armand Harkless
The Idiot	Tenor	Michael Pollock

Drummers, Soldiers, Townspeople, Children, Musicians

SYNOPSIS OF STORY
TIME AND PLACE: Germany, 1830's

✳

ACT I

SCENE 1—An office in the barracks; Marie's lodgings; the street in a small garrison town

Wozzeck, an uneducated, slow-witted militiaman, is seen in the barracks shaving the Captain, for whom he is personal servant. The Captain is philosophizing, to which Wozzeck only responds with mechanical agreement; however, after a short time, he launches into a complaint about his poverty.

SCENE 2—In the woods by a pond

Wozzeck and Andres are seen cutting sticks

386

in a field at sunset. Wozzeck is in terror of the place and imagines strange sights and sounds. Andres attempts to calm him by singing a hunting song, but Wozzeck's fears grow wilder and both leave as night falls.

SCENE 3—Same as Scene 1

It is evening; Marie, Wozzeck's mistress, is standing with their child watching as a military band passes beneath the window. She responds to the wave of the Drum Major and is chided by her neighbor, Margaret, for her wandering eyes. Turning angrily from the window, Marie sings a lullaby to the child. Wozzeck passes the window but only terrifies her with tales of his visions.

SCENE 4—Same as Scene 1

The next day, Wozzeck, who, to earn extra money, has placed himself at the disposal of the Doctor for experimentation, is seen in the Doctor's study. Wozzeck becomes more confused and incoherent as the Doctor tells him how bad he is and that he is probably going crazy. The Doctor exclaims ecstatically that this case will make him immortal.

SCENE 5—Same as Scene 1

In the street in front of Marie's house, Marie is admiring the Drum Major, who struts and boasts how handsome he is for the Sunday parade. Marie easily succumbs to his advances, and they disappear into her house.

ACT II

SCENE 1—Marie's lodgings; the street

Marie preens herself before a broken mirror and admires a pair of gold earrings she is wearing. When Wozzeck enters she attempts to hide the earrings, and his suspicions are aroused. He laments over the sleeping child, who lies in a sweat. He gives Marie his wages and leaves her pondering her wickedness.

SCENE 2—The same

The Captain and the Doctor meet on the street, and the Doctor frightens the Captain by telling

him he looks as if he will have paralyzing apoplexy someday. When Wozzeck passes by, the two turn their malice on him, making references to Marie's unfaithfulness and frightening him about his health.

SCENE 3—The same

Wozzeck, meeting Marie on the street, wildly accuses her of being faithless. When he seems about to strike her, Marie exclaims that rather than being hit she would prefer a knife in her heart, and Wozzeck leaves repeating the phrase.

SCENE 4—A beer garden

In the crowded beer garden, everyone is high-spirited and slightly drunk. Wozzeck sees Marie dancing with the Drum Major and is about to attack him when the music stops; Andres leads a drunken song, and an apprentice gives a mock sermon. The Idiot appears, only to implant visions of blood in Wozzeck's brain.

SCENE 5—Part of the dormitories in the barracks

Wozzeck moans in his sleep about his visions and a knife blade. The Drum Major enters, boasting of his conquests; he attacks Wozzeck and beats him till he is bloody. The Drum Major then leaves and the other soldiers go back to sleep.

ACT III

SCENE 1—Marie's lodgings

Marie is alone with the child; she is reading biblical passages about an adulterous woman brought before Christ and Mary Magdalene; she prays to God for mercy.

SCENE 2—In the woods by the pond

Wozzeck and Marie appear at dusk. Wozzeck first expresses love to Marie, but he becomes incoherent; as the moon rises, Marie exclaims that it rises red; Wozzeck then draws a knife and stabs her in the throat.

SCENE 3—A tavern with a garret

Wozzeck is shouting wildly and then dancing

with Margaret; she suddenly notices blood on his hands, and in the outcry he rushes madly from the tavern.

ing and drowns. The Captain and the Doctor pass and hear the noise but hasten away in fear.

SCENE 4—Same as Scene 2

Wozzeck rushes back to the pool, searching for the knife; when he finds it, he tosses it into the pool, but, fearing it will be found and the blame for the murder placed on him, he attempts to retrieve it and toss it farther into the pool. As he walks into the water he loses his foot-

SCENE 5—The street; Marie's lodgings

In the street in front of Marie's house, children are playing; among them is Marie's child on a hobbyhorse. Other children rush in shouting that his mother is dead. They rush off to the pool, but the child continues to ride his horse and then rides off after the others.

Wuthering Heights

→)))∗(((←

MUSIC BY: Carlisle Floyd

WORLD PREMIERE: Santa Fe, New Mexico,
July 16, 1958

LIBRETTO BY: Carlisle Floyd
After the novel by Emily Brontë

NEW YORK CITY OPERA PREMIERE:
(Sung in English) April 9, 1959

CONDUCTOR: Julius Rudel
STAGE DIRECTOR: Delbert Mann (debut)
SCENIC DESIGNER: Lester Polakov
COSTUMES: Patton Campbell (debut)
CHOREOGRAPHER: Robert Joffrey

CHARACTERS (In order of appearance)	VOICE (type)	PREMIERE CAST (New York City Opera)
Lockwood	Tenor	Jack De Lon
Heathcliff	Baritone	John Reardon
Joseph	Tenor	Grant Williams
Isabella	Soprano	Jacquelynn Moody
Catherine Earnshaw	Soprano	Phyllis Curtin
Nelly	Mezzo	Patricia Neway
Mr. Earnshaw	Bass	Arnold Voketaitis
Hindley Earnshaw	Tenor	Jon Crain
Edgar Linton	Tenor	Frank Porretta
Guests		

SYNOPSIS OF STORY
TIME AND PLACE: English moor country, early 19th century

∗

PROLOGUE

SCENE—Wuthering Heights, 1832

Lockwood, a nearby tenant, enters from the storm, seeking shelter, as he has lost his way. Heathcliff, the owner of Wuthering Heights, coldly offers him a blanket beside the fire. Heathcliff's unhappy wife, Isabella, gives Lockwood several books to read in case he can't sleep. One of them is the diary of Catherine Linton. He is interrupted in his reading by the banging of a shutter, which he tries to close. But as he reaches for the shutter a white arm extends through the window; its owner asks to be let in and names herself Catherine Linton. Lockwood's shrieks bring Heathcliff, and upon being told the name of the apparition, he rushes out into the night calling for Cathy.

389

ACT I

SCENE 1—Wuthering Heights, February 1817

Fifteen years earlier, Cathy, her brother Hindley, and her father, Earnshaw, argue over the behavior of Heathcliff, an orphan taken in by Earnshaw who is a moody and difficult boy. Cathy defends him against her brother, who wants him disciplined. The tutor, Joseph, supports Hindley, and the argument culminates in the father's death of a heart attack. Cathy comforts Heathcliff and they vow eternal devotion.

SCENE 2—Wuthering Heights, April 1817

Cathy and Heathcliff are being read to by Joseph, but presently Cathy rebels and tears up the book. They are punished by Hindley by being banished to the kitchen, and they promptly escape to the crag on the moor. After a wildly lyrical exchange, Cathy proposes that they visit Thrushcross Grange, where the Lintons live. The scene changes to the Lintons'; and Heathcliff and Cathy are discovered looking in the window. They attempt to escape, but Cathy falls, hurting her ankle. Cathy remains with the Lintons, and Heathcliff returns to Wurthering Heights to inform Cathy's family.

ACT II

SCENE 1—Wuthering Heights, May 1817

Cathy returns to Wuthering Heights, to the delight of Nelly, the cook, but to Heathcliff's sullenness. He finally combs his hair and makes a respectable appearance; however, Edgar Linton makes a remark about Heathcliff's manners, which prompts Heathcliff to throw tea in his face. Edgar and his sister, Isabella, leave quickly, and Cathy comforts Heathcliff, who has been punished by Hindley for his display of anger.

SCENE 2—Wuthering Heights, June 1817

Cathy is preparing for a visit from Edgar, and Heathcliff shows his jealousy. Edgar arrives, and finally, after a display of temper followed by tears on Cathy's part, he proposes marriage. She accepts, but feels uneasy about the future and confides in Nelly. She asks, finally, for Heathcliff but Nelly tells her that he has gone. She frantically runs into an oncoming storm to look for him.

ACT III

SCENE 1—Thrushcross Grange, August 1820

Cathy is living with Edgar, as his wife, and with Isabella, his sister. Nelly admits Heathcliff dressed in formal attire, very much the gentleman. A party is in progress, and Cathy dances with Heathcliff, to the chagrin of Edgar. Heathcliff announces that he has gambled with Hindley, who drinks too much, and has won Wuthering Heights. Heathcliff will now be a neighbor. After Heathcliff leaves, Cathy tells Nelly that she will right matters with Edgar, who is unhappy to see Heathcliff again. Nelly warns Cathy about Heathcliff's ruthless nature, but Cathy is too happy to pay attention.

SCENE 2—Thrushcross Grange, September 1820

Cathy and Isabella argue about Heathcliff. Isabella confesses her love for him, and Cathy warns her of his hatred for her family and his fierce nature. Heathcliff enters with Hindley, now a broken man. Cathy tells him of Isabella's love for him in her presence. Isabella, horrified at Cathy's forwardness, runs from the room. In an argument, Heathcliff calls Cathy's marriage a "sham and pretense." Cathy orders him away, and he goes out the door to find Isabella waiting for him. They plan to run away to be married that evening. Cathy discovers them and, when Edgar arrives, confronts him with the new situation. But finally Edgar and Heathcliff both incur the wrath of Cathy, and she denounces them both. Left alone with Nelly, Cathy asks, in a long, incoherent speech, "What have I done?"

SCENE 3—Thrushcross Grange, April 1921

Cathy, with Nelly, is expecting a child she doesn't want. Heathcliff arrives and demands to see Cathy. Cathy begs him to carry her to the moor after he accuses her of abandoning her. But as he stands in the doorway holding her, she dies in his arms. Heathcliff places her back on the couch and cries out that she may never find peace. He begs that if he has killed her, she will haunt him the rest of his days.

The Young Lord

-»»*«‹-

MUSIC BY: Hans Werner Henze

WORLD PREMIERE: Berlin, Germany,
  April 7, 1965

LIBRETTO BY: Ingebord Bachmann
English translation by Eugene Walter,
  revised by Julius Rudel
NEW YORK CITY OPERA PREMIERE:
  (Sung in English) March 28, 1973

CONDUCTOR: Julius Rudel
PRODUCTION DEVISED and DIRECTED BY: Sarah Caldwell (debut)
SCENIC DESIGNER: Herbert Senn (debut)
COSTUMES: Eleonore Kleiber
CHOREOGRAPHY: Thomas Andrew

CHARACTERS (In order of appearance)	VOICE (type)	PREMIERE CAST (New York City Opera)
Herr Voightlander, the photographer	Mute	Jack Sims
Chief Magistrate Harethrasher	Baritone	James Billings
Professor von Mucker	Tenor	John Lankston
Town Comptroller Sharp	Baritone	David Ronson
The Burgomaster	Bass-baritone	Richard T. Gill
Luise, ward of the Baroness	Soprano	Patricia Wise
Three young men	Tenor	Joaquin Romaguera
	Tenor	Melvin Lowery (debut)
	Baritone	William Ledbetter
Ida, Luise's friend	Soprano	Ruth Welting
Frau von Hoffnail	Mezzo	Diane Curry
Frau Harethrasher	Soprano	Barbara Hocher (debut)
Wilhelm, a student	Tenor	Gary Glaze
Jeremy, the Turkish page	Mime	Mark Waymmann
Meadows, the butler	Mime	Cornelius Frizell
The Schoolmaster	Baritone	Don Yule
Begonia, the cook	Mezzo	Betty Allen
Sir Edgar's secretary	Baritone	Richard Fredricks
Sir Edgar	Mime	Rudolf Bing (debut)
Monsieur La Truiare	Mime	Michael Rubino
Baroness von Greenweasel	Mezzo	Muriel Greenspon
A parlormaid	Soprano	Diane Kehrig
Vulcan, the Fire-Eater	Mute	Presto
Rosita, "The Cloud-Walking Maiden"	Dancer	Esperanza Galan
Brimbilla, the juggler	Mute	Harry De Dio
Amintore la Rocca, director of the circus	Tenor	John Stamford

391

The Young Lord, 1973. Kenneth Riegel, Richard Fredricks, Rudolf Bing, and members of the ensemble.

CHARACTERS (In order of appearance	VOICE (type)	PREMIERE CAST (New York City Opera)
A lamplighter	Baritone	J. B. Davis
Lord Barrat, nephew of Sir Edgar	Tenor	Kenneth Riegel

Ladies and Gentlemen, Young People of Good Society, Common People, Children, Lackeys, Servants, Animals

SYNOPSIS OF STORY
TIME AND PLACE: German town of Hulsdorf-Gotha, 1830

*

ACT I

SCENE 1—The main square

Sir Edgar, a British nobleman who wishes solitude in which to pursue his scientific studies, has engaged a house in a peaceful little German town. The town, eager to profit from the visit of a rich Englishman, plans an elaborate welcoming ceremony, which is slightly soured by his late arrival. Sir Edgar, far from being flattered, is appalled by the ostentatious reception and the drabness of the faces of the gentry. The gentry are equally appalled by the exotic nature of Sir Edgar's entourage.

SCENE 2—Baroness von Greenweasel's salon

Flora von Greenweasel, social leader of Hulsdorf-Gotha, has invited Sir Edgar to tea. She secretly hopes that the unmarried Sir Edgar will prove to be a suitable match for her ward, Luise. Sir Edgar sends a polite note of refusal, infuriating the Baroness and her friends, who invent ugly and vicious rumors about him.

SCENE 3—The main square

A small traveling circus is performing outside Sir Edgar's house. Although the children and the common folk are on obvious good terms with Sir Edgar, the gentry are deeply offended by his attendance at the circus, since he has refused to participate in their social life. When they try to close the circus for lack of a license, Sir Edgar, shocked by their boorish behavior, pays for the license and invites the circus performers into his home. The parents of the children are further incensed when the children cheer Sir Edgar's action.

ACT II

SCENE 4—A park at the rear of Sir Edgar's house, a winter evening

The now-bigoted children of the town attempt to drive Jeremy from the park. The lamplighter, making his rounds, runs for help when he hears screams coming from Sir Edgar's house. Wilhelm and Luise meet in secret for a bleak and unsatisfactory rendezvous. When the town fathers come to investigate the screams, Sir Edgar's secretary explains that the cries are from Lord Barrat, Sir Edgar's nephew, who occasionally must have his knuckles rapped. He is being taught German and will soon be presented at a party to which they will all be invited.

SCENE 5—Sir Edgar's house

Sir Edgar and the members of his household relax together on the day of his long-awaited party. The guests soon arrive. Lord Barrat is presented to the ladies, and Luise finds herself attracted to him, his eccentric behavior affording a welcome contrast to the pallor and propriety of Wilhelm.

SCENE 6—The main square

Luise finds it difficult to understand her strong feelings for Lord Barrat. When he arrives to escort her to the town dance, the entire populace eavesdrops on them, lamenting that the sophisticated young Lord will soon be taking their most eligible young lady away from them. Lord Barrat's frenzied dancing is copied by the young people of the town, who ape him in every way. As the evening progresses, Lord Barrat grows wilder and wilder, as do his followers, to the extent of tearing off their clothes when he does. It is then that they discover his real identity.

Credits

-»»*«««-

Since it is impossible in a book of this nature to include every person involved in the production of the operas, the Committee wishes to recognize all of the artists whose contributions to various premiere productions will long be remembered, especially the following:

Assistants to Production Designers and Stage Directors
Cynthia Auerbach, Julie Bellisle, Elena (Gigi) Denda, Donald Eastman, Roger Englander, Richard Getke, Barbara Karp, Jay Lesenger, Steve Presnell, John Primm, Francis Rizzo, Christian Smith, Antonio Tauriello

Assistants to Choreographers
Susan Hendl, Buzz Miller

Chorus Masters
George Branson Gray, Margaret Hillis, William Jonson, Chris Nance, Gino Smart, Lloyd Walser

Lighting Directors, Designers, and Assistants
Ken Billington, Charles Elson, Jules Fisher, Gilbert V. Hemsley, Jr., Kliegl Bros., Nananne Porcher, Jean Rosenthal, Hans Sondheimer, Lee Watson, Richard Nelson

Makeup, Masks, and Wigs
Michael Arshansky, Charles Elsen

General Footnotes

-»»*«««-

Even though every effort has been made by the Committee to report accurate information on the productions, stories, and performers, in some cases it was impossible to report all the information. For example,

(1) In the lesser roles there may be a contradiction in voice type listing. This is due to the unavailability of the voice type of the artist. In such cases the voice type was listed as it appeared in the libretto.

(2) In some instances the names of artists are spelled differently. This, in part, is because the artists changed the spelling of their names. It may also be due to the inadvertent variation in the printing of the names in the playbill.

(3) There were subsequent new productions of many of the operas. However, for the purpose of this book only the premiere performances are listed.

(4) In some cases it was impossible to place the characters in order of appearance. In these cases a footnote indicates this fact.

References

→)))✳(((←

Davidson, Gladys. *The Barnes Book of the Opera*. New York: A. S. Barnes & Co., 1962.

Eaton, Quaintance. *Opera Production: A Handbook*. Minneapolis: University of Minnesota Press, 1961.

_____. *Opera Productions II*. Minneapolis: University of Minnesota Press, 1974.

Ewen, David. *Encyclopedia of the Opera*. New York: Hill & Wang, Inc., 1955.

Fellner, Rudolph. *Opera Themes and Plots*. New York: Simon & Schuster, 1958.

Grabbe, P., and Nordoff, P. *Minute Stories of the Opera*. New York: Grosset and Dunlap, 1932.

Green, Stanley. *The World of Musical Comedy*. New York: Grosset and Dunlap, 1960.

Johnson, H. E. *Operas on American Subjects*. New York: Coleman-Ross Co., 1964.

Kobbe, Gustave. *The Complete Opera Book*. New York: G. P. Putnam's Sons, 1950.

Marek, George R., ed. *The World Treasury of Grand Opera*. New York: Harper and Bros., 1957.

Simon, Henry W. *One Hundred Great Operas and Their Stories*. New York: Doubleday & Co., 1957.

Westrup, J. A. *The New College Encyclopedia of Music*. New York: W. W. Norton, 1959.

Appendix A

-»»*«« -

NEW YORK CITY OPERA PRODUCTIONS
(Composers and Operas, Alphabetically Arranged)

ARGENTO
Miss Havisham's Fire

BARTOK
Bluebeard's Castle

BEESON
Lizzie Borden

BELLINI
I Puritani

BERG
Wozzeck

BERNSTEIN
Trouble in Tahiti

BIZET
Carmen

BLITZSTEIN
The Cradle Will Rock
Regina

BOITO
Mefistofele

BORODIN
Prince Igor

BRITTEN
Albert Herring
A Midsummer Night's Dream
The Rape of Lucretia
The Turn of the Screw

BUCCI
Tale for a Deaf Ear

CHARPENTIER
Louise

CHERUBINI
Medea

COPLAND
The Tender Land

DALLAPICCOLA
The Prisoner

DEBUSSY
Pelléas et Mélisande

DELIUS
A Village Romeo and Juliet

DELLO JOIO
The Triumph of Saint Joan

DONIZETTI
Anna Bolena
The Daughter of the Regiment
Don Pasquale
Lucia di Lammermoor
Lucrezia Borgia
Maria Stuarda
Roberto Devereux

EGK
The Inspector General

EINEM
Danton's Death
The Trial

ELLSTEIN
The Golem

FALLA
El Amor Brujo
La Vida Breve

FLOTOW
Martha

FLOYD
The Passion of Jonathan Wade
Susannah
Wuthering Heights

GERSHWIN
Porgy and Bess

GIANNINI
The Servant of Two Masters
The Taming of the Shrew

GINASTERA
Beatrix Cenci
Bomarzo
Don Rodrigo

GIORDANO
Andrea Chenier

GOUNOD
Faust

HANDEL
Giulio Cesare

HENZE
The Young Lord

HERBERT
Naughty Marietta

HOIBY
Natalia Petrovna
The Scarf
Summer and Smoke

HONEGGER
Jeanne d'Arc au Bucher

HUMPERDINCK
Hansel and Gretel

JANÁČEK
The Makropoulos Affair

KERN
Show Boat

KIRCHNER
Lily

KORNGOLD
Die Tote Stadt

KURKA
The Good Soldier Schweik

LEHÁR
The Merry Widow

LEONCAVALLO
Pagliacci

LIEBERMANN
The School for Wives

MARTIN
The Tempest

MASCAGNI
Cavalleria Rusticana

MASSENET
Manon
Werther

MENOTTI
Amahl and the Night Visitors
Amelia Goes to the Ball
The Consul
Help! Help! the Globolinks!
Maria Golovin
The Medium
The Most Important Man
The Old Maid and the Thief
The Saint of Bleecker Street

MONTEVERDI
La Favola d'Orfeo
Il Ritorno d'Ulisse in Patria
L'Incoronazione di Poppea

MOORE
The Ballad of Baby Doe
Carry Nation
The Devil and Daniel Webster
The Wings of the Dove

MOROSS
Gentlemen, Be Seated!

MOZART
The Abduction from the Seraglio
Così fan Tutte
Don Giovanni
Idomeneo
The Impresario
The Magic Flute
The Marriage of Figaro

MUSGRAVE
The Voice of Ariadne

MOUSSORGSKY
Boris Godunov

NICOLAI
The Merry Wives of Windsor

OFFENBACH
La Belle Hélène
Les Contes d'Hoffmann
Orpheus in the Underworld

ORFF
Carmina Burana
Catulli Carmina
The Moon

POULENC
The Dialogues of the Carmelites
La Voix Humaine

PROKOFIEV
The Flaming Angel
The Love for Three Oranges

PUCCINI
La Bohème
La Fanciulla del West
Gianni Schicchi
Madama Butterfly
Manon Lescaut

Suor Angelica
Il Tabarro
Tosca
Turandot

PURCELL
Dido and Aeneas

RAVEL
L'Heure Espagnole

RIMSKY-KORSAKOV
Le Coq d'Or

ROREM
Miss Julie

ROSSINI
Il Barbiere di Siviglia
La Cenerentola
The Turk in Italy

SHOSTAKOVICH
Katerina Ismailova

SMETANA
The Bartered Bride

STILL
Troubled Island

J. STRAUSS
Die Fledermaus
The Gypsy Baron

R. STRAUSS
Ariadne auf Naxos
Le Bourgeois Gentilhomme (ballet)
Capriccio
Der Rosenkavalier
Salome
The Silent Woman

STRAVINSKY
L'Histoire du Soldat
The Nightingale
Oedipus Rex

SULLIVAN
The Mikado
H.M.S. Pinafore
The Pirates of Penzance

399

TAL
Ashmedai

TAMKIN
The Dybbuk

TCHAIKOVSKY
Eugene Onegin
The Golden Slippers

THOMAS
Mignon

VERDI
Aida
Un Ballo in Maschera
Falstaff
Macbeth
Rigoletto
La Traviata
Il Trovatore

WAGNER
Der Fliegende Holländer
Die Meistersinger

WALTON
Troilus and Cressida

WARD
The Crucible
He Who Gets Slapped

WEILL
Die Dreigroschenoper
Lost in the Stars
Street Scene

WEISGALL
Nine Rivers from Jordan
Six Characters in Search of an Author

WOLF-FERRARI
The Four Ruffians

Appendix B

-»»*«««-

NEW YORK CITY OPERA PRODUCTIONS
(In Chronological Order)

	OPERA	COMPOSER	1st PERF	LANGUAGE
1.	Tosca	Puccini	2/21/44	Italian
2.	Martha	Flotow	2/22/44	English
3.	Carmen	Bizet	2/24/44	French
4.	La Bohème	Puccini	5/ 5/44	Italian
5.	Cavalleria Rusticana	Mascagni	5/ 5/44	Italian
6.	Pagliacci	Leoncavallo	5/ 5/44	Italian
7.	La Traviata	Verdi	5/ 8/44	Italian
8.	Manon Lescaut	Puccini	11/ 9/44	Italian
9.	The Gypsy Baron	J. Strauss	11/14/44	English
10.	Der Fliegende Holländer	Wagner	4/12/45	German
11.	Faust	Gounod	4/16/45	French
12.	The Bartered Bride	Smetana	10/ 3/45	English
13.	Rigoletto	Verdi	5/ 9/46	Italian
14.	Pirates of Penzance	Gilbert & Sullivan	5/12/46	English
15.	Madama Butterfly	Puccini	5/15/46	Italian
16.	Ariadne auf Naxos	R. Strauss	10/10/46	German
17.	Eugene Onegin	Tchaikovsky	11/14/46	Russian
18.	Andrea Chenier	Giordano	4/ 9/47	Italian
19.	Salome	R. Strauss	4/16/47	German
20.	Werther	Massenet	10/ 2/47	French
21.	Il Barbiere di Siviglia	Rossini	10/ 5/47	Italian
22.	Don Giovanni	Mozart	10/23/47	Italian
23.	Pelléas et Mélisande	Debussy	3/25/48	French
24.	The Old Maid and the Thief	Menotti	4/ 8/48	English
25.	Amelia goes to the Ball	Menotti	4/ 8/48	English
26.	The Marriage of Figaro	Mozart	10/14/48	English
27.	Aida	Verdi	10/28/48	Italian
28.	Troubled Island	Still	3/31/39	English
29.	Les Contes d'Hoffmann	Offenbach	4/ 6/49	French
30.	The Medium	Menotti	4/ 7/49	English
31.	Der Rosenkavalier	R. Strauss	10/ 6/49	German
32.	The Love for Three Oranges	Prokofiev	11/ 1/49	English
33.	Turandot	Puccini	4/ 6/50	Italian

OPERA	COMPOSER	1st PERF	LANGUAGE
34. Die Meistersinger	Wagner	10/13/50	German
35. Manon	Massenet	3/22/51	French
36. The Dybbuk	Tamkin	10/ 4/51	English
37. The Four Ruffians	Wolf-Ferrari	10/18/51	English
38. Wozzeck	Berg	4/ 3/52	English
39. Amahl and the Night Visitors	Menotti	4/ 9/52	English
40. Bluebeard's Castle	Bartok	10/ 2/52	English
41. L'Heure Espagnole	Ravel	10/ 2/52	English
42. The Consul	Menotti	10/ 8/52	English
43. La Cenerentola	Rossini	3/26/53	Italian
44. Regina	Blitzstein	4/ 2/53	English
45. Die Fledermaus	J. Strauss	4/ 8/53	English
46. Hansel and Gretel	Humperdinck	10/14/53	English
47. The Trial	Von Einem	10/22/53	English
48. The Tender Land	Copland	4/ 1/54	English
49. Show Boat	Kern	4/ 8/54	English
50. Falstaff	Verdi	4/15/54	English
51. Don Pasquale	Donizetti	3/24/55	Italian
52. The Merry Wives of Windsor	Nicolai	3/31/55	English
53. The Golden Slippers	Tchaikovsky	10/13/55	English
54. Troilus and Cressida	Walton	10/21/55	English
55. Il Trovatore	Verdi	4/ 4/56	Italian
56. The School for Wives	Liebermann	4/11/56	English
57. The Impresario	Mozart	4/11/56	English
58. Orpheus in the Underworld	Offenbach	9/20/56	English
59. Mignon	Thomas	9/25/56	French
60. Susannah	Floyd	9/27/56	English
61. The Tempest	Martin	10/11/56	English
62. The Moon	Orff	10/16/56	English
63. L'Histoire du Soldat	Stravinsky	10/16/56	English
64. La Vida Breve (ballet)	Falla	10/16/57	Spanish
65. El Amor Brujo	Falla	10/16/57	Spanish
66. Macbeth	Verdi	10/24/57	Italian
67. The Merry Widow	Lehár	10/27/57	English
68. The Abduction from the Seraglio	Mozart	10/30/57	English
69. The Ballad of Baby Doe	Moore	4/ 3/58	English
70. Tale for a Deaf Ear	Bucci	4/ 6/58	English
71. Trouble in Tahiti	Bernstein	4/ 6/58	English
72. Lost in the Stars	Weill	4/10/58	English
73. The Taming of the Shrew	Giannini	4/13/58	English
74. The Good Soldier Schweik	Kurka	4/23/58	English
75. The Silent Woman	R. Strauss	10/ 7/58	English
76. The Rape of Lucretia	Britten	10/23/58	English
77. Maria Golovin	Menotti	3/30/59	English
78. Street Scene	Weill	4/ 2/59	English
79. The Scarf	Hoiby	4/ 5/59	English
80. The Devil and Daniel Webster	Moore	4/ 5/59	English
81. Wuthering Heights	Floyd	4/ 9/59	English
82. He Who Gets Slapped	Ward	4/12/59	English
83. The Triumph of St. Joan	Dello Joio	4/16/59	English
84. Six Characters in Search of an Author	Weisgall	4/26/59	English

OPERA	COMPOSER	1st PERF	LANGUAGE
85. Oedipus Rex	Stravinsky	9/24/59	Latin
86. Carmina Burana	Orff	9/24/59	Latin
87. The Mikado	Gilbert & Sullivan	10/ 1/59	English
88. Così fan Tutte	Mozart	10/ 8/59	English
89. The Cradle Will Rock	Blitzstein	2/11/60	English
90. The Prisoner	Dallapiccola	9/29/60	English
91. La Favola d'Orfeo	Monteverdi	9/29/60	Italian
92. The Inspector General	Egk	10/19/60	English
93. Il Tabarro	Puccini	10/ 5/61	Italian
94. Suor Angelica	Puccini	10/ 5/61	Italian
95. Gianni Schicchi	Puccini	10/ 5/61	Italian
96. The Wings of the Dove	Moore	10/12/61	English
97. H.M.S. Pinafore	Gilbert & Sullivan	10/15/61	English
98. The Crucible	Ward	10/26/61	English
99. The Golem	Ellstein	3/22/62	English
100. The Turn of the Screw	Britten	3/25/62	English
101. Porgy and Bess	Gershwin	3/31/62	English
102. Louise	Charpentier	10/ 4/62	French
103. The Passion of Jonathan Wade	Floyd	10/11/62	English
104. A Midsummer Night's Dream	Britten	4/25/63	English
105. The Nightingale	Stravinsky	10/ 3/63	English
106. Jeanne D'Arc au Bucher	Honegger	10/ 3/63	English
107. Gentlemen, Be Seated!	Moross	10/10/63	English
108. Boris Godunov	Moussorgsky	10/ 1/64	English
109. Natalia Petrovna	Hoiby	10/ 8/64	English
110. Katerina Ismailova	Shostakovich	3/ 4/65	English
111. Die Dreigroschenoper	Weill	3/11/65	German
112. The Saint of Bleecker Street	Menotti	3/18/65	English
113. Lizzie Borden	Beeson	3/25/65	English
114. The Flaming Angel	Prokofiev	9/22/65	English
115. Capriccio	R. Strauss	10/27/65	English
116. Miss Julie	Rorem	11/ 4/65	English
117. Don Rodrigo	Ginastera	2/22/66	Spanish
118. The Dialogues of the Carmelites	Poulenc	3/ 3/66	English
119. Danton's Death	von Einem	3/ 9/66	English
120. Giulio Cesare	Handel	9/27/66	Italian
121. The Magic Flute	Mozart	10/13/66	English
122. The Servant of Two Masters	Giannini	3/ 9/67	English
123. Le Coq d'Or	Rimsky-Korsakov	9/21/67	English
124. Bomarzo	Ginastera	3/14/68	Spanish
125. Carry Nation	Moore	3/28/68	English
126. Nine Rivers from Jordan	Weisgall	10/ 9/68	English
127. Prince Igor	Borodin	2/27/69	English
128. Mefistofele	Boito	9/21/69	Italian
129. Lucia di Lammermoor	Donizetti	10/ 9/69	Italian
130. Catulli Carmina	Orff	10/30/69	Latin
131. Roberto Devereux	Donizetti	10/15/70	Italian
132. The Makropoulos Affair	Janáček	11/ 1/70	English
133. Help! Help! the Globolinks!	Menotti	11/28/70	English
134. The Most Important Man	Menotti	3/ 7/71	English
135. Un Ballo in Maschera	Verdi	3/21/71	Italian

OPERA	COMPOSER	1st PERF	LANGUAGE
136. Albert Herring	Britten	9/15/71	English
137. Maria Stuarda	Donizetti	3/ 7/72	Italian
138. Summer and Smoke	Hoiby	3/19/72	English
139. L'Incoronazione di Poppea	Monteverdi	3/ 8/73	Italian
140. Beatrix Cenci	Ginastera	3/14/73	Spanish
141. The Young Lord	Henze	3/28/73	English
142. A Village Romeo and Juliet	Delius	10/ 6/73	English
143. Anna Bolena	Donizetti	10/ 3/73	Italian
144. I Puritani	Bellini	2/21/74	Italian
145. Medea	Cherubini	3/ 7/74	Italian
146. Idomeneo	Mozart	3/16/75	Italian
147. Die Tote Stadt	Korngold	4/ 2/75	German
148. The Daughter of the Regiment	Donizetti	9/ 7/75	English
149. Il Ritorno d'Ulisse in Patria	Monteverdi	2/29/76	Italian
150. Lucrezia Borgia	Donizetti	3/18/76	Italian
151. Ashmedai	Tal	4/ 1/76	English
152. La Belle Hélène	Offenbach	9/21/76	English
153. Lily	Kirchner	4/14/77	English
154. La Voix Humaine	Poulenc	4/22/77	English
155. The Voice of Ariadne	Musgrave	9/30/77	English
156. La Fanciulla del West	Puccini	10/16/77	Italian
157. Naughty Marietta	Herbert	8/31/78	English
158. The Turk in Italy	Rossini	9/24/78	English
159. Miss Havisham's Fire	Argento	3/22/79	English
160. Dido and Aeneas	Purcell	4/ 8/79	English
161. Le Bourgeois Gentilhomme (ballet)	R. Strauss	4/ 8/79	English